WRONGFUL
CONVICTION

WRONGFUL CONVICTION

International Perspectives on Miscarriages of Justice

C. Ronald Huff *and* Martin Killias

EDITORS

TEMPLE UNIVERSITY PRESS
Philadelphia

TEMPLE UNIVERSITY PRESS
1601 North Broad Street
Philadelphia PA 19122
www.temple.edu/tempress

⊚ The paper used in this publication meets the requirements of the American National Standard for Information Sciences—Permanence of Paper for Printed Library Materials, ANSI Z39.48-1992

Library of Congress Cataloging-in-Publication Data

Wrongful conviction : international perspectives on miscarriages of justice / edited by C. Ronald Huff and Martin Killias.
    p. cm.
  Includes bibliographical references and index.
  ISBN-13: 978-1-59213-645-2 (cloth : alk. paper)
  ISBN-13: 978-1-59213-646-9 (paper : alk. paper)
 1. Judicial error. I. Huff, C. Ronald. II. Killias, Martin.
  K5560.W76 2008
  347'.012—dc22
  2008002888

032210-P

This book is dedicated to the victims of wrongful convictions throughout the world.

CONTENTS

PART III EUROPEAN AND ISRAELI PERSPECTIVES AND ISSUES

PART IV CONCLUSIONS

I

CROSS-NATIONAL
PERSPECTIVES
AND ISSUES

1

INTRODUCTION

~

C. RONALD HUFF AND MARTIN KILLIAS

The subject of wrongful conviction attracted some attention in the United States beginning in the 1930s, but most of the earlier literature focused primarily on discussions of individual cases (see, for example, Borchard, 1932; Gardner, 1952; Frank and Frank, 1957; Ehrmann, 1962; Radin, 1964). Some literature has dealt extensively with the most high-visibility cases, such as the Dreyfus affair in the nineteenth century (Chapman, 1955; Tuchman, 1962; Bredin, 1986); the infamous case of the "Scottsboro boys" in the 1920s (Carter, 1969); the Lindbergh baby kidnapping and murder in the 1930s (Kennedy, 1985); and more recent cases such as that of Randall Dale Adams, whose wrongful conviction, imprisonment, and near execution in Texas led to both his own book (Adams, 1991) and Errol Morris's prize-winning documentary, *The Thin Blue Line* (1988). Some cases have captured the attention of the general public, including some of those already mentioned as well as the Sam Sheppard case, which led to a long-running television series and a very successful movie by the same name (*The Fugitive*); the "Birmingham Six" case, which inspired extensive analyses and the film *In the Name of the Father*; the controversy surrounding John Demjanjuk, accused of being the notorious "Ivan the Terrible," a Nazi death camp guard who helped in the mass murder of Jews; and the wrongful conviction of Michael and Lindy Chamberlain for the death of their daughter in Australia, which attracted international attention and inspired the movie *A Cry in the Dark*.

Both scholarly attention and public attention to this issue have been greatly accelerated by the exonerations of hundreds of wrongfully convicted individuals who had been imprisoned and, in a number of cases, sentenced to death. Advances in forensic science, including DNA testing of biological evidence, have greatly facilitated the discovery of these errors. In one state, Illinois, the governor became so concerned about these errors and the possibility of executing innocent persons, that he declared a moratorium on the death penalty. A number of other states have discovered similar problems and have undertaken studies, imposed moratoria, or proposed possible moratoria while attempting to address the underlying problems that generate wrongful convictions and imprisonment.

Since the 1990s, scholars have begun to pay more attention to the issue of wrongful conviction, especially in the United States (Huff, Rattner, and Sagarin, 1986, 1996; Radelet, Bedau, and Putnam, 1992; Scheck, Neufeld, and Dwyer, 2000; Westervelt and Humphrey, 2001; Forst, 2004) and in Great Britain (Walker and Starmer, 1999; Nobles and Schiff, 2000). These studies were preceded by a monumental survey of some 1,600 cases overturned in Germany over a period of more than three decades (Peters, 1970–1974). However, none of these scholarly publications has systematically addressed the problem of wrongful conviction from a cross-national perspective. Following a 2001 presidential address to the American Society of Criminology and a subsequent article in *Criminology* (Huff, 2002), the co-editors of this book organized an international network of scholars for the purpose of analyzing wrongful convictions across different nations and different types of criminal justice systems. With the sponsorship of the Swiss National Science Foundation, we held the first international workshop on wrongful conviction in Switzerland and subsequently decided to undertake this book project. We believed that it was important to pursue this cross-nationally because there were major unanswered questions to be addressed.

This book represents what is, to our knowledge, the first that addresses the issue of wrongful conviction from a cross-national perspective. Beginning with a discussion of cross-national issues and the importance of a cross-national perspective, the book offers analyses of wrongful conviction and related issues from eighteen contributors from nine different nations. The chapters provide a balance of (1) detailed discussions of specific nations and (2) considerations of cross-cutting issues that transcend national boundaries. The traditional dichotomy of "adversarial" versus "continental-inquisitorial" legal systems will be both explained and revisited to determine (1) what impact each system may have on preventing or generating wrongful convictions and (2) whether this traditional dichotomy remains a viable one or is in need of revision. The book also includes a number of public policy recommendations intended to reduce the number of wrongful convictions and compensate more fairly those who are the victims of these miscarriages of justice.

What is wrongful conviction? In developing our approach to the subject and in producing this volume, we have relied on the definition utilized by Huff, Rattner, and Sagarin (1996), focusing exclusively on those who have been arrested on criminal charges, who have either pleaded guilty to the charges or have been found guilty, and who, notwithstanding their guilty plea or verdict, are actually innocent. This restrictive definition excludes many other types of injustice, such as those cases in which persons were detained for long periods of time without ever having been found guilty of anything. It also excludes cases in which the initial conviction was overturned due to procedural errors without any determination of factual innocence, for example. We also prefer the term *wrongful conviction* instead of *miscarriages of justice*, which is often used synonymously but is, in our judgment, much broader and more inclusive. The latter term might be interpreted to include other types of injustice and errors of law, rather than errors of fact and could, for some, even include cases where the accused, although guilty, "got away with murder," as that result certainly represents a miscarriage of justice for the victim and his or her family.

Why study the problem of wrongful conviction across different nations as opposed to focusing on only one nation? Of course, such research is justified for its own sake in terms of the intellectual opportunities represented by such comparative studies. That is, satisfying our curiosity about other nations' systems of justice is, by itself, an important benefit. However, among the several benefits to be derived from cross-national studies is one that we regard as most important: We often can learn more about our own system of justice by looking at it in the context of other nations' systems. It is only by way of comparison and contrast that we can intelligently decide whether our system might be improved so that justice might be better served. It is, ultimately, the *improvement* of justice through the reduction of error that motivated us to undertake this research. We have, therefore, formed a network of scholars, represented in the chapters that follow, who are committed to this kind of cross-national analysis and committed to learning from each other about the ways in which other nations' criminal justice systems generate or avoid producing wrongful convictions. As one prominent scholar recently noted:

> . . . For a long time, transnational comparative studies were a peripheral and none-too-important suburb of the empirical study of crime and social control . . . [but] . . . how do we know whether, and to what extent, the United States is unique without implicit or explicit comparisons between the United States and elsewhere? (Zimring, 2006: 615).

It is our hope that this volume will help address that need. In conducting cross-national research, one must first consider the unit of analysis and in what way the study will be cross-national in scope. Kohn (1989) formulated a useful typology of cross-national research, advocating that the typology be viewed as representing gradations of emphasis, rather than sharp demarcations. The purpose of this book, the analysis of wrongful conviction across nations, is consistent with Kohn's discussion of cross-national studies in which the nations provide the *context* for the study. In this case, we are interested in studying wrongful conviction in the context of various nations and their respective criminal justice systems.

Part I focuses on some cross-national perspectives and issues. Sometimes wrongful convictions occur in a context of "moral panic" due to certain highly inflammatory crimes or allegations of crimes that are especially detested by the public. This phenomenon seems to occur in many different nations. In Chapter 2, Grometstein discusses a series of cases allegedly involving the ritual and sexual abuse of children by day care workers and other caregivers. Those cases led to "moral panics" on several continents beginning in the 1980s and continuing for two decades (most recently in France in 2004). These cases were termed "organized child sexual abuse" and led to the convictions of many suspects, only to have a number of those convictions overturned later by appellate courts. The chapter discusses moral panic theory and the factors present in those cases that increased the likelihood of error, such as the weakening of evidentiary standards for proving the elements of crimes.

The advent of DNA technology and other high-tech tools for fighting crime and identifying perpetrators promises to revolutionize the criminal justice systems of a number of nations. In Chapter 3, Schiffer and Champod discuss the risks involved in using forensic science to link suspects to the crimes that they committed, but also to exonerate innocent persons. Two British case examples illustrate points such as the admissibility of scientific evidence, uniqueness, the notion of match, confirmation bias, false inferences, lack of transparency, and contradictory physical evidence.

Part II includes contributions focusing on the United States and Canada. Much of the world's attention to the issue of wrongful conviction has been centered on the United States due to a number of highly publicized cases and due, in part, to the vast magnitude of the U.S. criminal justice system. Even a small error rate generates thousands of cases of wrongful conviction each year. In Chapter 4, Huff provides an overview and analysis of the U.S. experience with wrongful conviction, including the leading causes of error; the consequences of wrongful conviction for the convicted but innocent and for public safety; the increasing role of forensic science, including DNA, in exonerations; and some recent developments and public policy recommendations intended to address this problem.

One of the most intriguing issues explored in this book is the question of whether the adversarial system of justice is itself an important factor contributing to wrongful conviction. Zalman (Chapter 5) analyzes the adversary jury trial and assesses its capacity to determine the objective truth. The debates concerning the adversarial jury trial versus the continental, "inquisitorial" system date back to differences in perspective between Blackstone and Bentham. Does the U.S. adversarial system require the courts to do their best to discover the truth? Zalman analyzes the role of the judge, rules of evidence, reforms to allow more jury involvement, and other ideas to determine whether technical modifications might make jury trials more accurate and reduce the number of wrongful convictions.

Another issue that continues to generate a great deal of public and scholarly debate is whether the death penalty should be retained in the United States. The problem of wrongful conviction has caused many observers to wonder whether it is worth retaining capital punishment when there is the possibility that innocent persons might be executed, as argued by Radelet, Bedau, and Putnam (1992), for example. In Chapter 6, Lofquist and Harmon analyze executions that occurred in the United States between 1972 and 2000 that involved "compelling claims of factual innocence" and a comparison group of eighty cases during the same time period in which prisoners were released from death row due to doubts about their guilt. They systematically examine the factors involved in cases resulting in execution compared with those resulting in exoneration. Their analyses produce some important insights into the dynamics of those cases and the judicial review process.

In Chapter 7, Campbell presents an analysis and discussion of the causes and effects of wrongful convictions in Canada, as well as the responses of the state, including the limitations of current policies and procedures designed to rectify miscarriages of justice. Her analysis includes the conviction review process, which allows those who assert that they have been wrongly convicted and imprisoned to apply to the Minister of Justice for case review, following all appeals. The chapter points out serious problems in that process and argues for the establishment of an independent system of review, similar to that utilized by the Criminal Cases Review Commission in Great Britain.

In Part III, the focus shifts from North American studies and concerns to European and Israeli perspectives and issues. In Chapter 8, Killias shows how Switzerland's legal system focuses on the search for "objective truth" and emphasizes even-handed investigations of the facts, whether they are favorable or unfavorable to the defendant. Guilty pleas without trial are possible only in cases involving minor offenses with minimal sanctions. Greater reliance is placed on scientific evidence than on oral statements, even including confessions. He discusses the Swiss system and its advantages and vulnerabilities, considering the results of a recent survey of all final convictions that have been overturned between 1995 and 2004. He concludes that wrongful convictions are far more likely to occur in apparently trivial cases where few resources are devoted to investigate the relevant facts, such as the possibility of error, shortcomings, or both in scientific investigations.

The Dutch "inquisitorial system" of criminal law and its vulnerability in producing wrongful convictions is the subject of Brants in Chapter 9. She notes that the Dutch system is one of the most inquisitorial in all of continental Europe and is based on a number of assumptions that are, in theory, strong protections against error. However, when any one of those assumptions is not met in practice, the safeguards against wrongful conviction are eroded accordingly. She also discusses the meaning of "wrongful conviction" and whether the usual dichotomy of the "adversarial" and the "inquisitorial" systems is a viable one.

Moving from the Netherlands to the United Kingdom, Walker and McCartney (Chapter 10) argue that although extensive safeguards exist to prevent the conviction of the innocent in England and Wales, errors nonetheless occur. Their chapter examines the nature of "residual error" in England and Wales, the mechanisms put in place to respond to such residual error, and the performance of those mechanisms in recent years.

Does the way in which prosecutors carry out their roles have an impact on the generation of wrongful convictions? That question is addressed by Kessler in Chapter 11, wherein she argues that miscarriages of justice are sometimes closely connected with prosecutorial performance. She asserts that at each stage, from the initial decision to begin criminal proceedings to the final conviction, prosecutors can manipulate or influence the presentation of evidence. The outcome of criminal proceedings largely depends on the charges and the way in which evidence is presented to judges and, especially, to lay justices. Kessler delineates the differences in the respective roles of prosecutors in Germany and in the United Kingdom, from initial investigations to trial proceedings, as examples of the "inquisitorial" and "adversarial" systems of justice. She also discusses both systems' vulnerabilities in generating miscarriages of justice.

Dongois (Chapter 12) argues that wrongful convictions tend to delegitimate the criminal justice system as well as the authority of final decisions. Therefore, she asserts, the procedures to "revise" final rulings by admitting and, if possible, correcting wrongful convictions need to remain exceptional. French law is similar to other European countries with respect to the consequences of a successful "revision"; that is, in terms of recognizing judicial errors and restoring the rights of the wrongfully convicted. However, the limits within which such redress is open are more narrowly defined, in terms of both material and formal requirements. Dongois reviews a number of prominent cases in an attempt to make clear the limits of this remedy in the French legal system.

Another example of wrongful conviction from an international perspective is provided by Rattner (Chapter 13), who discusses the Israeli criminal justice system and the review mechanisms that exist to correct errors. He identifies one of the major constraints as the problem of denial—the opinion that such errors rarely occur—and the strong tendency to defend "the sanctity of the criminal law."

The concept of wrongful conviction may also have different meanings within different political systems. For nations such as Poland and others in Eastern Europe that have evolved from communist control to developing democracies, the question of wrongful conviction is one that must be carefully analyzed over time. In Chapter 14 Plywaczewski, Górski, and Sakowicz trace the evolution of Poland's legal and public policy responses to the problem of wrongful conviction, including both those miscarriages of justice that occurred during the earlier, repressive Stalinist legal system and those that have occurred since Poland's legal and political systems underwent democratization. In redressing errors from the Stalinst era, Poland decided that rather than nullifying those convictions that were related to political repression, they would simply be declared invalid (i.e., they were not ever valid and the persons involved were formally declared "not guilty"). Poland's current legal and public policy approaches are discussed, using actual cases to illustrate how the system works today.

Finally, in Chapter 15, the editors discuss some of the recurrent themes that emerged from the collective research represented in this volume and offer some conclusions and recommendations. As the studies in this volume clearly demonstrate, it should be possible to reduce the frequency of wrongful conviction in each of the criminal justice systems we have analyzed. Through improved understanding of the structural, organizational, and human causes of error in our systems of justice, we should be able to undertake reforms that will result in the improvement of justice—one of the most important objectives of this volume.

References

Adams, R. D., with Hoffer, W., and Hoffer, M. M. (1991). *Adams v. Texas*. New York: St. Martin's.

Borchard, E. M. (1932). *Convicting the innocent: Sixty-five actual errors of criminal justice*. Garden City, NY: Doubleday.

Bredin, J. (1986). *The affair: The case of Alfred Dreyfus*. New York: George Braziller.

Carter, D. T. (1969). *Scottsboro: A tragedy of the American South.* Baton Rouge, LA: Louisiana State University Press.

Chapman, G. (1955). *The Dreyfus case: A reassessment.* New York: Reynal.

Ehrmann, S. (1962, March). For whom the chair waits. *Federal Probation,* pp. 14–25.

Forst, B. (2004). *Errors of justice: Nature, sources and remedies.* New York: Cambridge University Press.

Frank, J., and Frank B. (1957). *Not guilty.* Garden City, NY: Doubleday.

Gardner, E. S. (1952). *The court of last resort.* New York: William Sloane.

Huff, C. R. (2002). Wrongful conviction and public policy. *Criminology, 40*(1), 1–18.

Huff, C. R., Rattner, A., and Sagarin, E. (1986). Guilty until proven innocent: Wrongful conviction and public policy. *Crime & Delinquency, 32:* 518–544.

Huff, C. R., Rattner, A., and Sagarin, E. (1996). *Convicted but innocent: Wrongful conviction and public policy.* Thousand Oaks, CA: Sage Publications.

Kennedy, L. (1985). *The airman and the carpenter: The Lindbergh kidnapping and the framing of Richard Hauptmann.* New York: Viking.

Kohn, M. L. (ed.) (1989). *Cross-national research in sociology.* Newbury Park, CA: Sage.

Morris, E. (Director) (1988). *The thin blue line* [film]. New York: Miramax Films.

Nobles, R., and Schiff, D. (2000). *Understanding miscarriages of justice.* New York: Oxford University Press.

Peters, K. (1970–1974). *Fehlerquellen im Strafprozess. Eine Untersuchung der Wiederaufnahmeverfahren in der Bundesrepublik Deutschland* [Sources of errors in criminal proceedings: A study of cases of successful petitions of revision in the Federal Republic of Germany), 3 vols. Karlsruhe, Germany: C. F. Müller.

Radelet, M. L., Bedau, H. G., & Putnam, C. E. (1992). *In spite of innocence: Erroneous convictions in capital cases.* Boston: Northeastern University Press.

Radin, E. (1964). *The innocents.* New York: William Morrow.

Scheck, B., and Neufeld, P. (2000). *Actual innocence.* New York: Doubleday.

Tuchman, B. W. (1962). *The proud tower: a portrait of the world before the war, 1890–1914.* New York: Macmillan.

Walker, C., and Starmer, K. (eds.) (1999). *Miscarriages of justice: A review of justice in error.* London: Blackstone Press.

Westervelt, S. D. and Humphrey, J. A. (eds.) (2001). *Wrongly convicted: Perspectives on failed justice.* New Brunswick, NJ: Rutgers University Press.

Zimring, F. E. (2006). The necessity and value of transnational comparative study. *Criminology and Public Policy, 5,* 615–622.

2

WRONGFUL CONVICTION
AND MORAL PANIC

*National and International Perspectives on
Organized Child Sexual Abuse*

~

RANDALL GROMETSTEIN

The study of wrongful conviction has focused on the conviction of individuals in spite of evidence that casts serious doubt on the defendant's guilt. This chapter examines a different type of case, in which several defendants may be convicted but in which doubt exists as to whether any crime was committed at all. The moral panic about organized abuse of children began in North America in the early 1980s, spread to other English-speaking countries, and is currently afflicting Western Europe. In this chapter I argue that the organized child abuse cases shed light on some weaknesses of Western legal systems that render them vulnerable to wrongful conviction. The structure of this chapter is as follows. I first discuss moral panic theory and the moral panic about organized child abuse. Then, using factors found by C. Ronald Huff (Huff, Rattner, and Sagarin, 1996; Huff 2004) to contribute to wrongful conviction, I discuss the role played by four of those factors—overzealousness by police and prosecutors; false and coerced confessions and improper interrogations; forensic errors, incompetence, and fraud; and the adversary system itself—in the organized abuse cases. Additionally, the moral panic concept suggests another source of error, namely, the weakening of traditional legal safeguards due to the perceived urgency of the danger threatening society. In conclusion, I recommend, as does Huff (2004), the establishing of criminal case review commissions, or "innocence commissions." In my view, the organized abuse cases demonstrate the need for such commissions.

The moral panic about organized child abuse began in the early 1980s in the United States and Canada, spread to the United Kingdom, the Netherlands,

Australia, and New Zealand, and more recently to France in the case in Outreau (Associated Press, 2004) and led to the arrest and charging of hundreds of defendants with serious crimes. Some of these were convicted and sentenced to severe punishment; others, although exonerated, found their lives and their businesses in ruins. In each jurisdiction, as the fear subsided, and many convicted defendants won new trials, the public was puzzled to find that so many defendants were acquitted on retrial or the charges against them were dropped altogether, although some defendants remain behind bars to this day. In each country, the cases occurred in a pattern of bizarre charges made against an expanding number of adults, based on therapists' interviews with child victims that have been criticized as unduly suggestive and coercive. Each case inspired controversy from the moment suspicions were first voiced, with the result that communities split between supporters of the prosecution and supporters of the accused. Regardless of outcome, the controversy continued to the level of the appellate courts, with whom convicted defendants have filed criminal appeals and exonerated defendants have filed civil suits seeking compensation for the loss of their reputations and livelihoods. There have been a number of governmental commissions of inquiry, which have criticized the prosecutions in question. Supporters of the prosecutions, however, remain convinced of the validity of the charges filed (see, for example, the Project Truth case in Cornwall, Ontario, described later).

Moral Panic Theory

The term *moral panic* was introduced by British sociologist Stanley Cohen in a study of how British society responded to confrontations between youth on motorcycles and the police (Cohen, 1972, 2002).[1] Historian Philip Jenkins explains that "[t]he word *panic* . . . implies not only fear but fear that is wildly exaggerated and wrongly directed . . ." (Jenkins, 1998, pp. 6–7). *Moral* indicates the evocation of deeply held beliefs about right and wrong. Moral panic theory is a branch of social construction theory, according to which, from time to time, societies "discover" social problems that are brought to collective attention by activists called claims-makers. A claims-maker presents assertions (claims) about the nature and extent of the problem; these are phrased in nonneutral terms that link them to important values or other well-established social problems (e.g., the newly coined "lawsuit abuse"). The definition of the problem is usually implied in the name (e.g., "thrownaway children"; cf. Best 1987).

Moral panics are a particular type of social problem. What distinguishes them from the general category, according to other sociologists (e.g., Goode and Ben-Yehuda, 1994; Victor, 1998), is that, in a moral panic, blame for the problem is attributed to deviant persons that Cohen (1972, 2002) called *folk-devils*. Blaming deviant people implies its own remedy, and, during a moral panic, claims-makers turn to social control authorities with demands that the deviants be dealt with. A second distinction is that, due to the urgent nature of the danger about which claims-makers warn, claims often outstrip the ability of scientific or law enforcement authorities to verify them. As a result, claims-makers themselves are acknowledged to be the experts in detecting the deviant individuals thought to be causing the problem. Claims-makers, therefore, although personally sincere, display a confirmatory bias due to their stake in having society take their claims—and their expertise—seriously.

A third distinction between ordinary social problems and moral panics is that frequently, during a moral panic, claims-makers demand a modification of traditional procedures or practices that are said to get in the way of dealing with the newly perceived problem. For example, the legal system may modify its rules of evidence and procedure to prosecute persons perceived to be so dangerous. With the subsiding of the moral panic, the modified investigative and legal procedures may remain in place to affect future cases. This chapter argues that these modified investigative and legal procedures are important for understanding some types of wrongful convictions.

Organized Abuse

Critics of the organized abuse cases often compared them to a witch hunt, a charge that claims-makers rejected indignantly. However, in the moral panic about organized child abuse, claims-makers' assertions about dangerous people operating in secret to harm vulnerable and innocent victims—while the authorities were helpless to halt these activities—persuaded many people that immediate action was necessary. Further, it was obvious that anyone who would conspire to commit these crimes must be evil, whether evil be understood in religious or secular terms. Fundamentalist Protestants and conservative Catholics viewed these cases in terms of satanic abuse or ritual abuse, while secular claims-makers such as feminists explained the very same cases as revealing evidence of organized criminal activity, such as a ring—a homosexual ring, pornography ring, prostitution ring, or pedophile ring. Fears of organized criminal rings found a ready audience, despite periodic official inquiries that failed to find supporting evidence. Along with the general public, therapists and child abuse professionals who specialized in the treatment of abused adults and children were similarly divided between those comfortable with the term *satanic ritual abuse* and those with a more secular frame of reference, who preferred either the term *sexual abuse* or the compromise term *ritual abuse*. In this chapter, *organized abuse* is used to denote both these beliefs, whether couched in religious or secular terms.[2]

Other Scares About Children's Safety

Jenkins argues that "panics emerge in groups rather than singly" (Jenkins, 1992, p. 12).[3] In North America in the 1980s, the moral panic about organized child abuse arose in a context that included the following scares: a moral panic about satanic activity (Victor, 1998); a scare about missing and murdered children (Best, 1987); great public anxiety about incest, redefined as child sexual abuse during the 1970s (Hacking, 1991); a wave of disputed custody cases in which women accused their former husbands of sexually abusing children during court-ordered visitations (Horner and Guyer, 1991a, 1991b); self-help books by women claiming to be "survivors" of incest and ritual abuse (e.g., Bass and Thornton, 1983, 1988); and therapists' claims that many of their adult women patients suffered from multiple-personality disorder as a result of severe childhood sexual and ritual abuse (Acocella, 1998). Of particular importance were claims that society was in denial about widespread child sexual abuse, and that any man could be guilty of such an offense. Thus, claims about organized child abuse by caregivers were made in a context of claims about similar issues, and the effect of claims in one panic was to reinforce claims in another.

The Moral Panic in North America

The organized abuse cases began in California, where a network of child abuse professionals and prosecutors met monthly in the early 1980s to discuss the ways in which the criminal justice system should respond to cases of incest, which was said to be a widespread but hidden problem. In the early months of 1984, the moral panic intensified when a reporter for a Los Angeles television station broke the story of the investigation into the McMartin Preschool case; he charged that adults at the school had engaged in rape, pornographic photography, and animal killing (Nathan and Snedeker, 1995, p. 87). One month later, reports on the burgeoning charges in the Jordan, Minnesota, case appeared in the national press. Following these sensational charges, a wave of cases broke across North America during the rest of 1984 (Nathan and Snedeker, 1995). In succeeding months and years, the number of new cases filed subsided quickly to a much lower level (Grometstein, 2001). The McMartin case has been extensively covered, so I give a brief summary of the Jordan, Minnesota, case.

Jordan, Minnesota

Although the Jordan case began at almost the same time as the McMartin case, it occupied national attention only for about six months, until a jury acquitted the first two of twenty-four defendants in September 1984. Despite its brief existence, the Jordan case was similar to many of the others that followed. After a woman living in a trailer park complained to police that her children had been molested by a young man who also lived in the trailer park, the children were interviewed and the young man was arrested. However, continued questioning of the four children, aged under ten, and of the young man resulted in accusations against many other residents of the trailer park, male and female, as well as a growing list of victims, who were questioned in their turn. Eventually, the list of accused included people with little or no connection to the inhabitants of the trailer park. Interestingly, the initial complainant was the fourth person arrested, and shortly thereafter her sister and brother-in-law were arrested as well, on the basis of their own children's testimony.[4] Authorities believed that the twenty-four accused were operating at least two child sex rings, that the children had witnessed the ritual slaying of babies, and that the children were forced to participate in child pornography (Malan, 1984; Rutchik, 1984). The twenty-four defendants were charged with hundreds of counts of abusing children.

In court, prosecutors concealed the satanic allegations and pursued the sexual abuse charges (Humes, 1999, p. 424). After the acquittal of the first couple, but before the trial of a second couple, the trial judge ordered the prosecution to turn over one hundred pages of police notes on a homicide investigation concerning whether some children had been murdered in sexual orgies. Rather than reveal the police notes, the prosecutor dismissed the charges against the remaining twenty-two defendants (Shipp, 1985). Even after the charges were dismissed, state authorities announced plans to dredge the Minnesota River to find the bodies of murdered children (Associated Press, 1984). The case collapsed shortly thereafter, frustrating both supporters and critics of the prosecutor, who was investigated by a commission appointed by the governor, and later defeated at the polls (Crewdson, 1988, p. 18).

In the ten years following the end of the Jordan case, organized abuse cases were filed in almost all of the fifty states and several Canadian provinces, with one of the largest occurring near the end of that period (i.e., Wenatchee, Washington, in 1993–1994). Although some defendants in these cases were acquitted at trial and others had their convictions overturned, nearly two dozen defendants remain in prison as of this writing.[5] In the meantime, however, the moral panic had spread to other countries.

Canadian Cases: Ontario and Saskatchewan

A number of important cases occurred in southern Ontario. For example, there were at least two large organized abuse cases, Project Jericho in Prescott

(1989–1995) and Project Truth in Cornwall (1996–2001).[6] In Project Jericho, fifty-two people were tried for sexually abusing children, and most of them were convicted. Social workers suspected satanic abuse, an idea that received support from the fact that one suspect was charged with the murder of an unidentified infant whose body was never found (Wilkes, 1990). Others, including the Ontario Provincial Police, rejected the satanic ritual abuse interpretation (Brent 1991). Newspapers continued to describe the arrests in Prescott as being part of a child-sex ring (Canadian Press, 1991). Project Jericho ended its six-year run in the summer of 1995, and it was considered such a success that "area police forces and the Children's Aid are considering setting up a permanent joint unit to investigate child sexual and physical abuse cases in Leeds-Grenville county" (Miller, 1995, p. B2).

By contrast, a second large organized abuse case that began fifty miles away in Cornwall, Ontario, as the Prescott case was coming to an end, had a different outcome. Project Truth was initiated to investigate allegations that a multigenerational "pedophile clan" had been operating in and around Cornwall for decades (Leroux, 1997). Fifteen men, including two priests, a doctor, and a lawyer, were arrested and charged in connection with Project Truth. In the meantime, a provincial legislator, unconvinced that all members of the pedophile clan had been identified and arrested, collected what he said were boxes of affidavits from victims and witnesses and threatened to name names on the parliamentary floor if his request for a public inquiry was not met (*Ottawa Citizen*, 2001). At least some of this material consisted of testimony about satanic ritual abuse (Rupert, 2001). Project Truth came to an end in August 2001 with the Ontario Provincial Police's announcement that they "found no evidence to substantiate allegations from at least 69 complainants that prominent members of the Cornwall community conspired to sexually prey on young boys over four decades" (Sands and Campbell, 2001). Of the fifteen men against whom charges had been laid, four men died before their cases went to trial, four were acquitted, three had charges against them withdrawn, two had charges stayed, one was deemed mentally unfit to stand trial, and one entered a guilty plea (Canadian Press, 2002). Police found no evidence of a pedophile ring and no evidence of a high-level cover-up. However, in response to calls from victim groups and other claims-makers, the Attorney General of Ontario promised to convene early in 2005 a commission of inquiry to examine, for the fourth time, whether Project Truth was properly conducted (Lajoie, 2004). Thus, the earlier Project Jericho did not challenge the existence of organized abuse, whereas Project Truth did, and that may explain the controversy at the latter's ending.

The capital of the province of Saskatchewan, Saskatoon, was the site of at least two important cases of organized child abuse that began at about the same time in 1991, the Sterling/Martensville case and the foster children case. The first involved a family home day care run by Ron and Linda Sterling and their 22-year-old son Travis in Martensville, a suburb of Saskatoon, in which the family, a female juvenile, and several members of the Martensville police force were accused of ritually abusing the children at the day care. Ron and Linda Sterling were acquitted at trial, but their son Travis and the young woman were convicted, although the latter's conviction was over-turned shortly thereafter. Charges against the police were dropped after the Sterlings' trial, but the Martensville police force was disbanded.

The Saskatchewan foster children case involved the children's accusations of extreme sexual and ritual abuse committed against them by the members of their extended foster family and another family. In 1991, an investigatory team of a police officer, a therapist, and two Crown prosecutors arrested six-teen adults. Eighteen months later, all charges were stayed against the defen-dants (except for one who entered a guilty plea), on the grounds that the children were too traumatized to undergo a trial. In 1994, the defendants, unable to clear their names, filed suit for malicious prosecution against the members of the investigatory team, and, in 2003, nearly twenty years after the case began, in a landmark decision, the Saskatchewan Court of Queen's Bench found on behalf of the sixteen people accused of abusing the children (*D.K. v. Miazga* 2003). The court found that the investigatory team had no reasonable basis for pursuing charges against the accused (Grometstein, 2007). Justice Baynton's exhaustive and carefully reasoned critique of the investigation conducted in this case should have far-reaching effects on this type of prosecution—unless the Crown's appeal is successful.[7]

England and the Netherlands

By 1986, England was experiencing a moral panic about organized child abuse similar to that in North America (cf. Jenkins, 1992). After pediatri-cians in Leeds began applying the new reflex anal dilation test (cf. Nathan and Snedeker, 1995, Chapter 9), the number of children suspected of being sexually abused grew at an alarming rate, and in 1986 Leeds became "the first British community to experience a child abuse crisis on a pattern that would shortly be experienced in other areas" (Jenkins, 1992, p. 135). By the spring of 1987, pediatricians in Middlesbrough, county of Cleveland, employed the same test and discovered startling numbers of sexually abused children, whom social services agencies then removed from their parents' custody. A series of "little Clevelands" followed (Jenkins, 1992, p. 148), many of which involved allegations of satanic ritual abuse. Examples in 1990 include the Rochdale case, the Manchester case, the Nottingham case, and the Orkney case, which culminated in the infamous dawn raids by social workers in February 1991 to remove children from their parents' care (Jenkins, 1992, Chapter 8). The public uproar over the Orkney raid ended the raids and led to an official inquiry in July 1991. In 1994 a comprehensive official study by anthropologist J. S. La Fontaine found that there was no basis for believing in the satanic ritual abuse of children in Britain (La Fontaine, 1994; see also La Fontaine, 1998). Although the moral panic appeared to subside, it flared up again in 2000 following the murder of an eight-year-old girl named Sarah Payne. For several weeks during that summer, the tabloid *News of the World* published the names and addresses of people it said were pedophiles, and mobs around the country stoned the houses of people whose names appeared on the list, or who had the same name as someone on the list (Cullen, 2000).

As pediatricians in Middlesbrough, Cleveland, were discovering a sexual abuse crisis in 1987, the moral panic spread to the Netherlands, where organized abuse was discovered in the village of Oude Pekela (Jonker and Jonker-Bakker, 1991), as well as to Australia and New Zealand.

Australia

The state of New South Wales made combating child sexual abuse a priority in 1984 (Jenkins, 1992, p. 230, n. 1). In November 1988, the "Mr. Bubbles" case began in New South Wales with the arrest of the owners of a kindergarten and two of their assistants on charges of sexual and ritual abuse of seventeen children said to have taken place over eleven months. After a six-week committal hearing, the magistrate dismissed the charges when experts testified that the testimony of the children had likely been contaminated by repeated, suggestive, and coercive questioning. While the parents of the alleged victims called for a commission of inquiry, the husband and wife who owned the kindergarten were awarded $227,000 in costs by the magistrate who had freed them. Some years later, in response to criticism from claims-makers who feared a cover-up had taken place, the Wood Commission conducted an inquiry, finding in August 1997 that the trail was "too old" and the evidence of the children "too contaminated" to ever establish what really happened in the Mr. Bubbles case. The kindergarten owners then sued the state of New South Wales for defamation based on statements made to the press by police during the investigation of the case. A jury awarded the couple $750,000 in damages, but an appeals court ordered a new trial of the husband's defamation case.

New Zealand

In 1992, in New Zealand, Peter Ellis and four female child care workers at the Christchurch Civic Crèche (child care center) were charged with abusing children in a bizarre fashion, although only Ellis was tried. He was convicted in June 1993 on sixteen counts of indecency with young children. In September 1994 he appealed, and three counts on which he had been convicted were overturned, due to the recantation of the child witness, but thirteen counts were affirmed. Two further appeals were unsuccessful (*Ellis v. R.*, 1998, 1999). The 1999 appeal specifically raised the issue of organized abuse prosecutions (using the term "mass allegations") and their flaws, but the court declared that it was not the forum in which to address these issues.

France: l'affaire d'Outreau[8]

In recent years, Europe has been inundated by charges of sex rings, pornography rings, Satanism, and sex crimes committed against children.[9] During the 1990s, "internationally-linked child abuse networks have been uncovered in France, Spain, Italy, Britain, Germany, Austria and Poland" (Pinon, 1997). In 1991, a young judge-magistrate in the northern French town of Outreau began investigating allegations that some children had been sexually abused. His inquiries led to charges of rape, torture, and bestiality from 1996 to 2000 in the home of a family named Delay in a housing project in Outreau, accompanied by the confessions of Thierry and Myriam Badoui Delay and a couple who were their neighbors (Smith, 2004). The four confessed abusers were arrested, along with thirteen other suspects who protested their innocence, including a neighborhood priest. Many of the seventeen accused were held before trial for three years, during which time one committed suicide. When the case finally came to trial in May 2004, the principal accused, Mme. Delay and her neighbor, Aurélie Grenon, stunned the courtroom when they recanted their accusations against their thirteen co-defendants. One defendant was released provisionally, but, despite public criticism, the presiding judge refused to release the other seven who had maintained their innocence. A week later, after indignant editorials in both left-wing and right-wing newspapers, the seven defendants were released, even though Mme. Delay then renewed her original accusations, including a statement that she had abused her own children, and accused her husband of murdering a young Moroccan girl (Agence-France-Presse, 2004b). The psychologists who had questioned the children were examined in court, as was the judge-magistrate who had begun the investigation. In early July 2004, the jury convicted ten people, including the two couples who had confessed and six of the defendants who had been released a few weeks earlier. Seven defendants (including the suicide) were acquitted. This result satisfied neither supporters nor critics of the prosecution. A day later, the French justice minister, promising a commission of inquiry, apologized to the exonerated defendants and stated, "This must not happen again" (Lichfield, 2004). More than a year later, as the appeal by the convicted defendants opened in November 2005, Thierry and Myriam Badoui Delay (now serving sentences of twenty years and fifteen years, respectively) reiterated that only they and their two neighbors were guilty; the other six had "done absolutely nothing" (Agence-France-Presse, 2005a). At the appeal hearing the state "deliberately failed to renew its case [against the six defendants]—a clear act of recognition that the six were victims of a miscarriage of justice" (Agence-France-Presse, 2005c). The senior prosecutor expressed his regrets to the convicted six. On December 7, 2005, French lawmakers voted to open a parliamentary inquiry into the Outreau case, to answer questions about "the willingness of social services and psychiatric experts to accept uncorroborated allegations made by young children, and about the power given to lone examining magistrates under the French system" (Agence-France-Presse, 2005b).

Contributing Factor 1: Overzealousness by Police and Prosecutors

Several of the factors identified by Huff and his colleagues (Huff, Rattner, and Sagarin, 1996) as contributing to wrongful convictions were important in the organized abuse cases. First, and most important, the organized abuse cases were characterized by a marked degree of police and prosecutorial overzealousness. For example, in a number of cases, prosecutors concealed the most bizarre charges of satanic ritual abuse from the defense, choosing instead to focus on the allegations of sexual abuse. In other cases, evidence disappeared (e.g., therapists' notes, as well as audiotaped or videotaped interviews by therapists with the children). Additionally, investigators were given manuals to follow, such as *Investigation and Prosecution of Child Abuse*, published by the American Prosecutors Research Institute (2003), in which the claims about organized abuse were fully set out, including a copy of the seminal paper by psychiatrist Roland Summit (1983) (discussed later). Three appellate court opinions detail this overzealousness: *California v. Pitts* (California Court of Appeal, 1990), *D.K. v. Miazga* (Saskatchewan Court of Queen's Bench, 2003), and *Valentin v. Los Angeles* (California Court of Appeal, 2000; see Grometstein, 2007). In general, police and prosecutors displayed a confirmatory bias that derived from their acceptance of the claims on which the moral panic was based.

Contributing Factor 2: False and Coerced Confessions and Improper Interrogations

Almost from the beginning of the moral panic, critics questioned the methods used to question the child victims (see, e.g., *New Jersey v. Michaels*, 1993, 1994). Recent research has supported the critics (Ceci and Bruck, 1995; Nathan and Snedeker, 1995). Although a number of suspects confessed initially to the accusations against them, these confessions were not supported by evidence. There are many reasons why suspects might confess falsely to a crime they did not commit. These reasons can include torture, brutality, threats, fear, fatigue, and deception by the interrogator (Huff, Rattner, and Sagarin, 1996; Huff, 2004). The chances of a false confession are increased when there is great community pressure to solve a crime (Huff, Rattner, and Sagarin, 1996); in a moral panic, the concept of "innocent until proven guilty" is often suspended. To this we may add that defendants who demand a trial of the charges against them may suffer the so-called trial penalty, in which a convicted defendant is sentenced more harshly because he or she is viewed as refusing to take responsibility through a plea of guilty (Givelber, 2000). In the organized abuse cases, convicted defendants in the United States were sentenced to such long sentences (e.g., 165 years in the case of Frank Fuster, Country Walk Babysitting, in Miami, Florida), that other defense lawyers routinely urged their clients to plead guilty. In the climate of public opinion prevailing during a moral panic, even an upright citizen with an unblemished record facing such heinous charges can expect a harsh response from judge and jury.

Contributing Factor 3: Forensic Errors, Incompetence, and Fraud

The organized abuse cases are replete with innovative investigative techniques that were developed under the perceived emergency conditions created by the moral panic. Subsequent research has established the weaknesses of the interviewing techniques used with young children who were believed (Summit, 1983) to be reluctant or afraid to disclose abuse (see review by Ceci and Bruck, 1995). Similarly, claims that sexual abuse could be diagnosed from children's drawings (Burgess, McCausland, and Wolbert, 1981), from children's play with anatomically correct dolls (Leventhal et al., 1989; Realmuto, Jensen, and Wescoe, 1990), and from examination of a child's hymen with a colposcope or from the reflex anal dilation test (McCann et al., 1989; McCann et al., 1990; Nathan and Snedeker, 1995) proved untenable. Additionally, laboratory tests for sexually transmitted diseases such as gonorrhea were criticized by the Centers for Disease Control.[10] Other than these unreliable forensic techniques, prosecutors only had testimonial evidence—from the very young victims or from a child abuse professional who had examined the children. We turn next to these two forms of evidence.

Contributing Factor 4: Legal Innovations

One of the claims of a moral panic is that existing lines of defense against danger are inadequate and new weapons are needed. This was true of the organized child abuse cases. First, and most important, was the fact that prosecutors and police were dependent on a finding by a child abuse professional that a child had been sexually abused. It often required months of therapy before the therapist determined to his or her satisfaction how and by whom the child had been abused, months during which police officers were assigned to look for corroborative evidence. By the time it became clear that no such evidence could be found (no pornographic pictures, no witnesses, no documents, and no other physical evidence was found to support the charges), police and prosecutors had become emotionally invested in the truth of the charges, and the lack of corroboration could be interpreted as evidence of the cunning of ruthless criminals. Lacking physical evidence of the crime, and aware that not only did parents not want their children to take the stand, but were eager to take the stand themselves, prosecutors turned to new procedural weapons that legislatures had recently created.

Modified legal rules included two exceptions to the general prohibition on hearsay testimony—the fresh complaint/spontaneous declaration rule and an expanded definition of when a child witness is "unavailable" to testify—as well as rules permitting children to testify from behind a screen or outside the courtroom via closed-circuit television. These modified rules resulted from the erosion of a long-standing skepticism about children's capacity to testify as witnesses, as well as the belief that child witnesses required special accommodation. Most important, it was necessary to explain to the judge and jury the prevailing claims about child sexual abuse, such as the claims in the seminal paper *The Child Sexual Abuse Accommodation Syndrome* (Summit, 1983); for example, that children are reluctant to disclose sexual abuse, and thus a child might not disclose abuse until months or years after its occurrence, and that children do not lie about these matters. Once these claims were accepted by courts, parents and therapists could be trusted to repeat in court what the children had told them because such statements were understood to be particularly reliable. A further claim in Summit's paper, that anyone who questioned a charge of sexual abuse risked revictimizing the victim, who was entitled to support and encouragement instead of skepticism, served to justify rules that permitted children not to face the accused caregivers directly in court but instead to testify via closed-circuit television or from behind a screen—if they testified at all.[11] In many states, judges were given great latitude in ruling that the child was "unavailable" to testify and thus permitting a parent and therapist to testify in the child's stead.

A long-standing evidentiary rule allows a party to present testimony from any expert concerning matters outside the ordinary knowledge of jurors. In the organized abuse cases, child abuse professionals explained to jurors how they used checklists of behaviors that sexually abused children were thought to display—checklists of ordinary behaviors, like difficulty falling asleep and reluctance to go to preschool—to diagnose sexual abuse.[12] Psychiatrists, psychologists, and even social workers were allowed to testify about the general characteristics of a sexually abused child, and then to continue testifying as to why, in their opinion, this particular child had been sexually abused, a practice that, as several appeals courts pointed out, invaded the province of the jury as fact-finder. The organized abuse cases represent an enormous expansion of the use of expert testimony to establish the *corpus delicti* (i.e., the fact that a crime had occurred), as well as, in many cases, the guilt of the defendant.[13] The central role of expert witnesses is the feature of the organized abuse cases that calls to mind most strongly Elliott Currie's (1968) description of witch finders in Renaissance Europe.

The Adversary System

Trial courts were as likely as prosecutors and police to be caught up in the moral panic about organized abuse. The severe sentences handed down to convicted defendants support this assertion, as do the criticisms of some of the appellate courts that overturned convictions. Furthermore, some appellate courts rebuffed numerous appeals of defendants in the organized abuse cases, for example, courts in Massachusetts,[14] Florida,[15] New York,[16] and North Carolina.[17] These courts retreated behind the traditionally narrow scope of appellate review,[18] and, in some cases, it is clear from the court's language that the appellate court itself believed the claim that the child victims had been abused.[19] By contrast, a few appellate courts faced up to the possibility that something can go fundamentally wrong in these types of prosecutions; see, for example, the New Jersey Supreme Court,[20] the Nevada Supreme Court,[21] the Ohio Court of Appeals,[22] the Utah Supreme Court,[23] and some of the judges of the Ninth Circuit Court of Appeals.[24] The Saskatchewan Court of Queen's Bench, as noted earlier in this chapter, wrote a particularly trenchant analysis of an organized abuse prosecution (*D.K. v. Miazga*, 2003).

The organized abuse cases underscore the limitations of appellate review in criminal cases, in light of the likelihood that no crimes were committed at all. The establishment, therefore, of criminal case review commissions, or "innocence commissions" (Huff, 2004), empowered to examine actual innocence and not just procedural violations, could provide protection for defendants caught up in a moral panic.

Conclusions

The organized child sexual abuse cases demonstrate that the Anglo-American and European legal systems are vulnerable to claims-makers advancing new and untested claims against those identified as deviants in an atmosphere of urgency and danger. In addition to the wider society, all participants in the court process—prosecutors, judges, and especially jurors—are vulnerable to being swept up in the moral panic. Claims-makers come forward with claims of special expertise and offer their guidance to the criminal justice system. As a result, they may be allowed to go beyond the traditional scope of expert testimony and testify that a crime was committed by the defendant on trial. Legislatures may weaken or eliminate time-tested legal safeguards; for example, California's retroactive extension of the statute of limitations for molestation in 1994, passed at a time when claims of "repressed memory" seemed compelling; however, the measure was recently struck down by the California Supreme Court (Finz, 2003).[25] Fortunately, as a moral panic subsides, it becomes possible for dissenting voices to make themselves heard, and for authorities to scrutinize closely the claims that have been made. However, whether or not claims-makers lose a particular case, they may still win the war. For example, innovative legal procedures may not be reexamined, and limitations on the scope of appellate review, as we have seen, may prevent an appellate court from correcting mistakes made at the trial level.

Moral panics are a useful tool for understanding how some situations are conducive to wrongful conviction. For example, Huff and his colleagues have identified a number of historical *causes célèbres* that may fit the moral panic model, for example, the cases of Leo Frank, the Scottsboro boys, and possibly the Lindbergh baby kidnapping (Huff, Rattner, and Sagarin, 1996, pp. 27–32); they also identify community pressure for conviction (p. 75) as a cause of wrongful conviction, and certainly community pressure is a feature of a moral panic. Furthermore, if police and prosecutorial misconduct is a cause of many wrongful convictions, as argued by Huff and his colleagues, as well as Humphrey and Westervelt (2002), that misconduct may be more readily understandable under moral panic conditions (cf. Grometstein, 2007). The theory of moral panic suggests a new avenue of inquiry into the subject of wrongful conviction, and the organized child abuse cases suggest that the incidence of wrongful convictions taking place in our system is not trivial.

Notes

1. *Moral panic* is not a completely satisfactory term; it has generated criticism from scholars (e.g., Cornwell & Linders 2002) and offended social actors in a moral panic with the implication that they acted blindly or irresponsibly. Despite these caveats, however, it has become a well-established term.

2. British anthropologist J. S. La Fontaine (1994), who studied the moral panic about organized child abuse in the United Kingdom, explains the origin of the term *organized abuse* as follows: "This term was adopted to cover paedophile rings and other cases . . . in which large numbers of abusers were identified, together with cases in which satanic abuse was alleged. . . . By using a neutral term both organizations hoped to avoid a damaging split in their ranks between those who believed the allegations of 'satanic' or 'ritual' abuse and those who did not" (La Fontaine 1998, p. 11). La Fontaine herself uses "organized abuse" thus: "Defined as cases involving multiple perpetrators collaborating to abuse children" (La Fontaine 1998, p. 196, n. 4). Other analysts have used other terms. For example, in his book on the moral panic in Britain, Jenkins (1992) refers to the panic as one of "mass abuse" and "mass organized abuse." In the United States, FBI behavioral specialist Kenneth Lanning used the term "multi-victim, multiple perpetrator" (MVMP) cases. This chapter uses the term *organized abuse.*

3. Jenkins further explains: "Problem construction is a cumulative or incremental process, in which each issue is to some extent built upon its predecessors, in the context of a steadily developing fund of 'socially available knowledge'" (Jenkins 1992, p. 13).

4. In a later televised interview, these two children described the grueling questioning they had undergone: "'They questioned us one time from 6 o'clock in the morning until 10 o'clock at night,' the girl told a reporter. 'I told them what they wanted to hear. I told them lies'" (Associated Press 1985).

5. For example, James Toward of the Glendale Montessori School in Stuart, Florida; Bernard Baran of Pittsfield, Massachusetts; Frank Fuster of Miami; Robert Halsey of Lanesborough, Massachusetts; Daniel and Frances Keller of Austin, Texas; Marilynn Malcom of Vancouver, Washington; Michael Alan Parker and Mildred Parker of Hendersonville, North Carolina; James Watt of Mount Vernon, New York; Debbie Runyan of Bainbridge Island, Washington; Michael Joseph Schildmeyer of Edgewood, Iowa; Nancy Smith of Lorain, Ohio; Stephen Boatwright of Reno, Nevada; the Rev. Lonnie Fawbush of Lower Brule, South Dakota; Walter West, Jr., of Hapeville, Georgia; Kenneth Holloway of North Little Rock, Arkansas; and John E. "Red" Baine of Clarksdale, Mississippi.

6. Prescott and Cornwall are located along the St. Lawrence Seaway, about fifty miles apart. Ottawa is about fifty miles northeast and northwest of the two towns, respectively.

7. The plaintiffs in the defamation case have received apologies from the provincial premier (Warick 2004a) and from the three officials criticized in Justice Baynton's ruling: the Crown prosecutor, the police officer, and the therapist (Warick 2004b). The province agreed to pay $1.5 million (Cdn.) to the twelve plaintiffs in June 2004 and made an interim payment, despite the fact that the Justice Minister and Attorney General of the province have applied for intervenor status in the appeal of the defamation case (Wood 2004).

8. This phrase recalls *l'affaire Dreyfus*, a case of wrongful conviction discussed by Huff, Rattner, and Sagarin (1996).

9. See "Italians arrested for Satanism and child abuse" (Agence-France-Presse 2002); the Casa Pia trial in Portugal, which appears to resemble strongly the Outreau case (EuroNews 2005); and the Marc Dutroux case in Belgium (Agence-France-Presse 2004a). When the bodies of four newborn babies were discovered in a French village near Mulhouse, in Alsace, some people blamed "Satanists, gypsies, and the eastern European prostitution rings which have colonized many French cities in the past five years" (Lichfield 2003).

10. See www.pbs.org/wgbh/pages/frontline/shows/terror/cases/medical.html, and sources cited therein (last accessed August 4, 2006).

11. In *Ortiz v. Georgia* (1988), the Georgia Court of Appeals asked: "Would the [child] victim be more likely to tell the truth if forced to stare the defendant in the face? Certainly not as a matter of law and certainly not as a matter of fact. We have no information as to such a proposition and only superstition would suggest it." By contrast, most other courts conceded the importance of the right of confrontation but found reasons to override it (cf. *Maryland v. Craig* 1990).

12. Cf. the case of Kelly Michaels/Wee Care, Maplewood, New Jersey (*New Jersey v. Michaels* 1993), in which a social worker listed thirty-two items on a behavioral checklist and stated that "clusters" of five to fifteen symptoms allowed her to diagnose sexual abuse (1993 N.J. Super. Lexis at 186).

13. In the French case in Outreau, for example, the court heard testimony from the psychologists who had interviewed the child victims, but not from the children themselves. The psychologists' belief that the children were credible witnesses sufficed.

14. Massachusetts cases include Bernard Baran of Pittsfield, Robert Halsey of Lanesborough, and the Amirault family of the Fells Acres Day School. Baran and Halsey remain in prison as of this writing. In refusing motions for new trials for Violet Amirault and her daughter, Cheryl Amirault LeFave, after their release from prison, the Supreme Judicial Court cited concerns for finality of judgment (*Mass. v. Violet Amirault* 1997, *Mass. v. Cheryl Amirault LeFave* 1999). Gerald Amirault was released on parole in May 2004 after spending eighteen years in prison (Ranalli 2004).

15. Two of the Florida cases have been the subjects of documentaries by the Public Broadcasting System show *Frontline*: the Frank Fuster/Country Walk case (*Frontline* 2002) and the Harold Grant Snowden case (*Frontline* 1998). Snowden was released following a habeas corpus appeal to the Eleventh Circuit Court of Appeals (*Snowden v. Singletary* 1998). In Stuart, Florida, James Toward of the Glendale Montessori School served a ten-year sentence and then was civilly committed as a violent sexual offender (Taylor 2002).

16. In 1984, five cases in the Bronx resulted in long sentences for Alberto Algarin, Jesus Torres, Franklin Beauchamp, Alberto Ramos, and the Rev. Nathaniel Grady. The minister was the last to obtain his release. In 1996 a federal district court granted Grady's petition for habeas corpus and ordered a new state appeal (*Grady v. Artuz* 1996). The New York Appellate Division reversed his conviction in one sentence (*New York v. Grady* 1997). The prosecution declined to retry him. In 2004, the Appellate Division affirmed the Court of Claims' dismissal of Grady's claim for unjust conviction and imprisonment (*Grady v. New York* 2004).

Another New York case is that of James Watt of Mount Vernon, Westchester County. In 1987 he was convicted, largely on the testimony of a social worker named Eileen

Treacy, who had interviewed the child victims and determined that they had been sexually abused. Ms. Treacy played a similar role in the well-known New Jersey case of Kelly Michaels and Wee Care Nursery School (*New Jersey v. Michaels* 1993, 1994), and the two New Jersey courts were critical of her role in that case, overturning Michaels's conviction and ruling that in the future a pretrial hearing would be required to show that the children's testimony had not been tainted by coercive or suggestive questioning. In the James Watt case, the New York courts did not share the skepticism of the New Jersey courts concerning Ms. Treacy's ability to diagnose child sexual abuse. Instead, in 1992 the New York Appellate Division reversed Watt's conviction on the grounds that the indictment had lacked specificity by stating that the children had been assaulted over a five-month period (*New York v. Watt* 1992). The Appellate Division also noted in passing that the prosecution had violated discovery rules by not providing the defense with any information about what the children had told the social worker until after they had taken the stand. The Appellate Division was overruled by the Court of Appeals (*New York v. Watt* 1993a), whereupon the Appellate Division dutifully agreed that five months did not constitute a lack of specificity (*New York v. Watt* 1993b). Finally, the Court of Appeals affirmed Watt's conviction (*New York v. Watt* 1994).

17. See, for example, the cases of Patrick Figured of Smithfield (*North Carolina v. Patrick S. Figured* 1994) and Michael Alan Parker of Henderson (*North Carolina v. Parker* 1995).

18. See, for example, the Saskatchewan Court of Appeal (*R. v. Sterling* 1995) and the Court of Appeal, Wellington, NZ (*R. v. Ellis* 1999). In the latter case, the court noted (paragraph 27) that the defense had supplied it with the *Report of the Inquiry into Child Abuse in Cleveland 1987,* the *Report of the Inquiry into the Removal of Children from Orkney in February 1991,* and the *Royal Commission into the New South Wales Police Service Final Report* of August 1997 (Vol. IV, *The Paedophile Inquiry*). The court stated: "It is impossible, and in our view it would be inappropriate, to attempt to undertake a comprehensive analysis of it with a view to reaching a conclusion on some particular aspect of relevance to the present appeal. Such an exercise is more the function of a formal commission, which is empowered to inquire into and report upon certain defined matters. This Court is not the forum for reviewing or evaluating the conclusions reached by the various authors, some of which understandably in these difficult and constantly developing areas are conflicting" (*R. v. Ellis* 1999, para. 27).

19. In *Maryland v. Craig* (1990), the U.S. Supreme Court affirmed a Maryland statute permitting child witnesses to present their testimony by closed-circuit television, thus weakening the accused's Sixth Amendment right to confront the witnesses against him or her. Justice O'Connor, writing for the court, cited authorities for the proposition that testifying in court could be stressful for children.

20. *New Jersey v. Michaels* (1994), as well as the New Jersey Appellate Division in *New Jersey v. Michaels* (1993).

21. *Nevada v. Babyan* (1990) and *Felix and Ontiveros v. Nevada* (1993). The Nevada Supreme Court, in the latter case, specifically noted the influence of both the McMartin Preschool case in Los Angeles and the Babyan case in Nevada on the conduct of the Felix and Ontiveros case.

22. *Ohio v. Aldridge and Wilcox* (1997).

23. *Utah v. Hadfield* (1990).

24. *Devereaux v. Abbey* (2001), Kleinfeld, J., dissenting. This was the unsuccessful civil suit brought by a wrongfully convicted defendant in the Wenatchee, Washington,

case, against the various law enforcement and social workers who had participated in the criminal case.

25. The Supreme Court of South Carolina reached the opposite result in Moriarty v. Garden Sanctuary Church of God (2000). The court stated that the repressed memory syndrome is valid in South Carolina, and a plaintiff may bring a timely cause of action under the discovery rule after recovering the memories. The plaintiff in this case attended the church's day care center from 1973 to 1976, and stated that she recovered memories of abuse while receiving mental health counseling in 1992.

References

Acocella, J. (1998, April 6). The politics of hysteria: Over the past twenty years, multiple-personality disorder has been used to explain the behavior of thousands of American women. How was it allowed to happen? *The New Yorker,* pp. 64–79.

Agence-France-Presse. (2002, October 16). Italians arrested for satanism and child abuse. Rome: Author.

Agence-France-Presse. (2004a, December 15). Belgium's top court throws out Dutroux appeal. Brussels, Belgium: Author.

Agence-France-Presse. (2004b, May 24). French child sex trial turns confused after accusations repeated. Saint-Omer, France: Author.

Agence-France-Presse. (2005a, November 18). Charges collapse in French child sex trial. Paris: Author.

Agence-France-Presse. (2005b, December 7). French Parliament backs inquiry into child sex legal fiasco. Paris: Author.

Agence-France-Presse. (2005c, December 1). Six cleared of child sex charges in France after judicial fiasco. Paris: Author.

American Prosecutors Research Institute (2003). Investigation and prosecution of child abuse. 3rd ed. Thousand Oaks, CA: Sage.

Associated Press. (1984, October 30). Officials to drag river for bodies in child abuse probe. *San Diego Union-Tribune,* p. A8.

Associated Press. (1985, May 19). Two children say they fabricated sex abuse stories. *Los Angeles Times,* p. 25.

Associated Press. (2004, May 21). Pedophile case shakes system: About-turn by accuser in France leads to a judicial shipwreck: Lawyer. *Montreal Gazette,* p. A19.

Bass, E., & Thornton, L. (1983). *I never told anyone: Writings by women survivors of child sexual abuse.* New York: Harper & Row.

Bass, E., and Thornton, L. (1988). *The courage to heal: A guide for women survivors of child sexual abuse.* New York: Perennial Library.

Best, J. (1987). Rhetoric in claims-making: Constructing the missing child problem. *Social Problems, 34*(2), 101–121.

Brent, B. (1991, January 23). Rising number of abuse cases has town baffled. *Toronto Star,* p. A12.

Burgess, A. W., McCausland, M. P., & Wolbert, W. A. (1981). Children's drawings as indicators of sexual trauma. *Perspectives in Psychiatric Care, 19*(2), 50–58.

Canadian Press. (1991, September 9). Sex trial charges stayed over delay. *Toronto Star,* p. A9.

Canadian Press. (2002, June 18). Last charges withdrawn in Project Truth probe. *Ottawa Citizen,* p. D8.

Ceci, S. J., & Bruck, M. (1995). *Jeopardy in the courtroom: A scientific analysis of children's testimony.* Washington, DC: American Psychological Association.

Cohen, S. (1972). *Folk devils and moral panics.* Oxford, UK: Blackwell.

Cohen, S. (2002). *Folk devils and moral panics.* London: Routledge.

Cornwell, B., & Linders, A. (2002). The myth of "moral panic": An alternate account of LSD prohibition. *Deviant Behavior, 23,* 307–330.

Crewdson, J. (1988). *By silence betrayed: Sexual abuse of children in America.* Boston: Little, Brown.

Cullen, K. (2000, August 13). Gossip fuels a mob's fury; Britons rage against suspected pedophiles. *Boston Globe,* p. A1.

Currie, E. P. (1968). Crimes without criminals: Witchcraft and its control in Renaissance Europe. *Law and Society Review, 3,* 7–32.

EuroNews. (2005, May 2). Alleged victims testify in Portugal's Casa Pia trial.

Finz, S. (2003, June 29). Repressed memory hysteria prompted molestation ruling; Defense lawyers have high praise for court decision. *San Francisco Chronicle,* p. A7.

Frontline. (1998, October 27). The child terror. *Frontline.* PBS. Retrieved September 1, 2006, from http://www.pbs.org/wgbh/pages/frontline/shows/terror/etc/script.html

Frontline. (2002, April 25). Did Daddy do it? *Frontline.* PBS. Retrieved September 1, 2006, from http://www.pbs.org/wgbh/pages/frontline/shows/fuster/

Givelber, D. (2000). Punishing protestations of innocence: Denying responsibility and its consequences. *American Criminal Law Review, 37,* 1363.

Goode, E., & Ben-Yehuda, N. (1994). *Moral panics: The social construction of deviance.* Oxford, UK: Blackwell.

Grometstein, R. (2001). *The activity and validity of claims-making during a moral panic: The example of the daycare center cases, 1983–1995.* Unpublished doctoral dissertation. Law, Policy and Society Program, Graduate School of Arts and Sciences, Northeastern University, Boston.

Grometstein, R. (2007/January/February). Prosecutorial misconduct and noble-cause corruption. *Criminal Law Bulletin, 43,* 63–75.

Hacking, I. (1991, Winter). The making and molding of child abuse. *Critical Inquiry, 17,* 253–288.

Horner, T. M., &. Guyer M. J. (1991a). Prediction, prevention and clinical expertise in child custody cases in which allegations of child sexual abuse have been made: (I) Predictable rates of diagnostic error in relation to various clinical decisionmaking strategies. *Family Law Quarterly, 25,* 217–251.

Horner, T. M., & Guyer M. J. (1991b). Prediction, prevention, and clinical expertise in child custody cases in which allegations of child sexual abuse have been made: (II) Prevalence rates of child sexual abuse and the precision of "tests" constructed to diagnose it. *Family Law Quarterly, 25,* 381–409.

Huff, C. R. (2004). Wrongful conviction: The American experience. *Canadian Journal of Criminology, 46*(2), 107–120.

Huff, C. R., Rattner, A., & Sagarin, E. (1996). *Convicted but innocent: Wrongful conviction and public policy.* Thousand Oaks, CA: Sage.

Humes, E. (1999). *Mean justice: A town's terror, a prosecutor's power, a betrayal of innocence.* New York: Pocket Books.

Humphrey, J. A., & Westervelt, S. D. (2002). Introduction. In S. D. Westervelt & J. A. Humphrey (Eds.), *Wrongly convicted: Perspectives on failed justice* (pp. 1–16). New Brunswick, NJ: Rutgers University Press.

Jenkins, P. (1992). *Intimate enemies: Moral panics in contemporary Great Britain*. New York: Aldine de Gruyter.

Jenkins, P. (1998). *Moral panic: Changing concepts of the child molester in modern America*. New Haven, CT: Yale University Press.

Jonker, F., & Jonker-Bakker, I. (1991). Experiences with ritualistic child sexual abuse: A case study from the Netherlands. *Child Abuse and Neglect, 15,* 191–196.

La Fontaine, J. S. (1994). *The extent and nature of organised and ritual abuse: Research findings*. London: Her Majesty's Stationery Office.

La Fontaine, J. S. (1998). *Speak of the devil: Tales of satanic abuse in contemporary England*. Cambridge, UK: Cambridge University Press.

Lajoie, K. (2004, November 30). Project Truth inquiry to be convened very soon. *Brockville (Ontario) Recorder and Times*, p. .

Leroux, J. (1997, July 26). OPP probes Cornwall sex "clan"; Town cop alleges clergy, public officials involved in child abuse. *Toronto Sun*, p. 2.

Leventhal, J. M., Hamilton, J., Rekedal, S., Tebano-Micci, A., & Eyster, C. (1989). Anatomically correct dolls used in interviews of young children suspected of having been sexually abused. *Pediatrics, 84,* 900–906.

Lichfield, J. (2003, October 31). French baby murders lead to macabre rumours of satanic ritual abuse. *The Independent (London)*, p. 13.

Lichfield, J. (2004, July 3). Minister apologises after child sex trial ends in farce. *The Independent (London)*, p. 28.

Malan, M. (1984, August 19). First trial set to begin in child abuse cases. Associated Press.

McCann, J., Voris, J., Simon, M., & Wells, R. (1989). Perianal findings in prepubertal children selected for nonabuse: A descriptive study. *Child Abuse and Neglect, 13,* 179–193.

McCann, J., Wells, R., Simon, M., & Voris, J. (1990). Genital findings in prepubertal girls selected for nonabuse: A descriptive study. *Pediatrics, 86,* 428–439.

Miller, J. (1995, March 25). Walls come down on child abuse; Social workers, police work together to seal convictions. *Ottawa Citizen*, p. B2.

Nathan, D., & Snedeker, M. (1995). *Satan's silence: Ritual abuse and the making of a modern American witch hunt*. New York: Basic Books.

Ottawa Citizen. (2001, October 25). Ontario tries to block probe into Project Truth case.

Pinon, B. (1997, August 10). Pedophilia. Brussels, Belgium: Agence-France-Presse.

Ranalli, R. (2004, May 1). Amirault is freed from prison; Conviction stands in day-care abuse. *Boston Globe*, p. A1.

Realmuto, G. M., Jensen, J. B., & Wescoe, S. (1990). Specificity and sensitivity of sexually anatomically correct dolls in substantiating abuse: A pilot study. *Journal of the American Academy of Child and Adolescent Psychiatry, 29,* 743–750.

Rupert, J. (2001, May 29). What Guzzo's got: MPP Garry Guzzo has amassed boxes of affidavits testifying to the existence of a pedophile "clan" in the Cornwall area. *Ottawa Citizen*, p. A1.

Rutchik, J. (1984, October 19). State takes over child porn probe. *United Press International*.

Sands, A., & Campbell, D. (2001, August 24). Project Truth cover-up "continues"; Ex-officer: End of investigation a "great win for the pedophiles." *Ottawa Citizen*, p. C1.

Shipp, E. R. (1985, August 20). County prosecutor defends dropping sex abuse cases. *New York Times*, p. A12.

Smith, C. S. (2004, May 20). French pedophilia case falls apart when main suspect recants. *New York Times*, p. A5.

Summit, R. C. (1983). The child sexual abuse accommodation syndrome. *Child Abuse and Neglect, 7,* 177–193.

Taylor, J. (2002, July 25). Molester denied release from treatment center. *Palm Beach (Florida) Post,* p. 1B.

Victor, J. S. [1998]. Moral panics and the social construction of deviant behavior: A theory and application to the case of ritual child abuse. *Sociological Perspectives, 41,* 541.

Warick, J. (2004a, February 20). Calvert apologizes to families: But won't discuss early settlement with wrongly accused. *The (Saskatoon, Saskatchewan) Star Phoenix,* p. A3.

Warick, J. (2004b, September 11). Klassens, Kvellos declared innocent in writing. *The (Regina, Saskatchewan) Leader-Post,* p. B1.

Wilkes, J. (1990, March 8). Prescott child sex inquiry extended. *Toronto Star,* p. A10.

Wood, J. (2004, December 15). Province must contribute to abuse case: Quennell. *The (Regina, Saskatchewan) Leader-Post,* p. A7.

Cases Cited

California v. Pitts. 223 Cal. App. 3d 606; 1990 Cal. App. Lexis 1004 (Cal. Ct. App. 1990).

Devereaux v. Abbey. 263 F.3d 1070; 2001 U.S. App. Lexis 19674 (9th Cir. 2001).

D.K. v. Miazga. 2003 SKQB 559; 2003 SK.C.Lexis 1696 (Sask. Ct. of Queen's Bench 2003).

Ellis v. R. . [1998] 3 NZLR 555; 1998 NZLR Lexis 580 (Ct. of App., Wellington, NZ 1998).

Felix and Ontiveros v. Nevada. 109 Nev. 151; 849 P.2d 220; 1993 Nev. Lexis 27 (S. Ct. of Nevada 1993).

Grady v. Artuz. 931 F. Supp. 1048; 1996 U.S. Dist. Lexis 8761 (U.S. District Court, S.D.N.Y. 1996).

Grady v. New York. 6 A.D.3d 308; 775 N.Y.S.2d 141; 2004 N.Y. App. Div. Lexis 4762 (N.Y. App. Div. 2004).

Maryland v. Craig. 497 U.S. 836; 110 S.Ct. 3157; 1990 U.S. Lexis 3457 (U.S. S. Ct. 1990).

Massachusetts v. Cheryl Amirault LeFave. 430 Mass. 169; 714 N.E.2d 805; 1999 Mass. Lexis 555 (Mass. S. Jud. Ct. 1999).

Massachusetts v. Violet Amirault. 424 Mass. 618; 677 N.E.2d 652; 1997 Mass. Lexis 74 (Mass. S. Jud. Ct. 1997).

Moriarty v. Garden Sanctuary Church of God. 341 S.C. 320; 534 S.E.2d 672; 2000 S.C. Lexis 149 (S. Ct. S.C. 2000).

Nevada v. Babyan. 106 Nev. 155; 787 P.2d 805; 1990 Nev. Lexis 28 (S. Ct. of Nev. 1990).

New Jersey v. Michaels. 264 N.J. Super. 579, 625 A.2d 489, 1993 N.J. Super. Lexis 174 (N.J. App. Div. 1993).

New Jersey v. Michaels. 136 N.J. 299, 1994 N.J. Lexis 504 (S. Ct. of N.J. 1994).

New York v. Grady. 1997 N.Y. App. Div. Lexis 10026 (N.Y. App. Div. 1997).

New York v. Watt. 179 A.D.2d 697; 579 N.Y.S.2d 429; 1992 N.Y. App. Div. Lexis 218 (N.Y. App. Div. 1992).

New York v. Watt. 192 A.D.2d 65; 600 NYS2d 714; 1993 N.Y. App. Div. Lexis 6999 (N.Y. App. Div. 1993a).

New York v. Watt. 81 N.Y.2d 772; 609 N.E.2d 135; 593 N.Y.S.2d 782; 1993 N.Y. Lexis 2 (Ct. App. N.Y. 1993b).

New York v. Watt. 84 N.Y.2d 948; 644 N.E.2d 1373; 620 N.Y.S.2d 817; 1994 N.Y. Lexis 4116 (Ct. App. N.Y. 1994).

North Carolina v. Parker. 119 N.C. App. 328; 459 S.E.2d 9; 1995 N.C. App. Lexis 523 (N.C. Ct. App. 1995).

North Carolina v. Patrick S. Figured. 116 N.C. App.1; 446 S.E.2d 838; 1994 N.C. App. Lexis 868 (N.C. Ct. App. 1994).

Ohio v. Aldridge and Wilcox. 120 Ohio App. 3d 122; 697 N.E.2d 228; 1997 Ohio App. Lexis 891 (Ct. App. Ohio 1997).

Ortiz v. Georgia. 188 Ga. App. 532; 374 S.E.2d 92; 1988 Ga. App. Lexis 1125 (Ga. Ct. App. 1988).

R. v. Ellis. [2000] 1 NZLR 513; 1999 NZLR Lexis 41 (Ct. App., Wellington, NZ 1999).

R. v. Sterling. 102 C.C.C. (3d) 481; 1995 Lexis 2487 (Sask. Ct. App. 1995).

Snowden v. Singletary. 135 F. 3d 732; 1998 U.S. App. Lexis 2624 (11th Cir. Ct. App. 1998).

Utah v. Hadfield. 788 P.2d 506; 1990 Utah Lexis 14 (S. Ct. Utah 1990).

Valentin v. Los Angeles. 78 Ca. App. 4th 212; 2000 Cal. App. Lexis 94 (Cal. Ct. App. 2000).

3

JUDICIAL ERROR AND
FORENSIC SCIENCE

Pondering the Contribution of DNA Evidence

BEATRICE SCHIFFER AND
CHRISTOPHE CHAMPOD

Judicial error or miscarriage of justice will "invariably identify at least some element of an earlier conviction as a mistake: whether evidential, procedural or material irregularity" (Edmond, 2002). In this chapter, we restrict ourselves to examining the contribution of forensic science as a catalyst of either enabling or detecting miscarriage of justice. New pieces of evidence and facts provide the evidence needed for successful appeal. With the advent of new techniques, forensic science can fill this gap. It allows for demonstrating errors without questioning the integrity of the legal system, being an extraneous factor to it. Because, in recent decades a number of criminal convictions have been reversed on appeal (Edmond, 2002), partially on the basis of problems associated with the use of scientific evidence adduced by the prosecution during the trial, we propose to explore the contribution of forensic science in this context using two case examples that we believe cover most of the issues and will serve as a basis for a more general discussion. They both involve an appreciable contribution of forensic science as inculpatory and exculpatory evidence.

Regina v. Dallagher: The Case

In May 1996, a delicate, deaf, elderly woman was smothered with a pillow at her home in Huddersfield by a burglar who had forced his entry through a transom window. When the scene was examined, ear prints were found on the window pane immediately below the transom window that had been forced. The inquiry revealed that the windows had been cleaned three or four weeks earlier. The investigators believed that the burglar had listened for the presence of persons inside by putting his ears to the victim's window. As there were no suspects, the police investigated the movements of well-known burglars. During this process Mark Dallagher, who offered no valid alibi and had supposedly confessed the murder to a jailhouse snitch, was arrested and his ear prints were taken. Two ear experts, Mr. Cornelis Van der Lugt and Professor Peter Vanezis (Forensic Medicine and Science at the University of Glasgow), found a match, the former qualifying it as "unique," and the latter corroborating the match in slightly less categorical terms ("very likely"). Based on this evidence, Dallagher was jailed for life in 1998 after his conviction by the Leeds Crown Court. The case received a lot of public attention, the verdict being hailed as a great step forward for forensic science (see http://news.bbc.co.uk/1/hi/uk/235721.stm). On appeal, experts for the defense questioned the scientific validity and strength of ear prints as identification evidence (see http://www.forensic-evidence.com). The Court of Appeal (*R v. Dallagher* [2003] EWCA Crim, 1903, July 25) allowed the admission of ear print evidence. However, based on additional information that might have affected the decision of the jury, the conviction was quashed and a new trial was ordered ("Cases in Brief," 2003).

Subsequent DNA tests were carried out on the lifted ear marks, and that analysis showed a partial nonmatching DNA profile, which was immediately interpreted as excluding Dallagher. The prosecution dropped the case. That causal relationship was trumpeted in the press and among scientific commentators (Fresco, 2004). Dallagher was freed in January 2004 after serving seven years in prison.

Regina v. Michael Shirley: The Case (Adapted from Johnson and Williams [2004])

Michael Shirley, an eighteen-year-old Royal Navy sailor, was arrested in 1987 for the brutal rape and murder of Linda Cooke, killed by her assailant who stamped violently on her head and neck after raping her. One important aspect of the original trial evidence against Shirley was the result of analysis carried out on semen recovered from Linda Cooke's body. As part of common techniques available at that time, blood group analysis was undertaken. Evidence presented to the court identified a blood group match between semen and Michael Shirley; the same blood group, it was asserted at the time, was shared by 23.3 percent of the British adult male population. Other physical evidence consisted of a footwear mark with a logo imprinted on the victim's body, which corresponded to the outsole of the shoes found in his possession. In addition, the prosecution mentioned cuts and scratches on his face and body and bloodstains on his trousers.

DNA profiling could not be undertaken at that time, but in 1999, new DNA profiling techniques were carried out. Two years later, in 2001, reference samples from Cooke and Shirley were obtained: "When Cooke's DNA bands were subtracted from those exhibited by the mixed profile 'there remained an array of "foreign" DNA bands which did not match either the victim or the appellant.'" The Appeal court interpreted these "foreign bands" to provide significant grounds for Shirley's appeal against sentence and the court quashed his conviction in July 2003.

Points of Discussion

From these two cases, we discuss three main themes:

1. The issues associated with assigning a proper weight to identification evidence as exemplified in Dallagher and its bearing on the question of admissibility in court.
2. The fact that new technology, such as DNA evidence, is gaining an international status of gold standard, especially when the evidence provides support for the defense.
3. The complexity of combining various items of scientific evidence when individually they may point in different directions.

We are fully conscious of the limitation of these themes in the grand scheme of intertwined issues between wrongful conviction and forensic science. We acknowledge the significant contribution of laboratory errors, sloppy work, mixed-up "probes" and deliberate falsification of results. Our purpose here is something else: How does well-processed forensic science impact on wrongful conviction, as a cause or as a remedy?

These three main topics are examined while bearing in mind Edmond's (2002) statement: "Previously safe and reliable convictions are destabilized by the identification of supposedly flawed scientific evidence and bad scientists. In stark contrast, the new evidence tends to be described, in largely idealized terms, as good or reliable science." And, "However, if a critical approach to scientific evidence in the criminal justice system is so important, it might appear curious that so little attention has been systematically dedicated to examining the scientific evidence sustaining acquittals." We agree that forensic science is largely criticized if it leads to a judicial error and is generally not at all "evaluated" if used to establish the innocence of a convict. The Michael Shirley and Mark Dallagher cases enable the illustration of these topics and help a more general discussion.

The Strength of the Identification Evidence

Two factors brought radical changes in the way we approach identification evidence today. First, the rapid and extraordinary development of DNA evidence, which, after important vigorous and scientific debate in court and the scientific literature, has established itself as a mature technique. The strength of the potential association between the DNA profile from a crime scene and the DNA profile from a known person is routinely expressed through the use of a statistical argument related to the selectivity of the DNA in a relevant population. It is fair to say that DNA evidence is becoming rightly or wrongly the new gold standard in forensic science (Lynch, 2003). The second factor is the admissibility of evidence. Although it is more specific to the United States, it impacts on all forensic disciplines around the globe. The path-making Supreme Court cases interpreting Federal Rule of Evidence (FRE) 702 on admissibility are the *Frye* case, superseeded by *Daubert v. Merrell Dow Pharmaceuticals, Inc.* (509 U.S. 579 (1993)) and *Kumho Tire Co.v. Carmichael* (526 U.S. 137 (1999)). These cases pinpointed the twin concerns of reliability and helpfulness. Five factors represent the reliability prong of *Daubert* and can be used by the judge, acting as a gatekeeper, to guide his or her decision on admissibility. These are, as summarized by the Advisory Committee on FRE 702:

1. Whether the expert's technique or theory can be or has been tested; that is, whether the expert's theory can be challenged in some objective sense, or whether it is instead simply a subjective, conclusory approach that cannot reasonably be assessed for reliability.
2. Whether the technique or theory has been subject to peer review publication.
3. The known or potential rate of error of the technique or theory when applied.
4. The existence and maintenance of standards and controls.
5. Whether the technique or theory has been generally accepted in the scientific community.

This combined effect of DNA and *Daubert* led to a resurgence of interest in the foundations of well-known identification evidence such as handwriting, toolmarks, firearms, and fingerprints (Saks and Koehler, 1991; Saks, 1998; Epstein, 2002; Steele, 2004).

To our knowledge, ear print evidence has not been submitted to any *Daubert* hearing in the United States. However in *State v. Kunze* (Court of Appeals of Washington, Division 2, 97 Wash. App. 832, 988 P.2d 977 (1999)), the Court heard twenty experts in identification evidence and came to the conclusion that earmark identification was not a field that had gained general acceptance among peers. The Court ruled that earmark evidence could not be accepted as scientific evidence under the *Frye* test.

Critical reviews have recently been published (van Koppen and Crombag, 2000; Champod, Evett, and Kuchler, 2001; Swift and Rutty, 2003). Compared to established identification fields, such as fingerprints or handwriting comparison, the body of literature pertaining to earmark identification is limited. Scientific research has been done, but it has mainly been devoted to the study of the variability of ear morphology based on the examination of ear photographs. The relevance of this body of knowledge to the case at hand—involving ear impressions found on a window pane—is questionable.

The Dangerous Tenet of Uniqueness

Considerable confusion exists among laymen, and among forensic scientists, about the use of a word such as unique. The phrase "all ears are unique" is no more than a statement of the obvious: Every entity is unique. As the Court of Appeal stated in *Kunze* in a generalized manner:

> We agree with and adopt the statements of a commentator who, after noting two generally held tenets—"that no two snowflakes are exactly the same," and "that no two fingerprints have ever been found to have the same ridge positioning"—states as follows: "In some quarters, these tenets have been scooped up and extended into a single, all- encompassing, generalized principle of uniqueness, which states that "Nature never repeats itself."
>
> This principle is probably true, although it would not seem susceptible of rigorous proof. But the general principle cannot be substituted for a systematic and thorough investigation of a physical evidence category. One may posit that no two snowflakes are alike, but it does not immediately follow that no two shoe soles are alike, since snowflakes are made in clouds and shoes are not. If no two shoe soles are alike, the basis for this uniqueness must rest on other grounds, and those grounds must be identified and enunciated.

Making parallels between ear prints, the uniqueness of the ear and fingerprint is certainly the best way to give more weight to the association that it really deserves.

Indeed what matters here is how objects can be distinguished. This distinguishability or variability of earmarks depends crucially on the examination method, but also on the intrinsic qualities of the marks to display selective features (extensiveness, clarity, etc.). One striking feature in this field is the constant confusion between the variability of objects (e.g., ears, shoe soles) and of the marks left by these objects.

All external ears are different but a high variability between ears does not necessarily imply that a high variability is expressed in marks left by different people. This "clarity bridge" from a complete three-dimensional malleable organ to a two-dimensional mark revealed on a surface, marred by distortions and artefacts, needs to be investigated in much more detail. The same position was recently reached for bite mark examinations. Following a review, the authors stressed its lack of fully established scientific basis (Bowers, 1999; Pretty and Sweet, 2001). Recent observations of close neighbors (Pretty and Turnbull, 2001; close agreement between bite marks originating from different sources) have led the authors to call for renewed interest in researching the replication of dental features on human skin and to raise a cautionary note on claiming individuality in terms of the suspect's teeth rather than the pattern they make on the bitten substrate. The *Dallagher* case shows analogies with the case against Krone in Arizona where a crucial piece of evidence was a bite mark left on the victim. Krone was freed in April 2002 after serving ten years in prison. In the case, the Arizona Supreme Court's en banc (*State v. Krone*, 182 Ariz. 319, 897 P.2d 621 (en banc, 1995)) decision said that the physical evidence could neither exclude nor include Krone as the perpetrator, and without the bite mark evidence the State had no case (see http://www.forensic-evidence.com/site/ID/bitemark_ID.html).

The Lack of Transparency in the Decision Process

The protocol used by practitioners to compare earmark(s) and ear prints is comparable to the process of well-accepted identification fields (e.g., fingerprints). It can be summarized by the following steps (van der Lugt, 2001). The earmarks and the ear prints are respectively and independently evaluated to assess which parts and features are visible, variable, and constitute pressure points. The earmark is compared with the ear prints using overlays. The examiners looked at agreement in pressure points and measurements. Differences in the comparison process are evaluated by the examiners in the light of the tolerances defined by the known effect of pressure and distortion. A decision is made as to whether any difference is significant (hence leading to an exclusion) or can be accounted for (hence leading to a "match"). From the quality and extensiveness of the overlay, a judgment is made as to whether or not the earmark and the ear prints share common origin.

The fundamental weakness is the evaluation process and the value of a match (the concept of "match" between an earmark and an ear print is not precisely defined). It might be surprising that the identification process is described as a matching process—an assessment of the adequacy of superimposition between the mark and the prints—but that the crucial question of the value to be given to a match is never addressed and is left to the examiner's judgment. This fundamental weakness is, however, not acknowledged in literature. When a match is declared, the assessment of the rarity of the shared features relies solely on the examiner's experience, whereas in other fields such as DNA it will be based on published scientific data and probabilities.

Confirmation Bias

Both prosecution experts referred to the use of ear image and ear print databases to check for the presence of matching candidates, when comparing the earmarks from the crime scene and the ear prints obtained from Dallagher. These comparisons have not been carried out before but after the comparison relevant to that case (between the crime scene earmarks and the ear prints from Dallagher) had been made. As the examination relies heavily on a subjective assessment of correspondence, it is imperative for any study of that kind that the examiner's judgment is not influenced by initial mindsets. Most published accounts for experiments of that type suffer from the same strong methodological bias in that examiners knew beforehand that they were comparing prints from different people.

Subjective bias or confirmation bias (Risinger et al., 2002) in identification techniques are a real risk that needs to be mitigated by appropriate working procedures. It is our view that the *Dallagher* case suffers from such unconscious bias. The recent case of incorrect identification by means of fingerprints may suffer from the very same issue (Loftus and Cole, 2004).

What's Next?

Earmark-to-ear print comparison relies at the moment on individual experience and judgment rather than on a structured body of research undertaken following strict scientific guidelines. Such subjective judgments should be monitored in a structured and disciplined environment (i.e., a large-scale program of collaborative studies and proficiency tests). The expertise of the forensic scientist would be demonstrated not by casework experience only, but by a portfolio recording his or her proficiency in a long series of independently conducted proficiency tests.

The need for scientific research in the field of ear print identification has been recognized and a research consortium has been initiated under the umbrella of the European community (www.fearid.com). Any fundamental and systematic study of that nature should precede and not follow the use of earmark as "conclusive" evidence in court. Such a cautious approach should apply to all identification fields that have not met the basic criteria under *Daubert*.

However, in *Dallagher* (*R v. Dallagher* [2003] EWCA Crim 1903, July 25), the Court of Appeal did not share this view, nor did the Court embrace a full assessment à la *Daubert*. The ear print evidence was held admissible, leaving the duty of highlighting its limits to the adversarial system itself through a proper voir dire or at trial (that decision was confirmed in another recent Appeal case, *R. v. Mark J. Kempster* [2003] EWCA Crim 3555).

The risk is that both parties may not have the same access to expertise and technology to make this adversarial battle a fair and informed assessment. Dallagher, no doubt, suffered from such an imbalance in his first trial.

Investigator/Evaluator

Are we saying that such forensic identification techniques have no place within the criminal justice system? Not entirely, but there is a need to distinguish between investigative and probative use. A valuable model that helps scientists focus on their role is called the Investigator/Evaluator dichotomy (Jackson et al., 2006). In reality, scientists operate in both investigator and evaluator modes in many of the cases they examine. Providing opinion in these two different modes requires different mindsets. In the investigator mode, it is the scientist's role to form a reasonable hypothesis from the observations.

The scientist will form and communicate what may explain the observations based on his knowledge, experience, or through the use of databases. Generally, scientists operate in this mode before a suspect is arrested and charged with an offense. Opinions provide directions and options for the investigation with the understanding that misleading directions may be offered. It should remain obvious that searching for someone in a database and finding a match does not automatically incriminate the person. It only represents an investigative tool (i.e., forensic intelligence) and other evidence will be needed for conviction. Thus, it is feasible to exploit fragmentary or contaminated (DNA) traces or marks that themselves could not be presented as proof in court.

The problem arises when these data are not further scrutinized and are used as confirmed evidence in court. In the evaluator mode, the scientist's role is to form a view on the weight of evidence to be assigned to scientific findings. This is the primary role of the scientist in what may be called post-charge cases, cases in which a suspect has been arrested and charged. In this role, the concept of weight of evidence associated with the findings should be approached more carefully.

For example, a partial mixed DNA profile (from more than two donors) may be searched against the national DNA database and provide tentative donors for further verification. Obviously, not all of them (and perhaps none) could have left the trace, as they cannot all be responsible for the offense. Only additional police investigation can reveal other evidence to narrow the enquiry. In itself, the DNA information can be crucial investigative information. However, considering the current state of knowledge regarding the assessment of complex DNA mixtures at the moment, we may not be in a position to guide the court with robustness as to the weight of evidence to assign for a given retained potential donor.

Applying the reasoning to ear prints, we think that they represent a very important investigative tool that should not be ignored, but when it comes to an evaluative use for court purpose such as in *Dallagher*, we need to be very careful about the way the evidence is presented to the jury. There is no scientific basis for the categorical conclusions expressed in this case and we would even be very careful at any vague probabilistic expression such as "consistent with" or "probable." Because of the constant (although fallacious) comparison between ear prints and fingerprints, even using a statement about a match between the mark and the print without further qualifying its significance could potentially be misleading (and has been). Adequate presentation of such evidence in court should be made using a very strong statistical and objective underpinning. That line of argument has recently been taken by the U.K. Court of Appeal dealing with facial mapping evidence (*R. v. Paul E. Gray* [2003] EWCA Crim 1001) and we would recommend treating all new forms of identification evidence in the same way, namely:

> We do not however wish to pass from this appeal without making general observations about the use of facial imaging and mapping expert evidence of a reliable kind. Mr Harrow, like some other facial imaging and mapping experts, said that comparison of the facial characteristics provided "strong support for the identification of the robber as the appellant." No evidence was led of the number of occasions on which any of the six facial characteristics identified by him as "the more unusual and thus individual" were present in the general population, nor as to the frequency of the occurrence in the general population, of combinations of these or any other facial characteristics. Mr Harrow did not suggest that there was any national database of facial characteristics or any accepted mathematical formula, as in the case of fingerprint comparison, from which conclusions as to the probability of occurrence of

particular facial characteristics or combinations of facial characteristics could safely be drawn. This court is not aware of the existence of any such database or agreed formula. In their absence any estimate of probabilities and any expression of the degree of support provided by particular facial characteristics or combinations of facial characteristics must be only the subjective opinion of the facial imaging or mapping witness. There is no means of determining objectively whether or not such an opinion is justified. Consequently, unless and until a national database or agreed formula or some other such objective measure is established, this court doubts whether such opinions should ever be expressed by facial imaging or mapping witnesses. The evidence of such witnesses, including opinion evidence, is of course both admissible and frequently of value to demonstrate to a jury with, if necessary, enhancement techniques afforded by specialist equipment, particular facial characteristics or combinations of such characteristics so as to permit the jury to reach its own conclusion—see Attorney General's Reference No 2 of 2002 [2002] EWCA Crim 2373; but on the state of the evidence in this case, and if this court's understanding of the current position is correct in other cases too, such evidence should stop there.

DNA Evidence: The New Gold Standard for the Defense

As mentioned earlier, more than any other forensic science disciplines, DNA and its use for evaluative and intelligence purposes was submitted to vigorous legal and scientific scrutiny before its acceptance in court (National Research Council, Committee on DNA Forensic Science, 1996).

The United Kingdom is considered a pioneer in the forensic use of DNA for analysis, interpretation, and databasing. Indeed, Alec Jeffreys from the University of Leicester was the first to apply, in 1985, DNA profiling for identification purposes. Since then, and thanks to the collaboration between Jeffreys and the Forensic Science Service, the United Kingdom has been a leader in the field of DNA analysis (development of new techniques such as LCN, SNP, and STR), interpretation, and databasing, even if the United States was the first to develop a database in 1994. A European comparison between DNA databases is currently carried out at the University of Durham (Williams and Johnson, 2005). Whereas a few years ago, there were clearly two types of regulations regarding the entry of DNA profiles (from known individuals) on a national DNA database (i.e., legislation allowing large categories of offenses to initiate the acquisition of a DNA sample vs. restricted rules limiting the acquisition of DNA samples in very restricted types of offenses). Today, most countries have enlarged their criteria in terms of the range of offenses allowing the collection of DNA samples from known individuals. England and Wales, Switzerland, and Austria had from their beginning adopted extensive criteria. Exposed to the United Kingdom's DNA hit rates across offense types, countries such as France and the different U.S. states have changed their legislation. Currently, the U.K. database includes more than 3.5 million individuals; in Switzerland there are 75,000 profiles; in the United States there are 3.6 million, and in France the database includes 400,000. Regarding innovative use of the DNA database, the United States and the United Kingdom have had success with familial searching and the use of partial profiles or mixtures.

Regarding analysis and interpretation, there is no common standard: Some countries use ten-loci systems (e.g., Switzerland and the United Kingdom use the SGM+ kit); others use thirteen-loci systems (e.g., United States). In Europe, thanks to the European Network of Forensic Science Institutes (ENFSI) DNA working group, agreement has been reached on seven markers that are used in common, which enables international exchanges. Interpretation is a domain where standardization is even harder to achieve, even in the same country (Taroni et al., 2002).

Evidence involving a DNA match between a crime scene stain and an individual is often presented as positive proof that this individual left the stain. Nonetheless, the DNA strength does not amount to factual certainty. The process is essentially probabilistic and by its nature, it requires well-thought-out and balanced communication at both the investigative and evaluative stages. The following case illustrates the dangers of overweighting DNA evidence during investigation. In 1999 a man was wrongly associated with a crime through a SGM DNA profile match (based on six loci). In the United Kingdom, Raymond Easton, suffering from Parkinson's disease, was accused of having committed a burglary 300 km away from his home, as a six STR (Short Tandem Repeat) DNA sample matched a blood stain recovered from a broken window at the crime scene. The "cold" hit produced a match probability of one in 37 million (see http://www.crimlaw.org/defbrief123.html). The result was obtained by comparing the crime scene sample to the 700,000 DNA profiles in the national database, one of them being that of Raymond Easton. Despite his protestations of innocence and alibi evidence, he was arrested and spent several months in jail. It was only on the suspect's solicitor demand that additional loci were tested subsequently, leading to the discovery of an exclusion on four loci.

How could this case have gone so far? As discussed before, scientific evidence can be used in investigator mode (e.g., searching a DNA database) or evaluator mode (e.g., as proof for the legal instances). These two notions were mixed up and the DNA cold hit was rightly used as an investigatory tool, then regarded by prosecution in isolation and regardless of the other circumstantial elements, as evidence with disproportionate strength (probably amounting to a moral certainty). Contemporary press releases speak of:

- "computer mismatched DNA evidence" and "DNA mistake" (http:// www.exn.ca/Stories/2000/02/18/04.asp).
- "Parkinson's disease sufferer Mr Easton was arrested on the basis of DNA evidence which later proved false" (http://www.thisiswiltshire .co.uk/wiltshire/archive/2000/08/15/swindon_news10ZM.html).

These statements are not correct, as the match was genuine, only the interpretation of its meaning was poorly understood, and that constitutes the biggest danger associated with DNA evidence. Today, according to the Association of Chief Police Officers (ACPO) good manual practice (United Kingdom), to convict or arrest a person based on a hit in the DNA database it is necessary to have other evidence. The DNA hit in itself is considered insufficient. Indeed, most people would be seduced by the argument that "when a DNA 'match' is reported with odds of one in 37 million, we will encounter a like match in the DNA pattern only once in 37 million people" (http://www.forensic-evidence.com/site/EVID/EL_DNAerror.html). Dr. Bramley, Chief Scientist of the Forensic Science Service, put it well in offering the following statement: "The number of CJ (suspect/offender) sample profiles on our National DNA Database at the time was about 700,000 and the number of scene of crime sample profiles about 70,000. If none of these were related to one another and we were checking for a match using the 6 SGM loci we would be carrying out something like 50 billion pairwise comparisons and would expect several hundred matches just by chance" (http://www.crimlaw.org/defbrief123.html).

The correct understanding of the value to attribute to DNA evidence is crucial. Most often when misunderstandings arise, as illustrated by the Easton case, the problem can be traced to an incomplete comprehension or communication of the statistics involved. In addition, DNA involves also other risks, such as the use of nonpertinent DNA samples, the (in)correct handling of items of physical evidence, and the neglect of other scientific and circumstantial evidence to thoroughly investigate a case (Coquoz, 2003). Therefore, as pointed out by Penacino, Sala, and Corach (2003): "it is important to underscore that DNA testing should be considered one more piece of evidence within the context of a criminal or forensic investigation."

DNA Does Free People . . .

Although these situations have no direct bearing on the *Dallagher* or *Shirley* cases, they do help to illustrate our reservations about DNA as the new gold standard and people's high expectations. On the other hand, by raising some critical points, we by no means attempt to diminish the importance of DNA as exoneration evidence. Indeed, the turning point in the cases of both Dallagher and Shirley has been the results from DNA analysis showing in both cases a DNA profile not matching those of the respective defendants. This is one of several ways judicial errors can be discovered. When forensic science is employed to reveal judicial error, DNA is involved most of the time.

Recent research data gathered by Gross et al. (2005) illustrates this fact by listing the number of exonerations in the United States from 1989 to 2003, the former being the year of the country's first DNA exoneration. Of 328 liberated persons, 145 were freed by DNA, or over 44 percent. The authors argue that their data are necessarily biased in several ways and mention the following most important reasons:

- Not all possible cases of wrongful convictions have been retained, as it is difficult to compile data of this type (e.g., pending cases).
- In the 145 DNA exonerations, only offenses "producing" physical evidence that may be tested for DNA are included, thus leading to an overrepresentation of rape cases, and less so murder cases (a total of 97 percent of all cases examined by the authors). Eighty-eight percent of the rape case exonerations were based on DNA evidence, compared to 20 percent for the murder exonerations (including rape charges). Thus, robberies, for instance, do not appear in their compilation, as this offense seldom involves DNA testing.
- The initial samples have to be available for retesting when they are needed by the defense.
- Only people convicted and given long prison sentences (and it may thus be deduced serious crimes) will "profit" from an exoneration, as the others will be released before the sentence is quashed, the average time from conviction to quashing being more than eleven years.

Unfortunately, Gross et al. (2005) do not mention how many wrongful convictions were based on (faulty) scientific evidence, although they mention that in twenty-four cases perjury by governmental forensic scientists could be detected. Although Saks et al. (2001) point to erroneous forensic science as one of the causes for wrongful conviction in fifty-three of the eighty-one cases, they do not specify precisely what this means (or which forensic science was involved). This is no surprise to us, as forensic science (to convict and to exonerate) is underrepresented and often wrongly understood in research concerning wrongful convictions.

... But Beware of False Inferences

Returning to both our cases, *Dallagher* and *Shirley*, it may be stated that the DNA results have been portrayed by some commentators (Fresco, 2004; Johnson and Williams, 2004) and the national press in the United Kingdom as demonstrating without any doubt the innocence of the two men. This status of gold standard for DNA evidence is more dominant when the evidence favors the defense. For instance, Saks et al. (2001) conclude, "When a person who has been wrongly convicted and imprisoned is later excluded as the perpetrator by DNA typing, that person is thereby exonerated more convincingly than had ever been true of cases of exoneration in the past." They pronounce DNA to be "the first method to expose those errors with virtual certainty." We would like to explain some reservations to such blind reliance on scientific evidence by referring to our case examples. It is very tempting (if not fully logical for any member of the jury) to progress the arguments in the following way in the *Shirley* case:

- The DNA profile shows a contribution of an unknown male.
- The DNA profile originates from the sperm recovered in intimate samples taken from the victim.
- The semen has been left by the rapist.
- Hence Michael Shirley cannot be that man.

This deductive progression is however, faulty, and we show that, although the DNA evidence lends some support for the defense position (in both cases), it is not powerful enough to end the debate in such a categorical manner. This is due to the probabilistic nature of the progression of arguments between the demonstration of common (or different) sources and the guidance as to the activities involved at the heart of the case.

The Need for Transparent Communication on the Hierarchy of Issues

One of the key principles for interpreting scientific evidence is that interpretation of evidence is not possible unless one considers the scientific findings in the light of at least two competing propositions. In most cases in the adversarial system, these represent, respectively, the prosecution (P_p) and defense positions (P_d). It places an emphasis on a balanced and impartial view of the evidence (Evett et al., 2000; Jackson, 2000). An appropriate assessment of the weight of the evidence is obtained by assessing the relative likelihood of the scientific findings given each proposition.

Managing the elicitation of propositions is without doubt the most difficult aspect of case interpretation. To assist the scientist, a "hierarchy of propositions" (Cook et al., 1998) has been suggested. In summary, the hierarchy has three levels: source, activity, and offense. The offense level question can be seen as the ultimate matter to be proven. The activity or source level questions could represent intermediate issues further away from the ultimate issue. The forensic findings can provide support for propositions at any level within that hierarchy. A clear understanding of their position within the hierarchy is a first step toward understanding their potential impact on the ultimate issue.

In the context of the cases against Mark Dallagher (earmark) and Michael Shirley (shoe mark and blood group test), the following sets of propositions can be put forward (with a lot of similarities) covering both the mark evidence and biological evidence:

Mark Dallagher: Hierarchy of propositions

Offence *Offense level*	P_p: Mark Dallagher killed Dorothy Wood. P_d: Some other man killed Dorothy Wood.	
Activity level	P_p: Mr. Dallagher listened at the window. P_d: Some other man listened at the window.	
Source level	P_p: The collected residue came from Mark Dallagher. P_p: The earmarks originated from the ears of Mark Dallagher.	P_d: The collected residue came from some other person. P_d: The earmarks originated from another unknown person.
Sub-source level	P_p: The DNA profile obtained is from Mark Dallagher. P_d: The DNA profile obtained is from an unknown person.	

Michael Shirley: Hierarchy of propositions

Offence *Offense level*	P_p: Michael Shirley raped and killed Linda Cooke. P_d: Some other man raped and killed Linda Cooke.	
Activity level	P_p: Michael Shirley had the last sexual intercourse with Linda Cooke. P_p: Michael Shirley trod on the body of Linda Cooke.	P_d: Michael Shirley is not the man who had the last sexual intercourse with Linda Cooke. P_d: Some other man trod on the body of Linda Cooke.

Source level	P_p: The sperm came from Michael Shirley.	P_d: The sperm came from some other man.
	P_p: The footwear mark originated from the right shoe seized from Michael Shirley.	P_d: The footwear mark originated from another unknown shoe.
Sub-source level	P_p: The DNA profile obtained is a mixture originating from Michael Shirley and Linda Cooke.	
	P_d: The DNA profile obtained is a mixture originating from an unknown male and Linda Cooke.	

To progress from subsource to source level, we need to consider uncertainties surrounding the relationship between the DNA profile obtained and the underlying body fluid assumed. This will depend on the type of presumptive tests conducted in an attempt to identify the body fluid, their specificity and sensitivity, the microscopic examination carried out, the efficiency of obtaining DNA profiles from targeted fluids, and so on. It is our understanding that in both cases, the DNA analysis has been carried out using Low Copy Number (LCN) techniques. The LCN technique, by increasing the number of PCR cycles and changing analytical conditions (reagents), allows greater sensitivity and enables profiles to be obtained from only a few cells of starting DNA, as is the case with epidermal contact traces (Gill, 2002). This sensitivity is a new powerful investigative tool allowing the reinvestigation of old cases. However, when it comes to interpreting its results for court purposes (evaluative role), the inference may be obvious at the subsource level: The DNA does not originate from the designated persons, but its significance in the context of the alleged actions (activity level) needs further consideration and guidance. We certainly observe a shift from questions such as "Whose DNA is this?" to "How does that DNA happen to occur in this item?" This progression is not straightforward and requires expert knowledge. Although we could reasonably argue that the progression from source level issues to activity level issues for mark evidence (e.g., finger marks, earmarks, or footwear marks) can be left to the court in a process mitigated by advocacy, when it comes to DNA evidence in such limited quantity, the scientist should guide the court because of the specialized knowledge he or she can bring to the debate. Indeed, the interpretation of LCN DNA profiles at the activity level requires consideration of issues such as the transfer of DNA, the persistence of DNA under different circumstances (Lowe et al. 2002; Wickenheiser 2002), the possibilities of contamination and so-called drop-in of spurious alleles, and also the determination of the reproducibility of profiles (Gill et al., 2000). This special knowledge is clearly the domain of expertise of the forensic scientist and no other. Considering technical aspects, Thompson, Taroni, and

Aitken (2003) argue that "ignoring or underestimating the potential for a false positive can lead to serious errors of interpretation, particularly when the suspect is identified through a 'DNA dragnet' or database search" and "even a small positive probability can, in some circumstances, be highly significant, and therefore [...] having accurate estimates [of] the false positive probabilities can be crucial for assessing the value of DNA evidence." Although they discuss "normal DNA" techniques, this argument, by analogy, equally applies to LCN DNA methods. The scientist will then have to articulate the key elements impacting on the move from subsource to activity level. The closer to the offense level the expert is able to assess the evidence, the more fit-for-purpose the interpretation will be, providing greater added value to the court. In essence, the process is probabilistic. However, it must be recognized that the amount of background information required from the framework of circumstances increases as the expert moves up the hierarchy from subsource to activity level. The final progression from activity to offense level should remain within the remit of the court.

When DNA Contradicts Other Scientific Evidence

In the *Dallagher* case, regardless of the discussion on the weight of the association provided through the examination of the earmarks, the case boils down to impression evidence providing support for the prosecution and DNA evidence pointing in the other direction. Similar results were obtained in the *Krone* case, when the DNA profile obtained from the swabbed bite mark revealed a DNA profile different from the DNA profile of the defendant. In these cases, the combined effect depends critically on two factors: (1) the probability of a DNA profile originating from sebaceous secretions left by the donor of the earmarks, and (2) the probability of detecting an extraneous DNA profile (present for other "innocent" reasons) from such surfaces. In *Dallagher*, the first probability is not equal to one (a certainty). Indeed, due to the age of the marks, the limited quantity of DNA left following such contacts, and the detection technique applied to reveal the marks, there is an appreciable chance that the DNA profile from the person who left the marks will not be detected. The second probability is not equal to zero (an impossibility), simply due to the extreme sensitivity of the LCN techniques and the uncertainty surrounding the exposure and preservation of the window. Taking into account both factors, although it is established that the DNA detected is not originating from Mark Dallagher, we cannot simply deduce that he is not the donor of the earmarks. The DNA evidence undoubtedly provides support for the defense proposition at the activity level but not to the point to demonstrate that the earmarks were left by another person.

In the case against Michael Shirley, the fact that a DNA profile was obtained that does not correspond to the appellant does not mean de facto that the sperm heads observed under the microscope did not originate from him. Due to the time elapsed between the preparation of the slides and DNA analysis, no DNA profile was detected from the heads, and the observed profile obtained came from another DNA source. To evaluate these findings further within a framework of propositions at the activity level, the scientist will need to take into account additional information on background levels of DNA and issues surrounding the transfer, persistence, and recovery of DNA. Addressing propositions at the activity level forces more detailed consideration of the nature of the relationships between the propositions and the result. We will have to then take into account the following:

1. The possibility that intercourse took place with an unknown man some time prior to the offense.
2. Whether or not ejaculation occurred during these acts of intercourse and also the nature of the seminal fluid produced.
3. The expectations of obtaining, respectively, the observation of sperm heads, an enzymatic serological result, and a DNA partial profile from the recovered fluids.
4. Other sources of an extraneous DNA profile either from the DNA contamination dating back to the preparation of the samples or due to today's laboratory process.

A difference here is that the interpretation of the biological results at the activity level requires both expert knowledge (3 and 4) and circumstantial information (1 and 2) that is outside the remit of the scientist. Interpreting such results at a fit-for-purpose level is then a communication challenge as well as a delicate task of finding the appropriate positioning for the scientist. Without any guidance (and likewise for the defense under different circumstances), prosecution tends to question a nonmatch and to advance alternative explanations for these findings. This happened in the *Shirley* case, as well as other cases (see http://www.prisonerlife.com/articles/articleID=49.cfm). If the forensic expert presents a scientific and objective account of his or her findings, the question will have to be discussed where it properly belongs: a balanced and informed advocacy.

Among the elegant tools, to be prepared for such an eventuality, are the Bayesian networks. They combine relevant probabilities according to the laws of probability (Evett et al., 2002) and thus avoid the pitfalls of intuition when it comes to probabilistic reasoning.

The Combination of Conflicting Pieces of Scientific Evidence

The combination of various pieces of scientific evidence can be very challenging. Bayesian Networks are promising tools that enable handling of complex situations. One important observation is that the combination of various pieces of scientific evidence, such as in these cases, cannot occur at the source level, but has to be handled higher in the hierarchy of propositions. If the various items of evidence help, through their respective strength, to address the same set of propositions, then the combination amounts to a multiplication of their respective values (their respective likelihood ratios in the jargon of forensic scientists) taking into account potential dependencies. That requirement for a correspondence in the propositions considered is met in the *Dallagher* case (at the activity level) and an overall weight of evidence could be offered. Remember that in this scenario, the knowledge and experience needed to progress from source to activity issues fall within the strict remit of the forensic scientist. Hence, the scientist should be encouraged to present evidence at this level: The court would certainly benefit from a combined figure instead of two elements pointing in opposite directions. Because of the dominance taken by the technical expertise in this combination, it does not usurp the jury's responsibility and we do not believe that it contradicts the Adams decision rejecting Bayesian procedures (*R. v. Dennis J. Adams* [1996] 2 Cr App Rep 467). Following the interpretation of Lynch and McNally (2003), "the Court in Adams did not discount the appropriateness of the Bayesian method for assisting judgments about scientific evidence . . .".

In the case against Michael Shirley, the matter is more complex. As we have seen before, the assessment of the biological results alone requires technical knowledge and assessments of the circumstances of the case. In addition, the combination of the biological results with the footwear mark result can only be undertaken if the inference is progressed higher in the hierarchy of propositions, toward the offense level:

P_p Michael Shirley carried out the offense as alleged.

P_d Michael Shirley is not that man; another man is the offender.

This combination has then to take into account the following:

- The strength of the relationship between Michael Shirley and the shoe under examination.
- The relevance to the offense of the last intercourse and the deposition of the mark on the victim's body.

- Whether or not the two activities (raping and treading) have been undertaken by one or two offenders.

As noticed before, these elements are related to an assessment of the circumstances of the case and are outside the remit of the scientist. In the absence of other evidence, we doubt that the scientist can assist with any additional competence (or added value) in such a combination, and think that this task should remain the duty of the fact finder.

Conclusion

We have explored two cases where scientific evidence played a critical role, both in leading to the first conviction, and also to the exoneration of the defendants. The first case (*R. v. Mark Dallagher*) allowed the discussion on the strength of identification evidence, especially when the means of identification rests on new possibilities or new technologies. The analysis of the earmark evidence shows that there is always a risk associated with features presented as unique to convey more strength than they actually deserved. In our opinion this risk is increased:

- When the opinion is an informed subjective opinion.
- When the descriptive and inferential models lack transparency.
- When the risks for confirmation bias have not been mitigated.
- When the field is not underpinned by a strong experimental and research background.

We recommend that these conditions (which are highly correlated with the *Daubert* factors) should be fulfilled before the findings are used as evidence in court, but acknowledge that there is room for investigative use of such techniques. In this case the Court of Appeal (*R v. Dallagher* [2003] EWCA Crim, 1903, July 25) adopted a more open position to the admissibility of the evidence putting responsibility on the adversarial system. To our surprise, the same Court has been more restrictive regarding facial mapping techniques (*R. v. Paul E. Gray* [2003] EWCA Crim 1001) and obviously treated differently identification evidence that we, as scientists, would have handled in the same fashion.

When DNA evidence comes into play, what mainly makes the difference is the point of view of the observer. Edmond (2002) discusses the "conceptual disparity (or asymmetry) between assessment of scientific evidence used to convict and the scientific evidence used to acquit." This was well illustrated by the perceived contribution of nonmatching DNA profiles in the case against

Dallagher. We observe a blind reliance on the "new" technique. Although DNA analysis per se is widely accepted, it might not be so clear-cut in certain situations. For instance, the LCN method is so sensitive that it will become more and more difficult to distinguish DNA evidence from "normal" background DNA present on a crime scene.

The risk of overstating the value of DNA was also present in the Michael Shirley case. Our analysis attempted to expose the complexity of interpreting such a framework of scientific evidence at the appropriate activity level. This task requires expert knowledge as well as specific assessment of key elements arising from the understanding and assessment of the circumstances of the case, to the point that only the framework of circumstances allows attributing the "proper" weight to the nonmatching DNA results.

Readers may have noticed that we did not explicitly discuss the scientific evidence leading to the first conviction of Michael Shirley, namely the shoe mark and the blood group test. Indeed arguments advanced on the subject of earmarks are, by analogy, applicable to both these items. However, we feel that considering "risk factors" possibly leading to judicial error will help better understand how wrongful convictions could happen in both cases (but especially Shirley's). Three features are common to both cases: the atrocity and severity of the crime committed, the initial lack of a suspect, and very poor circumstantial evidence. In our opinion, the need for (any) (scientific) proof to convict outweighed the limitations of the latter. In conclusion, we cite Edmond (2002): "Just as police and forensic scientists are portrayed as routinely oriented toward producing cases sufficiently robust (or tainted) to warrant and produce successful prosecutions, so too, many legal commentators appear equally confident in the unreliability of prosecution forensic science and the reliability of the scientific evidence designed to acquit in the high profile miscarriage of justice cases."

References

Bowers, C. M. (1999). A statement why court opinions on bitemark analysis should be limited. *Newsletter of the International Organization for Forensic Odontology-Stomatology, 21*(2), 11–12.

Cases in brief. (2003, September 19). *Archbold News*, p. 8.

Champod, C., Evett, I. W., & Kuchler, B. (2001). Earmarks as evidence: A critical review. *Journal of Forensic Sciences, 46*, 1275–1284.

Cook, R., Evett, I. W., Jackson, G., Jones, P. J., & Lambert, J. A. (1998). A hierarchy of propositions: Deciding which level to address in casework. *Science and Justice, 38*, 231–240.

Coquoz, R. (2003). *Preuve par l'DNA: la Génétique au Service de la Justice* [Proof by DNA: Genetics to the service of justice. Lausanne, Switzerland: Presses Polytechniques et Universitaires Romandes.

Edmond, G. (2002). Constructing miscarriages of justice: Misunderstanding scientific evidence in high profile criminal appeals. *Oxford Journal of Legal Studies, 22*(1), 53–89.

Epstein, R. (2002). Fingerprints meet Daubert: The myth of fingerprint "science" is revealed. *Southern California Law Review, 75,* 605–655.

Evett, I. W., Gill, P. D., Jackson, G., Whitaker, J., & Champod, C. (2002). Interpreting small quantities of DNA: The hierarchy of propositions and the use of Bayesian networks. *Journal of Forensic Sciences, 47,* 520–530.

Evett, I. W., Jackson, G., Lambert, J. A., & McCrossan, S. (2000). The impact of the principles of evidence interpretation on the structure and content of statements. *Science and Justice, 40,* 233–239.

Fresco, A. (2004). Earprint evidence a "grotesque injustice." *Fingerprint Whorld, 30*(116), 57.

Gill, P. (2002). The role of short tandem repeat (STR) DNA in forensic casework in the UK: Past present and future. *Biotechniques, 22,* 366–385.

Gill, P., Whitaker, J. P., Flaxman, C., Brown, N., & Buckleton, J. S. (2000). An investigation of the rigor of interpretation rules for STRs derived from less than 100pg of DNA. *Forensic Science International, 112,* 17–40.

Gross, S. R., Jacoby, K., Matheson, D. J., Montgomery, N., & Patil, S. (2005). Exonerations in the United States 1989 through 2003. *Journal of Criminal Law and Criminology, 95,* 523–560.

Jackson, G. (2000). The scientist and the scale of justice. *Science and Justice, 40,* 81–85.

Jackson, G., Jones, S., Booth, G., Champod, C., & Evett, I. W. (2006). The nature of forensic science opinion: A possible framework to guide thinking and practice in investigations and in court proceedings. *Science and Justice, 46*(1), 33–44.

Johnson, P., & Williams, R. (2004). Post-conviction DNA testing: The UK's first "exoneration" case. *Science and Justice, 44*(2), 77–82.

Loftus, E. F., & Cole, S. A. (2004). Contaminated evidence. *Science, 304*(5673), 959.

Lowe, A., Murray, C., Whitaker, J., Tully, G., & Gill, P. (2002). The propensity of individuals to deposit DNA and secondary transfer of low level DNA from individuals to inert surfaces. *Forensic Science International, 129*(1), 25–34.

Lynch, M. (2003). God's signature: DNA profiling, the new gold standard in forensic science. *Endeavour, 27*(2), 93–97.

Lynch, M., & McNally, R. (2003). "Science," "common sense," and DNA evidence: A legal controversy about the public understanding of science. *Public Understanding of Science, 12,* 83–103.

National Research Council, Committee on DNA Forensic Science: An Update & Comission on DNA Forensic Science: An Update. (1996). *The evaluation of forensic DNA evidence.* Washington, DC: National Academy Press.

Penacino, G., Sala, A., & Corach, D. (2003). Are DNA tests infallible? *International Congress Series, 1239,* 873–877.

Pretty, I. A., & Sweet, D. (2001). The scientific basis for human bitemark analyses: A critical review. *Science and Justice, 41*(2), 85–92.

Pretty, I. A., & Turnbull, M. D. (2001). Lack of dental uniqueness between two bite mark suspects. *Journal of Forensic Sciences, 46,* 1487–1491.

Risinger, D. M., Saks, M. J., Thompson, W. C., & Rosenthal, R. (2002). The Daubert/Kumho implications of observer effects in forensic science: Hidden problems of expectation and suggestion. *California Law Review, 90*(1), 1–56.

Saks, M. J. (1998). Merlin and Solomon: Lessons from the law's formative encounters with forensic identification science. *Hastings Law Journal, 49,* 1069–1141.

Saks, M. J., Constantine, L., Dolezal, M., Garcia, J., Titus, C., Horton, G., Leavell, T., Muntz, J., Rivera, L., Stewart, J., Strumpf, F., & van der Haar, H. (2001). Towards a model act for the prevention and remedy of erroneous convictions. *New England Law Review, 35,* 669–683.

Saks, M. J., & Koehler, J. J. (1991). What DNA "fingerprinting" can teach the law about the rest of forensic science? *Cardozo Law Review, 13,* 361–372.

Steele, L. J. (2004). The defense challenge to fingerprints. *Criminal Law Bulletin, 40,* 213–240.

Swift, B., & Rutty, G. N. (2003). The human ear: Its role in forensic practice. *Journal of Forensic Sciences, 48*(1), 153–160.

Taroni, F., Lambert, J. A., Fereday, L., & Werrett, D. J. (2002). Evaluation and presentation of forensic DNA evidence in European laboratories. *Science and Justice, 42*(1), 21–28.

Thompson, W. C., Taroni, F., & Aitken, C. G. (2003). How the probability of a false positive affects the value of DNA evidence. *Journal of Forensic Sciences, 48*(1), 47–54.

van der Lugt, C. (2001). *Earprint identification.* Gravenhage, The Netherlands: Elsevier Bedrijfsinformatie.

van Koppen, P. J., & Crombag, H. F. M. (2000). Oren, Lippen en Vingers: De Waarde van oud en Nieuw Identificatiebewijs [Ears, lips, and fingers: The value of old and new identification evidence]. *Nederlands Juristenblad, 75,* 6–12.

Wickenheiser, R. A. (2002). Trace DNA: A review, discussion of theory, and application of the transfer of trace quantities of DNA through skin contact. *Journal of Forensic Sciences, 47,* 442–450.

Williams, R., & Johnson, P. (2005). *Forensic DNA databasing: An European perspective.* University of Durham.

II

NORTH AMERICAN
PERSPECTIVES
AND ISSUES

4

WRONGFUL CONVICTIONS
IN THE UNITED STATES

~

C. RONALD HUFF

The U.S. experience with the problem of wrongful conviction extends throughout the nation's history, of course, and predates the formation of the United States as an independent nation. As citizens of a British colony, the colonists were often subjected to secret accusations without the right to question their accusers and were generally denied the types of due process rights that U.S. citizens have taken for granted since the development of the Constitution and the Bill of Rights. Although status differences were generally less important in the colonies than was the case in England, the American colonies were certainly not egalitarian, and some regions (especially Virginia) were quite conscious of distinctions in socioeconomic class (Whitman, 2003). This fact, along with the inferior social status assigned to blacks, suggests that class and race discrimination influenced decisions regarding who was guilty and how they should be punished. Sadly, such discrimination continues to occur today despite important social and legal reforms, and such discrimination is evident in many cases of wrongful conviction in the United States.

This chapter is not, however, the place in which to dwell on the colonial roots of wrongful conviction, but rather to discuss the contemporary American experience and the need for cross-national, comparative research and policy discussions. As noted elsewhere (Huff, 2002), scholars, jurists, journalists, and activists have documented and analyzed cases of wrongful conviction since Borchard's (1932) pioneering work more than seven decades ago. For more than half a century, the documentation and analyses focused almost exclusively on individual cases, but beginning in the 1990s and continuing today, a decided shift has occurred in scholarly research, as well as in media attention and public opinion. The public policy importance of wrongful conviction has recently grown in the United States. The increasing awareness of this issue among citizens and policymakers has been closely linked to the highly publicized postconviction DNA exonerations of individuals who served long prison sentences and the increasing abolition of or moratoria on the use of the death penalty in the United States. Recent studies involving the possibility of error in capital cases have brought even further attention—and a sense of urgency—to this issue. In their seminal study, Radelet, Bedau, and Putnam (1992) argued that at least twenty-three innocent persons have already been executed in the United States. In a more recent and highly publicized study examining thousands of capital sentences over a twenty-three-year period (1973 to 1995), Liebman et al. (2000; see also Liebman, 2002) found serious, reversible errors in nearly seven of every ten cases. Although the great majority of those who are wrongfully convicted in the United States do not face the death penalty or life in prison, such errors often result in many years of unwarranted punishment and serious damage to the lives of the wrongfully convicted, while the actual offenders in those cases are free to commit additional crimes, thus compromising public safety.

What Is the Frequency of Wrongful Conviction in the United States?

No systematic data on wrongful conviction are kept in the United States and certainly it is not possible at this point to accurately estimate or compare the magnitude or frequency of this problem across jurisdictions. In fact, estimating the extent to which wrongful conviction occurs is a much greater challenge than estimating the true incidence rate of crime, since victimization surveys (including cross-national surveys) have greatly facilitated that task, allowing us to extrapolate between official crime reports and victimization data. No similar credible methodology has been developed to estimate the true extent of wrongful conviction, as many cases go undiscovered and analogous surveys of prisoners, for example, would lack public credibility.

A colleague and I conducted a survey, utilizing an intentionally conservative sample dominated by prosecutors, judges, and law enforcement officials, and a national sample of attorneys general (Huff, Rattner, & Sagarin, 1996). The total sample size was 353 and we received 229 responses (a 65 percent response rate). We asked our conservative sample to *estimate* what proportion of all felony convictions resulted in wrongful convictions. Based on the responses we received, we then estimated an error rate of 0.5 percent, and we decided to see what it would really mean if the U.S. criminal justice system is, indeed, 99.5 percent accurate and errs in only 1/2 of 1 percent of all felony cases. Based on Uniform Crime Report data for 2000, if we assume that the system is 99.5 percent accurate, we can estimate that about 7,500 persons arrested for index crimes are wrongfully convicted each year in the United States. The United States has such a large base rate of arrests for serious crimes that only a small error rate will produce thousands of wrongful convictions each year. Also, Scheck, Neufeld, and Dwyer (2000) reported that in DNA testing conducted in 18,000 criminal cases, more than 25 percent of prime suspects were excluded prior to trial. Since the great majority of criminal cases do not produce biological material to be tested, one can only speculate as to the error rate in those cases. These findings raise serious questions about the accuracy of the U.S. criminal justice system.

What Are the Causes of Wrongful Conviction in the United States?

Research in the United States has consistently found that the principal factors contributing to wrongful conviction include eyewitness error; overzealous law enforcement officers and prosecutors who engage in misconduct, including withholding evidence; false or coerced confessions and suggestive interrogations; perjury; misleading lineups; the inappropriate use of informants or "snitches"; the ineffective assistance of counsel; community pressure for a conviction; forensic science errors, incompetence, and fraud; and the "ratification of error" (the tendency to "rubber stamp" decisions made at lower levels as cases move up through the system). Usually, more than one factor contributes to the error and there are interaction effects among these factors. For example, police or prosecutorial overzealousness might be combined with perjury, withholding of evidence, and the inappropriate use of jailhouse informants, all occurring in a case in which the defendant has inadequate assistance of counsel and is therefore unable to discover these errors. Let us consider some of these factors.

Eyewitness Error

The great majority of extant research suggests that eyewitness identification error is the factor that is most often associated with wrongful convictions. In our survey, 79 percent of our respondents ranked witness error as the most frequent type of error resulting in wrongful conviction (Huff et al., 1996, p. 67). Scheck et al., (2000) reported that 84 percent of the DNA exonerations that they examined rested, at least in part, on mistaken eyewitness identification. Loftus (1979), Wells and his colleagues (Wells et al., 1998) and other scholars have written extensively concerning eyewitness perception; how it can be significantly affected by psychological, societal, cultural, and systemic factors; and how police lineups should and should not be conducted in fairness to suspects.

Overzealous or Unethical Police and Prosecutors

Of the postconviction DNA exonerations reported by Scheck et al. (2000), 63 percent involved police or prosecutorial misconduct. They also reported that in examining 381 murder convictions that had been reversed due to police or prosecutorial misconduct, not once was a prosecutor disbarred, even when knowingly allowing perjured testimony or deliberately concealing exculpatory evidence. Most of the time, they were not even disciplined. A recent study by the Center for Public Integrity (2003) found that since 1970, individual judges and appellate court panels cited prosecutorial misconduct as a factor when dismissing charges at trial, reversing convictions or reducing sentences in more than 2,000 cases. An analysis of these cases revealed the following types of misconduct:

- Courtroom misconduct (includes making inappropriate or inflammatory comments in the presence of the jury; introducing or attempting to introduce inadmissible, inappropriate, or inflammatory evidence; mischaracterizing the evidence or the facts of the case to the court or jury; committing violations pertaining to jury selection; or making improper closing arguments)
- Mishandling of physical evidence (includes hiding, destroying, or tampering with evidence, case files, or court records)
- Failing to disclose exculpatory evidence
- Threatening, badgering, or tampering with witnesses
- Using false or misleading evidence
- Harassing, displaying bias toward, or having a vendetta against the defendant or defendant's counsel (including selective or vindictive prosecution, which includes instances of denial of speedy trial)
- Improper behavior during the grand jury proceedings (Center for Public Integrity, 2003)

False and Coerced Confessions and Improper Interrogations

Another important factor in wrongful convictions is false and coerced confessions, often related to suggestive interrogations. Scheck et al. (2000) reported that fifteen of the first sixty-two postconviction DNA exonerations in their database, or about one in four, involved false confessions.

Some law enforcement units seem especially prone to unethical behavior. These include "elitist" units that tend to operate with more independence from the rest of the organization, such as elite narcotics enforcement and street gang units. For example, in a recent highly publicized scandal in the Los Angeles Police Department, an excerpt from one officer's own testimony illustrates the problem:

> Well, sir, make no bones about it, what we did was wrong—planting evidence . . . fabricating evidence, perjuring ourselves—but our mentality was us against them. . . . We knew that Rampart's crime rate, murder rate, was the highest in the city. . . . (L)ieutenants, captains, and everybody else would come to our roll calls and say this has to end and you guys are in charge of things. Do something about it. That's your responsibility. . . . And the mentality was, it was like a war, us against them. . . . (McDermott, 2000, p. A22)

Inappropriate Use of Jailhouse Informants or "Snitches"

Another important contributing factor is the widespread and often unprincipled use of informants, or "snitches," by police, prosecutors, and jail officers. Five of the first thirteen Illinois death row inmates found to have been wrongfully convicted were prosecuted using jailhouse informants, and 21 percent of the DNA exoneration cases reported by Scheck et al. (2000) involved the use of jailhouse snitches. Such informants, many of whom have been used repeatedly, are often willing to shape their stories to fit whatever is needed, in return, of course, for favorable considerations of various kinds (or, sometimes, simply because they do not like the defendant or the nature of the crime with which he or she has been charged; e.g., violent crimes against children, such as molestation or rape). These unreliable informants have often played key roles in helping convict defendants, including those in capital cases. Major investigations concerning the use of jailhouse informants have been conducted in both the United States and Canada in recent years, culminating in recommendations for reform (Bloom, 2003).

Ineffective Assistance of Counsel

Ineffective assistance of counsel has been a basis for appeal in the United States since the famous Scottsboro Boys case (*Powell v. Alabama*, 1932), but such appeals are rarely successful, despite the widespread acknowledgment by judges at the state and federal levels that many attorneys are inadequately prepared for trial work. Unfortunately, being inadequately represented by defense counsel is a widespread problem that is likely to worsen due to the inadequate budgets allocated for defense work. Given the assumptions of the adversarial system of justice, ineffective assistance of counsel poses a special problem and challenges those assumptions. Even more threatening to our adversarial system's assumptions are the "guilty plea wholesalers" (Huff, Rattner, and Sagarin, 1996, p. 55) who make comfortable livings by pleading defendants guilty without investigating cases or even interviewing the defendants.

Forensic Errors, Incompetence, and Fraud

The important advances in forensic science offer tremendous opportunities to improve the accuracy of our criminal justice system. However, the technology is ahead of the quality control, training, and in some cases, ethics, of those working in crime labs. On the positive side, Scheck and Neufeld's Innocence Project has relied on DNA analyses to exonerate many wrongfully convicted persons. On the negative side, some "junk scientists" have mishandled, misinterpreted, and even intentionally distorted evidence that has helped secure the convictions of innocent defendants.

Forensic labs where evidence in criminal cases is analyzed should be accredited, independent scientific laboratories with their own line item budgets, and their analyses should be equally available to both the prosecution and the defense. Unfortunately, in the United States these labs are nearly always part of a law enforcement organization. This organizational locus often subjects them to organizational cultures that emphasize convicting defendants ("We arrest them and you help convict them") instead of emphasizing scientific objectivity.

The Adversarial System

A major contextual factor in the production of wrongful convictions in the United States is the adversarial system in which the U.S. criminal justice process unfolds. The adversarial system relies on the skill and resources of the prosecution and the defense, and nearly always in criminal cases, the prosecution enjoys considerably more resources than does the defense. These resource advantages include human resources (investigators, staff, etc.) and budgetary resources. In all too many cases, the defense counsel relies heavily, if not entirely, on the police investigation, rather than conducting an independent investigation to establish the facts. This means that the police investigation must be both thorough and objective, which is not always the case due to the organizational pressures to move on to the next case (time and caseload pressures) and to press for a conviction (public and political pressures).

Although both the adversarial and the inquisitorial systems replace private vengeance with state authority, the adversarial system places much greater emphasis on *process* than on simple truth-finding. This is apparent in a number of cases involving wrongful convictions, wherein the convicted defendants sought reversals of their verdicts on the grounds that they were factually innocent (and in some cases, had new evidence that could potentially exonerate them), only to learn that since they claimed no procedural violations, their chances for success were remote at best. A humorous story is told to illustrate this point with respect to the British system of adversarial justice. A frustrated English judge had just finished listening to conflicting witness accounts, when the judge turned to the barrister and asked, "Am I never to hear the truth?" The barrister's reply: "No, my lord, merely the evidence."

Defenders of the adversarial system argue that it is superior because justice is better served when the two sides present vigorous cases and the trier of fact decides the outcome. This, of course, assumes that both sides will present vigorous arguments and will have conducted thorough investigations to determine the facts of the case. These assumptions are highly questionable, given the resource issues already noted. On the other hand, defenders of the adversarial system argue that without such individual-level responsibility for representing the defendant, the inquisitorial system does not ensure a thorough investigation and presentation of the facts, either.

Recent and Current Developments

The Innocence Protection Act

The Innocence Protection Act of 2003 represented a comprehensive package of criminal justice reforms aimed at reducing the risk that innocent persons may be executed. The bill would (1) ensure that convicted offenders are afforded an opportunity to prove their innocence through DNA testing; (2) help states provide competent legal services at every stage of a death penalty prosecution; (3) enable those who can prove their innocence to recover some measure of compensation for their unjust incarceration; and (4) provide the public with more reliable and detailed information regarding the administration of the nation's capital punishment laws. The chief sponsor of the bill in the Senate, Senator Patrick Leahy (D-Vermont), made the following comments at a press conference:

... (T)he death penalty machinery is broken.... More than 100 people have been released from death row—not on technicalities, but because they were innocent. The Innocence Protection Act addresses the very same problems that the public is concerned about.... Thirty-one members of the Senate and 246 members of the House are cosponsors of the bill. Cosponsors are Democrats and Republicans, supporters of the death penalty and opponents, liberals and conservatives.... If we put ourselves in the place of those who are wrongly convicted, we surely would act. A year may not seem like a long time on Capitol Hill, but it is an eternity for someone sitting, wrongfully convicted, in a death row prison cell. For every wrongfully convicted person on death row there is a true killer who may still be on the streets. The parade of wrongfully convicted people being released from death row undermines public confidence in our system of justice. These close calls should concentrate our minds and focus our will ... (Leahy, 2002)

Major parts of the Innocence Protection Act were later incorporated in the Justice for All Act of 2004, which became law on October 30, 2004, after approval from the U.S. Senate on a voice vote and approval from the U.S. House of Representatives (393 to 14). The U.S. Senate has approved a bipartisan amendment sponsored by Judiciary Committee leaders to secure over $200 million in funding over five years for several Justice Department programs authorized by the Justice for All Act. The bulk of the funding would go to key programs authorized by the Innocence Protection Act. Senator Leahy and Chairman Arlen Specter (R-Pennsylvania) offered the amendment, which would provide $82.5 million to support a variety of DNA education, training, research and identification programs; invest $13 million in the Kirk Bloodsworth Post-Conviction DNA testing grant program, and provide $111 million in Capital Litigation Improvement Grants to improve the quality of legal representation for indigent defendants in capital cases. Congress will determine the final funding level for this important act, which represents an important step forward for innocent people who might otherwise be sentenced to death. By providing funds to test the backlog of as many as 300,000 untested rape kits, this legislation will help ensure that perpetrators are caught and punished. In addition, the bill establishes the Kirk Bloodsworth Post-Conviction DNA Testing Program to test the DNA evidence of those already convicted of crimes who may be innocent, including death row inmates, some of whom have already been exonerated through the use of DNA testing. It is also important to ensure that death penalty trials are fair and accurate by helping states provide professional and experienced lawyers at every stage of a capital case.

Innocence Projects and Innocence Commissions

The Innocence Project was cofounded by Barry Scheck and Peter Neufeld in 1992 at the Benjamin Cardozo Law School in New York City. It is a clinical law program for law students supervised by law professors and several administrators. It provides pro bono legal assistance to inmates who are challenging their convictions based on DNA testing of evidence, although clients must obtain funding for testing. The Project has represented or assisted in more than 160 cases where convictions have been reversed or overturned in the United States.

The Project is currently working on (1) legislation that would provide statutes in every state allowing for easier access to postconviction DNA testing of evidence; (2) proper compensation of wrongly incarcerated citizens; and (3) development of an Innocence Network in law schools across the country, which would enable the Innocence Project to act as a conduit and pass these cases on to other law schools that are equipped to handle them.

Another important development is the increasing advocacy for criminal cases review commissions, or "innocence commissions" (see, e.g., Scheck and Neufeld, 2002). Such commissions should be established at the federal and state levels in the United States. As Griffin (2001) has noted, the commissions could review appeals, then refer appropriate cases to trial-level courts that could then entertain collateral attacks on the conviction. They could hold hearings and decide to dismiss the appeal or referral, order a new trial, or vacate the conviction.

Although state and local bar associations and the courts must become more active in punishing and deterring such behavior, that is not likely to be sufficient, nor will the efforts of Scheck's and Neufeld's Innocence Project, Jim McCloskey and Centurion Ministries, and a number of journalists and activists. The time has come to do what the United Kingdom has done. We should establish commissions similar to their Criminal Cases Review Commission (CCRC) to review postappellate claims of wrongful conviction and, where appropriate, refer those cases to the appropriate courts.

According to Griffin (2001), at the time of her analysis, the CCRC had received 3,680 appeals, had reviewed 2,381 and had referred 203 cases (4.3 percent) to courts of appeal. Of those 203 cases, forty-nine had been heard by the courts, resulting in thirty-eight convictions having been overturned. These thirty-eight overturned convictions represent 77.5 percent of the cases referred to the courts by the CCRC but only 1.6 percent of all appeals. Thus, the argument that has been advanced by some critics that such a review commission would overburden the courts does not find empirical support thus far, at least with respect to the British experience.

In addition to the important benefit of postconviction reviews based on claims of innocence, innocence commissions can also serve as investigative bodies to analyze "system failures" to see what went wrong and what might be done to prevent such miscarriages of justice. We are struck by the contrast in what occurs when a plane or a train crashes as compared with what occurs when innocent persons are wrongfully convicted. The former tragedies lead to immediate and thorough investigations to determine what went wrong, but the latter tragedies do not. Innocence commissions could undertake such investigations if given proper resources. Finally, innocence commissions have been created in several states and countries. In 2002, North Carolina, in response to highly publicized wrongful convictions, became the first state in the nation to announce the creation of an innocence commission. In 2003, Connecticut became the first state in the United States to use legislative action to create an innocence commission. Several other state legislatures have considered or are considering proposals for similar commissions.

The Death Penalty

The highly publicized DNA exonerations mentioned previously, especially those involving prisoners under death sentences, have called into question the continuing use of the death penalty as a sentencing option in the United States. In Illinois, former Governor George Ryan imposed a moratorium on the death penalty in that state, following a period of time in which more death row inmates had been exonerated than had been executed. He was concerned about the clear-cut evidence that the criminal justice system had made a number of errors and, therefore, the possibility that innocent persons might be executed.

These developments, coupled with the fact that the United States is increasingly isolated, especially among the developed nations of the world, in its use of the death penalty, may ultimately result in its abolition. As Zimring (2003) recently noted:

> [A] process of social engagement with capital punishment that is without precedent in American history has already begun. The end game in the effort to purge the United States of the death penalty has already been launched. The length and the intensity of the struggle

necessary to end the death penalty are not yet known, but the ultimate outcome seems inevitable. . . . (p. 205)

The death penalty should be abolished in the United States and replaced with sentences of twenty years, thirty years, or life imprisonment without parole, depending on the facts of each case. Since all convictions are based on a probabilistic assessment of guilt and are subject to error, they should be reversible, allowing the innocent person to be freed and compensated. All criminal sentences *except* the death penalty allow this opportunity, but execution of the innocent forecloses this option. Samuel Gross (1998) recently found that a majority of Americans surveyed, both supporters and opponents of the death penalty, indicated that the issue of innocence caused them concern about the propriety of the death penalty. In a subsequent study, Gross et al. (2005) also found that during a recent fifteen-year period (1989 to 2003) in the United States, there were 328 exonerations, mostly involving those sentenced either to life imprisonment or death. Finally, this would bring the United States in line with other nations that have abolished the death penalty. Such abolition is, for example, a requirement of membership in the European Union of nations, and Russia has had a moratorium in place for a number of years and shows no intention of resuming capital punishment.

In 360 B.C., one of the world's greatest philosophers, Plato, made the following observation in *The Republic*, perhaps the finest of his Socratic dialogues: "Mankind censure injustice fearing that they may be the victim of it, and not because they shrink from committing it." In that regard, it seems that not much has changed. It is therefore imperative that we continue to develop a better understanding of this particular type of injustice known as wrongful conviction and reduce its occurrence, both to protect the innocent and to protect society from continued victimization by criminals who may remain free while innocent persons go to prison or, perhaps, to their deaths in those societies that retain capital punishment as a sentencing option. As Forst (2003, 2004) has argued, the U.S. criminal justice system's accuracy is essential to its perceived legitimacy, and systematic attention must be paid to the errors that are committed and how those errors might be reduced.

References

Bloom, R. M. (2003). Jailhouse informants. *Criminal Justice, 18*(1), 20–26, 78.

Borchard, E. M. (1932). *Convicting the innocent: Sixty-five actual errors of criminal justice.* Garden City, NY: Doubleday.

Center for Public Integrity. (2003). *Harmful error: Investigating America's local prosecutors.* Washington, DC: Author.

Forst, B. (2003, August 26). *If wrongful conviction were a disease, what would be the cure?* Paper presented at the First International Workshop on Wrongful Convictions, Breil/Brigels, Switzerland.

Forst, B. (2004). *Errors of justice: Nature, sources and remedies.* New York: Cambridge University Press.

Griffin, L. (2001). The correction of wrongful convictions: A comparative perspective. *American University International Law Review, 16,* 1241–1308.

Gross, S. R. (1998). Update: American public opinion on the death penalty—It's getting personal. *Cornell Law Review, 83,* 1448–1475.

Gross, S. R., Jacoby, K., Matheson, D. J., Montgomery, N., & Patil, S. (2005). Exonerations in the United States 1989 through 2003. *The Journal of Criminal Law and Criminology, 95,* 523–560.

Huff, C. R. (2002).Wrongful conviction and public policy. *Criminology, 40*(1), 1–18.

Huff, C. R., Rattner, A., & Sagarin, E. (1996). *Convicted but innocent: Wrongful conviction and public policy.* Thousand Oaks, CA: Sage.

Leahy, P. (2002, September 24). [Comments at press conference.] Washington, DC.

Liebman, J. S. (2002). Rates of reversible error and the risk of wrongful execution. *Judicature, 86*(2), 78–82.

Liebman, J. S., Fagan, J., West, V., & Lloyd, J. (2000). Capital attrition: Error rates in capital cases, 1973–1995. *Texas Law Review, 78,* 1839–1865.

Loftus, E. F. (1979). *Eyewitness testimony.* Cambridge, MA: Harvard University Press.

McDermott, T. (2000, December 31). Perez's bitter saga of lies, regrets, and harm. *Los Angeles Times,* pp. A1, A22–A24.

Penrod, S. (2003). Eyewitness identification evidence: How well are witnesses and police performing? *Criminal Justice, 18*(1).

Plato. (1998). *The republic* (Book I, 344-C; trans. R. Waterfield). New York: Oxford University Press.

Radelet, M. L., Bedau, H. A., & Putnam, C. (1992). *In spite of innocence: Erroneous convictions in capital cases.* Boston: Northeastern University Press.

Scheck, B. C., & Neufeld, P. J. (2002). Toward the formation of "innocence commissions" in America. *Judicature, 86*(2), 98–105.

Scheck, B. C., Neufeld, P. J., & Dwyer, J. (2000). *Actual innocence: Five days to execution and other dispatches from the wrongly convicted.* New York: Doubleday.

Wells, G. L., Small, M., Penrod, S., Malpass, R. S., Fulero, S. M., & Brimacombe, C. A. E. (1998). Eyewitness identification procedures: Recommendations for lineups and photospreads. *Law and Human Behavior, 22,* 603–647.

Whitman, J. Q. (2003). *Harsh justice: Criminal punishment and the widening divide between America and Europe.* New York: Oxford University Press.

Zimring, F. E. (2003). *The contradictions of American capital punishment.* New York: Oxford University Press.

Cases Cited

Powell v. Alabama 287 U.S. 45 (1932)

5

The Adversary System and Wrongful Conviction

~

MARVIN ZALMAN

This chapter addresses two questions: What role is played by the adversary system and by the American adversary trial in generating miscarriages of justice? Are modifications to the American adversary trial and system that can reasonably hope to reduce miscarriages of justice feasible (see Huff, 2002: 15)? Given the great complexity of the adversary trial and the large scope of the adversary system, an attempted answer in a chapter must be partial, so I describe one potential modification suggested by an expert on evidence law (Risinger, 2004) and suggest a single improvement to the adversary system. Any comprehensive review of the adversary system, compared to the inquisitorial system, is beyond the scope of this chapter.[1] The terms *adversary trial* and *adversary system* are often used interchangeably, but I use the latter term to encompass the entire criminal justice system to the conclusion of adjudication and sentencing. It is easier to separate the two in the United States than it is in the so-called inquisitorial system, given the centrality of the investigation and the dossier in a country like France.

A consensus of sorts exists among those who think about the conviction of factually innocent people in the United States about what "causes" and what must be done to reduce wrongful convictions. The Innocence Commission for Virginia (ICVA, 2005; Gould, 2008), for example, recently identified eight factors found to "underlie" the wrongful convictions that preceded eleven exonerations: mistaken eyewitness identification, suggestive identification procedures, police tunnel vision, antiquated forensic testing, inadequate assistance of defense counsel, failure to disclose exculpatory evidence, high-pressure interrogation with vulnerable suspects, and inconsistent or suspicious statements by defendants (ICVA, 2005: xvi, 6–12). The eighty-five recommendations of the Illinois Governor's Commission on Capital Punishment (Illinois, 2002), following the exonerations of thirteen death-row inmates, included many that are applicable to noncapital cases: Reduce police tunnel vision and improve investigation (Recommendations, 1, 2, 16, 19), videotape and improve interrogations (Recommendations, 4–9, 58), reform identification procedures (Recommendations 10–15, 55–57), test DNA (Recommendations, 26), expand discovery (Recommendations, 34, 46–49), assure attorney qualifications (Recommendations, 40–45), and limit snitch evidence (Recommendations, 50–52).[2] Notice that the adversary structure of the American criminal justice system and the mode of adjudication are not included in these lists.

Such catalogs of error are not a recent innovation. As Richard Leo (2005) points out, this method was used in the fountainhead of wrongful conviction scholarship, Edwin Borchard's study of "sixty-five actual errors of criminal justice." In the conclusion of *Convicting the Innocent*, Borchard (1932: 367–372) counted twenty-nine cases of mistaken identity, thirteen cases in which no crime had been committed (including eight murder convictions), eleven in which the conviction rested only on circumstantial evidence, fifteen involving witness perjury, and sixteen associated with police and prosecutor error or overzealousness. In another five cases, Borchard noted that confessions were obtained by physically or psychologically coercive methods. Finally, to not extend these catalogues indefinitely (see Givelber, 1997: 1348, n. 102, 103), the widely circulated account of Scheck et al. (2001: 361) refines Borchard's method and identifies eleven flaws that were apparent in more than one false conviction: mistaken eyewitness identification, serology inclusion, police misconduct, prosecutor misconduct, defective or fraudulent science, microscopic hair comparison, bad lawyering, false witness testimony, snitches, false confessions, and other forensic inclusions. Again, the adversary system and the adversary trial itself are not identified as relevant factors.

The similarity of some "causes" in these catalogs may reflect enduring sources of error in criminal prosecutions, most notably, mistaken identification. The differences may be due to variations in the samples of cases examined or to temporal changes, such as the increased use of forensic science leading to more instances of junk science and expert witness fraud in recent years. Writing in a critical vein Leo (2005) suggests that these catalogues reflect their origin in the writings of journalists and lawyers, beginning with Borchard (1932); that these catalogs reflect legal causes and not "root causes" of wrongful convictions; and that they impede the development of a criminological and social science theory of wrongful conviction. Leo's critique is a good starting point. What the Virginia and Illinois commissions and Borchard and Scheck et al. reported was indeed present in the cases they studied. However, I wish to hypothesize that what was observed, and what was not observed, was in a sense formed by and formative of a socially constructed reality of wrongful conviction.

The social construction of reality, a sociological perspective, holds that "reality is a social construction, an interpretation of symbols and images negotiated through interactions" (Herda-Rapp, 2003: 547). The social construction of reality, akin to the public policy agenda setting perspective of policy studies (Zalman, 2005, 2006), focuses on the meaning attributed to perceived phenomena, and to variations in attention paid to problems. Philip Jenkins's (1998) study of the problem of child sexual abuse over the course of a century noted enormous variations in the amount of attention given to that problem. At times public attention was driven by comprehensible reasons (e.g., growing levels of sexually transmitted diseases), but at other times "the perceived significance of a given problem grows or diminishes without any change in the real threat-potential of the condition itself" (3). The constructionist approach is typically wide-angled—paying attention to social, political, ideological, and media influences (Beckett, 1997; Herda-Rapp, 2003; Jenkins, 1998). Unlike an "objectivist" approach to social problems that "accepts that something is a problem when it harms or disturbs a significant section of society, constructionism may or may not accept that the phenomenon exists or, if it does, that it is indeed harmful, but the central question is how the condition comes to be viewed as a problem in the first place" (Jenkins, 1998: 4). Thus, the social construction of reality is about individuals' *interpretations* of events and phenomena, whether accurately or inaccurately perceived, and even of nonexistent phenomena (e.g., ritual sex abuse cases; Rabinowitz, 2003).

My concern here, however, is not with the social construction of wrongful conviction itself as a significant policy issue. It is now generally accepted that accounts of miscarriages of justice had little social, political, or professional impact before 1990 (Leo, 2005; Zalman, 2004). The reasons for this lack of social response, although not studied in depth, were connected to a deeply conservative refusal in the legal community to acknowledge a systemically flawed criminal justice system.[3] The "DNA Revolution," fostered by the Justice Department (Connors et al., 1996) and amplified by the news media (Warden, 2002), was the critical factor that forced complacent professionals to admit to systemic problems, thus leading to the acceptance of "wrongful conviction" as a problem area (Scheck et al., 2001; Zalman, 2005). "Recent years have brought a torrent of public attention to the phenomenon of wrongful conviction" (Raymond, 2001: 449).

What I wish to suggest instead is that the "normal science" within which scholars and scientists work (Kuhn, 1970) has produced something akin to an *"expert* socially constructed understanding" of the very complex problem of wrongful conviction. What is curious about this construction is not so much what is included but what is left out of the list of causes: the adversary system and the jury trial itself. Most of the known false convictions resulted from jury trials rather than guilty pleas. In each wrongful conviction the jury did not filter out the errors that were later identified. One would think that an important question is whether the trial process itself contributed to these miscarriages of justice.

The hypothesis, then, begins with the assumption that the jury trial, the adversary system in general, or both, contribute to wrongful convictions either by injecting error because of its inherent features, or are inefficient in weeding out errors that arise during the investigation of crimes. The issue then becomes, why is it that the mode of adjudication does not make the list of standard factors associated with wrongful convictions? Several reasons may account for this. One is that *trial* factors that generate wrongful convictions have been identified as factors in their own right: ineffective assistance of counsel, witness perjury, prosecutorial misconduct, and the withholding of exculpatory evidence (Center for Public Integrity, 2003). Another is that several "offstage" errors are so potent that they overwhelm the jury's decision-making abilities when introduced in a trial (false confessions, perjury by forensic expert witnesses, erroneous eyewitness identification). Perhaps there would be little residual error if such problems could be corrected by improved lineup and interrogation procedures, improved training and monitoring of prosecutors, laboratory accreditation, and the like. It is also possible that trial factors may not have been highlighted as causes of wrongful convictions because they are hard to find without inspecting trial transcripts. It is relatively easy to pick out a gross error, such as a live murder "victim" reappearing some time after a conviction, which is likely to be touted by the newspapers (Borchard, 1932: 39–44). In comparison, erroneous motions by judges that do not allow the examination of disputed evidence, or the effect of gory evidence on the jury (Barthel, 1976: 194–198), or prosecution cross-examination that is not legal error that nevertheless clouds an issue of fact, or a myriad of other fine points that arise in the course of a trial that could turn a case around, are found only by the painstaking examination of trial transcripts. By trial factors that lead to miscarriages of justice, I do not mean only tactics that constitute legal error, but include practices in trials that operate properly and within procedural, evidentiary, and constitutional rules. Support for this point comes not only from the idea that known exoneration cases have not been studied in sufficient depth, but also from the reasonable belief that only a small fraction of wrongful convictions have been uncovered. Given the likelihood that a large number of wrongful convictions are not being identified (Gross et al., 2005; Huff, Rattner, and Sagarin, 1996), there may be an unknown set of cases in which the primary causes of error are flaws inherent in the jury trial or in the adversary system.

Another explanation for the hypothesis that writers on wrongful conviction, led by legal writers, have not identified trial errors as causes of wrongful convictions, is the "ostrich head-in-the-sand" position taken by the legal community—a refusal to face facts bred by an inherent professional conservatism. This position, larded with a crime control ideology (Packer, 1968), was classically stated by the noted jurist, Learned Hand, in his oft-quoted 1923 decision in *U.S. v. Garsson* (see Givelber, 1997: 1328–1336) denying to the defendant access to the full transcript of the grand jury:

> Under our criminal procedure the accused has every advantage. While the prosecution is held rigidly to the charge, he need not disclose the barest outline of his defense. He is immune from question or comment on his silence; he cannot be convicted when there is the least fair doubt in the minds of any one of the twelve. Why in addition he should in advance have the whole evidence against him to pick over at his leisure, and make his defense, fairly or foully, I have never been able to see. No doubt grand juries err and indictments are calamities to honest men, but we must work with human beings and we can correct such errors only at too large a price. Our dangers do not lie in too little tenderness to the accused. Our procedure has been always haunted by the ghost of the innocent man convicted. It is an unreal dream. What we need to fear is the archaic formalism and the watery sentiment that obstructs, delays, and defeats the prosecution of crime. (*U.S. v. Garsson*, 1923: 649)

Finally, the adversary system and the adversary trial are hard to see as individual factors in specific cases because they form the context, the backdrop, of the cases; as a result their influence is easily missed. Just as criminal justice officials in earlier decades failed to "perceive" the influence of the age structure of the population on crime rates, until criminologists drew their attention to this "invisible" factor, the very structuring of our institutions become invisible.

Before proceeding, I wish to raise some doubts about the hypothesis. It is not possible to prove with scientific certainty that the jury trial itself causes erroneous convictions. Indeed, it may be the case that the errors identified by Borchard and his successors are not only the prime, but virtually the entire set of reasons for wrongful convictions; and that searching for deeper structural error in the trial or the criminal justice system for the causes or "cures" of wrongful convictions is entering a blind alley. The mid-twentieth-century jurists and writers Edwin Borchard (1932), Erle Stanley Gardner (1952), and Jerome and Barbara Frank (1971 [1954]) were sufficiently iconoclastic to have been willing to take on the adversary system, and Frank (1950) has won an enduring intellectual niche by doing just that. One would think that if they did not find errors in the processes of the jury trial that such errors were not present. Note also that the experienced attorneys who wrote detailed case studies of exonerations in the Virginia wrongful conviction study, after reading the trial transcripts, did not identify trial practice as a generator of error (ICVA, 2005).[4] Indeed, were it not for two striking articles on the subject, by Givelber (1997) and Risinger (2004), I would not have proceeded even this far on the hypothesis that the adversary process itself is a contributor to erroneous convictions.

Still, there is some specific evidence that the trial, operating lawfully (if not as it should), contributed to wrongful convictions. An interesting example of the way in which the normal operation of the jury trial can be overlooked, or submerged in an examination of other factors, is found in Scheck et al. (2001). The first chapter of their book tells the sad story of Marion Coakley, a hapless fellow with a low IQ who was identified as the perpetrator of a vicious rape and robbery because his mug shot was left in police sex crimes files. This happened when a woman he picked up at a bar, a prostitute, apparently asked for payment after services were rendered. An indignant Coakley, refusing to pay, was charged with rape. The complaint against him was dismissed after the woman failed to show, but his photograph was later picked out by the victim of a real rape.

There was a string of error in Coakley's prosecution: honestly mistaken eyewitness identification after less-than-optimal lineup procedures, an overworked and ill-prepared public defender, and sloppy police forensic investigation. Coakley, however, not only passed a polygraph examination, but had a seemingly rock-solid alibi: He was at a regularly scheduled Bible study meeting at his sister's apartment on the night of the rape. He had been at that apartment building for several hours before the study meeting, chatting with friends, and he "had nine witnesses ready to say he was there, including the minister" (Scheck et al., 2001: 25). What happened at trial was not an evidentiary or constitutional violation, but rather was standard operating procedure in an adversary trial. As Scheck et al. put it, "Through pinpoint cross-examination, Assistant District Attorney Reiser was able to spin the preacher like a child's top" (25). In a series of questions about the time and place of the meeting, the weather conditions, the number of men present, and their precise participation, the District Attorney was able to befuddle the preacher. The testimony did establish that Coakley was at the meeting, but Reiser established doubt about the time it ended, allowing her to argue that Coakley had enough time to commit the crime (Scheck et al., 2001: 27–28). One might argue that a prosecutor adhering to the "minister of justice" model would not have used cross-examination in such a manner—that sprinkling doubt on honest witnesses is a cross-examination tactic that is only proper for defense lawyers (Friedman, 1966). Nevertheless, what Reiser did was allowable under adversary trial rules of combat.

What is significant about this episode, from our perspective, is that the prosecutor's cross-examination is not cataloged among others as a "cause" of wrongful conviction in Scheck et al. or in other books or reports. One is not sure how such a factor would be categorized if indeed it were identified in transcripts. Perhaps "the excesses in ordinary trial procedures" is the right label. I certainly am not suggesting that the prosecution should be divested of the right to cross-examine, only that when searching for the truth of a precisely provable fact (like the time of events), the way in which the litigator's questions were used against Coakley might serve to obfuscate as much as to enlighten.

In addition to this episode, there is a whole genre of writing that raises serious doubts about the capacity of juries to find facts accurately. Indeed, a colleague and I have written (Zalman & Gates, 1993) that the best that can be achieved in change-of-venue applications in a racially charged situation is a jury of "practical impartiality," and after that is achieved we should accept de Tocqueville's (1969: 272) observation that juries are institutions of local democracy that will inevitably reflect local values. The most sophisticated voir dire study demonstrates that white predominance on Philadelphia capital juries produces a higher rate of death penalties and black predominance leads to a statistically significantly higher rate of life sentences (Baldus et al., 2001). Jeffrey Abramson (1994), commenting on a less-than-ideal aspect of the cross-sectional ideal of jury composition, writes:

> The new and competing ideal for the jury is a group-representation model, one that seeks to redesign the jury so that it basically fits the pluralistic paradigm of democracy and interest group politics. This model is openly skeptical about whether deliberation inside the jury room matters; it insists, in the name of realism, that there is no one justice to share, that juries are not above the political fray but are a microcosm of the biases and prejudices, the bartering and brokering among group interests that dominate democratic deal making in general. According to this point of view, the key to jury verdicts becomes whom the jurors are, not what the evidence shows. (245)

This model may be overdrawn, as Abramson suggests in the pages following this quotation. In-depth stories of jury service support the anecdotal evidence that juries work hard at examining the evidence and following jury instructions (Burnett, 2002; Caplow, 2002).

Nevertheless, George Fletcher's (1995) review of a train (or train wreck) of such jury verdicts as the Dan White "twinkie defense" murder prosecution resulting in an exceedingly light and possibly homophobic verdict; the original Rodney King case in which an almost all-white Simi Valley, California, jury failed to convict Los Angeles police officers whose continuous beating of a downed King, captured on videotape, raised the specter of a racially biased verdict; and the initial acquittal of Lemrick Nelson in the killing of Yankel Rosenbaum during a pogrom in New York City—verdicts that all sparked riots or mass demonstrations—hardly inspire confidence in the jury trial to render accurate verdicts, although the erroneous verdicts in those cases (as borne out by later federal civil rights suits) were errors of impunity rather than errors of due process (Forst, 2004). An attorney speaking about plea bargaining during a *Nightline* episode hosted by Ted Koppel referred to going to trial as a "roll of the dice" (*Nightline*, 2000), an assessment that many attorneys share.

The failure to focus on the adversary system and trial by most writers on wrongful conviction cannot be attributed to a lack of scholarship in these areas. In recent decades a substantial amount of perceptive scholarship has been devoted to comparative trial systems (e.g., Damaška, 1986; Frase, 1990; Pizzi, 1999: 89–116, comparing trials in four European countries, and in the United States: 117–153). According to one author, "We are fortunately in the midst of a renaissance in comparative criminal procedure" (Lerner, 2001: 796; see McKillop, 1997). In parallel, the comparative study of evidence, a critical component in the truth-finding process of the trial, has been flourishing (e.g., Damaška, 1997a ; Nijboer and Reijntjes, 1997). A common theme in writings about comparative criminal procedure and evidence, perhaps going back to Wigmore and earlier to Bentham, has been the supposed superiority of continental trials to ascertain the truth (Bergman, 1991). The last decades have also been a rich time for the study of the American jury trial and a good deal of work has been done on improving the accuracy of jury verdicts via such innovations as allowing jurors to take notes, ask questions, discuss the case before the conclusion of testimony, and improvements in jury instructions (Cohen and Cohen, 2003; Dann and Hans 2004; Hans, 2002; Kelso, 1996). At the same time, of course, a very large literature has grown in the various "subfields" of wrongful conviction.[5] The number of articles on various standard factors range from the thousands (eyewitness identification; Wells et al., 1998) to the scores (e.g., false confessions). What is curious is that so few studies have bridged the gap between the wrongful conviction area of study and the work of trial system and evidence specialists and comparativists. Two important articles that have explored trial and wrongful conviction are closely reviewed later (Givelber, 1997; Risinger, 2004). I have identified only one article on the equally important issue of plea bargaining and wrongful conviction, but do not address it herein (Hessick & Saujani, 2002).

To conclude this section, it is not possible to prove that otherwise properly functioning jury trials contribute to wrongful convictions, directly or by filtering out investigation error, but there is a good deal of evidence that raises this inference. In recent decades comparative legal scholars have closely examined criminal procedure, evidence law, and European and American trials. Most of this literature has not directly addressed the question of wrongful conviction. At least one leading scholar has warned against making quick judgments about the superiority of one system over the other and of thinking that it is easy to transplant procedures from one "system" into another (Damaška, 1997a, 1997b). It is beyond the scope of this chapter to review the comparative literature on criminal trials, procedure, and evidence. In the remainder of this chapter, I examine the adversary trial and the adversary system. The exploration of the adversary trial reviews two important law review articles, the first (Givelber, 1997) a pioneering work that provided a perceptive analysis of the issue but included no prescriptions for change, and the second (Risinger, 2004) a breakthrough in proposing a feasible avenue of reform in the adversary trial. The last section explores one issue in the adversary system, the control of investigations.

Tinkering with the Adversary Trial

Givelber (1997) hammered home the point that blind faith in jury verdicts is no longer justified in a world of DNA testing. He was writing fairly early in the DNA testing era, shortly after the publication of the National Institute of Justice (NIJ) report that established beyond doubt the existence of a worrisome number of exonerations (Connors et al., 1996). The title and lead quote to his article, suggesting that a guilty defendant has a better chance of acquittal in a common law court whereas an innocent would fare better in a continental court, set the stage for exploring the trial process. This was only partly the case as he also reviewed other factors associated with wrongful convictions. The article set up the classic legal position that false confessions are rare or nonexistent, and then undermined that position by citing more than thirty exonerations in then recent news accounts (Givelber, 1997: 1317–1321). After discussing the "legal invisibility" of exonerations that feeds the presumption of guilt (1322–1328) he reviewed the argument that a system rich with procedural protections and quick to acquit the guilty does not really protect the innocent (1328–1336), a position supported with substantial empirical evidence of likely and actual miscarriages of justice (1337–1358). The evidence included (1) high rates of dismissals and acquittals (1336–1338); (2) American and English studies of trial courts (Baldwin and McConville, 1979; Kalven and Zeisel, 1966) that threw "into question the claim that only the guilty are charged and convicted" (Givelber 1997: 1339); (3) the Huff, Rattner, and Sagarin (1996) study in which justice system personnel estimated that one-half of 1 percent of all convictions convict the innocent (Givelber, 1997: 1342); and (4) a close analysis of the NIJ Report (Connors et al ., 1996; Givelber, 1997: 1346–1358).

Much of this material placed the major responsibility for wrongful convictions on police errors. Givelber (1997: 1358) then turned to a review of the adversary system itself, asking "why our procedures do not protect the innocent." This lengthy analytic section dissected central aspects of the adversary system and the adversary trial, exposing several weak points. First, he dismissed the protections afforded by the palace of constitutional rights erected to "insure that the innocent are acquitted; these rules have not succeeded in minimizing false convictions to the extent practicable" (1359). The major reason is the chronic imbalance between the resource-rich prosecution and the resource-poor defense. Although this criticism does not go to the inherent structure of the adversary system, the imbalance is so pervasive in the United States that it might be treated as a structural error. Correcting this problem does not require constitutional change, but its intractability must be considered in any practical exploration of improvements to the adversary system. In this section, Givelber (1997: 1361) briefly mentions that adversarialness breeds a competitive spirit among prosecutors that leads to withholding evidence, a point requiring greater attention. Givelber's second, somewhat discursive critique looks at the pretrial process and finds it wanting as an effective screening of innocent suspects. This is largely because the police wish to close cases as quickly as possible and because of the relative insulation of the prosecutor at the charging stage.[6] I discuss one aspect of the investigation and pretrial process in the concluding section.

The last section in this part of Givelber's article assesses the adversary system's capacity to get to the truth and finds it severely wanting. A fundamental aspect of the adversary system is the multiple functions of the trial and the extraconstitutional status of ascertaining the truth.

The Supreme Court has read the United States Constitution as embracing an adversarial system of justice in which the passive fact-finder must be convinced of a criminal defendant's guilt beyond a reasonable doubt. The Court has not found in the Constitution any requirement that the adversaries themselves seriously consider the elimination of reasonable doubt before presenting a case to the fact-finder, nor has the Court held that the conviction of an innocent person offends the Constitution. Factual accuracy is desirable, but as a Constitutional matter, hardly paramount. (Givelber, 1997: 1370–1371, footnotes omitted)

Thus, for all of the judicially expanded textual constitutional rights designed to protect the defendant that exist, the criminal justice system has not been constitutionally required to do its best to ascertain the truth.

But the Court has refused to concern itself with the obligations of the police or prosecutor to conduct a thorough investigation, to maintain comprehensive records, or even to choose wisely which potential defendants to charge. These matters—the very essence of a system concerned with actual innocence—are extra-constitutional. (1371, footnotes omitted)

Further, the classic role of the defense in raising a reasonable doubt in the prosecution case is undermined by the "background" jury bias in favor of the prosecution that can be exploited by some prosecutors to refute even scientific evidence, by the numerous ways in which exculpatory evidence in police and prosecution hands is never divulged to the defense, and by judicial passivity in the face of highly improbable evidence such as the testimony of jailhouse snitches (Givelber, 1997: 1372–1378). These points were well made by Givelber but not completely original. Yet, by pulling them together he made a significant advance in the legal scholarship of wrongful conviction and raised important questions about the role of the adversary system and the adversary trial.

Givelber sheds much light on the adversary system–wrongful conviction interface but suggests that meaningful reform is possible only on the periphery of the adversary system and trial. His silence about jury trial reform implies that modifications to the constitutionally embedded jury trial are not possible. The lack of studies on the role of the jury in perpetuating wrongful convictions seems to confirm the view that an "expert social construction" of the reality of wrongful conviction has avoided this central institution. I believe that D. Michael Risinger's (2004) recent article is a significant breakthrough; it points the way to further speculation and practical modifications that could make the jury trial an arena for preventing wrongful convictions.

Before turning to Risinger (2004), I wish to add a word about the use of "adversary system" and "adversary trial" in this article. The terms are often used interchangeably, but I believe they are separable. To advance feasible reforms, it is necessary to "unpack" the adversary system and trial, and to be clear about what these terms encompass. To Stephen Landsman (1984), the adversary system includes three components: a neutral and passive fact finder, party presentation of evidence, and a highly structured forensic procedure. Paradoxically, the jury is central to the adversary system but is not essential for a valid adversary trial. Landsman's "unpacking" of the elements leads to an appreciation of Risinger's advances.[7]

Risinger (2004) unpacks the jury trial by briefly outlining what he calls the "standard rationalist" model, also known as the "search for the truth" model among evidence theorists. He notes that the model coexists uneasily with "the adversary system," which encompasses party presentation of evidence and a highly structured forensic proceeding (1288), and with the jury trial (1290). By thus unpacking the adversary trial, Risinger is able to examine the jury trial in a way that advances the search for truth while not undermining traditional jury functions.

To oversimplify somewhat, Risinger (2004: 1290–1295) points out that juries, as bearers of social norms, are best at determining value questions in civil and criminal law. He then, again oversimplifying, divides the kinds of issues that confront criminal juries into polyvalent issues of intent and the like and binary issues of whether a specific fact occurred. When, for example, there is no doubt that a defendant committed the act but the issue involves ascertaining his state of mind, this in effect requires "the resolution of . . . complex, no-one-right-answer, normatively charged judgments about what was going on in his head" (1299). Risinger allows, somewhat uncomfortably, that lawyers' emotional appeals, or the "story theory of lawyering" (Schrager, 1999), are inevitable and may be permissible up to a point in trials dominated by multivalent issues such as inferring a state of mind from the known facts. But "heartstrings and gore" lawyering, or the "spinning" of an honest alibi witness (Scheck et al., 2001: 25), can produce miscarriages of justice in what Risinger calls cases involving "brute fact innocence" (Risinger, 2004: 1298). "[B]inary fact determinations of the nontechnical type are the kinds of decisions where ordinary juries can most often be led to miscarry by adversary excess, especially in the context of high profile and highly dramatic cases" (1309). Here is Risinger's tentative proposal:

> It is well beyond the scope of this Article to recommend any such changes in detail, but tentatively, such proposed rules might look something like this: The defendant would be required to isolate the one (or perhaps two) binary exterior ultimate facts that underlie his claim of innocence. All other elements of the case would be conceded

by binding judicial admission, a circumstance to be explained to the jury in the most unambiguous fashion after alternative proposals for the explanatory charge have been made by the defense and the prosecution. Thereafter, in the actual trial, all proffers of evidence by both sides would have to be found "usably" relevant to the factual issues as limited. Prosecution use of expert testimony would be closely screened for reliability, and the court would be prevented from excluding, on the ground of "invasion of the province of the jury," any defense-proffered expert evidence on the weaknesses of eyewitness identification, false confessions, the commonness of false testimony by jailhouse snitches, and the weaknesses of any expert evidence proffered by the prosecution. Closing arguments would be expected to stick closely to the factual issues raised in the application. The cross-sectional jury would be retained, together with the finality rule for acquittals. Convictions would be reviewable not merely on the basis of sufficiency, but also on the issue of whether they were "unsafe." (1311–1312, footnotes omitted)

Risinger warns that this tentative proposal ought to be treated only as a preliminary idea, given the "law of unintended consequences." Undoubtedly, tinkering with the guts of the jury trial is not a matter that the legal world (think judges, prosecutors, trial attorneys and bar associations; state law reform commissions; legislative judiciary committees; state supreme courts, innocence commissions) would rush into willy-nilly. However, scholars, especially legal scholars, who have grappled with the awful injustices of wrongful convictions, should begin to take up Risinger's insight and considers its pros and cons in greater depth.[8]

Tinkering With the Adversary System

I distinguish the adversary system from the adversary trial by defining the former as the structural relationships within the criminal justice system focusing on the police, prosecution, defense, and judiciary. The United States and France (as a stand-in for the so-called inquisitorial system) differ greatly around the themes of separation and connectedness. The American system is marked by the constitutional separation of powers that sets police and prosecutors on one podium and the judiciary on another. Police and prosecutors, while walking arm-in-arm during the opening credits of the popular television show *Law and Order* are institutionally separated by jurisdiction (e.g., county prosecutor, municipal police department), provenance (e.g., elected prosecutor, appointed police executive), historic redundancy (e.g., city police, county sheriff, state police), and federalism (e.g., local and federal prosecutors with functionally concurrent jurisdiction; nonfederal police departments and a multiplicity of federal law enforcement agencies). This inherently inefficient "system" works as well as it does largely because of a substantial amount of cooperation, although interagency dynamics always carry the seeds of friction (Cole, 1970).

In contrast there appear to be fewer agencies and a greater degree of connectedness in France. There are only two major national police agencies that investigate major crimes and a centralized judiciary with a branch for the investigatory function that oversees major investigations. The lines of decision making between the investigating magistrate (*juge d'instruction*) and the prosecutor appear to be relatively clear cut. Investigatory power is heavily weighted in favor of the state, but the investigating magistrate has a duty to seek exculpatory evidence. Several aspects of the French process will strike Americans as dangerous to civil liberties, incomprehensible, or entirely unconstitutional: gathering complete background information on the defendant and entering it into evidence, having the suspect participate in the police investigation, detention for up to forty-eight hours with limited access to counsel at the end of that period, and the deferential role of defense counsel (see Cohen, 1999; Daly, 1999; McKillop, 1997).

Despite the deep structural difference between the United States and France, there has long been an attraction among American jurists for aspects of the French system.[9] One suggestion that is "sporadically suggested as a desirable innovation" is to allow the judge to take the lead in cross-examining witnesses (Damaška, 1997b: 849). Damaška takes the air out of this proposal. He forces the reader to see that the proposed change would not work unless other institutional and professional arrangements also changed. Effective cross-examination requires solid knowledge of a case, and "[a]s things presently stand, however, the Anglo-American judge knows very little about the facts of the case in which he is sitting" (Damaška, 1997b: 850). If this continues to be the situation, the judge's

> questioning would seldom elicit more than a thin narrative account from a witness. Counsel, who are aware of information available from the witness, would soon take over, and resume their dominant role in the interrogation process. The "thin" initial questioning from the bench would only bedevil their planning for orderly and clear presentation of evidence. A measure of repetition and confusion would most likely result. The enforcement of the present regime of rules of admissibility would also become more difficult: the freer narrative generated by broad questions from the bench would inject far more

inadmissible material into the case than the now prevailing technique of narrow questions put by counsel. (850)

Further, judicial questioning "would seriously strain the traditional common law understanding of judicial impartiality" (851). The more general lesson of Damaška's caution is that thought must be given to the possible rejection of any proposed legal transplant by the host system.

Having been duly forewarned, I believe that some procedures in the French system of judicially directed inquiry have the potential to catch potential wrongful convictions early in the process. Bron McKillop's (1997) detailed account of a French murder case discloses a feature of the French system that could advance the accuracy of police investigation when a defendant claims to be innocent. In France, as more generally in continental law countries,[10] the defendant (and the victim who is joined in the case as a civil party) has the right to request of the investigating magistrate that further investigations be carried out (McKillop, 1997: 539–540), and when confronted with experts' reports "to ask for a 'counter-expertise' or a complementary expertise within ten days" (538). A defense request has to be filtered through the investigating magistrate.

Clearly, a criminal defendant's request that police conduct an investigation along specific lines strikes at the heart of adversarialness. The defendant is supposed to do his or her own investigation. Yet, for an indigent defendant, or any defendant who is confronted with an issue for which the prosecution is uniquely positioned to investigate, the matter carries some logic. One could imagine a statutorily created practice that allows a defense motion to the court to consider, and order where reasonable preconditions have been met, specific investigation on the part of the police, to obtain exculpatory evidence or to clarify evidence that is questionable. I do not develop this idea any further here, although I think that it deserves greater exposition, at least as a thought experiment.[11]

By analogy, something like this is beginning to happen in regard to DNA testing. For a decade after the initiation of DNA testing in criminal cases, a large number of prosecutors fought bitterly to prevent convicted defendants from getting access to DNA samples to prove innocence, while happily using DNA to prove guilt (Medwed, 2004). This attitude, which flies in the face of basic fairness, has exposed the worst aspects of the culture of prosecutorial overzealousness. It is now slowly beginning to change. The ICVA recommends that "When prosecutors seek to use expert testimony about scientific evidence against a criminal defendant, it is vital that the defense have the opportunity to challenge or rebut the findings and conclusions of the government's experts" (ICVA, 2005: 85). The resistance of prosecutors to DNA testing shows how difficult it would be to initiate anything. The trend toward allowing postconviction testing indicates that change is possible.

For a trial practice that authorizes investigation by the prosecution for the defendant to be feasible, a number of changes would have to occur. Creating an investigating magistrate role in the United States is impossible. The separation of powers is not the only reason. American judges, elected or appointed from the diverse world of law practice, simply have no expertise in such a role. What is more feasible, although far from easy, is for police and prosecutors to develop a cooperative regime that mimics the investigating magistrate in some respects.[12] A change directed at making prosecution more effective in developing cases against the guilty—an investigation focused on eventual prosecution and not one that seeks to "clear" a crime as quickly as possible—would be a precursor to a defense request for investigation. Such police–prosecutor cooperation already exists in complex federal investigations, so a model exists, although it is one in which there appear to be very few controls on prosecutors (Moohr, 2004:198, 219; Richman and Stuntz, 2005: 602). Nevertheless, defense requests for investigation would begin to make sense in a system of police and prosecutorial investigation that has shifted more toward developing something like a dossier, that developed internal review rather than relying on the weak argument that the grand jury acts as a check, and that took seriously the practice of seeking exculpatory evidence.

It is not likely that prosecutors would initiate limits on their existing broad powers. Yet, were legislatures to begin to reverse the trend toward creating a prosecutorial juggernaut, including a defendant's right to petition for a specific investigation before trial would be an important element. Indeed, such legislation would be compatible with the due process and equal protection values if not, perhaps, the specific holdings of a Supreme Court case overturning a conviction where a psychiatrist, necessary for the proper defense of an indigent defendant, was denied (*Ake v. Oklahoma*, 1985). The underlying concern in that case was the "accuracy of a criminal proceeding (78), a concern of both the individual and the state that should be a prime concern in an adversary system of justice.

Conclusion

Wrongful conviction scholars for the most part have avoided serious discussion of the adversary trial, and comparative law scholars and experts on evidence law have, on the whole, not applied their knowledge to considering miscarriages of justice. It may be that some years of thinking about wrongful conviction had to pass before serious reflection on the adversary trial (e.g., Givelber, 1997) would begin to bear fruit in potentially workable alterations to present practice with a chance of reducing miscarriages of justice (Risinger, 2004). Legal scholars should heed Leo's (2005) challenge to criminologists to get involved in the study of wrongful conviction (see Huff, 2002), and to think the subject anew. The formulaic "catalog of errors" approach to thinking about wrongful conviction needs to be amplified. A broader way of seeing the issues, one that involves a panoramic understanding of the criminal justice system, and that looks to possible solutions in other legal systems, must be entertained.

Notes

1. It should go without saying that there are great risks in using these terms. All comparative legal scholars say that nothing like an "inquisitorial system" really exists (Nijboer 1997), although there are clusters of commonalities that differentiate continental from English and American legal practices and institutions (Damaška 1986, 1997a).

2. These lists may give the erroneous impression that single factors "cause" a wrongful conviction. Wrongful conviction cases usually involve a cascade effect where one error "infects" a case and opens the way to a train of other errors. Castelle and Loftus (2001:19) note that the cascade effect "is poorly understood within the judicial system and the law enforcement community and is rarely acknowledged." In fairness, most scholars of wrongful convictions are aware that multiple errors typically occur in a miscarriage of justice.

3. Edwin Borchard, a professor at Yale Law School, apparently wrote *Convicting the Innocent* (1932) as a refutation to a prosecutor's statement that innocent men are never convicted (v). It appears that this belief was widely held and is reflected in Learned Hand's assertion that "the ghost of the innocent man convicted . . . is an unreal dream" (*U.S. v. Garsson* 1923: 649).

4. The ICVA (2005) report includes one- to two-page summaries of the cases of each of eleven exonerees that formed part of the empirical basis for the report. More detailed studies of these cases, approximately thirty pages each, are found on the IVCA Web site (http://www.icva.us/).

5. Leo (2005) posits that three specialized literatures exist that can be seen as subfields of wrongful conviction: studies of eyewitness identification, child suggestibility, and false confession, to which he adds a more popular genre of true-crime-style case studies. It is possible, however, to construe from the existing literature additional subfields, such as repressed memory, the use of informants, prosecution error, the withholding of evidence, forensic error, and the like.

6. For a detailed and thoughtful defense of not turning the pretrial stage into another trial, at least in federal prosecutions, see Henning (1999).

7. A masterful "unpacking" is found in Damaška (1997a), which deconstructs the adversary trial system along three dimensions: the bifurcation of the tribunal between lay and professional judges, the temporal compression of trials, and the adversary proper— party control of evidence.

8. Risinger (2004: 1313–1333) goes on to suggest that the "unsafe verdict" as a standard for review, the standard now used in England, be considered. Reviewing this proposal is beyond the scope of this chapter, but legal scholars ought to examine it closely.

9. Any wholesale adoption of a French-style investigatory system in American states is probably impossible given the deep structural and constitutional differences between the polities (Damaška 1986). Proponents of the civil law system's approach should be aware of a disquieting scandal about its flaws (Bell 2004). See also the chapter by Brants on miscarriages of justice under the continental system.

10. See also the chapters on The Netherlands, France, and Switzerland, as well as the chapter comparing German and English prosecutorial systems.

11. See on this issue the chapter by Schiffer and Champod.

12. The model could be the kind of police-prosecutorial cooperation in most continental law countries. See especially the chapter by Kessler.

References

Abramson, J. (1994). *We, the jury: The jury system and the ideal of democracy.* New York: Basic Books.

Baldus, D. C., Woodworth, G., Zuckerman, D., Weiner, N. A., & Broffitt, B. (2001). The use of peremptory challenges in capital murder trials: A legal and empirical analysis. *University of Pennsylvania Journal of Constitutional Law, 3,* 3–170.

Baldwin, J., & McConville, M. (1979). *Jury trials.* New York: Oxford University Press.

Barthel, J. (1976). *A death in Canaan.* New York: Dutton.

Beckett, K. (1997). *Making crime pay: Law and order in contemporary American politics.* New York: Oxford University Press.

Bell, R. (2004). *Joanna.* Court TV's Crime Library. Retrieved May 11 2005, from http://www.crimelibrary.com/serial_killers/predators/auxerre/

Bergman, P. (1991). Book review: Of Bentham, Wigmore, and Little Bo Peep: Where evidence lost its way, and a map for scholars to find it (*Rethinking Evidence-Exploratory Essays,* by Twining, W. & Blackwell, B., 1990). *Notre Dame Law Review, 66,* 949–964.

Borchard, E. M. (1932). *Convicting the innocent: Sixty-five actual errors of criminal justice.* Garden City, NY: Doubleday.

Burnett, D. G. (2002). *A trial by jury.* New York: Knopf.

Caplow, S. (2002). The impossible dream comes true—A criminal law professor becomes juror # 7. *Brooklyn Law Review, 67,* 785–825.

Castelle, G., & Loftus, E. F. (2001). Misinformation and wrongful conviction. In S. D. Westervelt & J. A. Humphrey (Eds.), *Wrongly convicted: Perspectives on failed justice* (pp. 17–31). New Brunswick, NJ: Rutgers University Press.

Center for Public Integrity. (2003). *Harmful error: Investigating America's local prosecutors.* Washington, DC: Author.

Cohen, G. D. (1999). Comparing the investigating grand jury with the French system of criminal investigations: A judge's perspective and commentary. *Temple International and Comparative Law Journal, 13*(1), 87–105.

Cohen, N. P., & Cohen, D. R. (2003). Jury reform in Tennessee. *University of Memphis Law Review, 34,* 1–71.

Cole, G. F. (1970). The decision to prosecute. *Law & Society Review, 4,* 331–343.

Connors, E., Lundregan, T., Miller, N., & McEwan, T. (1996, June). *Convicted by juries, exonerated by science: Case studies in the use of DNA evidence to establish innocence after trial* (National Institute of Justice Ref. No. NCJ 161258). Washington, DC: National Institute of Justice.

Daly, M. C. (1999). Legal ethics: Some thoughts on the differences in criminal trials in the civil and common law legal systems. *Journal for the Study of Legal Ethics, 2,* 65–73.

Damaška, M. (1986). *The faces of justice and state authority: A comparative approach to the legal process.* New Haven, CT: Yale University Press.

Damaška, M. (1997a). *Evidence law adrift.* New Haven, CT: Yale University Press.

Damaška, M. (1997b). The uncertain fate of evidentiary transplants: Anglo-American and continental experiments. *American Journal of Comparative Law, 45,* 839–852.

Dann, B. M., & Hans, V. P. (2004). Recent evaluative research on jury trial innovations. *Court Review, 41,* 12.

de Tocqueville, A. (1969). *Democracy in America* (J. Mayer, ed. & G Lawrence, Trans.). New York: Anchor Books.

Fletcher, G. (1995). *With justice for some: Victims' rights in criminal trials.* Reading, MA: Addison-Wesley.

Forst, B. (2004). *Errors of justice: Nature, sources, and remedies.* New York: Cambridge University Press.

Frank, J. (1950). *Courts on trial: Myth and reality in American justice.* Princeton, NJ: Princeton University Press.

Frank, J., & Frank, B. (1971). *Not guilty.* New York: DaCapo Press. (Original work published 1957)

Frase, R. (1990). Comparative criminal justice as a guide to American law reform: How do the French do it, how can we find out, and why should we care? *California Law Review, 78,* 539–683.

Friedman, M. H. (1966). Professional responsibility of the defense lawyer: The three hardest questions. *Michigan Law Review, 64,* 1469–1484.

Gardner, E. S. (1952). *The court of last resort.* New York: William Sloane.

Givelber, D. (1997). Meaningless acquittals, meaningful convictions: Do we reliably acquit the innocent? *Rutgers Law Review, 49,* 1317–1396.

Gould, J. B. (2008). The Innocence Commission: Preventing wrongful convictions and restoring the criminal justice system. New York: New York University Press.

Gross, S. R., Jacoby, K., Matheson, D. J., Montgomery, N., & Patel, S. (2005). Exonerations in the United States, 1989 through 2003. *Journal of Criminal Law and Criminology, 95,* 523–560.

Hans, V. P. (2002). U.S. jury reform: The active jury and the adversarial ideal. *St. Louis University Public Law Review, 21,* 85–97.

Henning, P. J. (1999). Prosecutorial misconduct in grand jury investigations. *South Carolina Law Review, 51*(1), 1–61.

Herda-Rapp, A. (2003). The social construction of local school violence threats by the news media and professional organizations. *Sociological Inquiry, 73,* 545–574

Hessick, F. A., III, & Saujani, R. M. (2002). Plea bargaining and convicting the innocent: The role of the prosecutor, the defense counsel, and the judge. *BYU Journal of Public Law, 16,* 189–242.

Huff, C. R. (2002). Wrongful conviction and public policy: The American Society of Criminology 2001 presidential address. *Criminology, 40*(1), 1–18.

Huff, C. R., Rattner, A., & Sagarin, E. (1996). *Convicted but innocent: Wrongful conviction and public policy.* Thousand Oaks, CA: Sage.

Illinois Governor's Commission on Capital Punishment. (2002, April). Governor's Commission on Capital Punishment. Retrieved March 1, 2008, from http://www.idoc.state.il.us/ccp/ccp/reports/commission_report/index.html

Innocence Commission for Virginia. (2005, March). *A vision for justice.* Arlington, VA: Innocence Commission for Virginia. Retrieved March 28, 2008 from http://www .icva.us

Jenkins, P. (1998). *Moral panic: Changing concepts of the child molester in modern America.* New Haven, CT: Yale University Press.

Kalven, H., Jr., & Zeisel, H. (1966). *The American jury.* Boston: Little Brown.

Kelso, J. C. (1996). Final report of the Blue Ribbon Commission on jury system improvement. *Hastings Law Journal, 47,* 1433–1520.

Kuhn, T. S. (1970). *The structure of scientific revolutions* (2nd ed., enlarged). Chicago: University of Chicago Press.

Landsman, S. (1984). *The adversary system: A description and defense.* Washington, DC: American Enterprise Institute for Public Policy Research.

Leo, R. (2005). Re-thinking the study of miscarriages of justice: Developing a criminology of wrongful conviction. *Journal of Contemporary Criminal Justice, 21*(3), 201–223.

Lerner, R. L. (2001). The intersection of two systems: An American on trial for an American murder in the French *Cour d'Assises. University of Illinois Law Review, 2001,* 791–856.

McKillop, B. (1997). Anatomy of a French murder case. *American Journal of Comparative Law, 45,* 527–583.

Medwed, D. S. (2004). The zeal deal: Prosecutorial resistance to post-conviction claims of innocence. *Boston University Law Review, 84,* 125–183.

Moohr, G. S. (2004). Prosecutorial power in an adversarial system: Lessons from current white collar cases and the inquisitorial model. *Buffalo Criminal Law Review, 8,* 165–220.

Nightline. (2000). Crime & punishment: Let's make a deal [videorecording]. New York: ABC News.

Nijboer, J. F. (1997). The American adversarial system in criminal cases: Between ideology and reality. *Cardozo Journal of International and Comparative Law, 5,* 79–96.

Nijboer, J. F., & Reijntjes, J. M. (1997). *Proceedings of the First World Conference on New Trends in Criminal Investigation and Evidence.* Amsterdam:Koninklijke Vermande bv/Open University of the Netherlands.

Packer, H. (1968). *The limits of the criminal sanction.* Stanford, CA: Stanford University Press.

Pizzi, W. T. (1999). *Trials without truth.* New York: New York University Press.

Rabinowitz, D. (2003). *No crueler tyrannies: Accusation, false witness and other terrors of our times.* New York: Wall Street Journal Books.

Raymond, M. (2001). The problem with innocence. *Cleveland State Law Review, 49,* 449–463.

Richman, D. C., & Stuntz, W. J. (2005). Al Capone's revenge: An essay on the political economy of pretextual prosecution. *Columbia Law Review, 105,* 583–639.

Risinger, D. M. (2004). Unsafe verdicts: The need for reformed standards for the trial and review of factual innocence claims. *Houston Law Review, 41,* 1281–1336.

Scheck, B. C., Neufeld, P. J., & Dwyer, J. (2001). *Actual innocence: When justice goes wrong and how to make it right.* New York: Signet.

Schrager, S. (1999). *The trial lawyer's art.* Philadelphia: Temple University Press.

Warden, R. (2002). The revolutionary role of journalism in identifying and rectifying wrongful convictions. *UMKC Law Review, 70,* 803–846.

Wells, G. L., Small, M., Penrod, S., Malpass, R. S., Fulero, S. M., & Brimacombe, C. A. E. (1998). Eyewitness identification procedures: Recommendations for lineups and photospreads. *Law and Human Behavior, 22,* 603–647.

Zalman, M. (2004/March 11). *A century of concern: Wrongful conviction in English and American culture, 1890–1990.* Paper presented at the annual meeting of the Academy of Criminal Justice Sciences, Las Vegas.

Zalman, M. (2005). Cautionary notes on commission recommendations: A public policy approach to wrongful convictions. *Criminal Law Bulletin, 41,* 169–194.

Zalman, M. (2006). Criminal justice system reform and wrongful conviction: A research agenda. *Criminal Justice Policy Review, 17,* 468–492.

Zalman, M., & Gates, M. (1993). Rethinking venue in light of the Rodney King case:An interest analysis. *Cleveland State Law Review, 41,* 215–277.

Cases Cited

Ake v. Oklahoma, 470 U.S. 68 (1985).

United States v. Garsson, 291 F. 646, 649 (S.D.N.Y. 1923) (Hand, J.).

6

FATAL ERRORS

Compelling Claims of Executions of the Innocent in the Post-Furman Era

⌒

WILLIAM S. LOFQUIST AND TALIA R. HARMON

No matter how careful courts are, the possibility of perjured testimony, mistaken honest testimony and human error remain too real. We have no way of judging how many innocent persons have been executed, but we can be certain that there were some.

—THURGOOD MARSHALL (*Furman v. Georgia*, 1972, PP. 367–368)

Naming Names: Identifying the Executed Innocent

With wrongful convictions firmly secure as a central issue in death penalty discourse, it is time to take the next logical step in the scholarly and political debates regarding wrongful convictions: identifying and examining compelling claims of innocence that resulted in execution rather than exoneration. Taking this step is difficult and controversial; difficult because the absence of legal recognition of error introduces an extra measure of uncertainty about the claims being made, controversial because what is at stake might be the most damning claim that can be made against the death penalty.

Although it is widely recognized in the abstract that some innocent individual or individuals have been executed in the post-*Furman* era[1] (see van den Haag, 1990; Radelet & Bedau, 1998; Will, 2000), no single case has gained broad recognition as a "fatal error." Bridging the gap between abstract recognition of the reality of fatal errors and identifying these errors—naming names, so to speak—requires scrutinizing all post-*Furman* executions in an effort to identify those cases in which there is a compelling claim that the executed defendant was "totally uninvolved in the capital offense of which they were convicted or were convicted of a capital offense that never occurred" (Radelet & Bedau, 1998, p. 106). This research undertakes this effort, identifying sixteen individuals executed despite compelling claims of factual innocence among the 784 executions in the thirty-year period beginning with the *Furman* decision on June 29, 1972.

Moving From Exonerations to Executions in the Innocence Debate

Efforts to narrow, pause, and even abolish use of the death penalty appeared moribund only several years ago (Kirchmeier, 2002). Death row populations were at historic highs and were growing rapidly (see deathpenaltyinfo.org for comprehensive post-*Furman* death penalty data). The pace of executions was increasing. Expansion of the death penalty to new offenses and new offenders was the subject of annual legislative one-upmanship (see Simon, 1999). Courts issued broad, even brazen endorsements of the death penalty, strongly rebuking efforts to challenge the legal apparatus of the death penalty (see *Coleman v. Thompson*, 1991; *Herrera v. Collins*, 1993; *Callins v. Collins*, 1994), and judicial opponents—real and imagined—of the death penalty were often attacked (see Bright & Keenan, 1995; Howarth, 2002). Searching self-criticism was widespread among anti-death-penalty scholars and activists (see Haines, 1996).

Within the last several years, and continuing into the present despite the vengefulness provoked by the events of September 11, 2001, and the execution of Timothy McVeigh earlier that same summer, the tide has turned. Public, media, and political voices have risen to challenge the death penalty (Lifton & Mitchell, 2001). Local and even state execution moratoria have been declared (Associated Press, 2002; Rimer, 2000; "Ryan Halts Executions," 2000). Legislative and executive efforts to study, reform, pause, and abolish the death penalty have been introduced across the nation (Associated Press, 2000; McDermott, 2002; Reed & Tysver, 2000; Yardley, 2001). Death row populations have ended their twenty-five-year increase, decreasing slightly from their peak in 2000. The pace of executions has slowed. Scholarly efforts to explain this change of course and discern its future direction have proliferated (Liebman, 2002; Sarat, 2002; Steiker & Steiker, 2002;). Although it is far too soon to declare the end of the death penalty—new statutory limitations on its use have been few and it remains well entrenched in its traditional Southern strongholds—it is clear that one moment has ended and another has begun.

Recognition of wrongful convictions has played a central role in the changing debate about the death penalty. Once viewed as a rare occurrence, marginal to the death penalty debate, wrongful convictions have moved to the top of the litany of concerns expressed about the death penalty (Farrell,

2000; Radelet & Borg, 2000; Rovella, 2000; Willing, 2001). Indeed, it was concern about wrongful convictions that figured most prominently in Illinois Governor George Ryan's decision to declare a moratorium on executions in 2000 and, more dramatically, in his decision to empty the state's death row through a blanket commutation in January 2003 (Wilgoren, 2003).

This shift in the death penalty debate began nearly twenty years ago, with the publication of a law review article identifying 350 wrongful convictions in capital and potentially capital cases and twenty-three wrongful executions in the twentieth century (Bedau & Radelet, 1987). Bedau and Radelet's article, later expanded to a book with Putnam (Radelet, Bedau, & Putnam, 1992), received an unexpected amount of attention, mostly favorable but also critical. Even the critical attention, coming as it did from the highest levels of the Justice Department (Markman & Cassell, 1988), served to legitimize the issue and move it into the death penalty debate.

Additional efforts to define and count the wrongly convicted (Dieter, 1997; Radelet, Lofquist, & Bedau, 1996), as well as a first-ever national conference dedicated to the issue (Terry, 1998; Zuckoff, 1998); a number of high-profile exonerations of death row inmates (Armbrust, 2002; Mills, 1999); technological advances, particularly in the area of DNA, which increased the ability to identify wrongful convictions (Scheck, Neufeld, & Dwyer, 2000); and the establishment of a series of university-based Innocence Projects, (see http://innocenceproject.org/about/other_projects.php) have followed. All of this culminated with federal legislative efforts to protect against wrongful convictions and with a federal court decision ruling that the Federal Death Penalty Act of 1994 was unconstitutional because of an "undue risk of executing innocent people" (*U.S. v. Quinones*, 2002, p. 418).

Even as the issue of wrongful convictions has achieved recognition and legitimacy, and the lists of 117 wrongful capital convictions (http://www.deathpenaltyinfo.org) and 153 DNA-based capital and noncapital exonerations (http://www.innocenceproject.org) have come to be widely accepted and cited, the issue has remained narrowly framed around the "exonerated" innocent. Every one of the names now appearing on the Death Penalty Information Center's list of wrongful convictions is on that list by virtue of formal appellate recognition of factual error in the original conviction. Claims originating from those still on death row and, more important and more pertinent to this research, those associated with executed individuals, are not recognized. Although perhaps understandable, given the political marginality of death penalty opponents and of the issue of wrongful convictions—at least until recently—there is also a perversity in relying exclusively on the courts to validate claims of innocence by recognizing its own errors.

Researching Cases: "A Meaningful Number of Innocent People"[2]

Combing through nearly 800 post-*Furman* executions to identify those with compelling claims of factual innocence is an unavoidably cumbersome process. In the absence of preexisting legal authority for limiting the scope of the inquiry, there is little choice but to wade into the entire population of executions and the claims of innocence associated with many of those cases, then attempt to evaluate them to identify meritorious claims. This was the approach taken by Bedau and Radelet (1987) in their original research. They began with exhaustive searches of newspapers, scholarly materials, and government publications, looking for innocence claims. To this, they added claims brought to their attention as a result of announcements they placed in the newsletters of criminologists, capital defense attorneys, and abolitionists. After gathering this initial group of cases, they collected appellate opinions, newspaper sources, archived information, and information provided, where possible, by parties to each case. They then evaluated this information and made their determinations of innocence. Although this approach is certainly imprecise and open to criticism, no clear alternative, short of rejecting all but legally sanctioned claims of innocence, is available.

Following Bedau and Radelet's approach, this research proceeded along multiple paths. The starting point was an exhaustive review of the existing literatures—scholarly, popular, activist, and electronic—on post-*Furman* claims of executions of the innocent. This effort produced approximately sixty cases involving independent claims (made by someone other than the defendant) of factual innocence. At the same time, the first author contacted death penalty scholars, activists, and defense attorneys in every state with a post-*Furman* execution and asked them to identify cases with which they were familiar that involved a credible innocence claim. This produced a list of forty-two cases. Closely examining each of these cases, particularly through newspaper accounts, appellate opinions, and published sources, allowed elimination of some cases that did not meet the narrow standards used to define innocence in this research, usually as a result of the determination that the executed individual was an accomplice to the capital murder.

With twenty-six cases remaining, questionnaires were sent to those individuals—usually defense attorneys, but also scholars and activists—most closely involved with each case. These questionnaires probed the views of the respondent about the innocence claim made regarding the case, as well as factors that contributed to the original wrongful conviction and to the failure to detect this error prior to execution. The results of this effort, as well as additional scrutiny of each case and examination of available clemency petitions, were sixteen cases presenting compelling claims of factual innocence.

Although these are the cases that meet the standards for compelling claims of factual innocence that we have established, it is unlikely that each person identified herein was in fact factually innocent of the crime for which he was executed. These are complicated cases, frequently involving individuals whose prior criminal records or troubled personal lives brought them to the attention of police, and whose trial and postconviction counsel were inadequate to counter the state's claims and unable to make effective use of a labyrinthine legal process. At the same time, it is at least as unlikely that all of the other nearly 800 individuals executed since 1977 were factually involved in the crimes for which they were executed.

Compelling Claims of Executions of the Innocent: The Cases

Timothy Baldwin, a white male, was convicted in 1978 for killing eighty-five-year-old Mary James Peters. He was executed in Louisiana in 1984. The victim, Baldwin's former neighbor and godmother to one of his children, was robbed and beaten. She died the next day. Baldwin's trial attorney had no capital experience. The main evidence presented against the defendant at trial consisted of the testimony of Baldwin's traveling companion at the time of the murder and Baldwin's girlfriend. The other primary witness for the state was the defendant's stepdaughter, Michelle Baldwin (for overviews of this case, see *Louisiana v. Baldwin*, 1980; *Baldwin v. Blackburn*, 1981; Ingle, 1990).

Michelle Baldwin's testimony is tainted by evidence that she was highly intoxicated the night of the murder and threatened by police to make a statement against her stepfather. A bank bag and bonds belonging to the victim discovered in the defendant's van were also tainted by having been found two days after police had gained possession of the van; the defendant claimed that the police planted the evidence.

Several additional factors raise significant doubt regarding Baldwin's guilt in Peters's murder. The victim regained consciousness at the hospital before she died. However, she did not identify her assailant, although surely she would have known Baldwin as a result of their extensive prior relationship. Baldwin's van did not match the van described by neighbors as parked outside Peters's house. These neighbors also picked out another man as the suspect in a police lineup. An eyewitness gave a description that did not match Baldwin. Finally, after the defendant's trial, a receipt was uncovered from a motel seventy miles from the crime scene. This evidence indicated that the defendant checked into the motel before midnight. The murder occurred at 11 p.m. Still troubled by Baldwin's execution, Louisiana Pardon Board Chair Howard Marsellus has stated that he had "grave misgivings" about Baldwin's guilt, but bowed to political pressure in voting for his execution (Rose, 1996, p. 8; see also Prejean, 1993).

Walter Blair, a black male, was convicted by an all-white jury in Missouri in 1980 and executed in 1993 for the killing of Katherine Jo Allen, a white female (see *Blair v. Armontrout*, 1990; Blair, 1993; *Blair v. Delo*, 1993). On August 19, 1979, Blair allegedly broke into Allen's apartment and found her and her boyfriend, Robert Kienzle, asleep in the living room. According to the state, Blair kidnapped Allen and stole Kienzle's ring. Several hours later, a witness heard screams and gunshots. The police found Allen's body four blocks away from Blair's mother's house, in a vacant lot. The state alleged Blair was paid $6,000 by Larry Jackson to kill the victim to prevent her from testifying against him. Officers arrested Ernest Jones—a friend of Blair's— after they learned that he and his brother, Fred Jones, had pawned Kienzle's ring. Kienzle identified Jones in a police lineup as the man who kidnapped Allen. After this identification, Jones accused Blair of the murder. Blair was then arrested.

The state's main witness against Blair at trial was Ernest Jones. Tina Jackson, Ernest Jones's girlfriend, also testified for the state at trial and implicated Blair. She later recanted her testimony and claimed that Ernest Jones had coerced her and her sister into testifying falsely against Blair. The only other evidence introduced against Blair at trial was several incriminating statements he made to the police. Blair alleged that these statements were coerced; he claimed an officer put a gun to his head until he confessed and he was told that his girlfriend would be charged with murder if he did not cooperate with the police. Evidence later surfaced that in return for his testimony, Ernest Jones received immunity for any part he may have played in the murder and received probation on pending charges of assault, burglary, and possession of a controlled substance (*Blair v. Armontrout*, 1990).

Blair's defense contended that Jones committed the murder. Evidence implicating Jones was provided by two witnesses who described a man who matched Jones's description leaving the crime scene; these witnesses were not called to testify at trial. Additional new witnesses came forward (providing a total of seven signed affidavits) stating that Ernest Jones admitted to killing the victim and framing Blair. After Blair's conviction, Ernest Jones was charged with another murder, but was not convicted. He was murdered in 1991.

The United States Court of Appeal for the Eighth Circuit granted Blair a stay of execution on July 20, 1993. Concurring in this opinion, Judge Gerald

Heaney asserted that "Blair did not receive a fair trial and . . . that the newly discovered evidence persuasively demonstrates that Blair is actually innocent of capital murder and that Katherine Jo Allen was murdered by another" (*Blair v. Delo*, 1993, p. 1220). Claiming the Eighth Circuit had abused its discretion, the United States Supreme Court vacated the stay on July 21, 1993. Blair was executed later that day.

Bernard Bolender, a white male, was convicted in Florida in 1980 and executed in 1995 for killing four men during a drug deal. Bolender and two co-defendants, Joseph Macker and Paul Thompson, were accused of robbing, torturing, and killing the victims in an attempt to locate twenty kilograms of cocaine. The victims apparently brought only one kilogram to Macker's residence, the location of the drug deal. Macker's involvement in the murders was not disputed; in exchange for a life sentence, he pled guilty to second-degree murder and became the state's main witness against Bolender. The only other evidence that was introduced against Bolender was his fingerprints, found on the trunk of the burning car that contained the victims (see generally *Bolender v. Singletary*, 1994; *Bolender v. Singletary*, 1995).

Bolender presented an alibi defense at trial. He claimed that he was home with his girlfriend, Dawn Poulis, and Claudia Merino, the wife of one of the victims. The jury rejected Bolender's alibi claims and convicted him of first-degree murder, kidnapping, and armed robbery of the four drug dealers. During the penalty phase, the jury deliberated for twelve minutes and unanimously recommended a life sentence for Bolender. According to Bolender's attorneys, this recommendation was the result of "doubts about his guilt" (Amnesty International, 2001). The judge overrode this recommendation and sentenced Bolender to death. Paul Thompson, ruled incompetent to stand trial due to a claim of mental illness later overturned, stated that if he had testified he would have supported Bolender's alibi (Amnesty International, 2001).

Newly developed postconviction evidence that challenged Macker's credibility was procedurally barred, preventing the courts from considering their merits. The testimony of six witnesses who claimed that Macker confessed to the murders and admitted to framing Bolender was also not permitted. Subsequent to his release from prison, Macker's former cellmates made statements supporting Bolender's innocence (*Bolender v. Singletary*, 1995).

Roger Coleman, a white male, was executed in Virginia in 1992 for the rape and murder of Wanda Fay McCoy, also white (see Tucker, 1998, for the definitive account of the Coleman case).[3] Coleman was the victim's brother-in-law. On March 10, 1981, Wanda's husband, Brad McCoy, came home from work and found her near death. The prosecution's theory of the crime was that Wanda McCoy had allowed the murderer into the house. This directed suspicion toward Coleman, who would have been allowed into the house and had a prior record for attempted rape. The prosecution claimed that within a thirty-minute time frame established by Coleman's work records, he parked his truck, waded across a creek (ten to twelve inches deep), climbed three hundred yards up a hill, raped Wanda twice, slit her throat, and escaped undetected.

Coleman was implicated by four main pieces of evidence, each of which can be called into question. However, Coleman's court-appointed trial attorneys were inexperienced; neither of the two attorneys had ever tried a murder case. Coleman presented an alibi defense at trial. His main alibi witness was Philip Vandyke, a friend and co-worker at the coal mine, whose claim that they had a conversation on the evening of the murder immediately prior to going to work was supported by his time card. After conviction, Coleman's attorneys were one day late in filing their appeal. As a result, federal and state reviews of the trial were denied and the merits of his appeal were never heard by the courts. Coleman appealed this ruling to the U.S. Supreme Court, which affirmed the denial (Tucker, 1998).

Beginning in 1988, Jim McCloskey, the founder of Centurion Ministries, an organization dedicated to exonerating innocent inmates, reinvestigated the case. He and his associates uncovered a great deal of evidence that raised doubt regarding Coleman's guilt, including Coleman's alibi placing him at work on the night of the murder and the absence of footprints found at the McCoy residence or mud or water on Coleman's pants, socks, or boots. The physical evidence contradicted the prosecution's theory that McCoy allowed her killer to enter her home; there was a pry mark on the door and a fingerprint on the screen door (that was never tested). Organic material found on the victim indicated an outdoor struggle probably occurred prior to the rape and murder. Coleman had no scratches on him.

Additional new evidence surfaced in late 1991. Teresa Horn came forward and claimed that another man, Donnie Ramey, a neighbor of the McCoys, attacked her in 1987 and during the course of the attempted rape admitted raping and murdering Wanda McCoy. Horn's mother and her boyfriend corroborated her story. On March 5, 1992, Teresa Horn granted an interview to a television station and repeated her charges against Ramey. Mysteriously, the next day, she was found dead. Three other women also came forward and claimed that Ramey had sexually attacked them. Ramey denied all the attacks, none of which had been reported to the police (Tucker, 1998).

Willie Darden, a black male, was executed in Florida in 1988 for the murder of Carl Turman, a white businessman (see Ingle, 1990). On September 8, 1973, a furniture store in Lakeland was robbed and the owner was shot and killed. At the time, Darden was on a weekend furlough from prison, where he was serving time for attempted rape. He became a suspect in Turman's murder as a result of a car accident he was involved in three miles away from the furniture store shortly after the murder; his car matched the description of a car seen leaving the murder scene. The main witnesses at trial were the victim's wife, Helen Turman, and Philip Arnold, a sixteen-year-old who was wounded during the robbery. Both of these witnesses identified Darden as the assailant (*Darden v. Wainwright*, 1986).

However, Mrs. Turman initially told the police that she could not identify the suspect. Later, at the preliminary hearing, she identified the defendant; however, he was the only black male in the courtroom at the time. While in the hospital, Arnold was given a six-photo array and he picked the defendant's picture. Darden's picture was one of two that had the notation "Sheriff's Department, Bartow, Florida," on the bottom of it (Ingle, 1990, p. 258). A gun presented as evidence against the defendant was never tied to the defendant or to the murder. Darden was convicted by an all-white jury in a racially charged trial.

Two new witnesses subsequently corroborated Darden's innocence claim. Christine Bass, who lived at the site of Darden's car problems, reported that he was in front of her house at the time of the murder; she was never called to testify at trial. This account was corroborated in part by Reverend Sam Sparks, who stated that he went to the victim's widow to comfort her immediately after the murder. This information helps to establish the time of the murder and, in combination with Bass's account, excludes Darden as the murderer. In his dissent to a Supreme Court decision denying Darden federal habeas corpus, Justice Blackmun asserted that the defendant did not receive a fair trial and castigated "a court willing to tolerate not only imperfection but a level of fairness and reliability so low it should make conscientious prosecutors cringe" (*Darden v. Wainwright*, 1986, p. 190).

Bennie Demps, a black male, was executed in Florida in 2000 for the 1976 murder of fellow inmate Alfred Sturgis, a black male, at Florida State Prison (see Mills, Possley, & Armstrong, 2000). At the time of the murder, Demps was serving two life sentences for a double murder; his death sentences for those murders had been commuted to life as a result of the *Furman* decision (*Demps v. Florida*, 2000).

According to the state's theory of the murder, Demps and two co-defendants, James Jackson and Harry Mungin, were responsible for killing Sturgis. They claimed that on September 6, 1976, with Mungin on the lookout at the door of Sturgis's cell, Demps held Sturgis down while Jackson repeatedly stabbed him. Prison personnel found Sturgis in his cell bleeding profusely from stab wounds. Seven months after Sturgis's killing, inmate Leroy Colbroth was murdered. Colbroth was widely considered by inmates to have killed Sturgis over nonpayment of a drug debt, and was in turn killed for having killed Sturgis (Mills et al., 2000).

There was no physical evidence linking Demps to the murder. The prosecution's main evidence was provided by one eyewitness, inmate Larry Hathaway, who was subsequently granted parole after serving four years of a ninety-nine-year sentence. Additionally, correctional officer A. V. Rhoden claimed that en route to the hospital, Sturgis named Demps as one of his three attackers (*Demps v. Florida*, 1981).

Considerable evidence supports Demps's innocence claim. Prison records indicated that Hathaway was "extremely manipulative" and had a "personality disorder" (Mills et al., 2000, p. 13). Before trial, Hathaway told a prisoners' rights group that he did not witness the stabbing. However, at trial, he changed his story and implicated Demps. Additionally, after trial, three inmates came forward to say that Hathaway was not near the crime scene when the stabbing occurred. In 1994, Hathaway admitted to an investigator that he committed perjury at trial (Mills et al., 2000).

New evidence discovered more than twenty years after the murder casts additional doubt on Demps's guilt. An internal investigation that was suppressed by the state revealed that Sturgis only implicated James Jackson, not Demps, as his assailant. Claiming this evidence did not necessarily exonerate Demps, the Florida Supreme Court ruled against him. Another suppressed internal document criticized Hathaway for lying in another investigation; this document could have been used by Demps's attorneys to undermine Hathaway's credibility at trial. Until his execution, Demps claimed that prison officials framed him because he had escaped an earlier death sentence as a result of *Furman* (*Demps v. Florida*, 2000).

Troy Farris, a white male with no prior adult record, was convicted in Texas in 1986 and executed in 1999 for the shooting death of Tarrant County Sheriff's Deputy Clark Rosenbalm, Jr., a white male. The police claimed that Rosenbalm was killed when he interrupted a drug deal in progress involving Farris and two co-defendants, Vance Nation and Charles Lowder (see *Farris v. Texas*, 1990).

Farris's trial was based entirely on circumstantial evidence–there were no eyewitnesses to Rosenbalm's murder and the murder weapon was never found. The three main witnesses testifying against him were Nation, Lowder, and Jimmy Daniels, Farris's brother-in-law. Nation testified that he asked Lowder to drive him to meet Farris for a drug deal. Leaving the scene, Nation noticed a patrol car approaching Farris. Although he said he did not hear any shots being fired or witness an altercation, he saw Rosenbalm lying motionless beside the road. Lowder gave an account similar to Nation's and also testified that his first statement to police—in which he implicated Nation—

was coerced. Lowder had claimed that he had witnessed a struggle between Nation and the victim at the crime scene (*In re Farris,* 1999).

Contrary to Nation's testimony, the physical evidence obtained from the crime scene indicated that a physical struggle took place between the assailant and Deputy Rosenbalm prior to the murder. In exchange for his testimony, capital charges against Nation were dismissed and he received a probated sentence of seven years for delivery of marijuana. Lowder received full immunity in exchange for his testimony. Police misconduct, a shoddy investigation, destruction of evidence, and misstatements by a police officer all cast doubt on the state's theory of the murder and contributed to an unfair trial (Sanders, 1999).

Several days before Farris's execution, Lowder told a reporter that he believed that Farris was innocent and indicated he believed Officer Rosenbalm was killed after he, Nation, and Farris drove away from the scene (*In re Farris,* 1999).

Billy Conn Gardner, a white male, was convicted in Texas in 1983 and executed in 1995 for killing Thelma Catherine Row, also white. On May 16, 1983, a man entered the back room of a high school cafeteria and, during a robbery, shot Row, the manager (see *Gardner v. Texas,* 1987). She died eleven days later. The key prosecution witness at trial was Melvin Sanders; he claimed that he and Gardner conspired to rob the cafeteria, with Gardner committing the robbery and Sanders driving the getaway car. Although Sanders was, in this depiction of the case, an accomplice to capital murder, he was granted "testimonial immunity in the capital murder case, probation on the robbery charge, and dismissal of [a] firearms charge" (Wiseman, 1996, p. 734). Melvin Sanders's wife, Paula, worked at the cafeteria with the victim and was also a witness against Gardner (*Gardner v. Texas,* 1987).

It was later discovered that Paula Sanders's co-workers, who were present at the crime scene and listed on the police report, were never interviewed by Gardner's trial counsel. During the appellate investigation, these witnesses claimed that Paula Sanders answered the phone numerous times before anyone else could on the afternoon of the murder, that she was nervous the entire morning and afternoon, and that she was directly facing the assailant, which contradicted her trial testimony. Although these behaviors are consistent with the defense theory that she was involved in the murder, she was never charged with any offense in connection with the crime.

Several additional factors raise significant doubt regarding Gardner's guilt. Before the victim died, she described her killer as more than six feet tall with reddish blond hair and a red goatee. Gardner was five feet, eleven inches tall, but had dark black hair and no facial hair. The only other eyewitness to the crime was a custodian at the school, who testified against Gardner at trial.

He also described the man as having red hair and a red goatee. Gardner's trial attorney interviewed him only one time for fifteen minutes prior to jury selection. He never interviewed witnesses who were at the scene or named on the police report (Wiseman, 1996).

Gary Graham, a black male, was convicted in Texas in 1981 and executed in 2000 for killing Bobby Grant Lambert, a white male. On the night of May 13, 1981, a young black male shot and killed Lambert in the parking lot of a Houston grocery store. Seven days later, police arrested Graham after a crime spree (see *Graham v. Collins*, 1993; *Graham v. Johnson*, 1996; *Graham v. Johnson*, 1999).

The state's case against Graham rested largely on the testimony of Bernadine Skillern; there was no physical or circumstantial evidence that tied Graham to the crime scene. Skillern claimed she saw the killer from inside her car in the grocery store parking lot; Skillern was thirty-five feet from the assailant. Graham's trial attorney was Ron Mock, who was three years out of law school and he boasted he had failed criminal law, and had already developed a reputation for his expeditious handling of capital cases. He called no witnesses during the guilt phase of the trial (Rimer & Bonner, 2000).

In 1992, new pro bono attorneys with substantial capital defense experience became involved in the case. By 1993, their investigation began to reveal new evidence that cast doubt on Graham's guilt. On closer inspection, many issues regarding Bernadine Skillern's eyewitness testimony undermined the veracity of her identification of Graham: Her initial description of the killer did not match Graham; a subsequent photo lineup was flawed; and a live lineup was also flawed. Other new evidence revealed that a police officer admitted that another eyewitness, Ron Hubbard, an employee of the grocery store, was also present at the lineup and claimed that Graham was not the shooter. Another eyewitness, Wilma Amos, also claimed that the killer was much shorter than Graham (*In re Graham*, 2000).

A police report turned over to the defense in 1993 revealed several additional exculpatory witnesses. Leodis Wilkerson, a twelve-year-old boy who was sitting in his father's car in the parking lot, and Sherian Etuk, a cashier at the grocery store, corroborated the discrepancy relating to the facial features and height of the shooter, claiming he was less than five feet, six inches tall (Graham was five feet, ten inches tall). Moreover, both of these witnesses claimed that they got a good look at the killer. Also, a Houston Police Department Firearms report indicated that the .22-caliber pistol that Graham had at the time of his arrest was not the .22-caliber pistol that was used to kill Lambert (*Graham v. Johnson*, 1999).

Continued defense investigation identified an alternative theory of Bobby Lambert's murder. Lambert and another man had been arrested with a plane full of illegal drugs in Oklahoma in 1980; the police did not have a search warrant for the plane so the evidence was suppressed. Unable to prosecute Lambert, the authorities pressured him to cooperate in their ongoing drug investigations, granting him immunity for his testimony. Lambert was reluctant to cooperate. At the time of his murder, Lambert had been issued a summons to testify. Years later, Lambert's attorney in Oklahoma informed Graham's attorneys of his belief "that Lambert was killed by a drug organization for whom he worked to prevent him from testifying before the grand jury" (*In re Graham*, 2000, p. 11). This theory was supported by the fact that Lambert was found with $6,000, which would likely have been taken if his murder occurred in the course of a robbery.

Larry Griffin, a black male, was convicted in Missouri in 1981 and executed in 1995 for the drive-by shooting death of Quinton Moss, a black male. The drive-by shooting occurred on June 25, 1980, in St. Louis, Missouri. Quinton Moss was a suspect in the murder of the defendant's brother, Dennis (see *Missouri v. Griffin*, 1983; Griffin, 1995).

The evidence against Griffin at trial consisted mainly of Robert Fitzgerald's testimony. Fitzgerald, the only eyewitness, picked Griffin out of a photo array and identified him as the shooter. Other evidence was provided by Officer Andre Jones. He testified that on the afternoon immediately prior to the murder, he saw the defendant and two other black men coming out of a house and that one of the men had a shotgun. This evidence corroborated Fitzgerald's testimony "that he saw three black males in the car perpetrate the drive-by killing of Mr. Moss" (Griffin, 1995, p. 3). Fitzgerald, a federally protected witness with a lengthy criminal record, was never questioned by the defense regarding the deal he received in exchange for testifying against Griffin.

On the day of the murder, police located the car that was used in the drive-by shooting. It contained the murder weapons and other physical evidence linked to the murder. None of the defendant's fingerprints were found in the car or on the other items. Subsequent investigations revealed additional evidence that cast doubt on Griffin's guilt. Kerry Caldwell, a federally protected witness, had called the defendant's attorney in April 1993 and claimed that he knew the defendant was innocent. Caldwell claimed responsibility for the murder under oath. He explained that in conjunction with his associates (all part of the drug trade), he had murdered Moss in retaliation for the murder of Dennis Griffin, their leader and the defendant's brother. Caldwell's descriptions of the murder weapons were identical to the physical evidence found by the police.

Another new witness, James Masey, came forward claiming he saw the drive-by shooting and he knew the defendant. However, he could not identify and did not recognize the three men in the car. His description of the incident corroborated Caldwell's testimony. While in prison, Fitzgerald admitted that he perjured himself at the defendant's trial and claimed that the police suggested he pick the defendant's photo before he actually did (Griffin, 1995).

Wilburn Henderson, a white male, was executed in Arkansas in 1998 for the robbery and murder of Willa Dean O'Neal, a white woman. On November 26, 1980, O'Neal was discovered dead by her daughter, in her furniture store in Fort Smith (see *Henderson v. Arkansas*, 1984).

Henderson was implicated by a piece of paper belonging to him that was found on the floor of the store at the time of the murder. Henderson claimed that he must have dropped the paper when he was shopping in the store several days before the murder. Henderson also made an incriminating statement to the police. Later, Henderson claimed that the statement was coerced by an officer who threatened to kill him (*Henderson v. Arkansas*, 1983).

Henderson presented an alibi defense. He claimed he was with his wife in another part of the state on the day of the murder. This was corroborated by Henderson's wife (*Henderson v. Sargent*, 1991).

Exculpatory evidence surfaced over the years prior to Henderson's execution that implicated other suspects in the robbery and murder. The primary suspect was Bob O'Neal, the victim's husband. Bob O'Neal had a history of violence and spousal abuse, was having an affair, and wanted a divorce. Additionally, the victim had a life insurance policy and a substantial estate that supplied a motive for the killing. O'Neal owned a .22-caliber pistol (the same type as the murder weapon) and, according to witnesses, he acted strangely in the days before and after the murder. The victim's daughter believed that O'Neal was the killer, claiming that "he was verbally abusive, mentally abusive, just a mean man" (Mills et al., 2000, p. 14). Moreover, his behavior the day of the killing suggested his effort to create an alibi for himself. When the police went to tell him about his wife's murder, he said "somebody has robbed and killed my—murdered my wife" before being told this by the police (*Henderson v. Sargent*, 1991, p. 711).

In 1991, a federal appeals court reversed Henderson's conviction due to trial counsel's failure "to investigate and develop evidence implicating other suspects in the murder. This evidence creates significant doubt about Henderson's guilt" (*Henderson v. Sargent*, 1991, p. 707). Henderson, the court noted, was "convicted on a circumstantial case with only a piece of paper to place him at the murder scene. In contrast, Bob O'Neal had several motives to kill his wife, had recently threatened her, owned the type of gun used in the murder, was with the victim during her last hour, made uncanny statements that indicated his involvement, and conducted himself in a bizarre and surprising manner" (*Henderson v. Sargent*, 1991, pp. 713–714).

While Henderson was on death row, O'Neal wrote a letter to the state claiming that Henderson was wrongfully convicted. Five years after the murder, O'Neal was committed to a mental hospital for paranoid delusions. He died of a heart attack in 1992 (Mills et al., 2000).

Edward Earl Johnson, a black male, was eighteen when he was arrested for the murder of J. T. Trest, a white male law enforcement officer murdered during the early morning hours of June 2, 1979. Johnson was convicted in Mississippi in 1980 and executed on May 20, 1987. Trest was killed after responding to a call from the home of Sally Franklin, an elderly white woman who was assaulted by a black man who had broken into her home (*Johnson v. Thigpen*, 1985).

Johnson became a suspect because his car matched the description of a car seen in the area at the time of Trest's killing and because he was reported to have been in the area earlier that day; Johnson had used a pay phone to call for assistance with his car, which had broken down. During a police lineup, Franklin, who knew Johnson, said he was not the intruder; the description she gave was of a taller, heavier, and fully bearded man. After releasing Johnson, the police met with him again, and asked him to submit to a polygraph examination. While Johnson accompanied police to the site of the test, police obtained a confession from him; the confession was in the form of a statement written by police that Johnson signed. Franklin then changed her testimony, identifying Johnson as the attacker. On the strength of his confession, Franklin's testimony, and reports he had been in the area around the time of the killing, Johnson was convicted and sentenced to death (*Johnson v. Mississippi*, 1987).

The murder weapon was never connected to Johnson; indeed, no physical evidence linked Johnson to the crime. The case against Johnson is weakened by his claim of inadequate counsel, his immediate recantation of his confession, and his claim that his confession was produced under threat of death. Also, after Johnson's execution, a young woman came forward claiming to have been with Johnson on the night of the murder, and claiming also that she had come forward during the investigation but was rebuffed by police (*Johnson v. Mississippi*, 1987).

Abetting Johnson's innocence claim, and distinguishing his case from other executions, is that Don Cabana, who as warden of Parchman State Prison presided over Johnson's execution, subsequently stated his belief that Johnson was not involved in Trest's murder (Tanney, 2000, p. 13).

Leo Jones, a black male, was convicted of killing a white male police officer in Florida in 1981. He was executed in 1998 (see Rauch, 1998). On the morning of May 23, 1981, three police cars were driving in a high-crime neighborhood in Jacksonville. Several shots were fired into the third car, striking the driver, Officer Thomas J. Szafranski. He died the next day. It was unclear from the start where the bullets came from. Some witnesses thought the bullets came from a vacant lot across the street; others, including an officer in another car, thought they came from a nearby duplex (see *Jones v. Florida,* 1983; *Jones v. Florida,* 1988).

Shortly thereafter, officers arrested Leo Alexander Jones, a drug dealer with a prior record, and his cousin, Bobby Hammonds. The evidence used against Jones came from witnesses who reportedly saw shots being fired from the defendant's residence, a confession from Jones, an incriminating statement from Hammonds, and a rifle of the same type as the murder weapon recovered from Jones's residence. In his defense, Jones alleged that the shots did not come from his building, that he had been beaten by the police, and that his confession was coerced. Hammonds also claimed police coercion (*Jones v. Florida,* 1983).

Defense witnesses claimed that the shots came from the open lot and not the defendant's apartment building. Additionally, despite reports of multiple shots fired, only a single shell was recovered from Jones's residence. The bullet removed from the victim was too badly damaged to match to any of the guns found in Jones's residence. Jones claimed that the rifle belonged to his friend, Glen Schofield. Schofield, a drug dealer with a prior record of violence, was on parole for manslaughter. He was originally a suspect in Szafranski's murder. He offered the police several alibis during the time period between Jones's arrest and execution (see *Jones v. Florida,* 1988; *Jones v. Florida,* 1996; Rauch, 1998).

After Jones's conviction, new evidence emerged. The officers who had arrested Jones and obtained his confession were forced to resign because of misconduct. A retired officer came forward and claimed that the officers were "enforcers" who had beaten suspects in the past to obtain confessions, and that police officers had been told to do everything in their power to put Jones in prison. Paul Marr, who was in prison with Schofield, claimed that Schofield boasted about the murder. Three more inmates came forward and said that Schofield had bragged to them about the murder. New witnesses also came forward claiming they saw Schofield running from the crime scene with a rifle. They stated that they did not come forward sooner because they were afraid of Schofield. Schofield's former girlfriend claimed that he was with her on the night of the murder. However, she claimed that she was not with him that evening and that he told her to corroborate his alibi and tell the authorities he was with her (Rauch, 1998).

In total, ten prison inmates reported that Schofield boasted about the killing. Six witnesses placed Schofield in the vicinity of the crime scene and several of these witnesses saw him with a rifle (*Jones v. Florida,* 1991).

Roy Roberts, a white male, was executed in Missouri in 1999 for the 1983 stabbing death of a prison guard, Thomas Jackson, also white. Roberts was serving time for a 1979 armed robbery conviction. Jackson's killing occurred during a disturbance at the prison. The state claimed that Roberts held Jackson down while two other inmates, Rodney Carr and Robert Driscoll, fatally stabbed him. Carr was convicted and sentenced to life in prison for his role in Jackson's killing. Driscoll was convicted and sentenced to death (see *Missouri v. Driscoll*, 1986).

No physical evidence tied Roberts to the murder. Although Jackson's stabbing death resulted in a significant amount of blood on Carr's and Driscoll's clothes, no blood was found on Roberts's clothes. The state's case was based on four eyewitness identifications. The main identification came seventeen days after the murder from Denver Halley, a corrections officer. Two other officers and an inmate also testified against Roberts (see Missouri v. Roberts, 1986; Roberts v. Bowersox, 1999; Roberts v. Missouri, 1989).

Roberts's court-appointed trial attorney only cross-examined one eyewitness. However, he did obtain testimony from a guard, Officer Kroeckel, who claimed he was having a "fist fight" with Roberts on the other side of the room during the murder. Eight inmates corroborated Kroeckel's testimony, testifying that Roberts was uninvolved in the stabbing. Nevertheless, the jury convicted Roberts and sentenced him to death (see Alter, 1999; *In re Roberts*, 1999).

Evidence was subsequently uncovered that raises additional doubt about the accuracy of the eyewitness testimony of the four state witnesses. Roberts weighed well over 300 pounds at the time of the murder, but the initial seventeen-page report by the Department of Corrections regarding the killing did not mention him. Rather, the report indicated that other than Carr and Driscoll, "additional participants [in Jackson's murder] might not ever be identified" (*In re Roberts*, 1999, p. 6). Given Roberts's weight, it seems unlikely that he would not have been identified initially.

In January 1999, Governor Mel Carnahan granted clemency to death row inmate Darryl Mease at the behest of Pope John Paul II, whose papal visit to St. Louis coincided with Mease's execution date. This left Roberts, whose execution was scheduled a short time later, in the position of presenting a compelling claim of innocence at precisely the time when such claims were least likely to be considered (see Alter, 1999).

David Wayne Spence, a white male, was executed in Texas in 1997 for the kidnapping and murder of Jill Montgomery, a white female, and Kenneth Franks, a white male. The victims (along with Raylene Rice) were last seen alive on the evening of July 13, 1982. Their bodies were found later that day. The women had been sexually assaulted and all three victims were bound, gagged, and stabbed to death (see generally *Spence v. Scott*, 1996).

An early investigation into the murders revolved around several suspects, including Terry "Tab" Harper. However, the Waco police were unable to solve the case until it was assigned to an officer who promised a quick resolution. That officer—Truman Simons—had already developed a suspect, Muneer Deeb. Simons's theory was that Deeb hired Spence in a failed murder-for-hire plot to kill Gayle Kelley, Deeb's employee and former girlfriend. Deeb held a life insurance policy on Kelley and other employees. Simons believed that Spence mistook Montgomery for Kelley and killed her.

In November 1983, Spence, alleged accomplices Gilbert and Anthony Melendez, and Muneer Deeb were charged with the murders. The evidence against Spence at trial included alleged incriminating statements that Spence made to two acquaintances and seven jailhouse informants. These inmates denied that they received any promises or favors in exchange for their testimony against Spence. The state also presented an odontologist who testified that Spence's teeth marks produced the bite injuries on the female victims (*Spence v. Scott,* 1996).

In his defense, Spence attacked the murder-for-hire theory, claiming that Deeb would not receive insurance money in the event of Kelley's murder and that he knew Kelley and therefore would not have accidentally killed Montgomery instead of her. Spence attempted to discredit the jailhouse informants, claiming that they had received deals for their testimony. Additionally, Spence pointed out inconsistencies with their testimonies. Finally, there was undisputedly "no hair or fiber evidence from the victims [that] was ever tied to Spence or his automobile" (*Spence v. Scott,* 1996, p. 1001).

New exculpatory evidence surfaced postconviction. Police reports suppressed by the state included incriminating evidence that pointed to another suspect in the case: Terry Harper, a convicted felon with a lengthy prior violent record. Several witnesses claimed that Harper bragged about the crimes and had inside knowledge of their circumstances. Other police reports indicated that numerous witnesses saw the victims or their car at the park on the night of the murders, none of whom identified Spence and several of whom identified Harper with the victims.

The state claimed that Harper had an alibi; however, the television show Harper claimed to have been watching the night of the murders did not air that night. In 1994, Harper committed suicide when police came to arrest him for the stabbing death of an elderly man during a robbery. Other police reports indicated that Kenneth Franks may have been a drug dealer and was a known associate of Harper (Texas Defender Service, 2002).

After Spence's conviction, three of the jailhouse informants admitted they fabricated their stories against Spence with the encouragement of Simons and had testified in return for favors. In 1993, both Melendez brothers recanted their testimony in spite of the fact that this left them open for prosecution and potential death sentences related to the murder of Raylene Rice. Additional new evidence was provided by five nationally renowned forensic odontologists, who concluded that the state's expert at trial was unreliable and Spence's teeth marks were not consistent with the bite marks on the victims' bodies (*Spence v. Scott*, 1996).

Muneer Deeb was also convicted in 1985 and sentenced to death. His conviction and sentence were overturned and he was acquitted at a retrial; the Melendez brothers are still in prison serving life sentences. Spence was executed despite sworn claims of his innocence by Waco police officers (see Herbert, 1997; Radelet et al., 1996; Texas Defender Service, 2002).

Dennis Waldon Stockton, a white male, was sentenced to death in Virginia in 1983 for the 1978 murder of Kenneth Arnder, who was shot in the head and had his hands cut off. Stockton was executed on September 27, 1995. Stockton's case is particularly complicated, even among usually complicated capital and wrongful conviction cases, in that it involves jurisdictional questions, multiple defendants, multiple murders, and prosecutorial deals for testimony (see *Stockton v. Angelone*, 1995).

What is clear is that Kenneth Arnder was killed sometime between July 20, 1978, when he was last seen by his mother in Mount Airy, North Carolina, and July 25, 1978, when his body was found in Patrick County, Virginia, and that his killing was associated with an unpaid drug debt he owed to Tommy McBride. In the state's theory of the case, McBride solicited Arnder's killing in North Carolina, while with a group of people including Stockton, Randy Bowman, and several others. Bowman was the state's sole witness against Stockton. Also figuring in the conviction was Stockton's admission of having killed Ronnie Tate on July 2, 1979. The state claimed Tate was killed to prevent him from talking about Stockton's role in killing Arnder; Stockton claimed self-defense.

The state's fragile case is weakened further in several ways. First, although McBride was charged in North Carolina for his role in the case, he was never tried. Despite Virginia's claim that McBride solicited murder-for-hire in the presence of a small group of people, no one corroborated Bowman's claim that Stockton accepted this solicitation, or even that such a meeting occurred. North Carolina authorities found no credible evidence to support his prosecution for murder-for-hire.

Second, McBride's credibility is challenged by the presence of multiple affidavits directly contradicting it and implicating McBride, as well as by evidence that McBride received a deal, in the form of substantially reduced prison time, in exchange for his testimony against Stockton. Prior to Stockton's execution, his attorneys obtained affidavits from Bowman's former wife, his son, and a friend, each claiming that Bowman confessed to having killed Arnder (Stockton, 1995).

Conclusions: The Future of Innocence Research

The debate over the number and identities of those with compelling claims of factual innocence among those who have been executed is certain to continue. The research presented here is much closer to the beginning of this debate than the end. It is intended to assist in defining the issue of executions of the innocent separate from but related to the issue of wrongful convictions, in framing the debate about this issue, and in providing a list of cases meriting careful consideration and further exploration.

We invite scholars to investigate these cases more fully, evaluate their innocence claims, eliminate those cases not appropriately included, include those cases not properly eliminated, and pursue posthumous exonerations for those who were innocent. We encourage policymakers to consider the implications of these cases: that executions of the innocent occur on a regular basis; that these executions are produced structurally, not through isolated and extreme examples of bad faith, but through systematic race, class, and resource biases and through a commitment to the death penalty—particularly in southern states—that overwhelms efforts to improve the machinery of death.

Notes

Acknowledgments: We would like to acknowledge the assistance and encouragement of Margaret Vandiver, Michael Radelet, James Acker, and Richard Leo.

1. The "post-*Furman* era" refers to the years following the Supreme Court's landmark *Furman v. Georgia* (1972) decision, which held, for the only time in U.S. history, the death penalty unconstitutional. State efforts to respond to the Court's concerns were endorsed by the Supreme Court in *Gregg v. Georgia* (1976), marking *Furman* as the impetus for a new, more procedurally complex era in death penalty practice.

2. *U.S. v. Quinones et al.* (2002, p. 418).

3. Subsequent to the completion of our research, long-delayed and much-contested DNA tests were conducted which confirmed Coleman's guilt. We have left the case in our study to protect the integrity of our research and as testimony to the difficulties in identifying the factually innocent among those executed.

References

Alter, J. (1999, March 22). How sure is sure enough? *Newsweek,* p. 37.

Amnesty International. (2001, March 20). *Case of Bernard Bolender.* Retrieved March 20, 2001, from www.derechos.net/amnesty/dp/bernbole.html

Armbrust, S. (2002). Chance and the exoneration of Anthony Porter. In D. R. Dow & M. Dow, *The machinery of death* (pp. 157–166). New York: Routledge.

Associated Press. (2000, May 20). New Hampshire veto saves death penalty. *New York Times,* p. A16.

Associated Press. (2002, May 9). Death penalty moratorium in Maryland. *New York Times,* p. A20.

Bedau, H. A., & Radelet, M. L. (1987). Miscarriages of justice in potentially capital cases. *Stanford Law Review, 40,* 21–179.

Blair, W. (1993). "Application for Commutation of a Sentence of Death," p. 1–26 (on file with volume chapter author [T. Harmon]).

Bright, S. B., & Keenan, P. J. (1995). Judges and the politics of death: Deciding between the Bill of Rights and the next election in capital cases. *Boston University Law Review, 75,* 759–835.

Dieter, R. C. (1997). *Innocence and the death penalty: The increasing danger of executing the innocent.* Washington, DC: Death Penalty Information Center.

Farrell, J. (2000, August 27). Cry of "Innocent!" trumps moral claim. *Boston Globe,* p. F1.

Farris, T. D. (1999). "Supplement to Application for Reprieve from Execution of Death Sentence and Commutation to Imprisonment for Life," p. 1–9. (on file with volume chapter author [T. Harmon]).

Graham, G. (2000). "Petition for a Recommendation of a Reprieve of Execution and Pardon or Alternatively a Conditional Pardon or Commutation of Death Sentence," p. 1–21 (on file with volume chapter author [T. Harmon]).

Griffin, L. (1995). "Application for Executive Clemency and/or Commutation of a Sentence of Death," p. 1–46, (on file with volume chapter author [T. Harmon]).

Haines, H. H. (1996). *Against capital punishment: The anti-death penalty movement in America, 1972–1994.* New York: Oxford University Press.

Herbert, B. (1997, July 28). The impossible crime. *New York Times,* p. 17.

Howarth, J. W. (2002). Executing white masculinities: Learning from Karla Faye Tucker. *Oregon Law Review, 81,* 183–229.

Ingle, J. B. (1990). *Last rights: 13 fatal encounters with the state's justice.* Nashville, TN: Abington Press.

Kirchmeier, J. L. (2002). Another place beyond here: The death penalty moratorium movement in the United States. *Colorado Law Review, 73,* 1–116.

Liebman, J. S. (2002). Opting for real death penalty reform. *Ohio State Law Journal, 63,* 315–342.

Lifton, R., & Mitchell, G. (2001, January 3). The death penalty's days are numbered. *Los Angeles Times,* p. B9.

Markman, S. J., & Cassell, P. G. (1988). Protecting the innocent: A response to the Bedau–Radelet study. *Stanford Law Review, 41,* 121–160.

McDermott, K. (2002, April 16). Death penalty needs sweeping reform, Illinois panel reports. *St. Louis Post-Dispatch,* p. A1.

Mills, S. (1999, February 12). Porter case had wrongs at each turn. *Chicago Tribune,* p. 1.

Mills, S., Possley, M., & Armstrong, K. (2000, December 17). Shadow of doubt haunts executions. *Chicago Tribune,* p. 1.

Prejean, H. (1993). *Dead man walking.* New York: Random House.

Radelet, M. L., & Bedau, H. A. (1998). The execution of the innocent. *Law and Contemporary Problems, 61,* 105–124.

Radelet, M. L., Bedau, H. G., & Putnam, C. E. (1992). *In spite of innocence: Erroneous convictions in capital cases.* Boston: Northeastern University Press.

Radelet, M. L., & Borg, M. J. (2000). The changing nature of death penalty debates. *Annual Review of Sociology, 26,* 43–61.

Radelet, M. L., Lofquist, W. S., & Bedau, H. A. (1996). Prisoners released from death row since 1970 because of doubts about their guilt. *Cooley Law Review, 13,* 907–966.

Rauch, J. (1998, May 30). Death by mistake. *National Journal,* pp. 1224–1231.

Reed, L., & Tysver, R. (2000, July 31). Studying Nebraska's death row: Results will be released soon from a two-year examination of the state's death penalty. *Omaha World-Herald,* p. 13.

Rimer, S. (2000, October 31). Support for a moratorium in executions gets stronger. *New York Times,* p. A18.

Rimer, S., & Bonner, R. (2000, June 11). Texas lawyer's death row record a concern. *New York Times,* p. A1.

Roberts, R. M. (1999). Application of Roy Michael Roberts to Governor Mel Carnahan for Executive Clemency," p. 1–18, (on file with volume chapter author [T. Harmon]).

Rose, D. (1996, April 21). Dead man stalking. *The (London) Observer,* p. 8.

Rovella, D. (2000, December 11). Scandals damage cop credibility: Jurors say brutality, corruption make police less believable. *National Law Journal,* p. A1.

Ryan halts executions while errors are probed. (2000, January 31). *Chicago Sun-Times,* p. A3.

Sanders, B. (1999, January 10). Execution of Farris would be mistake. *Ft. Worth Star Telegram,* p. 1.

Sarat, A. D. (2002). The "new abolitionism" and the possibilities of legislative action: The New Hampshire experience. *Ohio State Law Journal, 63,* 343–369.

Scheck, B. C., Neufeld, P. J., & Dwyer, J. (2000). *Actual innocence: Five days to execution and other dispatches from the wrongly convicted.* New York: Doubleday.

Simon, J. (1999). Tokens of our esteem: Aggravating factors in the era of deregulated death penalties. In A. D. Sarat (Ed.), *The killing state: Capital punishment in law, politics, and culture* (pp. 81–114). New York: Oxford University Press.

Texas Defender Service. (2002). *State of denial: Texas justice and the death penalty.* Retrieved May 3, 2002, fromhttp://www.texasdefender.org/study/chapter9.html.

Steiker, C., & Steiker, J. (2002). Should abolitionists support legislative "reform" of the death penalty? *Ohio State Law Journal, 63,* 417–432.

Tanney, P. (2000). The painful world of a six-times executioner. *Irish Times,* p. 13.

Terry, D. (1998, November 16). Survivors make the case against death row. *New York Times,* p. A14.

Tucker, J. C. (1998). *May God have mercy.* New York: Norton.

Van den Haag, E. (1990). Why capital punishment? *Albany Law Review, 54,* 501–514.

Wilgoren, J. (2003, January 12). Citing issue of fairness, governor clears out death row in Illinois. *New York Times,* p. 1.

Will, G. (2000, April 6). Innocent on death row. *Washington Post,* p. A23.

Willing, R. (2001, May 4). Even for death penalty foes, McVeigh is the exception: Worst mass murderer in US history tilts debate over capital punishment. *USA Today,* p. A1.

Wiseman, C. M. (1996). Representing the condemned: A critique of capital punishment. *Marquette Law Review, 79,* 731–758.

Yardley, J. (2001, August 19). Of all places: Texas wavering on death penalty. *New York Times,* p. D4.

Zuckoff, M. (1998, November 15). Death row survivors tell how justice errors. *Boston Globe*, p. A1.

Cases Cited

Baldwin v. Blackburn, 653 F2d 924 (1981).

Blair v. Armontrout, 916 F2d 1310 (1990).

Blair v. Delo, 509 U.S. 935 (1993).

Blair v. Delo, 999 F2d 1219 (1993).

Bolender v. Singletary, 16 F3d 1547 (1994).

Bolender v. Singletary, 898 F. Supp 876 (1995).

Callins v. Collins, 510 U.S. 1141 (1994).

Coleman v. Thompson, 501 U.S. 722 (1991).

Darden v. Wainwright, 477 U.S. 168 (1986).

Demps v. Florida, 395 So.2d 501 (1981).

Demps v. Florida, 761 So.2d 302 (2000).

Farris v. Texas, 819 S.W.2d 490 (1990).

Furman v. Georgia, 408 U.S. 238 (1972).

Gardner v. Texas 730 S.W.2d 675 (1987).

Graham v. Collins, 506 U.S. 461 (1993).

Graham v. Johnson, 94 F3d 958 (1996).

Graham v. Johnson, 168 F3d 762 (1999).

Gregg v. Georgia, 428 U.S. 153 (1976).

Henderson v. Arkansas, 652 S.W.2d 26 (1983).

Henderson v. Arkansas, 281 Ark. 406 (1984).

Henderson v. Sargent, 926 F2d 706 (1991).

Herrera v. Collins, 506 U.S. 390 (1993).

In re Gary Graham, clemency petition (2000).

In re Roy Roberts, clemency petition (1999).

In re Troy Farris, clemency petition (1999).

In re Troy Farris, supplement clemency petition (1999).

Johnson v. Mississippi, 508 So.2d 1126 (1987).

Johnson v. Thigpen, 623 F. Supp. 1121 (1985).

Jones v. Florida, 440 So.2d 570 (1983).

Jones v. Florida, 528 So.2d 1171 (1988).

Jones v. Florida, 591 So.2d 911 (1991).

Jones v. Florida, 678 So.2d 309 (1996).

Louisiana v. Baldwin, 388 So.2d 664 (1980).

Missouri v. Driscoll, 711 S.W.2d 512 (1986).

Missouri v. Griffin, 662 S.W.2d 854 (1983).

Missouri v. Roberts, 709 S.W.2d 857 (1986).

Roberts v. Bowersox, 1999 U.S. App. LEXIS 3757 (1999).

Roberts v. Missouri, 775 S.W.2d 92 (1989).

Spence v. Scott, 80 F3d 989 (1996).

Stockton v. Angelone ,70 F3d 12 (1995).

U.S. v. Quinones, 196 F Supp. 2d 416, p. 418 (2002).

7

THE FALLIBILITY OF JUSTICE

IN CANADA

A Critical Examination of Conviction Review

∼

KATHRYN M. CAMPBELL

The concept of miscarriages of justice or justice in error has become an accepted phenomenon in most Western jurisdictions in recent years. A burgeoning body of literature in the United States has demonstrated that not only do wrongful convictions and wrongful imprisonments occur far more frequently than expected, but several specific, systemic factors clearly contribute to their occurrence (Drizin & Leo, 2004; Gross et al., 2005; Huff, 2004; Scheck, Neufeld, and Dwyer, 2000; Westervelt & Humphrey, 2001). Factors such as eyewitness error, false confession, overreliance on jailhouse informants, errors in forensic analysis, and police and prosecutorial misconduct have been established as causative of these miscarriages of justice (Castelle & Loftus, 2001; Leo & Ofshe, 1998; Martin, 2001; Parker, Dewees, & Radelet, 2001; Scheck, Neufeld, & Dwyer, 2000; Zimmerman, 2001). Several high-profile cases have demonstrated that rarely does one error occur in isolation, but rather several factors often work in conjunction to contribute to these erroneous convictions. It is often only after many years of exhaustive legal research that the interplay of one error with others focused police attention on innocent individuals or caused evidence to be fabricated or misinterpreted in an incriminating manner, resulting in a wrongful conviction.

The Canadian context, consistent with the experiences in other common law jurisdictions, has evinced a number of wrongful convictions and imprisonments in recent years. Research has pointed to the existence of the usual contributing factors that foster these miscarriages of justice in this context (Denov & Campbell, 2005). A number of individuals in Canadian society and Canadian prisons have suffered at the hands of overzealous police, prosecutors, and jailhouse informants and have been subject to errors in eyewitness identification and forensic science. Moreover, what is unique to the Canadian situation is the means of redress available to individuals who believe they are victims of such miscarriages of justice. After exhausting all of their appeals, these individuals may apply to the federal Minister of Justice for a conviction review. This process involves an extensive review of the circumstances of the initial conviction and in essence provides a last ditch effort at exoneration. It is the objective of this chapter to outline this process and provide a critical analysis of its shortcomings. While seemingly available to anyone, it will be demonstrated that the process is protracted and onerous and the chances of a positive outcome for the convicted individual are very slight. Case illustrations are used to demonstrate the difficulties inherent in this process, and arguments are made regarding the need for an independent body to conduct reviews.

Conviction Review Process

The power to revisit a conviction has long been part of the Canadian legal landscape. The Royal Prerogative of Mercy was the first of such remedies, which continues to be part of the Canadian Criminal Code and allows for the granting of pardons. This authority has been used in the past to correct judicial errors, but this role is now undertaken mainly by criminal appellate courts (Trotter, 2001). The right to appeal criminal cases in the manner done today was introduced in Canada in 1923. Then section 1022 of the Criminal Code dealt with ministerial review and allowed the Minister of Justice to order new trials and refer cases or points to the Court of Appeal for its opinion (Department of Justice, 1998a). Since 1968, the Criminal Code has contained an explicit provision (section 690) that provided for conviction review, undertaken by lawyers appointed by the Department of Justice. Following many years of ad hoc review, in 1993 the Criminal Conviction Review Group (CCRG) was formed, reporting to the Assistant Deputy Minister of Justice. The CCRG, a group of lawyers working for the Department of Justice, reviews convictions thought to be in error and makes recommendations to the Minister regarding remedies. For a variety of reasons, which are discussed later, the conviction review process was considered inadequate and section 690 of the Criminal Code was amended and replaced by sections 696.1 to 696.6 in 2002.

The opportunity for conviction review is available to most individuals who have been convicted of an offense under criminal law. This includes both summary and indictable offenses, as well as convictions under the Criminal

Code or the Controlled Drugs and Substances Act. Furthermore, conviction review is also available to individuals who have been designated as dangerous or long-term offenders. However, in all cases conviction review does not occur until all avenues of appeal have been exhausted (provincial Court of Appeal and the Supreme Court of Canada), and must be based on new and significant information. The conviction review process takes place in four stages.[1]

1. *Preliminary assessment.* At this stage, legal counsel, working as part of the CCRG, assesses the merit of a case for review. This first step involves assessing the extent to which a case file contains all the necessary information given the extent of the information needed (factums from previous decisions, trial transcripts, etc.), which can take considerable time. However, essential to a case being accepted for review is that new and significant information is presented that was previously unavailable at trial or appeal and could arguably have affected the outcome of the case. The applicant is not required to convince the Minister of innocence, per se, but rather that there is a reasonable basis to conclude that a miscarriage of justice likely occurred.

2. *Investigation.* During this stage the investigative lawyers examine the extent to which the new information presented in support of an application is reliable, or reasonably capable of belief, and relevant (related to guilt or innocence; Department of Justice, 2003, p. 3). Each case is unique and thus demands the examination of specific issues during the investigation, which could include the following:

- Interviewing witnesses
- Scientific or forensic analysis (DNA testing, polygraph examinations)
- Consultation with police, prosecutors, and defense lawyers involved in the original prosecution or appeal
- Obtaining all relevant personal information and documents

3. *Investigation report.* Following the completion of the report, the applicant has the opportunity to view the report and make any comments. At this time any further investigation is completed and the report and legal advice from the CCRG lawyers are forwarded to the Minister. While the applicant can view the investigation report, he or she is not privy to the advice that the CCRG makes to the Minister as solicitor–client privilege is said to apply in this instance.

4. *Decision by the Minister.* The lawyers[2] investigating the case for the CCRG then forward all submissions, the investigation report, and legal advice to the

Minister of Justice. The Minister reviews the information and makes a decision whether to dismiss or allow the application. If the Minister is "satisfied by the application that there is a reasonable basis to conclude that a miscarriage of justice likely occurred" (Criminal Code, section 696.3), he or she may do the following:

1. Order a new trial.
2. Order a new hearing in the case of dangerous or long-term offender.
3. Refer the matter or a specific question to the Court of Appeal of a province or territory as if it were an appeal by the convicted person.

Statistics

While the numbers of applications for conviction review received in a given year appear to be increasing, the actual number of applications completed in the same year remains relatively small. This is in part due to the complexity of the process, the amount of information needed to assess the merits of an application, and the protracted nature of the investigation.[3] As Table 7.1 indicates, applications received in a year significantly outnumber decisions and outcomes. Nonetheless, the number of applications received for conviction review in a year is clearly not indicative of the actual numbers of convictions in error occurring in a jurisdiction.

When an application is declined, in reality it indicates that in assessing the merits of a case, legal counsel for the Department of Justice is of the opinion that there is insufficient information available on a case to warrant a review.

TABLE 7.1.   APPLICATIONS TO THE MINISTER OF JUSTICE FOR CONVICTION REVIEW

Fiscal Year	Application Requests	Investigations Completed	Ministerial Decisions	Outcome of Decision
April 2002 to March 2003	11	3	1 decision	1 new trial ordered
April 2003 to March 2004	29	11	6 decisions	6 dismissals
April 2004 to March 2005	35	6	5 decisions	1 dismissal, 2 referrals to the Court of Appeal, 3 new trials ordered
April 2005 to March 2006	39	2	1 decision	1 referral to the Court of Appeal

Source: Adapted from Denov and Campbell (2003).

Criticisms of the Process

The conviction review process has been criticized[4] over the years for a variety of reasons. It is useful to examine these criticisms as falling within two specific areas, the first being criticisms aimed at the process itself and the second stemming from the role of the Minister of Justice as the arbiter of conviction review.

Process/Procedural Criticisms

Length of Time
One main criticism of conviction review stems from the fact that the process is protracted (Braiden & Brockman, 1999; Campbell, 2005). The application process itself is onerous as individuals must supply all the necessary documentation on their case, including appeal factums and trial transcripts, prior to the start of the investigation. Furthermore, any new evidence must be investigated thoroughly, new witnesses questioned, and so on. It is likely that this sense of delay is exacerbated given that by the time a conviction review is filed an individual has exhausted all of his or her appeals, which has already taken a considerable amount of time. According to Boyd and Rossmo (1994), the standard of due process is not addressed in these cases. Two examples, discussed in more detail later, clearly illustrate this difficulty: David Milgaard's first request for conviction review received a response after three years, and Clayton Johnson's request received a response after three-and-one-half years. The Department of Justice (1998a) justifies the inordinate delays that occur through a conviction review as simply part of the thoroughness of the process. They also attribute some of the delay to the applicants who adjust or supplement their application with further submissions. It would appear that the team at the CCRG of six full-time lawyers is insufficient to process the number of applications received in a year.

Costs
The conviction review process is costly to the applicant, and there is a lack of financial assistance for a review (Rosen, 1992). Applicants must supply all completed transcripts, appeal factums, and copies of support materials, representing a considerable amount of documentation in most cases and likely to incur extensive legal and photocopy costs.[5] However, many lawyers represent their clients pro bono when making review applications. Further, some individuals are incarcerated when applying for conviction review, which increases the costs as well as the delays, although imprisoned applicants are given priority.

Review of Evidence

One great concern with the conviction review process surrounds how evidence is assembled, reviewed, and evaluated. Specifically, questions surround the types of evidence and documents collected by the Minister and the evidentiary burden of proof (Rosen, 1992). There appear to be few established rules of procedure or guidelines regarding this process (Braiden & Brockman, 1999, p. 24). Furthermore, the language used to describe the process is very broad, as is the discretion of the Minister, resulting in much discrepancy in interpretation.

In recent years, the Minister of Justice outlined specific principles[6] meant to guide discretionary powers in cases of conviction review (Department of Justice, 1998a), including the following:[7]

1. The remedy applicable under section 690 (now 696.1–696.6) is extraordinary. It is intended to ensure that no miscarriage of justice occurs when all conventional avenues of appeal have been exhausted.
2. The section does not exist to permit the Minister to substitute a Ministerial opinion for a jury's verdict or result on appeal.
3. The procedure is not intended to create a fourth level of appeal.
4. Applications should ordinarily be based on new matters of significance that either were not considered by the courts or that occurred or arose after the conventional avenues of appeal had been exhausted.
5. Where the applicant is able to identify such "new matters," the Minister will assess them to determine their reliability (as they must be reasonably capable of belief and relevant to the issue of guilt).
6. The applicant need not convince the Minister of innocence or prove conclusively that a miscarriage of justice has actually occurred, but demonstrate that there is a basis to conclude that a miscarriage of justice likely occurred.

These guidelines provide little direction for counsel in submitting a review application, but function more as a codification of the process as it already functioned. Furthermore, there is no statutory test that dictates what specific remedy should be ordered once the Minister is satisfied that a remedy is required (Department of Justice, 1998b).

Secrecy and Accessibility

Once an investigation has begun, there is also a perception that the process itself is inaccessible to interested parties, and that it is conducted behind closed doors (Braiden & Brockman, 1999, p. 23). Defense counsel, applicants, members of Parliament, and advocacy groups are often denied access to information during the investigation, as the Minister's final recommendations are considered protected due to solicitor–client privilege. Moreover, as part of the investigation the investigators need not reveal the nature of the information sought from interviews with legal professionals and witnesses or make the responses public (Boyd & Rossmo, 1994). Since 1994 counsel has been permitted to comment on the investigation brief, which discloses all of the information gathered and which is considered by the Minister in reaching a decision. The Department of Justice (2005) has recently addressed the issue of transparency in its annual report and argues that privacy protections safeguard the information contained in the brief and appendices from the public.[8] The applicant can make written submissions with respect to these findings, but these submissions have no legal weight with respect to the Minister's final decision.

Criticisms Relating to the Role of the Minister of Justice

Conflict of Interest

The notion of conflict of interest is an inherent part of the conviction review process. It is the Minister of Justice, as Chief Prosecutor, who is being asked to review his or her own practices or that of his or her provincial counterparts (Braiden & Brockman, 1999, p. 25). In other words, having the power to grant a remedy in a case where a miscarriage of justice occurred is essentially incompatible with the role of prosecution of crimes. On the one hand, a prosecutor must balance his or her function as an adversary with the responsibility to exercise discretion as a guardian of the public interest (Bloomenfeld & Cole, 2005). At the same time this individual is asked, through conviction review, to critically examine those very same practices undertaken by a member of that very same "team." It is akin to the practice whereby one police force polices the errors and malpractices of another—outside the realm of independent review—something that is frowned on in most jurisdictions as violating commonsense rules (Markham, 1992). In those rare instances where a remedy is ordered by the Minister, a member of the executive branch of government is essentially overruling the judiciary. Rosen (1992, pp. 15–16) believes that this practice reflects a prosecutorial bias on the part of the Department of Justice, resulting in "deference to judicial determinations of guilt and an insufficiently rigorous questioning of the foundations of criminal convictions." The exceedingly low number of remedies granted per year (of 137 applications received between the years 2000 and 2004, only five were granted a remedy) may be reflective of this reticence.

Adversarial System

A further criticism, centered on the role of the Minister of Justice, focuses on the fact that the review process is essentially using the adversarial system to address errors made in the adversarial system (Braiden & Brockman, 1999, p. 27). Many of the remedies the Minister of Justice relies on in addressing wrongful convictions involve referral back to the adversarial system itself. Whereas this critique in essence demonstrates a difficulty with the system per se, it also reflects a bias, related to the preceding criticism that the system should not be used to police itself. The Department of Justice clearly delineates what a conviction review is not meant to be: It is not another level of appeal or a substitution for a judicial review[9] of a case. Political relationships, individual roles, and the climate of this bureaucracy have contributed to the delicate balancing of these issues. However, using the adversarial system to address its own errors limits the possibility of remedies and the possible remedies. In essence, as the final voice in the conviction review process, the Minister of Justice is not meant to second-guess decisions rendered by the courts or determine guilt or innocence.

Principle of Finality in Law

In the Canadian jurisdiction the principle of finality,[10] embedded in the procedural rules of the court, is founded on the notion that an appellate system should not enable the endless relitigation of the same issues (Criminal Lawyers Association, 2000). It is quite likely that this principle influences, directly and indirectly, the conviction review process. When revisiting a conviction, the Minister of Justice must question this principle, and in some cases set it aside when considering possible remedies. The principle of finality may lead appellate courts to take a restrictive approach to interfering with a criminal conviction (Braiden & Brockman, 1999, p. 21), as well as reticence on the part of the Minister of Justice when undertaking a conviction review (Kaiser, 1989, p. 133). The following quote, from an International Labour Board decision,[11] illustrates the natural limits to the principle of finality:

> This article [Article IV] embodies the finality principle which in one form or another is a feature of all jurisdictions. There is however another principle which likewise in one form or another is to be found in most jurisdictions and this is that no court or tribunal is tied to what it has written per incuriam. The principle of finality is vital to the administration of justice but judges are human and can make slips and the principle does not go so far as to require that errors arising through accident or inadvertence or the like can never

be corrected; if it went as far as that, the principle could be made an instrument of injustice. The article does not therefore preclude the exercise of a limited power of review.

Other Issues

Language of the Guidelines

"Extraordinary" remedy: As noted earlier, the guidelines that established the parameters for the Minister of Justice in making decisions around conviction review ascertained that, above all, it is considered to be an extraordinary measure. Such language establishes precedent for how this process is not only used, but also how it is interpreted. Continuing to refer to conviction review and, by extension, the specter of miscarriage of justice, as extraordinary, exceptional, and infrequent likely serves to perpetuate myths about the infallibility of the judicial process and creates an unrealistic portrait of the reality. Huff, Rattner, and Sagarin (1996) have demonstrated that an approximation of the percentage of wrongful felony convictions in one jurisdiction in the United States was half of 1 percent, which translates to between 5,000 and 10,000 annual convictions for index crimes alone, a frighteningly high number. While there are no comparable Canadian figures to date, a number of high-profile cases in recent years demonstrate that the problem of wrongful conviction and imprisonment occurs in that country at alarming rates as well. To continue to provide an "extraordinary" response to a problem that is increasingly becoming ordinary belies reality and allows for the issue of miscarriages of justice to remain obfuscated.

New and Significant Information: The preceding guidelines also establish that for case information to be considered in a conviction review it must be "based on new matters of significance that either were not considered by the courts or that occurred or arose after the conventional avenues of appeal had been exhausted." According to the Department of Justice (2003, p. 2), information is considered to be significant if it is reasonably capable of belief, it is relevant to the issue of guilt, and could have affected the verdict if it had been presented at trial. Furthermore, information that would support a conviction review application as both new and significant would include information that:

1. Establishes or confirms an alibi
2. Includes another person's confession
3. Identifies another person at the scene of the crime

4. Provides scientific evidence that points to innocence or another's guilt
5. Proves that important evidence was not disclosed
6. Shows a witness gave false testimony
7. Substantially contradicts testimony at trial

Furthermore, information considered by the CCRG is "new" if the courts have not examined it during the original trial or appeal, or if the applicant becomes aware of it following court proceedings.

However, it is questionable as to whether the bar has been set too high in this regard. In some cases, it may not be new information, per se, that will exonerate an individual, but rather a reinterpretation of old information, which is not possible or acceptable under this process. It is likely that many erroneous convictions cannot reach this gold standard and thus go unchallenged. The standard of new and significant information will be of little value to the wrongly convicted individual who was represented by incompetent counsel, unless it can be established that he or she failed to introduce important evidence. Furthermore, the issue of erroneous eyewitness identification, the most frequent cause of wrongful convictions (Huff, Rattner, & Sagarin, 1986; Kassin, Tubb, Hosch, & Memon, 2001; Wells & Olsen, 2003), would require much concrete evidentiary and contradictory proof to be refuted through this process. Witnesses who unequivocally identify suspects at trial are viewed as inherently believable, in spite of the demonstrated unreliability of human memory. Finally, those who falsely confess to committing crimes due to the powerful nature of police interrogation tactics (Drizin & Leo, 2004; Leo & Ofshe, 1998) must in turn reinvestigate and eventually solve the crimes for which they have been convicted. A confession, even a false one, goes a very long way to convincing a judge and jury of culpability. Thus, these individuals must fight very hard to establish their innocence and the "new and significant information" standard for conviction review creates an enormous burden of proof for them.

"Likelihood" of a Miscarriage of Justice: As stated in the preceding guidelines, an applicant, to succeed, need not convince the Minister of innocence or prove conclusively that a miscarriage of justice has actually occurred, but that it *likely* occurred. Following this, the Minister of Justice may order a new trial or refer the matter to the Court of Appeal. Importantly, this notion of the likelihood of occurrence of a miscarriage of justice is not a legislative standard, per se, but rather it is a matter of policy for the exercise of the powers of the Minister under section 696.1 of the Criminal Code. Consequently, this "satisfaction" is inherently a subjective matter, to which precedent cannot be

followed. Each case is thus decided on its own merit, with little guidance as to what exactly constitutes "satisfying" proof to the Minister.

2002 Amendments

The conviction review process has gone through some transformations in recent years, as it was amended in 2002 in part to address dissatisfaction with the process. In particular this dissatisfaction centered around the role of the Minister of Justice, procedural delays, secrecy, lack of accountability, and prosecutorial bias (Department of Justice, 1998a). At that time extensive consultations with the provinces occurred and some changes were implemented. According to the Department of Justice, the review process was transformed into the "Reform Model," in essence meant to represent "a compromise between a separate review body similar to the English model and the status quo of section 690 of the *Criminal Code*" (Department of Justice, 2003). The amendments to this section included the following:

1. Guidelines regarding when a person is eligible for review
2. Criteria for when a remedy may be granted
3. Expanded categories of offenses for which a review is available, to include summary convictions (i.e., more minor offenses)
4. Authority for investigators to compel the production of documents and the appearance of witnesses
5. Regulations that set out how to apply and govern the review process generally
6. Requirement that the Minister of Justice submit an annual report to Parliament

Other nonlegislative changes, which were an attempt to distance the process from the Department of Justice, included the following:

1. A more separate CCRG (physically separate in another building)
2. Proposal to appoint a Special Advisor[12] to oversee the review process and provide advice directly to the Minister

The amendments have served to make both the procedures and criteria for review somewhat more explicit for applicants. The investigative lawyers now have the power to compel witnesses and investigate summary convictions ("Regulations Respecting Applications," 2002). However, given the expense and protracted nature of this process, it is unlikely that individuals convicted of summary convictions, the least serious of criminal offenses, will begin this onerous process for anything other than exceptional circumstances. Most of the other amendments address procedural issues, such as annual report, set eligibility criteria, and so on. This raises the question as to whether the amendments were a genuine attempt by the government to address the gaps and difficulties with the review process or to appease the various groups who lobbied for change, by appearing to actually "do something."

Case Examples

David Milgaard

Gail Miller, a twenty-year-old nurse's aide, was raped and murdered in Saskatoon, Saskatchewan, in 1969. At that time David Milgaard, a sixteen-year-old youth, considered to be a drifter and drug user, happened to be in Saskatoon on the day of the murder. Through the coercion of juvenile witnesses by the police, Milgaard become the prime suspect and was ultimately convicted of Miller's murder, receiving a sentence of life imprisonment in 1970. In 1971 Milgaard's appeal was rejected by the Saskatchewan Court of Appeal and his leave to appeal to the Supreme Court of Canada that same year was dismissed. Milgaard's legal team applied for a conviction review in December 1988 based on new evidence. The new evidence indicated that there was a serial rapist in the vicinity during that time and one of the key witnesses implicating Milgaard had later recanted his testimony. In February 1991, the Minister of Justice denied this application. A second application was made in August 1991, which was almost identical to the first. However, during that time the Milgaard case had gained prominence in the media and, in reversing her original opinion, the Minister of Justice then directed the Supreme Court[13] to review Milgaard's conviction and consider whether:

- "the continued conviction of David Milgaard in Saskatoon, Saskatchewan for the murder of Gail Miller, in the opinion of the Court constitutes a miscarriage of justice?"
- "depending on the answer to the first question, what remedial action under the Criminal Code, if any, is advisable?" (*Reference re. Milgaard* Can, 1992).

In 1992, the Supreme Court of Canada set aside Milgaard's conviction and ordered a new trial based on the fresh evidence regarding the serial rapist who had not been pursued by the police at that time and the recanted testimony of several of the original witnesses. According to the Court this evidence "constitutes credible evidence which taken together with the evidence adduced at trial could reasonably be expected to have affected the jury's verdict" (*Reference re. Milgaard,* 1992). The Attorney General for the province of Saskatchewan decided not to pursue another trial and stayed the charges against Milgaard. While Milgaard was freed from prison in 1992, after almost twenty-three years in prison, he was not formally acquitted or exonerated at that time. It was only five years later that DNA identification evidence proved unequivocally Milgaard's innocence and the Saskatchewan government formally apologized for his ordeal. In 1999, Milgaard and his family received ten million dollars, the largest compensation settlement for a case of wrongful conviction to date in Canada. Milgaard's case is of particular interest when discussing the issue of conviction review as it illustrates how the process initially failed to prove that a miscarriage of justice occurred, in spite of his innocence. It was only after a second review was requested, following much lobbying from Milgaard's family and political advocacy groups, that his case was reconsidered. Larry Fisher was convicted of the rape and murder of Gail Fisher in 1999.[14]

Clayton Johnson

Clayton Johnson was found guilty of murdering his wife in 1993 and sentenced to life imprisonment. His wife's death in 1989 was initially ruled as an accident due to a fall down the basement stairs, alleged to have occurred shortly after Johnson left for work. However, suspicion fell on Johnson due to his involvement with a younger woman shortly following his wife's death and when it was revealed that he had taken out a life insurance policy on his wife's life six months prior to her death. Pathologists initially called in to reinvestigate Mrs. Johnson's accidental fall declared that her head injuries could have been the result of blows from either a baseball bat or a two-by-four piece of wood. Furthermore, during Johnson's trial there was a blurring of the line between experts and opinionated witnesses, as well as an overreliance on suspicion and speculation surrounding this case in the small town where it occurred (Ontario Lawyers Gazette, 2003). Johnson's appeal to the Nova Scotia Court of Appeal was dismissed in 1994, and one year later the Supreme Court of Canada also dismissed the appeal.

In March 1998, with the assistance of AIDWYC, a lobby group for the wrongly convicted,[15] Johnson applied for conviction review. The new and significant information to support the review included opinions solicited from twenty-two experts in forensic pathology, engineering, biomechanics, physics, and human postural dynamics and further evidence that supported the improbability of the alleged crime (Public Prosecution Service, 2002). Moreover, it was established that crucial blood splatter evidence was not given to experts who testified at the original trial. In September 1998, the Minister of Justice referred the case back to the Nova Scotia Court of Appeal to allow the new forensic evidence to be heard. The Minister specifically asked the court:

> In the circumstances of this case, would the information provided by or on behalf of the Clayton Johnson or obtained during the review of his section 690 application for the mercy of the Crown be admissible as fresh evidence on appeal to the Court of Appeal?
> and
> If the Court of Appeal concludes that the information would be admissible on appeal, the Minister has asked the Court, pursuant to paragraph 690(b) of the Criminal Code, to proceed to hear the case as if it were an appeal by Mr. Johnson.

Johnson was released from prison while awaiting arguments from both the Crown and the defense following the testimony of several pathologists that concluded that Mrs. Johnson's death was due to a freak accident that resulted in her fatal head injuries. In 2002, after three-and-one-half years, the Nova Scotia Court of Appeal overturned Johnson's first-degree murder conviction and ordered a new trial. Given that expert witnesses had been found to refute the murder claims and present evidence of accidental death, the Crown decided not to proceed. Mr. Johnson's case illustrates how the conviction review process can work, but also demonstrates its flaws, as it took three-and-a-half years before a remedy was given, and this occurred only after a lengthy, extensive, and expensive investigation took place. Mr. Johnson recently received 2.5 million dollars in compensation for the five years he spent in prison.

Conclusion

This brief overview of the conviction review process, as a last resort for the wrongly convicted in Canada has served to illustrate its many challenges, deficits, and difficulties. For those individuals who believe they have suffered a miscarriage of justice, the conviction review process truly represents the last resort. With sufficient time, resources, and the introduction of new and significant evidence pertaining to their case, such individuals can apply for review, but as the numbers indicate, the chances of being granted a remedy are improbable. The creation of an independent review commission in Canada, similar to the Criminal Cases Review Commission (CCRC) in the United Kingdom is worthy of further consideration. The CCRC in the United Kingdom came about as a result of the Criminal Appeal Act 1995 and functions as an executive nondepartmental public body. Similar to the conviction review process in Canada, the CCRC requires that cases have already gone through the Appeal courts, or leave to appeal had been refused and there is a new factor or new evidence that the courts have not considered before. While the eligibility criteria are roughly similar, it would appear that the time to process cases is considerably longer in Canada.

As indicated in Table 7.2, in about a decade, the CCRC has reviewed more than 8,300 cases and referred more than 340 to the appeal courts; it receives two or three new applications every working day. The time frame for investigating cases is one or two months, and more complex cases take from one to two years, depending on whether an individual is incarcerated. This time frame is considerably shorter than the wait for conviction review in Canada, and many more cases are examined in a year, perhaps due in part to a larger number of investigators and legally trained professionals working for the Commission.[16]

The consultation that occurred about the amendments to the conviction review process in Canada in 2002 involved examining the possibility of establishing an independent review commission, similar to the CCRC. However, this suggestion was rejected, as it was stated that the provinces were satisfied that the review process remain in the hands of the federal Minister of Justice, and that the Canadian prosecutorial system was too dissimilar to that of the United Kingdom for such a commission to work in Canada ("Regulations Respecting Applications," 2002). Furthermore, the Department of Justice has argued elsewhere that a review mechanism similar to the CCRC would detract from the notion of judicial finality by creating another level of appeal, would be too costly, and would result in many more requests, pro forma. Finally, the Department of Justice (1998a) contends that as it is, the review process is considered independent from the prosecutions conducted by the provincial Attorneys General and thus satisfies the requirement for an independent review mechanism.

TABLE 7.2.   FIGURES FROM THE CCRC THROUGH SEPTEMBER 30, 2006

Total applications	9,044
Open	278
Actively being worked on	424
Completed	8,342 (including ineligible)
Referrals	341
Heard by Court of Appeal	291 (199 quashed, 89 upheld, three reversed)

Source: Data are from http://www.ccrc.gov.uk/cases/case_44.htm

The arguments put forth by the Department of Justice against the establishment of an independent commission are spurious and rejecting the idea outright appears to be somewhat shortsighted for a number of reasons. Primarily, the CCRG is not, nor will it ever be, independent from the Department of Justice. A truly independent commission would have enhanced credibility within the legal community. Establishing a commission that is at arm's length both literally and figuratively, from the federal government would allow it to function outside of the purview of prosecutorial bias, and also allow for a more expeditious processing of cases. Moreover, the principle of finality, as mentioned earlier, is not meant to be an instrument of injustice; errors made at an earlier point in the process must and should be later acknowledged and rectified. The idea that such a commission would result in an increased number of requests is likely, but it is impossible to estimate exactly how many more cases would come forward or be dealt with if an independent commission were established. However, that this would occur pro forma is unlikely.

The many high-profile cases heard in Canada, the United States, and abroad attest to the fact that a wrongful conviction is no longer an "extraordinary" occurrence. Therefore, it makes sense that measures in existence to address this problem are no longer out of the ordinary, but become accessible, affordable, and readily available to those who believe they have been wrongly convicted. Furthermore, the onerous nature of the process would likely dissuade those whose cases were questionable from undertaking a review. In addition, including input from other experts, such as forensic specialists, psychiatrists, and police, as is evidenced in the CCRC, would strengthen the investigation report and likely result in more convictions being sent back to the Court of Appeal. Given that the causes of wrongful convictions are multifaceted, the importance of including a number of voices, functioning outside of the legal realm, cannot be overstated. An independent commission that would have greater access to such professionals would likely process cases faster and in turn, foster greater confidence in its ability to address miscarriages of justice expediently, transparently, and equitably. Investing more resources in an independent commission is far less costly than the millions of dollars regularly spent on commissions of inquiry that investigate the circumstances of individual cases of wrongful convictions (cf. Campbell, 2005).

The ultimate goal of individuals seeking conviction review is exoneration. The hardship and misfortune that accompany a wrongful conviction are difficult to manage at best and untenable at worst. When a conviction review results in an acquittal or the setting aside of a conviction, it does not necessarily constitute exoneration, per se. Clearly, the advent of DNA identification practices has raised the bar on exonerating those wrongly accused and convicted. It is one of the few tests that can provide true exculpatory evidence in some cases. However, it is limited to those cases where physical evidence exists and the unfortunate reality is that wrongful convictions can occur in cases where there is no physical evidence linked to the accused, or even in cases where no crime has actually occurred. In the language of conviction review, a preponderance of factors that indicate a miscarriage of justice likely occurred does not constitute exoneration. To avoid future miscarriages of justice, perhaps what is needed is a greater awareness of the causes of wrongful conviction for those who contribute to these errors at the earlier stages (i.e., police and prosecutors). Preventing wrongful convictions from occurring in the first instance is far less costly, in both fiscal and human terms, than are the years of heartache involved in attempting to overturn a conviction at a later date.

An overview of the conviction review process in Canada has made clear that the justice system is not in a credible position to review itself. Much can be learned from the U.K. experience with the CCRC. While not without its own flaws, the system is at arm's length from the Home Secretary, is responsible for reviewing several hundred cases per year, has been successful in many of the cases sent back to the Court of Appeal, and employs many experts in compiling its investigative briefs. Individuals who have been wrongly convicted suffer a great deal psychologically, morally, physically, and financially. As long as the power to determine whether the system fails remains in the hands of lawmakers, the Canadian government will ultimately continue to fail these individuals.

Notes

1. The following information was summarized from Department of Justice (2003).

2. In most cases, the lawyers working at the CCRG conduct the review process. However, in high-profile cases or where the prosecution of the applicant was undertaken by the Department of Justice itself (drug offenses, those occurring in Northern regions) outside counsel will be appointed to conduct the review.

3. However, in a given year a number of new and old applications are actively under review. For example, in 2005 and 2006, twelve preliminary assessments were completed, and twenty were underway, six investigations were completed and eighteen were underway, and six reports were completed and twelve were underway (Department of Justice, 2005).

4. Some of these criticisms are also discussed in Campbell (2005).

5. It has been previously noted that most of these materials are necessary for each level of appeal and are likely already available (Campbell, 2005).

6. These are contained in the Thatcher 690 application decision. W. Colin Thatcher was convicted of murdering his wife in 1984. He applied for a conviction review in 1989 and received the Minister's response in 1994. At that time, the Minister of Justice denied the application and further set out the nature of the conviction review process and the role of the Minister in this decision.

7. Parts of these guidelines have been codified in law (Criminal Code, section 696.4) through amendments to the conviction review process, which occurred in 2002.

Furthermore, regulations accompanied these amendments containing information on the application process.

8. Following much lobbying, the Minister of Justice waived solicitor–client privilege in the case of *Truscott (Re)*, and publicly released an edited copy of the brief of that case in 2005.

9. In the Canadian jurisdiction, a judicial review is a mechanism of administrative law. It constitutes an appeal from the decision of an administrative tribunal, whereby a court rules on the appropriateness of the decision made by a tribunal or administrative agency.

10. This principle does not apply in the same manner in the United States, as American appellate courts have greater and more liberal powers and the possible grounds for appeal are more numerous (Department of Justice, 1998b). American states vary in terms of remedies and more collateral remedies such as civil action are available.

11. Available online at http://www.ilo.org/public/english/tribunal/fulltext/0570.htm.

12. Bernard Grenier, a retired Quebec provincial court judge, was appointed as special advisor in November 2003.

13. This request was considered to be unprecedented at that time, as in essence the Minister of Justice was asking the Supreme Court, which normally interprets law, to interpret fact (Boyd & Rossmo, 1994).

14. In 2004, the Supreme Court of Canada refused to hear Fisher's appeal, thus allowing for an inquiry to proceed on this case in 2005. The mandate of the Commission of Inquiry, ongoing at the time of writing, is to examine the investigation into the death of Gail Miller and the criminal proceedings against David Milgaard.

15. The Association in Defense of the Wrongly Convicted (AIDWYC) is a nonprofit organization located in Toronto, Ontario, that champions the cause of the wrongly convicted and is staffed by lawyers working pro bono. Their last director, Reuben "Hurricane" Carter, himself served twenty-three years in a New Jersey prison on a wrongful conviction for a multiple murder.

16. This is also due in part to the much larger relative population numbers of the United Kingdom, as compared to Canada.

References

Bloomenfeld, M., & Cole, D. (2005). The roles of legal professionals in youth court. In K. M. Campbell (Ed.), *Understanding youth justice in Canada*, pp. 198–220. Toronto: Pearson Education.

Boyd, N., & Rossmo, K. (1994). David Milgaard, the Supreme Court and Section 690: A wrongful conviction revisited. *Canadian Lawyer, 18,* 28–32.

Braiden, P., & Brockman, J. (1999). Remedying wrongful convictions through applications to the Minister of Justice under Section 690 of the *Criminal Code. Windsor Yearbook of Access to Justice, 17,* 3–34.

Campbell, K. M. (2005). Policy responses to wrongful conviction in Canada: The role of conviction review, public inquiries and compensation. *Criminal Law Bulletin, 41*(2), 145–168.

Castelle, G., & Loftus, E. (2001). Misinformation and wrongful conviction. In S. D. Westervelt & J. A. Humphrey (Eds.), *Wrongly convicted: Perspectives on failed justice* (pp.17–35). New Brunswick, NJ: Rutgers University Press.

Criminal Lawyers Association. (2000). Submissions on behalf of the Criminal Lawyers Association, addressing miscarriages of justice: Reform possibilities for Section 690 of the Criminal Code. Retrieved December 31, 2004, from http://www.criminallawyers .ca/publicmaterials/press&submissions/690submissions.htm

Denov, M., & Campbell, K. (2003). Wrongful conviction. In J. Roberts & M. Grossman (Eds.), *Criminal justice: A reader*, pp. 228–243. Toronto: Harcourt.

Denov, M., & Campbell, K. (2005). Criminal injustice: Understanding the causes, effects and response to wrongful conviction in Canada. *Journal of Contemporary Criminal Justice, 21*(3), 1–26.

Department of Justice. (1998a). Addressing miscarriages of justice: Reform possibilities for Section 690 of the Criminal Code, A consultation paper. Retrieved December 31, 2004, from http://Canada.justice.gc.ca/en/cons/amj/coverre.html

Department of Justice. (1998b). The Section 690 application of Clayton Johnson. Retrieved December 31, 2004, from http://canada.justice.gc.ca/en/news/nr/1998/ johnsonNote.html

Department of Justice. (2003). *Applying for a conviction review.* Ottawa, Canada: Minister of Justice, Communication Branch, Department of Justice.

Department of Justice. (2005). *Applications for ministerial review: Miscarriages of justice: Annual report 2005.* Ottawa, Canada: Minister of Justice, Communication Branch, Department of Justice.

Drizin, S., & Leo, R. (2004). The problem of false confessions in the post-DNA world. *North Carolina Law Review, 82*(3), 892–1007.

Gross, S. R., Jacoby, K., Matheson, D. J., Montgomery, N., & Patil, S. (2005). Exonerations in the United States 1989 through 2003. *The Journal of Criminal Law and Criminology, 95*, 523–560.

Huff, C. R. (2004). Wrongful convictions: The American experience. *Canadian Journal of Criminology and Criminal Justice, 46*(2), 107–120.

Huff, C. R., Rattner, A., & Sagarin, E. (1986). Guilty until proven innocent: Wrongful conviction and public policy. *Crime and Delinquency, 32*, 518–544.

Huff, C. R., Rattner, A., & Sagarin, E. (1996). *Convicted but innocent: Wrongful conviction and public policy.* Thousand Oaks, CA: Sage.

Kaiser, H. A. (1989). Wrongful conviction and imprisonment: Towards an end to the compensatory obstacle course. *Windsor Yearbook of Access to Justice, 9*, 96–155.

Kassin, S. M., Tubb, V. A., Hosch, H. M., & Memon, A. (2001). On the "general acceptance" of eyewitness testimony research. *American Psychologist, 56*(5), 405–416.

Leo, R., & Ofshe, R. (1998). The consequences of false confessions: Deprivation of liberty and miscarriages of justice in the age of psychological interrogation. *Journal of Criminology and Criminal Law, 88*, 429–496.

Markham, G. R. (1992). Organized crime and corruption: The police. *Police Studies, 15*(4), 175–178.

Martin, D. (2001). The police role in wrongful convictions: An international comparative study. In S. D. Westervelt & J. A. Humphrey (Eds.), *Wrongly convicted: Perspectives on failed justice* (pp. 77–95). New Brunswick, NJ: Rutgers University Press.

Ontario Lawyers Gazette. (2003, Spring). The Law Society of Upper Canada news and reports page. *Ontario Lawyers Gazette, 7*(2). Retrieved December 31, 2004, from http://www.lsuc.on.ca/news/gazette/gazette34/gazette34_focus.jsp

Parker, K. F., Dewees, M. A., & Radelet, M. L. (2001). Racial bias and the conviction of the innocent. In S. D. Westervelt & J. A. Humphrey (Eds.), *Wrongly convicted:*

Perspectives on failed justice (pp. 114–131). New Brunswick, NJ: Rutgers University Press.

Public Prosecution Service. (2002, February 18). *Crown halts Johnson murder prosecution*. Retrieved December 31, 2004, from http://www.gov.ns.ca/news/details .asp?id=20020218002

Regulations respecting applications for ministerial review : Miscarriages of justice, part 1. (2002, September 28). *Canada Gazette*, pp. 136–139.

Rosen, P. (1992, January). *Wrongful convictions in the criminal justice system* (Background Paper No. 285E). Ottawa, Canada: Library of Parliament.

Scheck, B. C., Neufeld, P. J., & Dwyer, J. (2000). *Actual innocence: When justice goes wrong and how to make it right.* New York: Doubleday.

Trotter, G. T. (2001). Justice, politics and the royal prerogative of mercy: Examining the self-defence review. *Queen's Law Journal, 26,* 339–395.

Wells, G. L., & Olson, E. A. (2003). Eyewitness testimony. *Annual Review of Psychology, 54,* 277–295.

Westervelt, S. D., & Humphrey, J. A. (2001). *Wrongly convicted: Perspectives on failed justice.* New Brunswick, NJ: Rutgers University Press.

Zimmerman, C. (2001). From the jailhouse to the courthouse: The role of informants in wrongful convictions. In S. D. Westervelt & J. A. Humphrey (Eds.), *Wrongly convicted: Perspectives on failed justice* (pp. 199–210). New Brunswick, NJ: Rutgers University Press.

Cases Cited

Reference re. Milgaard (Can), [1992] S.C.J: No. 35.

Truscott (Re) [2005] O.J: No. 2667.

III

EUROPEAN AND ISRAELI PERSPECTIVES AND ISSUES

8

WRONGFUL CONVICTIONS
IN SWITZERLAND

The Experience of a Continental Law Country

∼

MARTIN KILLIAS

T he risk of wrongfully convicting the innocent is, obviously, related to the extent to which the criminal justice system seeks to establish the truth in a balanced and fair manner. This, in turn, has to do with the legal safeguards and their respect, but also with the legal culture surrounding the establishment of relevant facts by the police and all other parties involved. In this chapter, I first give an overview of basic features of the Swiss criminal justice system.[1] In the second part, I review some cases of known wrongful convictions and highlight the critical role of police and prosecutorial behavior. In a final section, some consideration is given to problems specifically in the fields of police, forensic science, and medical examinations. I argue that professionals in these fields need to become more open to recognize the risks of errors at all levels of an investigation, and develop strategies to deal with such risks.

Features of Switzerland's Criminal Justice System

Switzerland has a typical continental criminal justice system, sharing many features with virtually all other continental and Scandinavian countries, and particularly with Germany, France, and Austria. In some respects, however, it also shares many features with the United States, its constitutional order being heavily influenced by the American model as it emerged in the late eighteenth and early nineteenth centuries.

Criminal Law and Criminal Courts

Traditionally (and before 1942), Switzerland's twenty-six cantons were autonomous in matters of criminal law, with the exception of a few federal offenses. Thus, the situation resembled, in many ways, what we find today in America. Since 1942, substantive criminal law is unified in a national criminal code. This code does not provide for the death penalty; before 1942, a few cantons had maintained it, and it had been abolished in most cantons between 1854 and 1874. The system of the code and the definitions of offenses have been influenced by the models of the neighboring countries, particularly Germany and France.

The law of criminal procedure has, so far, remained a cantonal domain, although a federal code is in preparation. The systems that survive in the twenty-six cantons are heavily influenced by France and Germany. About half of the cantons follow the French system of the examining magistrate (*juge d'instruction, Untersuchungsrichter*), whereas in others, the prosecutor (*procureur, Staatsanwalt*) dominates the pretrial investigation. Some cantons (e.g., Geneva) maintain a jury system, whereas others have largely replaced it either by professional benches of judges, or by benches of lay judges with at least one professional judge in the chair. All judges (lay or professional), including jurors, participate in reaching a verdict and in sentencing. The Federal Supreme Court (*Tribunal fédéral, Bundesgericht*) has largely shaped defendants' rights over the decades, particularly since the European Convention of Human Rights and European jurisprudence started to address issues related to criminal procedure. Although the Federal Supreme Court of Switzerland serves mainly as the highest court of appeals in all areas of law, it is fair to compare its role with its American counterpart with respect to criminal procedure. Thus, despite the great variety of systems in the twenty-six cantons, there is more uniformity than one might expect at first glance, due to dozens of Supreme Court rulings.

Basic Safeguards: The Right to Be Heard

Among the important rules developed by the Federal Supreme Court from the late nineteenth century is the right to be heard. Today explicitly guaranteed in Article 29 (§ 2) of Switzerland's new Constitution of 1999, this principle imposes on all authorities (in all fields) the strict obligation to fully disclose the file prior to making any decision about a citizen. Any person who, directly or indirectly, is affected by a decision, must have the opportunity to present his or her view on all relevant issues. This right to be heard (*droit d'être entendu, rechtliches Gehör*) is one of the very basic rules of Swiss law and continental law in general. Therefore, there are no specific rules of disclosure, as in the United States, since full disclosure of the prosecution's file is the strict rule under all circumstances. As a further consequence of the right to be heard, the defendant (and his or her lawyer) has the right to comment on all relevant aspects of the file. Although it is usual to hear the defendant at the beginning of the hearing, his or her counsel will have the right to comment on all declarations made by witnesses, experts, or any other party. Another consequence of the right to be heard is the obligation of all courts to cite their rationale for both the verdict and the sentence. This rule had the side effect of obliging juries to move away from the former "roll a dice" (Pizzi, 1999) system. Although juries, wherever they still exist in the traditional form, do not draft opinions like professional judges, they are obliged to indicate, in a few words, why they considered a certain fact to be established beyond a reasonable doubt. As a result of this requirement and the difficulties juries necessarily have in meeting it, most cantons have abolished or substantially reshaped their traditional jury systems. Most cantons now have courts composed of lay and professional judges.

The right to be heard and other constitutional safeguards were developed by the Federal Supreme Court during the late nineteenth and early twentieth century. They were further extended once Switzerland ratified, in 1974, the European Convention of Human Rights. These civil rights are now formally guaranteed in the new Swiss Constitution, effective since January 1, 2000. The right of the defendant to remain silent and to receive a warning inspired by *Miranda* is guaranteed in Article 31 (§ 2). Articles 29 (§ 3) and 32 (§ 2) guarantee the right to counsel. Several rules further provide for compensation in favor of any person detained without a valid reason.

Limited Role of the Defense

As a result of the right to be heard and the full disclosure of the prosecution's file, the role of the defense is more limited in the establishment of the relevant facts. Defense lawyers typically do not conduct their own investigation.[2] Whenever they believe that the police have neglected evidence that might be favorable to the defendant, they ask for an extension of the police investigation, usually at a pretrial hearing before the examining magistrate or the prosecutor. In practice, the police often invest considerable resources to rule out the implication of any third party.

Defense lawyers thus do not play a very active role in the factual side of a case, but concentrate on seeing that rules of due process and substantive criminal law are respected. Given his or her rather limited role, the job of attorney-at-law is probably "easier" in criminal cases than in damage suits, and the resources available do not have the same bearing on the quality of the defense as in American trials. Finding the truth is indeed considered the Court's business, and parties are merely expected to assist the judges in this task.

The defense counsel is not bound to disclose his or her file, as only the Government and its branches are required to respect the right to be heard. However, late disclosure of decisive evidence is discouraged because the court will, as a rule, order a complementary investigation by the examining magistrate (or the prosecutor) whenever new aspects come up at trial that cannot be cleared immediately. In practice, virtually all witnesses, experts, and other evidence are heard first by the police or the prosecutor (with the defendant and his or her counsel being present) during the pretrial investigation. Usually, witnesses are heard during trial only if the presiding judge, at the request of the parties, considers their statement as essential to allow the court to make up its mind. Uncontested evidence is usually not presented again at trial, but is recorded in the file that is known to professional and lay judges as well as to both parties.

"Inquisitorial" Traditions and Truth in Verdicts

Following the continental inquisitorial tradition, the interrogation of witnesses and experts (e.g., physicians, coroners, forensic scientists) will be conducted first by the presiding judge, who then will turn to the other judges on the bench (including the lay judges) for additional questions, and then let the prosecutor and the defense counsel continue the interrogation.[3] Unpleasant comments concerning witnesses, particularly the victim, are, whenever unwarranted, regularly reprimanded by judges.[4] It also would be unthinkable for attorneys to interrupt the victim while he or she is telling his or her story. Similarly, "preparing" witnesses and experts before their hearing is strongly discouraged, and there are no "witnesses for the prosecution" or "for the defense," but just individuals who contribute and assist the court in finding the truth.[5] Judges may also occasionally ask witnesses whether they have discussed the matter with the defendant or any other parties before; if they admit to having done so, their deposition will likely be seen as somewhat "colored" or "interested." Witnesses and experts who are lying or hiding relevant facts may be prosecuted for perjury. Defendants and codefendants, although always extensively heard by the court, do not have the status of a witness, which means that they are not liable to prosecution whenever they lie.[6]

Another fundamental rule of Swiss (and continental) procedural law is the principle that the judge should never admit facts as being proven unless he or she is "intimately" convinced (*conviction intime du juge*) that they are true. This means that the formal status of a person as a witness has no direct bearing on the verdict, since the court, if it feels that the witness did not tell the true or the full story, can always find the defendant's version more credible. The protection against self-incrimination is achieved by not making an offense any "perjury" a defendant might commit.[7] Witnesses have a right to remain silent (but not to lie) on all issues that might prove legally damaging to themselves, or to any member of their family. A suspect never can be questioned as a witness, even in his or her codefendant's case. Thus, there is no figure such as the "witness of the crown." If a witness turns out later to be a suspect rather than a third party, the testimony will be nil, and no punishment for perjury can be imposed.

Plea Bargaining as a Marginal Phenomenon

As in virtually all European continental systems, Swiss law allows guilty pleas whenever the sentence the prosecutor requires does not exceed a few months of imprisonment. In such cases, the prosecutor or examining magistrate issues a penal order (*ordonnance pénale*, *Strafbefehl*), in which the facts are summarized and the sentence summarily motivated. Such warrants are possible only if (1) the facts are obvious and not contested, (2) the defendant agrees to his or her legal qualification and the sentence, and (3) the prosecutor sees no reason to impose a sentence beyond a certain limit.[8] The defendant is entitled to declare, within a certain deadline (usually thirty days), not to agree. In that case, the penal order becomes an indictment, and the case is transferred to the local court, who will hear it according to the ordinary rules.

"Justice without trial" is mostly used in cases of traffic offenses, minor thefts, possession of drugs, and so on. In such cases, facts are usually obvious and hard to contest, their legal qualification easy, and the sentence at stake moderate. Under such circumstances, it certainly is legitimate to divert the system's scarce resources to more important cases. From the defendant's perspective, the interest in accepting this kind of settlement is often that it is not getting public attention. Since the penal order can only be issued for an offense that is in line with established facts, there is no option to reduce more serious charges. Similarly, the defendant does not risk being punished more severely by the court if he or she does not accept the penal order. Therefore, continental law lacks incentives to lure an innocent defendant into entering an "Alford"[9] guilty plea to avoid a worse outcome in case of a full trial.

Plea bargaining, however, is not available in cases involving contested or unclear facts. Under such circumstances, the court will always need to convince itself of the defendant's guilt. If a defendant admits (in a police interrogation) having committed an offense, the police will try to obtain from him or her as many technical details as possible to search for evidence that may corroborate that the crime happened exactly as the defendant described it. Even a confessing defendant will have a full trial. If facts are uncontested, the focus will turn, of course, to legal issues or the sentence, which in Switzerland (and generally in Europe) is determined during the same hearing by the same bench of justices who have wide discretion. The confession itself is, at best, a mitigating circumstance of limited impact on the sentence. According to Swiss jurisprudence, it entitles the defendant to a reduction of the sentence by roughly ten percent (Killias, 2001). Most defendants confess before or during trial, but try to obtain a relatively lenient sentence.

Although the limited scope of "transactions" in Switzerland may produce fewer wrongful guilty pleas than American-style plea bargaining, some recent developments should be viewed with reservation. For example, the sentencing powers of prosecutors have, generally in Europe, been extended over the last decades to make this summary procedure available in cases in which the offense was not trivial. Another trend is to allow prosecutors to issue a penal order without hearing the defendant.[10] As I show later, these "simplifications" may be the origin of several wrongful convictions.

The System of Appeals

Prosecutors and defendants and, in some instances, victims have the right to appeal verdicts and sentences. Within Europe, as well as among Switzerland's cantons, some differences exist in the extent of judicial controls over decisions made by lower courts. Certain systems allow the full appeal of verdict and sentence, implying that all facts and legal as well as sentencing issues can be brought up again. Eventually, new experts may be appointed, and witnesses may be heard again. Other countries (and some cantons) allow appeals only on limited issues, such as the violation of due process, serious factual errors, or errors in the interpretation of substantive criminal law. Switzerland and most European countries allow, after the first appeal, a second appeal, usually limited to legal and technical issues.[11] Once all procedural remedies are exhausted, the ruling becomes definitive (final; i.e., *res iudicata*), meaning that it cannot be challenged again, except under a few exceptional circumstances.

In Switzerland, appeals are successful relatively often. Statistics are available at the cantonal level only. In the canton of Zurich that, for one-seventh of Switzerland's population, handles roughly one-third of the national case load, 22 percent of all rulings by lower courts were appealed in 2003.[12] Over 35 percent of all appeals were successful, representing about 8 percent of all decisions by lower courts. Despite substantial differences between cantons, a fair estimate would be that roughly one decision in four is brought before a higher court, and one in three first appeals is successful. Most appeals, however, are directed at the sentence, or based on legal or technical grounds, and do not concern the verdict as such. Further, not only the defense, but also the prosecution can appeal. In assessing these estimates, it should be kept in mind that by far most defendants plead guilty, and that, therefore, the verdict is usually not often contested during and after the trial. About 700 criminal cases (or 1 percent of all convictions) are brought, after a first (unsuccessful) appeal at the cantonal level, to the Federal Supreme Court (*Tribunal fédéral, Bundesgericht*), out of which about one in seven is successful.[13] From these figures (and keeping the French, the English, or the Israeli experience in mind, as described by Dongois [Chapter 12], Walker and McCartney [Chapter 10], and Rattner [Chapter 13], respectively), it seems that Swiss higher courts review decisions brought before them rather critically. Obviously, the risk of wrongful conviction can be reduced if many errors are discovered and, eventually, corrected through appeals to higher courts. A high risk of having a decision overturned by a higher court may also be a strong incentive for lower courts to avoid errors of all kinds.

Exceptional circumstances that allow one to challenge a final decision include new evidence not available at trial or evidence pointing to the serious possibility that the "facts," as established during trial, may not be true. For example, a witness may have lied, or an expert may have drawn erroneous or excessive conclusions from the material he or she had at hand, or a DNA test conclusively proves that the facts differ from what the court had concluded. Under these situations, all European countries allow for a procedure by which the defendant can call for a new trial, which usually has to be granted by a superior court. The terminology varies greatly,[14] but the basic conditions are fairly similar across Europe.

Instances of Wrongful Convictions, Prosecutorial Misbehavior, and Good Police Practice

If, after a new trial, the defendant is acquitted, the implication is not necessarily that the defendant actually was innocent. Indeed, the witness who makes contradictory statements at the two trials may have been lying at the first or the second trial. Similarly, an expert's error may not necessarily imply that the defendant did not actually commit the crime for which he or she was convicted. In line with the study by Huff, Rattner, and Sagarin (1996) in the United States, I look for *wrongful* convictions; that is, instances where, after a first conviction, the defendant turns out to be innocent beyond any reasonable doubt, either because no crime occurred, the crime in question actually was committed by a third party, or DNA or other conclusive evidence exonerates the defendant. Further, a wrongful conviction will be considered as such only if the first (wrong) verdict had become legally effective, either because all appeals were rejected, or because no appeals had been filed. In sum, for this Swiss study, only cases where the defendant was found not guilty at a second trial, after a successful petition of revision, meet this requirement.

Unfortunately, there is no nationwide index of successful petitions of revision (*pourvoi en révision, Revisions-Gesuch*) in Switzerland. Therefore, a complete survey of all exonerations has been initiated among all courts of Switzerland.[15] So far, few exonerations of persons convicted for serious offenses have been located, but there are a surprisingly high number of exonerations after a penal order (involving misdemeanors).

A "Typical" Case

The first case concerns a district attorney who was in charge of the prosecution of a suspected drug dealer. The defendant, a Turkish immigrant, was stopped at the border with nearly one kilogram of a substance that appeared to be heroin. The forensic science department of the Zurich police (which conducts this kind of analysis centrally for many cantonal police forces) discovered, a few weeks later, that the substance seized contained less than 1 percent of pure heroin. Thus, the defendant had been caught with less than twelve grams of pure heroin, a quantity below the limit that, according to Swiss law, qualifies for a longer sentence (of up to twenty years). Despite its obvious relevance, the prosecutor failed to present this piece of evidence in court. The defendant, who had first admitted being involved in trafficking 200 to 300 grams of pure heroin, but later revoked that confession, had been convicted for serious drug trafficking and sentenced to 6.5 years in prison. An appeal was cancelled before the hearing, and the lower court's ruling became legally effective. Had the Court known the small quantity at stake, the sentence would presumably have been a suspended sentence of a few months.[16] A few years later, after the defendant had already served most of his sentence,[17] a police officer informed the defendant's former defense lawyer, who filed a petition of revision. The revision was granted, but the defendant was convicted once again and sentenced to four years. On appeal, that sentence was overturned by the Court of Appeals, basically because the case was "prescribed," given the long time that had passed since the offense, meaning that no sanction could be imposed any longer. For the unjust incarceration, the Court of Appeals allowed the defendant a sum of 100,000 Swiss francs.[18]

With this decision, the case was closed for the defendant, but not for the prosecutor, whose behavior was subjected to considerable media attention.

The Chief Prosecutor decided not to open an investigation, but the former defense counsel, in the meantime elected Minister of Justice, ordered the district attorney to be investigated and charged. The prosecutor was charged with "abuse of power,"[19] convicted, and sentenced to a suspended custodial sentence of forty-five days. A first appeal was not successful, but the defendant was acquitted on a second appeal. The High Court held that there was not sufficient evidence that the prosecutor had knowingly and willingly withheld relevant information from the court. In substance, the High Court held that the possibility could be ruled out that the prosecutor had acted negligently rather than intentionally.

This case illustrates how, unlike in America (Huff, 2002), prosecutors are subject to criminal prosecution whenever they withhold evidence that might be favorable to the defendant. The rule that prosecutors (as well as police officers) have to investigate all circumstances of an offense, including those that might be favorable to the defendant, is thus not without practical importance. As this case illustrates, this rule applies even in circumstances unknown to the defense counsel.

A Wrongful Conviction, and a "Model Prosecutor"

The second case that was brought to our attention offers an interesting illustration of how prosecutors see their role. Three robbers had committed an armed robbery in a large jewelry shop in downtown Geneva. They stole expensive watches and jewelry worth more than a million dollars (U.S.). Two of the robbers were armed with handguns; the third threatened the owner and two employees with a knife. More than seven years later, the police arrested a man for drunken driving. During the search of his vehicle, the police officer in charge believed that there might be a connection with the robbery of the jewelry shop. At a lineup, the manager and the two employees identified the suspect as "the man with the knife." Although contesting the facts, the defendant was convicted in 1991 by a jury for participation in robbery and sentenced to five years. Several years after the sentence was served, the Chief Prosecutor of Geneva received a request for legal cooperation from an Italian prosecutor. From the Italian file, a different version of that old hold-up emerged. It had, apparently, been committed by an Italian gang under circumstances that excluded any participation of the defendant convicted in Geneva. Seeing this potentially exonerating evidence, the Chief Prosecutor inquired in Italy to see whether the facts really excluded the participation of the man convicted in Geneva. Once he ascertained that they did, the Geneva prosecutor filed a petition of revision in favor of the defendant, who finally was acquitted, receiving an unknown amount in damages for unjust detention.

In this case, the reasons that led to the wrongful conviction are not unusual. Witnesses often are mistaken in identifying an individual in a lineup,[20] particularly if the time elapsed since the encounter is long, as in this case (seven years). There were also a couple of strange pieces of evidence in the defendant's car. However, the case is unusual in the sense that it was the prosecutor, not the defense counsel, who initiated the additional investigations that determined that the defendant had been wrongfully convicted, and who filed the petition to cancel the former conviction. Had the prosecutor decided to remain passive, or had he been less fluent in Italian and unable to find, rather coincidentally, a connection to that hold-up in 1983 in a bulky Italian file drafted in a highly technical language, the conviction would never have been challenged. This case illustrates that the impartiality maxim plays a real role in prosecutorial culture.

Prosecutorial Misbehavior

That prosecutors sometimes fail to investigate impartially has been illustrated already by the first case. Another prosecutor offers an even more extreme illustration of how critical the role of such officials can be.[21] Being short of cash, he abused his position by extorting money from defendants in exchange for dismissing their cases or bailing them out. This case is unusual since he dropped cases, rather than obtaining a wrongful conviction. The prosecutor was convicted not for corruption, but for causing a miscarriage of justice (i.e., "abuse of power") because he dismissed cases that, according to the Swiss system of compulsory prosecution (and given their merit) would have called for prosecution and a trial. In sum, the prosecutor was convicted for wrongful dismissals. Given American prosecutors' absolute powers in this respect,[22] it may be noteworthy that, in some European countries at least, prosecutors are subject to criminal punishment if they drop cases without adequate justification.

Good Police Practice

Just as looking at near accidents is helpful in accident prevention, analyzing cases where a wrongful conviction of an innocent defendant was avoided may be just as relevant as studying cases of actual wrongful convictions in preventing such miscarriages of justice. Several cases have come to my attention where false accusations of rape or child abuse have been cleared thanks to good police work.[23] In all instances reported here, the alleged victims admitted coming forward with a false accusation, and the reasons why they did so were reasonably clear, so that the defendants can indeed be considered innocent. In all instances, the cues that discharged arrested defendants after a few days were trivial details that the police corroborated. In one instance, the victim claimed to having been pushed to drink excessively in a pub before being taken home and raped. The two suspects were immediately arrested and interrogated separately. The police interviewed, over the next days, the waiter who had served the three, and the taxi driver who had brought them home. As it turned out, no one had noticed any signs of intoxication. Finally, the woman admitted having wrongfully accused the two out of frustration about one suspect's lack of ongoing interest in her. In a case of alleged abuse by a (female) teacher, a fifteen-year-old boy told the police that everyone at the school was aware of the love affair between him and that teacher. The police interrogated many fellow students and the entire school staff, but no one was aware of a romantic affair between the two persons. Finally, the boy admitted having to exacting revenge for the bad grades his brother had received the year before from that same teacher.

In these two (and several more) cases, a wrongful conviction was avoided thanks to the police officers' critical judgment, rapid reaction, and attention to apparently trivial details. In all cases, however, the victim seemed perfectly credible at first interview. It is easy to imagine what might have happened if the police had been less zealous at checking seemingly trivial details. Ironically, arresting the defendants was helpful to their cause, since no one could suspect them of coordinating their version with what the witnesses told the police. Indeed, interviewing witnesses, victims, and suspects separately and before any common story can be agreed on may be critical in finding the truth and avoiding the conviction of innocent persons.[24]

Wrongful Convictions in "Trivial" Cases

Our survey of all final convictions that were cancelled, over the entire country in the years 1995 to 2004 (Killias, Gilliéron, & Dongois, 2007), has found 237 successful petitions of revision. In 230 cases, the former decision has been cancelled in favor of the defendant; in six cases, the decision has been overturned because the defendant later turned out to be guilty, or guilty of a more serious offense than assumed at the first trial.[25] In 180 cases, the convicted defendant had filed the petition of revision; in forty-five cases, the exoneration had been initiated by the prosecutor[26]—an excellent illustration that prosecutors understand their role of impartiality.[27] In 125 cases, the defendant had originally been found guilty of a criminal code offense, among which were four cases of murder, six cases of assault, twenty-two cases of theft, five cases of robbery, and twelve cases of serious sexual offenses including three cases of rape. There were also 129 convictions concerning traffic offenses, including thirteen cases of drunken driving and fourteen cases of driving despite a withdrawn (or missing) driver's licence, and fourteen convictions for drug offenses (mostly selling of drugs). In sixty-two cases, the defendant had been sentenced to an unsuspended custodial sentence, and in fifty-two cases, a custodial sentence was suspended. In seventy-three cases, the sentence was six months or less; in thirty cases, it was longer than six months but less than two years; in ten cases, up to five years; and in two cases, above that limit (life in one case). Fines were 500 Swiss francs or less (or approximately $400 U.S.) in 77 percent of cases, and more than 1,000 Swiss francs in only 6 percent. In 196, or 84 percent of all cases, a new trial was granted because new evidence could be presented. In twenty cases (or 9 percent), the reason was that a second (later) court decision was in contradiction with the cancelled one, and in eight cases, the defendant had been convicted twice based on the same facts. In 159 cases (representing 67 percent), the overturned decision had been a penal order. Although this is not out of proportion, considering the number of cases that are dealt with in this way throughout the country, there are important differences among cantons regarding the frequency of overturned final decisions, with some cantons ranging far above their caseload. Most of these cantons allow issuing penal orders without the prosecutor hearing the defendant. Indeed, 77 percent of all overturned decisions concern just seven out of twenty-six cantons.

What do these figures show? The good news is that in only a handful of cases innocent people had been convicted for serious offenses, and none among these exonerations was due to DNA evidence. In roughly two out of three cases, the court had not considered the defendant's (partial) insanity, which often was recognized only in connection with a later offense. In these cases, the verdict as such had been correct, but the sentence needed to be mitigated to take the offender's mental condition into account. This was the case in three out of four cases where defendants had been convicted for murder; the fourth case concerned a killer of multiple children who had finally been exonerated of one among several murders, without mitigating the life sentence imposed after the first trial. In about one third of successful petitions of revision, the verdict as such had been erroneous, mostly because of perjury by rape and sexual assault victims, or, in some cases, due to a wrong confession by the defendant that he or she later repealed. Only three cases concerned incorrect identification of suspects by witnesses. In sum, wrongful convictions rarely concerned defendants who were convicted for serious crimes they never had committed.

However, more than 200 cases where defendants were wrongfully convicted of minor offenses have been found over ten years. Most of these defendants were convicted, without previous hearing,[28] under the form of a penal order. The story behind these exonerations is all too often the same: Less competent[29] defendants fail to contest the penal order, which then becomes a final decision. Once the sentence is to be executed, after the commutation of an unpaid fine into a short jail sentence, or if, at a later conviction, the suspension of a short custodial sentence is repealed, defendants who never were heard before come forward with potentially exonerating evidence showing, for example, that they were not driving the car at the critical moment. Usually in such cases, the relevant facts never were adequately assessed before issuance the penal order. Exonerations are, in such instances, rather generously granted, and defendants often are acquitted after a new trial. Although tentative, these findings show how vulnerable decisions are whenever defendants or other key figures in the case are not adequately heard, in sum, whenever justice is becoming too "summary." Of course, the number of exonerations discovered so far through our survey may seem negligible in comparison to the more than 500,000 penal orders issued by Swiss prosecutors over the same decade.[30] On the other hand, only a few among all miscarriages of justice will ever be discovered, especially because defendants may give up worrying about a conviction that led to a moderate sentence (especially a fine they were able to pay without too much trouble).

Despite the dramatic consequences of wrongful convictions in serious cases, it should not be forgotten that roughly three in four convicted defendants are found guilty without trial, but under the form of a penal order,[31] and that, therefore, such errors are probably far more frequent whenever minor offenses are at issue. Thus, the integrity of this simplified procedure has a great impact on the quality of the criminal justice system overall. Therefore, in connection with miscarriages of justice, trivial cases may warrant far more attention by practitioners and scholars. In conclusion, Switzerland (and Europe generally) are far from being immune to judicial errors, particularly in minor cases where procedural safeguards (such as the officiality maxim and the focus on "truth") may lose their protective force, just as the guarantees of dues process under the accusatorial system become more or less irrelevant whenever most cases are settled through plea bargaining rather than trial.

Quality Control in Scientific Expertise

In this connection, it should be noted that Swiss procedural rules are not favorable to second expert opinions. To obtain a second opinion, the defendant, according to a long-standing tradition of case law, has to establish that the expertise is (1) obviously incomplete, unreliable, or does not meet professional standards; and (2) that the expert is unable to respond adequately to eventual critiques of this sort.[32] These rules were obviously developed in view of psychiatric opinions on the defendant's eventual insanity (i.e., his or her capacity to understand and control his or her acts), but may be inappropriate for forensic and medical opinions on scientific issues where errors and contradictions are hard to discover for legal professionals. In contested cases, second opinions and peer review should, therefore, become part of a standard procedure of quality control. This implies, of course, that items of physical evidence will be preserved even over extended periods, and possibly long beyond the case becomes *res iudicata*. The current research project is expected to produce more insights into current quality standards of forensic expertise in Swiss criminal procedures.[33]

Conclusions

The cases presented here all illustrate the role of distinctive features of the Swiss (and more generally the continental) procedural system. The Geneva case shows how magistrates comply with the principle of impartiality in conducting investigations. The Zurich case further illustrates how prosecutors and police officers are subject to criminal prosecution whenever they fail to disclose (or collect) evidence that is potentially favorable to the defendant. Although convictions of prosecutors are exceptional, such rules may work as a powerful deterrent for individuals whose career can be seriously damaged by rumors of having behaved unfaithfully. In sum, controlling police and prosecutorial misbehavior by making an offense a serious violation of professional standards may be efficient to control this source of wrongful convictions. Finally, attention should no longer be limited to serious crimes and harsh sentences, but should extend to "trivial" cases, dealt with in summary proceedings, where miscarriages of justice are, although less dramatic, far more frequent and concern far larger numbers of defendants.

Notes

Acknowledgment: Parts of this chapter are based on an ongoing survey on wrongful convictions in Switzerland, supported by grant 100012 -105817 from the Swiss National Science Foundation.

1. In this chapter, no specific court rulings and other detailed sources are given. Readers familiar with either German or French will find a complete overview of procedural rules in Schmid (1997) and in Piquerez (2000). English-speaking readers can find a short introduction in Trechsel and Killias (2004).

2. An excellent comparison of American and Swiss (European) procedures can be found in Schmid (1993).

3. Medical, forensic, and other scientific experts are mandated by the examining magistrate (eventually the prosecutor). Usually, the magistrate consults with the parties whether they have any reservations concerning the presumed expert's reputation and

"objectivity." Once appointed, experts give a written statement, which can be commented on by both parties before the case goes to trial. Whenever any party comes forward with serious criticisms, the expert will be offered an opportunity to respond, or, eventually, to complement his report. He or she will be heard in court only if his or her oral statement is considered crucial by the court.

4. As a result, there are far fewer rules on barred questions, such as those concerning the victim's previous sexual conduct, in continental procedure compared to Common Law systems (Ries, 1984). Such questions are considered unfair and are barred whenever their relevance to the case is not obvious.

5. They are legally obliged to appear before the court and to answer any questions that might be asked.

6. According to a recent overview of exonerations in the United States from 1989 to 2003, perjury (particularly by supposed participants, jailhouse snitches, and police informants) is the leading cause of false convictions in murder cases (Gross, Jacoby, Matheson, Montgomery, & Patel 2004). The ban on such evidence may be an important factor in reducing wrongful convictions.

7. This feature was probably one of the reasons why Europeans were puzzled about the procedure directed by the U.S. special prosecutor (Kenneth Starr) against President Clinton regarding the allegation of perjury regarding the denial of his relationship with Monica Lewinsky. In a European court, a lying defendant would never be liable for perjury, let alone that, according to court practice in Europe, questioning any witness or party on a sexual matter without plausible connection with the offense at stake (in Clinton's case, a real estate transaction) would be seen as unprofessional.

8. The limits vary among jurisdictions (cantons). Usually the prosecutor's powers are limited to jail sentences not exceeding three or six months, or a fine.

9. 400 U.S. 25 (1970).

10. This is not seen as incompatible with the constitutional "right to be heard" as long as the defendant remains entitled to ask for a full-fledged (court) hearing. This (majority) view is not uncontested, however.

11. All appeals are to be heard, "certiorari" being unknown in Switzerland.

12. This estimate is based on figures given in the Report of the Cantonal High Court (Obergericht) to the Zurich Parliament (*Rechenschaftsbericht des Obergerichts des Kantons Zürich*, 2003, pp. 120–122, 131, 148).

13. Estimates based on the 2003 annual report of the *Bundesgericht* (Bericht des Bundesgerichts über seine Amtstätigkeit im Jahre 2003).

14. In Germany, the petition for a new trial is called *Wiederaufnahme-Gesuch*. In France the term used is *pourvoi en révision*. In German-speaking Switzerland, the term is *Revisions-Gesuch,* which is the term used in Germany for limited appeals (on technical issues).

15. It is inspired by Professor Karl Peters's monumental inventory of wrongful convictions in Germany (Peters, 1970–1974).

16. American readers may be surprised by such a lenient sentence, but it is not out of balance given the generally short sentences handed out in Switzerland (where the incarceration rate fluctuates between eighty and ninety per 100,000, compared to about 700 in the United States). On comparative sentencing patterns in Switzerland and other European countries, see the *European Sourcebook of Crime and Criminal Justice Statistics—2003* (pp. 158–183).

17. He was paroled, as usual, after two-thirds of the sentence.

18. Approximately $80,000 (U.S.).

19. Section 312 Swiss Criminal code.

20. Indeed, such errors are among the most prominent in wrongful convictions, as American research has shown (Huff, Rattner, & Sagarin 1996). A recent overview of exonerations since 1989 in the United States (Gross, Jacoby, Matheson, Montgomery, & Patil, 2005) confirms that nearly 90 percent of the false convictions for rape were due to eyewitness misidentifications.

21. The conviction of that prosecutor garnered considerable attention in the late 1960s. The facts and the legal problems are summarized in an article in the *Swiss Criminal Law Review* (Riesen, 1971).

22. Confirmed in the decision *Bordenkircher v. Hayes* 98 S. Ct. 663 (1978).

23. The sources are papers of students of the University of Lausanne Master's program in criminology on their stage in local police departments. The examples quoted here are from the reports by Sonia Lucia and Florence Ribaux.

24. Crombach (1999) illustrates the risks of "coordinated" accusations in such cases.

25. The low frequency of revisions that were unfavorable to defendants illustrates the limited practical role of double jeopardy under the continental system.

26. In two cases, the petition of revision was launched by another authority, and in one case, it is not clear who initiated the proceedings.

27. See also Chapter 11 by Kessler on the role of prosecutors in Germany and in England.

28. As noted earlier (note 11), this is not impossible in some cantons.

29. According to survey estimates, about 10 percent of Switzerland's adult population is functionally illiterate, or unable to understand more complex communications (www .gfs-zh.ch/content.php?pid=164). When one adds to this the high proportion of immigrants (more than 20 percent), the problem of defendants who are unable to understand a penal order may be considerable. It should be noted that defendants are not necessarily assisted by defense counsel when minor offenses are at issue.

30. Estimate based on data concerning prosecutorial decision making from the *European Sourcebook* (2003, pp. 94–95).

31. Estimate based on three major cantons (*European Sourcebook,* 2003, pp. 94–95).

32. Schmid (1997) and Piquerez (2000).

33. See Chapter 3 by Schiffer and Champod regarding these issues.

References

Crombach, H. (1999). Collaborative story-telling: A hypothesis in need of experimental testing. *Psychology, Crime and Law, 5,* 279–289.

European Sourcebook of Crime and Criminal Justice Statistics. (2003). 2nd edition. The Hague, Netherlands: WODC.

Greberding, P. (2005). *Das Rechtsmittelsystem im US-amerikanischen Strafverfahren* [The system of appeals in American criminal procedure]. Frankfurt, Germany: Peter Lang.

Gross, S. R., Jacoby, K., Matheson, D. J., Montgomery, N., & Patil, S. (2005). Exonerations in the United States 1989 through 2003. *The Journal of Law and Criminology, 95,* 523–560.

Huff, C. R. (2002). Wrongful conviction and public policy: The American Society of Criminology 2001 presidential address. *Criminology, 40,* 1–18.

Huff, R. C., Rattner, A., & Sagarin, E. (1996). *Convicted but innocent: Wrongful conviction and public policy*. Thousand Oaks, CA: Sage.

Killias, M. (2001). *Précis de Droit Pénal Général* [Introduction to general principles of criminal law] (2nd ed.). Berne, Switzerland: Stämpfli.

Killias, M., Gilliéron, G., & Dongois, N. (2007). *A survey of exonerations in Switzerland over ten years* (Report to the Swiss National Science Foundation). Lausanne and Zurich, Switzerland: University of Lausanne and University of Zurich.

Langbein, J. H. (1977). *Torture and the law of proof: Europe and England in the ancien regime*. Chicago: The University of Chicago Press.

Peters, K. (1970–1974). *Fehlerquellen im Strafprozess. Eine Untersuchung der Wiederaufnahmeverfahren in der Bundesrepublik Deutschland* [Sources of errors in criminal proceedings: A study of cases of successful petitions of revision in the Federal Republic of Germany] (3 vols). Karlsruhe, Germany: C. F. Müller.

Piquerez, G. (2000). *Procédure Pénale Suisse* [Swiss law of criminal procedure]. Zurich, Switzerland: Schulthess.

Pizzi, W. T. (1999). *Trials without truth*. New York: New York University Press.

Ries, P. (1984). *Die Rechtsstellung des Verletzten im Strafverfahren* [The victim's position in criminal procedure]. Munich, Germany: Beck.

Riesen, W. (1971). Amtsmissbrauch durch Staatsanwalt [Abuse of power by a prosecutor]. *Revue Pénale Suisse, 87,* 292–305.

Schmid, N. (1993). *Strafverfahren und Strafrecht in den Vereinigten Staaten: Eine Einführung* [Criminal procedure and criminal law in the United States] (2nd ed.). Heidelberg, Germany: Müller.

Schmid, N. (1997). *Schweizerisches Strafprozessrecht* [Swiss law of criminal procedure] (3rd ed.). Zurich, Switzerland: Schulthess.

Trechsel, S., & Killias, M. (2004). Criminal law/criminal procedure. In F. Dessemontet & F. Ansay (Eds.), *Introduction to Swiss law* (3rd ed., pp. 245–286). The Hague, Netherlands: Kluwer Law International.

9

THE VULNERABILITY OF DUTCH
CRIMINAL PROCEDURE TO
WRONGFUL CONVICTION

~

CHRISJE BRANTS

he problem of wrongful convictions has only recently arrived on the
public agenda in the Netherlands. Even so, it appears to be a question that vexes defense lawyers, the media, and some legal scholars
and criminologists, rather than representatives of the criminal justice system
or judges. When, in 1992 a multidisciplinary study—the first of its kind—
examined thirty-five cases that had been sent in by defense lawyers who were
not convinced of their clients' guilt (Crombag, Van Koppen & Wagenaar,
1994), the reaction in the legal community was one of disbelief and skepticism. Although the authors did not contend that all of these cases actually
were wrongful convictions and merely pointed to possible mistakes caused
mostly by flawed reasoning on the part of the court in the face of the available
evidence, judges, prosecutors, and legal scholars denounced the study itself
as flawed and legally unsound.[1] Several other (case) studies followed, some
by the same authors, some by ex-policemen or journalists, and some by ama-
teurs who set up Web sites to convince the public that "their" man, although
convicted, was really innocent.

Defense lawyers have managed to get new hearings for some of those
convicted in these cases; some have had their convictions overturned and
some have not. Even in a number of the successful cases, however, prosecutors and judges have insisted they still believe the original verdict to be correct.[2] Indeed, at a recent conference one of the authors of the 1992 study, Van
Koppen, also declared that of the thirty-five cases it covered, probably only
two, at most three, actually were wrongful convictions.[3] If we take the term

wrongful conviction to mean a conviction whereby the defendant has been found guilty after all avenues of appeal have been exhausted, although he or she did not commit the offense and the verdict was factually wrong, then very few of these cases are utterly convincing. Of all the instances highlighted over the years, only in a very few has it (later) become obvious that the convicted person could not, by any stretch of the imagination, be guilty.

So, although there is much ado in the media, it would nevertheless appear that the Netherlands is singularly lucky in the percentage of rightful convictions its criminal justice system manages to produce. The problem is that we do not know, and can never know for sure. We know and accept that someone who has been acquitted after a fair trial is not necessarily actually innocent. The logic of justice dictates that we can never be absolutely certain whether a guilty person has gone free, only that we may never punish those found innocent in a court of law. By the same token, though, it is often impossible to know if a wrongful conviction has actually occurred and an innocent person has been found guilty. Leaving aside cases in which it is later established that no crime occurred (e.g., the victim of the convicted "murderer" turns up in good health) or that it was physically impossible for the convicted person to have committed the offense (at the relevant time he was attached to a life support machine in a hospital), even if another person is found guilty, we can never be absolutely sure that we now have "the" truth. Although the advent of DNA has brought us greater certainty in cases where there is physical evidence, even that has its pitfalls.[4]

More often than not, what has been called wrongful convictions in the Netherlands is based on some sort of gut feeling on the part of a lawyer, researcher, or journalist. More often than not, if cases are overturned it is not because it has been established that the original verdict was definitely, factually wrong, but because of procedural flaws in the evidence or its evaluation by the court that should have resulted in an acquittal, but wrongly did not. For these reasons, and because there are no statistics or empirical research available in the Netherlands that would allow us to even remotely determine the number of wrongful convictions that actually occur,[5] I want to approach the problem from a different angle, using the only—legally—objective standard that exists: the rules that govern criminal procedure and allow us to judge, with hindsight, whether a conviction meets the norms we set for fair truth finding.

If the prosecution is found to have withheld exculpatory evidence; if the defendant who continues to protest his or her innocence did not have a chance to challenge incriminating evidence; if he or she confessed under duress, or if the trier of fact misunderstood or gave undue weight to an expert's opinion, any one of these factors (and there are many more) could give rise to doubt about the accuracy of a conviction, although not necessarily imply that the defendant is actually innocent. In the Netherlands, the authors of the 1992 study coined the phrase "dubious cases" to cover such situations: cases in which, with hindsight, there is room for reasonable doubt because the legal rules that should provide the safeguards for accurate truth finding were infringed on, while such mistakes were not corrected later in the process (see also Van Koppen, Hessing, & Crombag, 1992; Van Koppen & Schalken, 2004). These may or may not be wrongful convictions in an empirical sense, but legally they must be regarded as miscarriages of justice. I do not propose to present any case studies of dubious convictions in the Netherlands, for these already exist. Rather I want to identify the features of Dutch criminal procedure that render it vulnerable to mistakes and that could prevent mistakes from being rectified, assuming that the Netherlands is no more likely to have near perfect justice than any other country.

Researchers of miscarriages of justice in the Netherlands have said that criminal procedure that relies on professional judges of fact and an impartial, state-appointed prosecutor (i.e., an inquisitorial system such as exists in the Netherlands) probably produces fewer miscarriages than a procedure built around autonomous parties, a jury, and partisan (and sometimes elected) prosecutors as in the adversarial system (Van Koppen, 2003b; Van Koppen & Schalken, 2004, p. 120). That is a belief shared by the professionals in the Dutch criminal justice system, where the idea of a party-driven adversarial process and lay participation is anathema to internalized notions of justice. I would beg to differ. The inquisitorial systems found on the continent of Europe and the adversarial systems in the Anglo-American world are probably both vulnerable to delivering wrongful verdicts, although probably not in the same respects.

Such errors are very difficult to quantify, but there is in theory no reason to suppose that the adversarial system of common law is more prone to mistakes than the inquisitorial system in the civil law countries. Indeed, on paper the adversarial system is greatly preferred. In practice, however it relies so heavily on procedural notions of equality of arms, individually ascertained defense rights, and partisanship, that the scope for wrongful convictions is greatly increased as soon as theoretical assumptions fail to come up to their almost utopian standard. This seems especially true of the United States. In continental Europe, prosecutors and police officers are basically nonpartisan, and verdicts can usually be fully reexamined by a higher court (and are quite often overturned).[6] However, recent developments, in the Netherlands at least, have increasingly undermined these fundamental guarantees of the inquisitorial system against wrongful convictions.

All criminal procedures work and, in the overwhelming majority of cases, produce legitimate and acceptable results. In a very small minority of cases, the safeguards fail and mistakes are made (although that could mean a substantial absolute number of errors). It is my contention that the great strengths of the two predominant procedural traditions in law (i.e., in the law of Western democracies), the adversarial and the inquisitorial, are also potentially their great weaknesses, so that each has its own specific and inherent weak spots with regard to wrongful convictions. In this chapter, I propose to explore this notion further by examining the vulnerability of Dutch inquisitorial procedure in this respect. Focusing on what are, in theory, its great strengths (the notion of impartial pretrial investigation and the role of the prosecutor, the exclusively professional trier of fact who is bound to legal limitations with regard to evidence, and the possibility of a full retrial on appeal), I try to show that when the assumptions on which these features are based are not met, the attendant safeguards against erroneous convictions are eroded accordingly.

Basic Assumptions in Dutch Criminal Procedure

Like all modern inquisitorial procedures,[7] Dutch criminal procedure is based on a notion that the state is fundamental to the rational realization of the "common good," and that the latter includes criminal justice. Individuals define their relationship to and expectations of the state in matters of justice in terms of the modern *Rechtstaat*. The state is expected to uphold both law and order and individual liberty. Because the powers needed for the former may threaten the latter, their exercise is curtailed by written rules of law, by entrenched abstract constitutional rights, and by the division of power within the state. This is reflected in the procedural and organizational arrangements that govern criminal justice. Truth finding in criminal cases is seen as best undertaken by state functionaries, but on the other hand actions on the part of the police and prosecution service, representatives of the executive branch of the state, require a basis in written law and are subject to judicial scrutiny and hierarchical monitoring and control within the executive itself. The fairness and outcome of a criminal trial in such a system depend less on the assertion of individual defense rights than on the integrity of functionaries of the state—police, prosecution, and judge—in performing their allotted tasks within the limits of the Code of Criminal Procedure.[8]

Given that it is the state that conducts the task of criminal investigation, the agenda for the case that is eventually presented to the court by the prosecutor is set by the trial dossier, compiled by the state investigator during pretrial investigation on the basis of what the police, under his or her direction, have discovered. The prosecutor, and sometimes an investigating magistrate, is a central figure, invested with all of the powers needed to conduct a fair and thorough investigation (i.e., a nonpartisan investigation), taking both possible guilt and innocence into account. It is not the duty of the defense to find and produce evidence. Rather, the defense reacts to the agenda set by the prosecution and cannot determine it once the dossier is completed, although during its compilation the defense lawyer may point the prosecutor toward avenues of investigation favorable to the defendant, and the nonpartisan prosecutor has a duty to (order the police to) investigate them.

Truth finding and fair trial do not therefore depend on, in theory, equal parties presenting their own case and asserting their own rights to investigate and produce all evidence relevant to their version of events, but on the completeness and impartiality of a state-led investigation and the correct exercise of prosecutorial and judicial power. The defense does not have equal rights on the same footing as the prosecutor, but proportionate rights, or rights that will allow scrutiny of and challenge to the pretrial investigation and the evidence it has produced. Once the case comes to court, the defense role is essentially an attempt to undermine the case for the prosecution. In some inquisitorial countries, although pretrial investigation is totally in the hands of the prosecution, the trial stage itself is adversarial in that the defense has full rights of challenge and cross-examination and that only evidence produced and challenged at an oral hearing may be considered: This is the so-called principle of immediacy that obtains in, for example, Sweden and to a lesser extent Germany. In other countries, and the Netherlands is one of these, the role of the defense is more limited and is often no more than prompting the judge to ask the relevant questions. Written evidence contained in the dossier may be used although it has not been debated in open court.

In the theory of the inquisitorial tradition, both the legitimacy of criminal justice and the fate of the individual in terms of fair trial depend to a large extent on the integrity of state officials and their visible commitment to nonpartisan truth finding. Guarantees that the verdict will reflect the truth lie first in the prosecutor's role of representing and guarding all interests involved and in his or her control over the police; second, in the role of the defense in pointing to factual and legal deficiencies in the prosecution case and the attendant rights necessary for this; third in the fact that appeal on the facts—a full retrial before a higher court—is a normal feature of judicial supervision in inquisitorial criminal process; and last, but certainly not least, in the type of evidence that judges may take into account, in the requirement that they actively involve themselves in the truth-finding process in court, and that they give reasoned decisions.

Dutch criminal procedure, which, together with the organization of the judiciary, in essence was inherited from the French,[9] meets all of these criteria of the inquisitorial system, more so perhaps than that of other continental European countries in that the Netherlands is one of the very few that view criminal process as an exclusively state-oriented institution, without any involvement of the lay public. The idea of a trial by one's peers fills both the majority of Dutch legal scholars and the public with horror, and there is in general an aversion to the influence of both lay participation and public opinion on criminal trials and the penal process, as these are viewed as matters that require the considered and distanced judgment of legal professionals. Transparency of procedure and the public nature of trials are recognized as democratic rights under the Code of Criminal Procedure (and required by the European Convention on Human Rights and Fundamental Freedoms), but such recognition is reluctant and in practice not regarded as the mainstay of a fair trial.

The Participants

The Dutch public prosecutor is employed by the state as a civil servant. Prosecutors are trained in the same way as judges: After obtaining a university degree in Dutch law they enroll for five years of training, during which they practice as both junior judges and prosecutors. The selection process to enter this training course is rigorous and based on both knowledge of the law and a succession of psychological and aptitude tests. Only during the course do trainees opt either for the judiciary or the prosecution service. Indeed, the Public Prosecution Service is regarded as part of the judiciary, known as the "standing judiciary" because the prosecutor stands during his or her performance in court. The ideology that the prosecutor is really some sort of judicial figure is reflected in the fact that prosecutors are expected to adopt a magisterial stance in the execution of their most important role: controlling and monitoring pretrial investigation by the police and the compilation of a trial dossier containing records of all relevant steps in the investigation and all relevant evidence, both against and for the defendant. Only then will he or she decide to prosecute or not, a decision on which he or she has the monopoly. Guarantees that prosecutors will actually fulfill this nonpartisan role are to be found in the hierarchical system of monitoring and control that governs both their relationship with the police and relations within the prosecution service, and especially in the professional ethics they internalize during training. As an extra safeguard, however, rules of disclosure allow the defense to play a role in shaping the dossier that is eventually presented to the court, which has the power to actively scrutinize the way the pretrial investigation was conducted and the evidence it produced, and is expected to use that power, if necessary at the prompting of the defense lawyer.

Those who have gone through judicial training but have opted to be judges rather than prosecutors, form the small body of the "sitting judiciary."[10] These professional judges sit alone in minor cases and in panels of three in more serious cases (where the maximum sentence exceeds one year imprisonment). There is no jury in any criminal case (or any other court case for that matter). There are nineteen district courts of first instance to which young judges may be appointed. Each court has a number of investigating magistrates who are appointed on a rotational basis to conduct preliminary judicial investigations in the most serious cases and to authorize invasive methods of investigation such as telephone tapping. Originally, the investigating magistrate was a figure who was called to investigate any serious cases at a stage in the investigation where further prosecution looked likely. This role has been reduced over the past ten years, and the investigating magistrate is now a judge whose main task is the authorization of telephone taps and bugs and the interviewing, under oath, of witnesses whom the defense wants to challenge but who will not be called in court. He or she still plays a limited investigative role if he or she considers it necessary to grant a defense request to do so.

Subject to certain limitations, there is a right to appeal on conviction to one of the five appeals courts that will result in a full retrial. Dutch judges form an exclusive and elite group, and they are recruited on the basis of both legal skills and psychological characteristics; recruitment policy seems to favor those with reasonably middle-of-the-road views, both politically and socially, with increasing numbers of women following a judicial career. Although the judiciary forms part of a state organization, appointment for life, a (very) good salary, and the absence of any government involvement in day-to-day matters provide guarantees of independence. Impartiality is part of the professional ethic: Although the judges will be fully acquainted with the dossier before trial, they are expected (and trained) to approach the defendant with an open mind as to guilt or innocence.

Every defendant in a criminal case has the right to be represented by a lawyer; if he or she cannot afford one, one is assigned. Most criminal defense lawyers take assigned cases (which pay substantially less) as a matter of course. Defense lawyers in the Netherlands, organized in the criminal branch of the Dutch Bar Association, are self-employed. Their role in criminal procedure is to represent the interests of the defendant: monitoring the compilation of the dossier, not only as to the nature of the evidence but also as to the legality of the police methods used to obtain it; pointing the prosecutor toward certain avenues of investigation (witnesses to be heard, alibis to be checked, etc.); and in court attempting to undermine the strength of the prosecution case and directing the judge toward evidence favorable to the defense. Defense lawyers in the Netherlands are not expected to undertake their own investigation and will certainly not approach and interview potential witnesses. They have no powers to call witnesses or experts themselves.

The right to call and examine witnesses or invoke expert opinion is dependent on first the prosecutor's willingness to grant a request that the witness be heard, and, in the final instance on the court that can overrule or uphold the prosecution's refusal to accede to a defense request. Experts are appointed to the court and do not appear as partisan witnesses. If forensic or psychiatric expertise is required, most experts will be drawn from state-run institutions, such as the state forensic laboratory or one of the psychiatric assessment centers that are part of the criminal justice system. Social workers from the probation service—which is a semipublic institution, heavily subsidized by government although recently subject to drastic cuts in public spending—may also be called as experts.

Finally, a recent development has afforded the victim some status as a participant in court, although this is limited. Victims can, of course, be called as witnesses (although as we see later, there are many ways in which their testimony can be used even if it was not given in open court). In line with developments all over Europe, the position of victims has now been improved, in the sense that they may give a statement in court—emphatically not as a witness, but as a victim—as to the impact the crime has had on their lives and well-being. This the court may, at its own discretion, take into consideration during sentencing, but it may not use such a statement as evidence. Another recent phenomenon is a limited right for victims (not granted by law but in official prosecution guidelines) to request a second opinion on the thoroughness and efficiency of the police investigation.

The Procedure[11]

The Limited Role of Hearings

One of the outstanding features of a Dutch criminal case always remarked on by foreigners is that it is usually a (short) trial based on documents, and that adversarial debate in court is extremely limited. Given that all participants (with the exception of the defendant) are professionals, there is little need to elaborate on legal details, which are understood by all in any case, while all of the evidence will have been carefully gathered—including most witness statements—and systematically added to the dossier beforehand. The European Convention (and the Court) of Human Rights (ECHR) puts the right to know and challenge the evidence that is embodied in article 6 ECHR, at the forefront of the guarantees of a fair trial. However, recognizing the existence of inquisitorial systems within its jurisdiction, it does not require that this take place in court: It is sufficient if at some point in the proceedings, the defendant has been able to challenge the evidence and examine witnesses against him or her. The European Court also allows, under the same restrictions, the use of anonymous testimony, as long as a conviction is not based exclusively or to a large extent on it. It is perhaps not surprising, in light of what follows, that several of the European Court's decisions limiting the use of anonymous or unchallenged testimony have been made against the Netherlands.

Although the Dutch Code of Criminal Procedure places the trial in open court at the center of proceedings, requires that witnesses be heard at trial, and gives the defense the right to have them called, in a practice based on numerous decisions by the Dutch Supreme Court, most evidence is gathered (and often challenged) beforehand, the use of hearsay testimony is widespread, and in general pretrial investigation is the focus of truth finding in criminal process.[12] Threatened witnesses and those who are too vulnerable to be able to give evidence in court (e.g., rape victims) are not usually called at trial. Although the defense may attempt to have them appear in court, the more usual solution is to have them heard under oath by the investigating magistrate.[13] The defense may challenge this testimony, although not always directly. Sometimes the defense lawyer—although not usually the defendant—will be present at the hearing. Sometimes, however, he or she will have to ask questions by telephone from another room to protect the witness's identity, and sometimes he or she will be allowed to do no more than give the investigating magistrate a list of questions that should be put to the witness. The investigating magistrate will then submit a written report to the court; like the defense (but not the investigating magistrate or the prosecution), it too will remain ignorant of the witness's identity.

These procedures were introduced after the ECHR made a number of judgments against the Netherlands in which convictions had been based on unchallenged or anonymous testimony.[14] As yet it has not found them deficient, although they are a poor substitute for direct confrontation of the evidence. They are, however, consistent with the ideology on which Dutch procedure in general is based. More important than the "principle of immediacy" that requires evidence to be presented at trial, is that of "internal transparency": All participants must be acquainted with the facts of the case as represented in the dossier on an equal footing, so that there can be no conviction on the basis of evidence not known to the defense.[15] Internal transparency is also a guarantee that the court will not base its decision on incomplete evidence; that is to say, prosecutor and defense cannot agree beforehand to leave some things unsaid, which rules out plea bargaining as a means of settling cases.[16] This corresponds to an important basic assumption of inquisitorial procedure, that in the final event it is the court that must arrive at the truth. Another is that the defense will have been able to assist in the compilation of the dossier before trial, and that only those points on which there is disagreement will come up for debate before the court. However, given that the right of the defense to examine the complete dossier only becomes absolute ten days before trial and can be severely curtailed before that "in the interests of the investigation," a more important assumption is that the prosecutor will, in his or her nonpartisan role, have included everything that is relevant and will have looked into all aspects of the case before the trial starts.

The active role of the court in assessing whether this is actually the case means that it, and not the prosecution or the defense, has the last word in determining what the relevant evidence is and what should or should not be included (although again, it is the prosecution that sets the agenda here). Although the defense may challenge the accuracy of the prosecution case and request additions to the dossier or the hearing of new witnesses at trial, it is the court that makes, within the criteria of the law, the final decision on which witnesses are to be heard, on whether the dossier is complete and relevant or whether documents should be added to it or may be left out, and on whether expert opinion may be challenged by the introduction of other experts—in short, on whether it considers itself to be in possession of all relevant facts. It is also the court that conducts the first and fullest questioning of witnesses. The defendant (never considered a witness in his or her own case and therefore never under oath) may speak in his or her own defense (and always has the last word), but only if he or she so wishes. Dutch trials are therefore essentially a debate on the relative weight to be given to the several pieces of evidence that the state has gathered in its nonpartisan search for the truth.

Guarantees Against Miscarriages of Justice

In deciding on matters of guilt or innocence, Dutch courts are not free in the evidence they may consider. The Code of Criminal Procedure provides rules on the different sorts of evidence that may be used to construe guilt, on the weight that may be attached to them, and on the relationship between the evidence and the court's decision that the defendant is guilty (articles 338–344a CCP). Only evidence that is legally regarded as evidence suffices and the Code of Criminal Procedure contains a limitative list of what sort of evidence that is: the court's own observations during trial, statements by the defendant, witness statements, other statements or written documents (such as expert reports), and official written statements by police officers and other officers charged with conducting criminal investigations.[17] However, of all of these, only the last are regarded as of sufficient weight in themselves, but only then if they do not substantively amount to the hearsay testimony of a single witness or the defendant: The CCP forbids that a conviction be based on the statement of a defendant alone (thereby ruling out conviction solely on the basis of a confession) or on the statement of a single witness, and anonymous testimony may never form the basis of a conviction unless it is corroborated substantively by other evidence. Normally therefore, evidence requires other evidence as corroboration.

Moreover, although a prescribed amount of a prescribed sort of evidence is necessary for a conviction, the court may only convict if it has been convinced of the defendant's guilt by that evidence. For this reason, the evidentiary rules in the Netherlands constitute what is known as a negative system of evidence: The court must have sufficient evidence of a certain sort and may not convict unless that evidence has convinced it of guilt. If this causal relationship is missing, *in dubio pro reo* prevails. An extra safeguard requires the court then to give a reasoned decision, setting out the (legal) evidence by which it has been convinced. Even then, the person convicted at first instance is entitled to appeal, which will result in a full retrial (the same applies if the prosecutor disagrees with an acquittal). The appeals court decision on the facts is final, although another avenue of appeal to the Supreme Court may be open—known as *cassation*—if there is any disagreement on points of law.[18]

What, however, if the person convicted continues to protest his or her innocence, and what if he or she is indeed innocent? In the knowledge that even the most secure of evidentiary rules and the most professional of courts in two instances may still leave room for mistakes, the Dutch legislature provided a system of review of cases by the Supreme Court if new evidence casts doubt on the original decision (CCP, articles 457ff). As it stands, the procedure is designed to prevent the Supreme Court from becoming a court of third instance, by requiring that it establish that new evidence has emerged, not known at the time to the original court (a so-called *novum*), and then that such evidence would have led the original court to acquit. If it so finds, the case is referred to one of the appeals courts for a full retrial (but never to the court that originally gave the final verdict on the facts). Obviously, if another person has been convicted by another court for the same offense, that constitutes a typical *novum* and this scenario is specifically provided for in the Code of Criminal Procedure. In many other cases, however, the requirement that the Supreme Court in effect second guess the original decision—and therefore also the decision that the referral court will reach on retrial—may lead to debate on whether a case does meet the requirements for review.

The Vulnerability of Dutch Procedure

General Risk Factors

All of these specific rules and regulations on evidence, appeal, and review cannot disguise the fact that Dutch criminal process is, at its core, dependent on the integrity and ability of the professional participants to adhere to the professional ethics that govern the roles they play, and on the efficacy of hierarchical and judicial monitoring and control: the nonpartisan gathering of evidence by the prosecutor; his or her control of the police and their integrity in conducting a nonpartisan investigation; the ability of the defense lawyer to "assist" in the compilation of the dossier, which is in turn dependent on the nonpartisan professional attitude of the prosecutor; the impartiality and professional truth-finding activities of the court at trial—in short, the integrity of the system and its ability to police itself (Brants & Field, 1995; Jörg, Field, & Brants, 1995). The whole procedure lacks the normal safeguards found in adversarial systems and, indeed, in a number of inquisitorial countries. The defendant has no right to have a lawyer present during police investigations; it is essentially the prosecution that decides the content of the dossier; the court has the final word on when it has sufficient information to come to a verdict; and debate in open court based on autonomous defense rights is not regarded as essential for truth finding. Add to this the absence of any lay participation in the decision-making process, and it becomes clear that all of these aspects reflect the fundamental assumption that state officials will indeed conduct an independent and nonpartisan investigation into the truth and that the court will be able, on the basis of this, to arrive at a reliable and therefore legitimate verdict.

It would go beyond the scope of this chapter to examine the roots of the supreme confidence that the Dutch appear to place in their criminal justice system and its officials. Suffice it to say that, for a number of historical, legal, political, and cultural reasons, confidence has always existed, perhaps more so than in other inquisitorial systems (Brants & Field, 2000). Although they may differ in detail, all such systems share the need to trust the integrity of the representatives of state institutions and, logically, a greater and perhaps more unquestioning faith that the legal guarantees of the system, rather than the assertion of individual rights, will prevent the state in whatever guise from going off the rails. Without such faith the very basis of the system would be called into question. Paradoxically, this is precisely one of its strengths: In theory, the nonpartisan, state-appointed prosecutor has no interest in securing a conviction, only in presenting the court with the facts on which a true verdict can be based; the defendant is not dependent on the ability of the defense or on his or her own ability to pay for an able, motivated lawyer. In strength, however, there is weakness, and the specific weak spots in Dutch procedure that could render it prone to miscarriages of justice are found precisely at the points where integrity of professional roles and nonpartisanship form the essential guarantees for a fair and truthful verdict.

Again, it would go beyond the scope of this chapter to chart the changes in Dutch society and politics that have led to a gradual decline in trust in the state in general and the criminal justice system in particular. Undeniably, the last two decades of the twentieth century saw increasing criticism of decisions and policy in the criminal justice sphere and public dissatisfaction, as fear of crime and general feelings of insecurity led to a call for more and better crime control.[19] Demands for greater participation rights for victims, and complaints that criminals are treated too leniently, that they abuse due process rights in criminal procedure, that the police and prosecution service make too many mistakes, and that the courts are too slow and the process too bureaucratic—in short, a greater assertiveness among the public in demanding the right to a say in the way the criminal justice system operates—have all meant that the fundamental assumption that such matters are best left in the competent hands of the relevant professionals has been undermined. Criminal justice might still be exclusively in the hands of a small professional elite, but whether they can be trusted to know what is best is now open to question in the public debate. The Netherlands is not alone in Europe in this development and, as everywhere, media have played an important and increasingly critical role and provided a platform for the airing of public dissatisfaction.

The system has responded with new legislation designed to increase the efficiency of pretrial investigation and court procedure and the number of cases brought to court that end in convictions. This has undermined the guarantees of fair trial and truth finding, and therefore the guarantees against miscarriages of justice, that the inquisitorial system relies on, not least the practical commitment of the police and the prosecution service to nonpartisanship and the legal requirements that should ensure that courts convict only on the basis of reliable and corroborated evidence and are forced to commit their reasoning for the conviction to paper. While the powers of the prosecutor have increased dramatically, and those of the investigative magistrate (designed as an extra and impartial safeguard in criminal investigation) have been reduced, defense rights have in some cases been curtailed as a result of both legislation and case law, most especially concerning disclosure of the dossier before the ten-day limit and the right to have witnesses called.

In any event, the relative paucity of the scope of rights available to the defense in Dutch procedure stands in direct relation to the presumed proportionality that is needed to make sure that the prosecutor, and under his or her supervision the police, is both able and actually does attend to all of the interests involved, including those of the defendant. If the faith in the ability of those participants to contribute to fair truth finding is, for any reason, misplaced, the Dutch defense lawyer may be empty handed in terms of defense rights to challenge the prosecution case on issues, or at a point in the procedure where it could make a difference. Already the inquisitorial arrangements in Dutch procedure contain a number of risks for wrongful convictions, but examination of actual cases and recent research into the attitude—and worries—of judges show that these have now been compounded.[20]

In what follows, I focus on pretrial investigation and the court of first instance. I do not deal with appeals procedure, for the simple reason that what applies to cases judged in the first instance also applies to appeals. It should be noted, however, that while theory has it that appeal is a full retrial, appeals courts may, and do, under certain circumstances rely on evidence and witnesses originally produced, without reexamining them. The appeals system does work, and there are many instances of convictions by a district court being overturned. However, there are also cases in which the appeals court failed to spot a potential miscarriage and added its own wrongful verdict to the process.

The procedure of review by the Supreme Court in the case of new evidence is also not dealt with here. Suffice it to say that it exists, that it sometimes leads to an original verdict being overturned, and that one of the problems in obtaining a review is the definition of what constitutes new evidence, especially in the light of the requirement that the Supreme Court must also determine that it is this "new" evidence that, had it been known to the trier of fact at the time, would have led to an acquittal.

Verification as a Means of Truth Finding and Nonpartisan Investigation

From a scientific point of view, the presentation of two versions of events and the attempted falsification of the prosecution case that is characteristic of the adversarial system is surely a better way of arriving at the truth than the verification of the prosecutor's version by the judge—however many (limited) opportunities the defense may have had to influence the dossier pretrial and however nonpartisan the investigation. An inherent risk in procedures that rely on verification is not only that the police may be inclined to focus too much on one suspect once an apparently reasonable case can be made out against him or her—that is no different, perhaps even more likely in party-driven procedures—but that this will also lead to the police not looking for possible exculpatory facts, or, should they find such facts, attaching too little weight to them. This "mistake," or rather confirmation bias, will then be passed on to the other participants in the investigation: the prosecutor and, in the final event, the judge. There are few indications that the Dutch police wilfully ignore findings for the suspect, but many that they narrow their focus, seeking confirmation of existing suspicions and therefore undermining the first assumption of their inquisitorial role: an open mind and nonpartisanship.

Police violence during interrogations—although not a certain amount of pressure and modern psychologically informed interrogation techniques—is unusual in the Netherlands, notwithstanding the absence of video cameras, tape recorders, or the defense lawyer. Because these are absent, however, there is also no way of knowing what exactly was asked during an interrogation and whether it was skewed to produce confirmation of a suspicion. Written police reports, on which a court may place great reliance as (corroborating) evidence, are not verbatim and do not contain the questions asked; rather, reports of police findings are written in the form of a continuous statement by the suspect.[21] It is, of course, up to the prosecutor to recognize and correct police bias. However, he or she will rarely be present during the interrogation of a suspect—or a witness for that matter—while the investigating magistrate is no longer much involved in pretrial investigation as such. It is up to the defense to request that the magistrate undertake certain aspects of the investigation, such as looking into new aspects of the case or hearing witnesses overlooked or ignored by the prosecution and police, but that request can be refused. Moreover, limited access to the police files and burgeoning dossier at this stage in the proceedings means that the lawyer will not always know in which direction the investigation is going and on the basis of what.

It is stating the obvious that the pressure of public opinion in cases that generate a great deal of publicity and social unrest is likely to produce more mistakes of confirmation bias, as the police and prosecution service struggle to get the desired result of a conviction. Although Dutch legal culture traditionally abhors the influence of public opinion and regards it as unwarranted interference in the due process of justice, the recent developments outlined at the beginning of this section have rendered the whole criminal justice system highly sensitive to media coverage and demands for results. Within the prosecution service, where careers depend on performance, there have over the past decades been significant changes in the way that prosecutors see themselves. Traditionally, the magisterial, nonpartisan prosecutor, able and willing to make "judicial" decisions in the name of the common good, was the predominant role model (Van de Bunt, 1985; Nijboer, 1997). Gradually this has been replaced among a substantial number of prosecutors by the model of the crime fighter (Brants & Brants, 2002). This also produces confirmation bias at the prosecution level. Nonpartisanship should lead the prosecution to attempt to critically examine the police case, but they are more likely to seek to verify it and to base on it their decision to prosecute and the evidence they present through the dossier and in court.

Judges, on the basis of their professional group ethics, should be least inclined to take heed of public opinion and indeed refute suggestions that they could be influenced by it in any way. Recent research, however, indicates a certain amount of influence, not directly but through prosecution policy and the way prosecutors build and present their cases (de Keijser, Van de Bunt & Elffers, 2004). Moreover, judges are also subject to confirmation bias by the procedural arrangement that they are presented with the prosecution dossier and then conduct their own active search for the truth in court on the basis of their prior knowledge of the prosecution case. A defense lawyer may have a hard time convincing the court that the dossier is incomplete or one-sided. At the same time, a number of procedural rules regarding the way in which the court goes about its verification of the case compound this problem. Case law increasingly requires the defense to show substantial reasons why the court should question the accuracy of the dossier, or the legality or reliability of the evidence it contains. The defense in an inquisitorial system, however, does not have the defense rights or adversarial means and skills—and most importantly does not conduct its own pretrial investigation—to easily challenge the prosecutor's version of events.

It is even more difficult to challenge an expert opinion. Experts in a Dutch court are not considered to be witnesses and do not represent either prosecution or defense, but are simply experts to and appointed by the court, often from state laboratories or forensic institutions. They are regarded and see themselves as nonpartisan. Even if experts come from outside agencies, and are, for example doctors or academics with specific knowledge of certain aspects of the case, they will still be required and assumed to present their findings as nonpartisan and disinterested appointees to the court. Because of this assumption, courts are not quick to allow the defense the "luxury" of producing their own counter experts. Appointment to the court has the great advantage of releasing experts from any (unconscious) obligation they may feel toward one party. The main danger is not that they are inherently partisan, but that, precisely because they are regarded (and regard themselves) as nonpartisan, a court may place too great a reliance on their findings without there being an automatic response from an expert from the other side to contradict them.

For all of these reasons and more than ever, in Dutch court procedure allegations that exculpatory evidence exists but has not been investigated or disclosed, must be very strong to be admitted to judicial decision making. Notwithstanding the obvious intention of the Code of Criminal Procedure to guarantee as far as humanly possible that wrongful verdicts are never handed down, truth finding in court is not geared to discovering whether the evidence points beyond reasonable doubt to the guilt of the defendant, but whether the available evidence does not contradict the prosecutor's assertion that he or she is indeed guilty (Van Koppen & Schalken, 2004, p. 122). It is the same mechanism that undermines the presumed nonpartisan gathering of evidence during pretrial investigation. This does not entirely contradict the presumption of innocence, but it comes very close to it.

Rules of Evidence and Judicial Decision Making

Dutch rules of evidence and the requirement that judges decide in collaboration on issues of guilt and innocence together should operate to ensure that doubts as to the accuracy of the prosecution case are debated in chambers on the basis of reliable direct and corroborative evidence and that any weak aspects of the case are fully tested against possible other versions. This should be even more so, since judges may not convict unless they have been convinced by the evidence and must commit this decision and the reasons for it to paper while taking the chance that it may later be scrutinized on appeal. However, several inherent weaknesses in this system, both legal and psychological, can work to produce the opposite effect.

To begin with, the threads of verification and confirmation bias that could have overshadowed the assumed procedural guarantees and that run through the whole procedure come together at the end in the information on which the panel of judges now embarks on its deliberations. The negative system of evidence and legal requirements as to sorts and amount of evidence necessary to convict are meant to ensure that (possibly false) confessions, the statement of a single (possibly biased or untruthful) witness or of a single expert may never lead to a conviction unless there is corroboration of guilt from an independent source, and requirements of due process mean that the defendant must have had the opportunity to challenge the evidence brought against him or her. In reality, however, it is possible to convict on two sources of evidence—admittedly independent—although the conviction nevertheless rests on one witness, one expert, or a confession. It is perfectly legal, for example, to base a conviction on the defendant's confession to the police (later retracted) that she forged a check and on two written police reports: the first that the check was cashed, the second that a handwriting expert has ascertained that the writing on the check did not belong to the owner of the checks (although he did not ascertain that it was the defendant's handwriting).[22]

The rules of evidence suggest that judges look first at the evidence and then decide whether they find it convincing. It is, however, impossible to escape the conclusion that, if their mind is already made up by the information they themselves consider sufficient during trial—itself based on mainly the prosecution dossier—they will then simply look for the legally permissible forms of confirmation of what they think.[23] This psychological process is compounded by the fact that, in their written reasoning, the court need not discuss all available evidence and any residual doubt there may have been,[24] but is merely required to enumerate the legally permissible sorts of evidence on which the decision is based. Unanimity among the panel members is not necessary.

In case law, exceedingly summary reasoning has long been accepted. The Supreme Court does require that the court explicitly refute any defenses that have been raised as to the reliability of expert testimony or any defenses that appear to throw a different light on the conclusion that could be reached on the basis of the evidence the judges are using. Failure to do so could invalidate the verdict. In practice, such defenses are raised, but, as we have seen, the inquisitorial defense lawyer is ill equipped to substantiate such doubts and introduce (or rather, in this context, have introduced) other, new evidence during trial. Moreover, new legislation, passed to increase the efficiency of the criminal courts, no longer requires that verdicts automatically include the full reasoning of the court. This is only added if the defendant lodges an appeal.

Expert testimony is a separate problem that, in some ways is no different from problems that may occur in other systems of criminal procedure. We have already seen that judges may be inclined to give too much weight to expert testimony and forensic evidence (especially true of DNA). It is especially problematic that, when it comes to deliberating, they will usually have the evidence of only one expert at their disposal. It is not impossible that they may have misunderstood the weight of that evidence. Neither they themselves nor the defense lawyer are usually knowledgeable enough to ask the relevant scientific questions at trial and the routine absence of an expert hired by the defense to refute the prosecution's assertions as to the meaning and importance of forensic evidence renders the court dependent on its own (often amateur) evaluation of it. Moreover, if the defense has requested counter expertise during trial and been refused because the court considered this unnecessary, it is unlikely that it will later doubt the opinion of the expert it first considered sufficient. Again, recent research points to such problems occurring (Njboer, Malsch & Sennef, 1999).

There is also the aspect in which the Dutch system places the most faith: the career judiciary that trains its judges to be impartial and open-minded, so that it is the rationality of the legally trained mind and the experience of highly qualified practitioners that guides judicial decision making, and not any irrational prejudice that may color the verdict of the inexperienced layman, who is probably also ignorant of the finer points of law. There is a case to be made for both professional judges and lay tribunals. However, be that as it may, one of the more troubling aspects of a career judiciary is that experience easily becomes routine, that panels of judges feel no need to explain to each other what the strength or weakness of the case is, as all will understand it and that, in general a process of groupthink will govern deliberations. This is especially true of younger judges, who are quickly socialized into such a process and may well find out that too independent a frame of mind is not appreciated.[25]

A Highly Publicized Illustration

Recently, one of the "dubious cases" (see Van Koppen, 2003a) was revealed as a definite miscarriage of justice: After another man had been convicted and spent four years (of an eighteen-year sentence) in prison, the actual perpetrator confessed and DNA traces were found to match his. Pending review by the Supreme Court, the convicted man was released provisionally and has now been formally acquitted. The case is a classic example of just how vulnerable the Dutch inquisitorial system is when it fails to live up to its own guarantees.

On June 22, 2000, a boy (eleven years old) and a girl (ten years old) were (sexually) assaulted by a man in the bushes of a park in the town of Schiedam.[26] The girl was strangled and the was boy seriously injured. He attracted the attention of passersby, one of whom, Kees B, called the police and was later to become the chief suspect. Although the boy gave a description of the attacker that did not fit B, and although other witness statements were contradictory, the police soon focused on B as the suspect: He had been in the park at the time and, most important, was a known pedophile. Under a certain amount of pressure during the police interrogation (although this was later not found to be in any way inadmissible pressure), Kees B confessed. He retracted the confession two days later, but according to the rules of evidence, it could still be used in court. The other evidence was weak and somewhat contradictory, yet B was convicted by the District Court in Rotterdam in May 2001 and on appeal by the Appeal Court in The Hague in March 2002. In 2003, the Supreme Court refused B's petition for cassation and in 2004 dismissed his request for review.

All of this is bad enough: Courts in four instances failed to spot that anything was amiss and convicted on evidence that was flawed enough to arouse serious doubts among academics studying the case. Even worse, however, was that there had been traces of DNA found on the girl's body and on the murder weapon that did not match B's DNA and were from a third unknown person. Because of this, a number of scientists at the state forensic laboratory had serious doubts about B's guilt and they took the unprecedented step of twice speaking to both the district and the appeal prosecutors before their report was compiled. Their doubts, however, did not find their way into the final version of the report and were not communicated by either expert witnesses or prosecution service to the courts or the defense team. Although the latter knew that unidentified DNA had been found on the body, they were not told it had also been on the murder weapon.

In this case, every single guarantee that should have been in place failed to operate. The police piled mistake on mistake in the belief they had their man, pressuring him to confess (although what was said exactly will never be known, the only source being the police transcript) and disregarding possible evidence in his favor to the point of exerting what was later described as inadmissible and intolerable pressure on a young and traumatized witness to withdraw a statement that undermined the police case: The police, backed up by a child psychologist, had subjected the boy victim to lengthy and extremely hard interrogation to make him admit that the description of his attacker was a fabrication. He stuck to his statement, but neither the prosecution nor the court took it seriously. The prosecutor at the District Court ignored anything that pointed to the suspect's innocence, including the doubts of the forensic scientists. The prosecutor at the Appeal Court did have doubts, but finally ignored them and communicated nothing of them to the court. The forensic scientists somehow identified enough with the prosecution to leave their doubts out of the report; what was said to persuade them during their two conversations with the prosecution is not known, except that the district prosecutor did tell them it was important to make sure that "the defense cannot run away with this DNA-business."

Two triers of fact were able to scrape together enough proof to convict, though only by disregarding contradictory evidence (such as an alibi that gave B practically no time to commit the crime, but that was explained away—although not very convincingly—by the prosecutor). The fact that unidentified DNA was found on the girl's body was also explained away: Anyone who had been in contact with her could have left it; the fact that B's DNA was not found was presented by the prosecution as proof of his guilt ("he had been careful not to leave evidence behind") rather than his innocence, and the court failed to investigate further. The defense lawyer, ignorant of the fact that only unknown DNA had been found on the murder weapon and with no right to be shown the full results of the forensic institute's tests other than what found its way into the final report, and no right of cross-examination, could do little more than argue the case on the face of it in court. Forensic experts who testified were never asked about doubts, because neither court nor defense knew about them (and the court did not think to question the final report).

Eventually, although a confession is not enough under Dutch law to convict and despite the fact that it had been retracted, B's confession weighed heavily against him. The boy victim's description of his attacker was dismissed as not credible, and the discrepancies between the prosecutor's time schedule and B's alibi were reasoned away. Confirmation bias set in, nonpartisanship went by the board, the rules of evidence allowed courts to scrape together a conviction without actively questioning the prosecution case, and defense lawyers depended in vain on the integrity of prosecutors to provide the information that would allow them to assert defense rights. Against the background of the changing attitude of Dutch prosecutors, changes in the law that make convictions easier and have undermined defense rights, and a case in which there was considerable public alarm and pressure on the police to get results, this was a miscarriage waiting to happen.

The report commissioned by the Public Prosecution Service (see note 1) was ready in August 2005 and revealed all of these problems. At what point this would have become public knowledge (if ever) is unclear. However, an investigation by television journalists added an extra detail: While B was in prison, his case had been used by scientists from the forensic institute during presentations to the police and prosecution service to show how DNA evidence demonstrated the convicted man's innocence. Although at least 200 police officers and prosecutors had attended these sessions, only one had spoken out: After getting no response from his superiors, this police officer had approached the media and set in motion a lengthy and detailed journalistic investigation. He was fired for his pains. As a result of the program that was broadcast in September, a considerable public debate has ensued about the state of Dutch justice and especially the Prosecution Service. Parliament demanded answers from the Minister of Justice, but eventually accepted his version of events: No one had acted intentionally but "serious mistakes" had been made. It remains to be seen what the eventual result will be and whether structural improvements will be made to the system. The Minister of Justice rejected calls for an independent commission along the lines of the Criminal Cases Review Commission for England and Wales. Instead, a commission under the prosecution service, although with an independent chairman and a number of independent members, has been installed to look into other possible miscarriages. Its work will come up for review after two years. The commission itself is expect to push for complete independence from the prosecution service.

Conclusion

This chapter began with the contention that not only is no one system is better than the other, but also that the inherent strengths of either the adversary or the inquisitorial system become their inherent weaknesses when underlying assumptions as to the best way to guarantee truth finding in a fair trial do not, or no longer, hold true. Certain types of procedure are prone to certain errors and the Achilles heel of Dutch procedure seems to be twofold.

First, truth finding is dependent on nonpartisan pretrial investigation by the police under the supervision of the prosecutor. Both are, in complex and highly publicized cases especially, subject to considerable pressure from the media to deliver the goods (i.e., a conviction). In general, public dissatisfaction with their perceived inability to provide security on the streets and to solve and bring to trial "enough" criminals has led to more external and internal pressure and to a prosecutorial role model that has more of the partisan, adversary crime fighter, than the nonpartisan inquisitorial "magistrate." However, a focus on delivering convictions is, in an inquisitorial setting, not their job: They are supposed to deliver the building bricks for truth finding in court, which should preclude suspect-oriented investigations conducted and shaped by confirmation bias. At this stage of the investigation, which is the stage at which the essential contours of what will become the truth at trial are shaped, there is only the prosecution case; inquisitorial defense lawyers have neither the rights nor the training and the professional attitude that would allow them to undertake independent investigation. The police and the prosecution service in the Netherlands do not set out to be deliberately partisan, to focus on one suspect, and to ignore indications that they may have the wrong man. However, the very arrangements in inquisitorial pretrial procedure that should produce even-handed, open-minded investigation allow police and prosecution to behave in what is, in that inquisitorial setting, a nonprofessional way.

The second major weakness is again in theory a major strength: the active, truth-finding, professional court, that is not dependent on what parties put forward or on their skill in cross-examination, but can control and conduct its own investigation at trial, can have witnesses appear, can order the prosecution to produce documents, and can examine witnesses at length. A court must then deliberate on the evidence but is curtailed by legal rules as to what it may use, and must subsequently give written reasons for its decision. However, courts, too, become victims of confirmation bias and professionalism has its darker sides in peer solidarity and routine. All are possible because of the system within which the court operates: rules of evidence that have been slackened under case law and in any event allow evidence to be cherry-picked to suit a preconceived decision, rather than the other way around; rules on reasoned decisions that reflect rather than prevent this; and most of all the lack of adversary debate at trial, which would force judges to listen to the other side of the story and to consider possible alternatives to the defendant's guilt.

Add to this the subtle pressure of public opinion and we have a heady mix of factors that render Dutch criminal procedure more vulnerable to miscarriages of justice than it seems at first sight. That they are, as far as we can tell, few and far between is a testimony to the inquisitorial system: It works, usually. However, there is one other major weakness: The trust that the professionals of the system enjoy, be they police officers, prosecutors, or judges, and that is reflected in the procedural rules and professional legal culture of the Netherlands, has, until very recently, prevented them from considering their own vulnerability to get it wrong. Only with greater awareness, not so much of their own fallibility but of that of the system itself, will the civil servants who are the mainstay of justice in the Dutch inquisitorial system be able to prevent, as far as humanly possible, the conviction of the innocent.

Notes

1. See, for example, Schalken (1992) and Schuyt (1992).

2. In one such case (in 2002), the defendants were convicted and spent seven years in prison. They were eventually acquitted (after their release), but only after two retrials for one defendant and three for the other. One journalist who, together with a retired police chief, spent years mobilizing public opinion, called it the miscarriage of the century, but there is still doubt within the legal community. In another case (in 2004), the defendant was convicted for a second time after a retrial, although some journalists and lawyers are still not convinced of his guilt. In yet another, a pressure group is pushing for a retrial through a Web site and the media. These cases, and many more can be found on the Internet. See, for example, http://www2.rnw.nl/rnw/nl/achtergronden/nederland/putten020424.html, http://www.recht.nl/strafrecht/dossiers/moord, and www.dickmoetvrij.com. See also Van Koppen (2003a).

3. Fourth European Society of Criminology Conference, Amsterdam, August 26, 2004.

4. See Chapter 3 by Schiffer and Champod regarding these issues.

5. It is possible to determine the number of cases that are admitted to a review procedure after the verdict has become definite. However, these tell us nothing about wrongful convictions, as most such cases are concerned with inequalities in sentencing, and the statistics do not make any distinction between the types of issue that led to the review.

6. One of the first attempts at quantifying wrongful convictions, later replicated in other studies, was by Huff, Rattner, and Sagarin (1986). In their later work (Huff, Rattner, & Sagarin, 1996), they also arrive at a figure of some tenths of a percent of all convictions, which seems to hold true for most, if not all, Western countries (always depending, of course, on how the concept of wrongful conviction is defined).

7. For a classic description of the features of inquisitorial process that distinguish it from the adversarial, see Damaška (1986). For the specific features of Dutch criminal procedure in relation to its legal cultural tradition, see Brants and Field (2000).

8. There is no full English translation of the Dutch Code of Criminal Procedure. Excerpts, for example, concerning the hearing of witnesses and new rights for victims, are available on the Internet and can be found by a simple Google search.

9. At the beginning of the nineteenth century, the Netherlands was occupied by French forces led by Napoleon Bonaparte. The administrative contours of the court system then established still exist along much the same lines today.

10. Conditions of appointment of judges, their tasks, the administrative division of courts, and so on, can be found in the Wet op de Rechterlijke Organisatie (Law on the Organization of the Judiciary).

11. This exceedingly summarized description of Dutch criminal procedure is based on a number of sources in Dutch, the most important of which is the extensive handbook by Corstens (2002). For overviews in English, see Swart (1993), Nijboer (1999), and Tak (2003).

12. When the current Code of Criminal Procedure was introduced in 1926, it specifically required that all witnesses be heard in court and ruled hearsay testimony out. In a landmark judgment not even a year later, the Dutch Supreme Court overturned this legal requirement and allowed hearsay testimony as legal evidence (HR: 20 December 1926, NJ 1927, 85).

13. See, for the new rules on witnesses, articles 263/264 and 287/288 CCP, and for the special procedure for the hearing of threatened witnesses anonymously, article 226a and following CCP.

14. *Kostovski v. The Netherlands* (11454/85) [1989] ECHR 20 (20 November 1989); *Van Mechelen and others v. The Netherlands* (21363/93) [1997] ECHR 22 (23 April 1997).

15. It could of course be argued—although the ECHR does not accept this—that the fact that the identity of a witness remains unknown to the defense (and the court) but not the prosecutor, is in itself an infringement of the principle of internal transparency, and therefore undermines the fairness of the trial.

16. Cases can be settled out of court, but—as yet, there is a legislative change in the making—such settlements, known as *transactions,* are seen as agreements under civil law and not as punishment. Because of this, they cannot technically be regarded as convictions and any settlement with an innocent person is not therefore a wrongful conviction. It should, however, be noted that, as in plea bargaining, a person may be induced to settle and keep the case out of court for many reasons other than the fact that he or she is guilty.

17. Such reports may contain firsthand evidence based on the officer's own experience (e.g., that he or she found drugs in the defendant's possession), but may also be the transcript (not verbatim) of an interrogation of a witness (i.e., hearsay).

18. At present, this course of action is not open to the prosecutor after an acquittal: The prosecution service itself may apply to the Supreme Court for clarification of the law, but without detriment to the person acquitted. New legislation will mean that in the future cassation will also be possible after an acquittal, which could result in its being overturned.

19. For an insightful overview of the change that has taken place in the discourse on criminal justice over the past years, see Pakes (2004).

20. See Van Koppen and Schalken (2004) for an overview of six recent "dubious" cases that well illustrate the vulnerable points of the Dutch criminal process outlined later.

21. The idea that the defense should be present during police interrogations has been floated many times by both legal scholars and the Bar Association, but has never made it into the CCP. A recent study again refuted the right to have a lawyer present at such times because this would hamper the police in their search for the truth, but did advocate the use of tape recorders and video cameras (Groenhuijsen & Knigge, 2002).

22. See Van Koppen and Schalken (2004) on a murder case, where the evidence was construed in just such a fashion.

23. It is not easy to research what actually goes on in chambers when judges debate a case. Faith in the judiciary, needed to uphold the legitimacy of the system, dictates that such debates remain secret. The judiciary, it is assumed, must speak with one voice: Dissenting opinions are unknown in the Netherlands and judges always refuse to reveal their discussions in chambers.

24. That is, for example, the case under German law.

25. See de Keijser et al. (2004, pp. 36–38), where they discuss panel interviews with judges on the procedure during deliberations.

26. The facts are taken from the official report commissioned in January 2005 by the Prosecution Service after it became apparent that someone else was most probably the perpetrator. The case was investigated by one of the appeal prosecutors at the Appeal Court in Amsterdam, seconded by a law professor and an ex-police chief. The full report is available on the prosecution Web site at www.om.nl.

References

Brants, C. H., & Brants, K. (2002). Vertrouwen en Achterdocht: de Driehoeksrelatie Justitie, Media, Publiek [Trust and Suspicion: the triangular relationship between justice, the media and the public]. *Justitiële Verkenningen, 6*, 8–28.

Brants, C. H., & Field, S. F. (1995). *Participation rights and proactive policing: Convergence and drift in European criminal process.* Pre-advies voor de Nederlandse Vereniging van Rechtsvergelijking [Advisory to the Dutch Society of Comparative Criminal Law]. Deventer, NL: Kluwer.

Brants, C. H., & Field, S. F. (2000). Political cultures and procedural traditions. In D. Nelken (Ed.), *Contrasting criminal justice: Getting from here to there* (pp. 77–107). Aldershot, UK: Ashgate.

Corstens, G. J. M. (2002). *Het Nederlands Strafprocesrecht* (4th ed.). Deventer: Kluwer.

Crombag, H. F. M., van Koppen, P. J., & Wagenaar, W. A. (1994). *Dubieuze Zaken: De Psychologie van Strafrechtelijk Bewijs* [Dubious Cases: The Psychology of Criminal Evidence] (2nd rev. ed.). Amsterdam: Contact.

Damaška, M. (1986). Evidentiary barriers to conviction and two models of criminal procedure: A comparative approach. *University of Pennsylvania Law Review, 121,* 506–589.

Damaška, M. (1986). *The faces of justice and state authority: A comparative approach to the legal process.* New Haven, CT: Yale University Press.

de Keijser, J. W., van de Bunt, H. G., & Elffers, H. (2004). Strafrechters over Maatschappelijke Druk, Responsiviteit en de Kloof tussen Rechter en Samenleving [Judges on Social pressure, Responsivity and the Gap between the Courts and Society]. In J. W. de Keijser & H. Elffers (Eds.), *Het Maatschappelijk Oordeel van de Strafrechter. De Wisselwerking tussen Rechter en Samenleving* (pp. 21–52). The Hague, Netherlands: Boom Juridische uitgevers.

Groenhuijsen, M. S., & Knigge, G. (2002). *Dwangmiddelen en Rechtsmiddelen. Derde Interimrapport Onderzoeksproject Strafvordering 2001* [Coercive Measures and Legal Remedies. Third Interim Report Research Project Criminal Procedure 2001]. Deventer, NL: Kluwer.

Huff, C. R., Rattner, A., & Sagarin, E. (1986). Guilty until proven innocent: Wrongful conviction and public policy. *Crime and Delinquency, 32,* 518–544.

Huff, C. R., Rattner, A., & Sagarin, E. (1996). *Convicted but innocent: Wrongful conviction and public policy.* Thousand Oaks, CA: Sage.

Jörg, N., Field, S., & Brants, C. (1995). Are inquisitorial and adversarial systems converging? In C. Harding, P. Fennell, N. Jörg, & B. Swart, *Criminal justice in Europe* (pp. 41–56). Oxford, UK: Clarendon.

Nijboer, J. F. (1997). The dynamics of a role: Public prosecutors in the Netherlands. *Northern Ireland Legal Quarterly, 48,* 378–388.

Nijboer, J. F. (1999). Criminal justice system. In J. Chorus, P. Gerver, E. Hondius, & A. Koekkoek (Eds.), *Introduction to Dutch law* (3rd ed., pp. 383–432). Deventer, NL: Kluwer Law International.

Nijboer, J. F., Malsch, M., & Sennef, A. (1999). Introduction. In M. Malsch & J. F. Nijboer (Eds.), *Complex cases: Perspectives on the Netherlands criminal justice system* (pp. 3–10). Amsterdam: Thela Thesis.

Pakes, F. (2004). The politics of discontent: The emergence of a new criminal discourse in the Netherlands. *Howard Journal, 43*(3), 284–298.

Schalken, T. (1992). *Nederlands Juristenblad* [Judges Should be Less Decent. An Answer to the Current Criticism of Dutch Criminal Justice], *28,* 889–891.

Schuyt, C. J. M. (1992). Het Juridische en het Sociaal-Wetenschappelijk Bewijs [Legal and Social-scientific Proof]. *Delikt & Delinkwent, 22,* 655–666.

Swart, A. H. J. (1993). The Netherlands. In C. van den Wyngaert (Ed.), *Criminal procedure systems in the European community* (pp. 279–316). London: Butterworths.

Tak, P. J. P. (2003). *The Dutch criminal justice system: Organisation and operation* (2nd rev. ed.). The Hague, Netherlands: Boom Juridische uitgevers.

Van de Bunt, H. G. (1985).*Officieren van Jsutitie, Verslag van een Participerend Observatieonderzoek* [Public Prosecutors, Report of a Participating Observation Project]. Zwolle, Netherlands: W. E. J. Tjeenk Willink.

Van Koppen, P. J. (2003a). *De Schiedammer Parkmoord: Een Rechtspsychologische Reconstructie.* Nijmegen, Netherlands: Ars Aequi Libri.

Van Koppen, P. J. (2003b). *Verankering van Rechtspraak. Over de Wisselwerking tussen Burger, Politie, Justitie en Rechter.* Deventer: Kluwer.

Van Koppen, P. J., Hessing, D. J., & Crombag, H. P. M. (1992). *Het Hart van de Zaak— Psychologie van Het Recht.* Gouda Quint.

Van Koppen, P. J., & Schalken, T. M. (2004). Rechterlijke Denkpatronen als Valkuilen: Over zes Grote Zaken en Derzelver Bewijs. In J. W. de Keijser & H. Elffers (Eds.), *Het Maatschappelijk Oordeel van de Strafrechter. De Wisselwerking tussen Rechter en Samenleving* (pp. 85–132). The Hague, Netherlands: Boom Juridische uitgevers.

10

CRIMINAL JUSTICE AND MISCARRIAGES OF JUSTICE IN ENGLAND AND WALES

~

CLIVE WALKER AND CAROLE McCARTNEY

One expects in a fair and effective criminal justice system that evidence of guilt will be both overwhelming and clearly more convincing than the defendant's claim to innocence. However, mistakes are inevitable. Memories are fragile and may be masked by emotion or even open to manipulation. In addition, strong inducements encourage both prosecution and defense to be selective in their versions of reality. How far should a criminal justice system be alert to these possibilities of error, and how should it respond?

The answer to the first question is that the values of liberty and justice demand that a very high priority be given to ensuring that state coercive powers are exercised only in justified circumstances. Ultimately, the imposition of official sanctions, such as imprisonment or the imposition of a fine must be justifiable to the individual affected and must also be acceptable within the norms of society. The result is that a special premium is placed on the values of liberty and justice—more so than on the righting of a criminal wrong: "It is better that ten guilty persons escape than that one innocent suffer."[1]

In answer to the second question, of how a criminal justice system should respond to the possibility of error, many of the safeguards must reside within the legal rules and the internal working cultures fostered by training and management within institutions such as the police, prosecution, forensic science, judiciary, and advocates. Of further relevance are the appeal courts, which provide an outlet for certain types of doubt and grievance to be addressed.[2] Yet, whatever care is expended at each stage of the criminal justice process,

the possibility of error remains. This possibility then demands effective processes for remedying error.

In this chapter we first consider a definition and typology of miscarriages
of justice and then the mechanisms in place to respond to residual error and
their performance. We conclude that there remains a need for a concerted
effort on the part of researchers of criminal justice not only to assist in the
campaign to raise the public profile of miscarriages of justice, but also to
impact effectively upon reform of the criminal justice process in England and
Wales to facilitate not only the overturning (and proper compensation for)
wrongful convictions but also their prevention.[3]

Criminal Process in England and Wales

The perception that the criminal process starts with an arrest and ends in a
trial and conviction is misguided at best. The majority of crimes are never
detected, and those suspects who are arrested are either released with no further action taken, cautioned, or appear briefly before magistrates who accept
a guilty plea in return for a reduced sentence. For example, in England and
Wales in 2003 and 2004,[4] the police recorded 5.9 million crimes (of an estimated 11.6 million said to have occurred by victims), of which just under 1.4
million were "detected."[5] Of these, just under a quarter resulted in an "administrative sanction" (i.e., a caution or fixed penalty) or no further action. In the
year ending June 2004, the Crown Prosecution Service prosecuted just 96,000
cases in the Crown Court, and over 1.5 million in the magistrates' courts.[6] Of
those prosecuted in the magistrates' courts in 2003–2004 (where 98 percent
of cases are heard), 63 percent entered a guilty plea. In the Crown Court,
just under three-quarters of all cases ended in a conviction with 61 percent
of defendants pleading guilty to at least some charges. Such statistics belie
popular notions of criminal justice, where a crime prompts an arrest and a
contested jury trial.

In addition to such common misconceptions, while the criminal process
in England and Wales remains adversarial overall, the propagation of inquisitorial principles is increasing, with ever greater reliance on expert witnesses
and forensic evidence during investigations and trials. An important step in
this direction was taken in the shape of the Criminal Justice and Public Order
Act 1994, which, after many years of dispute on the issue, allowed potential penalties for the failure to answer police questions and failure to testify at trial.[7] More recent reforms in the Criminal Justice Act 2003 were said
to aim to achieve, "a fair balance between the rights of the prosecution and
defence."[8] The Act included the curtailment of jury trials, radical changes
to the evidential rules on hearsay, bad character, and previous convictions,

as well as the imposition by police of bail conditions before charging. Other legislative changes have seen an increase in prosecutorial rights of appeal, including provision for dealing with "tainted acquittals" by section 54 of the Criminal Procedure and Investigations Act 1996,[9] and Part X of the Criminal Justice Act 2003 removed double jeopardy protection for some defendants. Both Acts also introduced new disclosure regimes, as well as protocols on the timing of pleas. The 1996 Act introduces mandatory defense disclosure, a direct response to accusations of "ambush" defenses (the presentation of defenses at court previously undisclosed or intimated, with the prosecution unable to respond effectively). In addition, the Criminal Justice Act 2003, Part V, demands the disclosure of all expert reports sought by the defense, whether used or not.

Laws concerning investigation, pretrial, and trial processes have thus been modified in recent years, in attempts to improve on the perceived poor record of conviction of guilty defendants, with the adversarial system increasingly adopting "the *instruments* of inquisitorial investigation."[10] The rhetoric is firmly against individual protection, signaled politically by then Home Secretary, Michael Howard, in his speech to the Conservative Party conference in October 1993:[11] "In the last 30 years the balance in the criminal justice system has been tilted too far in favor of the criminal and against the protection of the public. The time has come to put that right."

Yet, the trend toward "narrowing the justice gap"[12] has increased the risk that the aversion to the conviction of the innocent receives less attention. At the same time, as there is argument concerning the "narrowly conceived" and "legalistic" nature of present perspectives on miscarriage of justice,[13] the processes to remedy wrongful convictions are coming under increasing pressure and criminal justice reform appears no longer to be informed by previously overturned convictions.

Residual Error

Meanings and Typology

A *miscarriage* means literally a failure to reach an intended destination or goal. A miscarriage of justice is therefore, *mutatis mutandis*, a failure to attain the desired end result of justice. Justice is about distributions, according persons their fair shares and treatment. As far as the impact of the criminal justice system is concerned, one could argue that fair treatment in the dispensation of criminal justice in a liberal, democratic society means that the state should treat individuals with equal respect for their rights and for the rights of others.[14] It does not follow that individual rights must always be treated as absolute, for it is rationally coherent to accept limitations for the sake of preserving the rights of others or competing rights. The primacy of individual autonomy and rights is central to the well-known due process model outlined by Packer,[15] which recognizes that the possibility of human fallibility and error can thereby yield grave injustice, as when the system convicts the innocent or even convicts without respecting procedural rights. As already indicated, the due process model does not underpin much of the daily operation of the English criminal justice system, especially those parts of the system that involve routinized and unsupervised encounters between police and citizen. Yet, it should certainly be to the fore when those encounters become more formalized and more is at stake in terms of rights, such as detention in a police station or when the suspect becomes formally charged, especially if liberty is at stake. This implies a strong duty on the part of the state to be vigilant about miscarriages and to be willing to rectify them, even if at some cost to aggregate (collective) welfare.

One possible definition of "miscarriage" in the context of criminal justice is one that reflects an individualistic rights-based approach to miscarriages of justice. A miscarriage occurs whenever suspects or defendants or convicts are treated by the state in breach of their rights, whether because of, first, deficient processes; second, the laws that are applied to them; or third, because there is no factual justification for the applied treatment or punishment; fourth, whenever suspects or defendants or convicts are treated adversely by the state to a disproportionate extent in comparison with the need to protect the rights of others; fifth, whenever the rights of others are not effectively or proportionately protected or vindicated by state action against wrongdoers; or, sixth, by state law itself. Each of these six categories is illustrated next.

1. The treatment of individuals in breach of their rights because of unfair processes will occur when individuals are subjected to arrest or detention without due cause or to unfair treatment to procure confessions. As well as these breaches of rights perpetrated by the police, a breach may occur at the trial stage. Failures can arise through biased judges, perverse juries, and the suppression or mishandling of evidence. A defendant may also be failed by lawyers through inadequate preparation or performance. Some observers attempt to distinguish between those who are really "innocent" and the wrongfully convicted, those who are acquitted "on a technicality." However, the emphasis here is on the breach of rights, and rights to due process have central importance in assuring righteous treatment Accordingly, even a person who has in fact and with intent committed a crime could be said to have suffered a miscarriage if convicted by processes that did not respect basic rights.

2. Another conceivable category of persons suffering a miscarriage because of a denial of their rights concerns those who fall afoul of laws that are inherently unjust rather than unjustly applied. In a responsive, liberal democracy, such failures of the system should be few and far between. However, claims along these lines have been made by persons convicted of failure to pay taxes to finance nuclear weapons or of homosexual activities by adults.

3. The third category of miscarriage occurs where there is no factual justification for the treatment or punishment. A conviction—perhaps because of mistaken identity—of a person who is in fact innocent would obviously fall into this category of breach of rights (ultimately of humanity and liberty) and indeed might be defined as a core case. Persons enjoy a "profound right not to be convicted of crimes of which they are innocent."[16]

4. Illustrations of miscarriages resulting from disproportionate treatment in terms of rights might include the granting of arrest or extensive search powers in respect to trivial antisocial conduct or excessively harsh charges or sentences. Similarly, the imposition of conditions during punishment that serve little purpose other than degradation (as opposed to deterrence or the objectives of restorative justice) and therefore do not ultimately bolster respect for rights should be treated as a miscarriage of justice.

5. The fifth type of miscarriage, a failure to protect and vindicate the rights of potential or actual victims, can arise in various ways. For example, a lack of police officers to guard against violent attackers could be a breach of rights.[17] A refusal to prosecute particular types of suspects, whether through intimidation, racial bias, or political manipulation or corruption, may also be viewed as a miscarriage.[18] A failure to vindicate rights may equally occur when a jury perversely refuses to convict an individual, through intimidation or bias. As well as substantive outcomes, victims may also be treated unjustly by the process, a point that is often raised in relation to rape survivors, especially those who have to face the cross-examination of their alleged assailants or are required to produce corroboration.[19]

6. A sixth type of miscarriage is the existence and application of laws that are inherently unfair to victims. To continue the theme raised in the last category, the treatment of the sexual history of rape survivors has raised concerns, although the difficulty of balancing fairness to the accused is acute, and the rights of the accused have tended to be treated as more important. One might offer two reasons for this priority: that the loss of rights tends to be more acute in the case of the suspect or convict in the sense that, for example,

liberty is immediately threatened; second, the loss of rights is entirely a matter of state responsibility, whereas the victim has suffered primarily through the actions of third parties.

These six categories might be termed direct miscarriages. In addition, we can derive from their infliction a seventh, indirect miscarriage that affects the community as a whole. A conviction arising from deceit or illegalities is corrosive of the state's claims to legitimacy on the basis of its criminal justice system's values such as respect for individual rights. In this way, the "moral integrity of the criminal process" suffers harm.[20] Moreover, there may be practical detriment in terms of diminished confidence in the forces of law and order, leading to fewer active citizens aiding the police and fewer jurors willing to convict even the blatantly "guilty." It is arguable that this indirect form of miscarriage can exist independently as well as contingently.

Notable Cases

We do not intend in this chapter to give a full chronology of *causes célèbres* around which discussions about miscarriages of justice have taken place in England and Wales. However, a few examples that have shaped the current agendas and laws regarding miscarriages of justice illustrate some of the categories already listed and also explain why reforms have occurred.[21]

1. The Guildford 4 (Paul Hill, Carole Richardson, Gerard Conlon, and Patrick Armstrong) were convicted of pub bombings on behalf of the Irish Republican Army (IRA) in Guildford and Woolwich.[22] An appeal against conviction failed in 1977 despite the fact that other IRA defendants awaiting trial had by then claimed responsibility. However, other new evidence was eventually amassed (including alibis and medical conditions) that convinced the Home Secretary to order further investigations and to refer the case back to the Court of Appeal. Once it was discovered that detectives in the Surrey Police involved in the case had fabricated statements (especially of Armstrong) and suppressed possible exculpatory evidence, the Director of Public Prosecutions (DPP) decided not to contest the convictions, which were quashed in 1989. This outcome immediately prompted reconsideration of the *Maguire 7* case.[23] Suspicion first fell on the Maguire household when Gerard Conlon (one of the Guildford 4) made statements to the police that his aunt, Anne Maguire, had taught him to manufacture bombs. The police raided her house, and convictions were obtained mainly on the basis of forensic tests that were said to show traces of nitroglycerine. The Court of Appeal, on a reference back in 1990,[24] grudgingly overturned the convictions

because of the possibility that third parties had left the traces in the house and so caused innocent contamination (the nondisclosure of evidence was also a material irregularity in the case). However, the May Inquiry's Interim and Second Reports on the Maguire case more realistically cast doubt on whether the tests used could in any event be taken to be conclusive proof of the knowing handling of explosives.[25]

2. The next blow to confidence in the criminal justice system was the *Birmingham 6* case in 1991.[26] The six (Patrick Hill, Gerry Hunter, Richard McIlkenny, Billy Power, Johnny Walker, and Hughie Callaghan) had been convicted along with three others of bombings in two Birmingham pubs in 1974. The attacks had caused the most deaths of any IRA incident in Britain and were the signal for the passage of the Prevention of Terrorism Acts. The prosecution evidence rested on three legs: confessions that the defendants claimed had been beaten out of them; forensic tests that the defendants claimed were inherently unreliable and had been performed negligently by Dr. Skuse (the forensic scientist employed by the police to examine the material); and highly circumstantial evidence, such as links to known Republicans, and the movements and demeanor of the defendants. After being refused leave to appeal in 1976, there was a referral back to the Court of Appeal in 1988. The Court was then not persuaded, but further revelations about the police fabrication of statements (especially of McIlkenny) and new uncertainties about the quality of the forensic tests eventually secured in their release in 1991. That outcome was swiftly followed by the establishment of the Runciman Commission (described later).

3. The next Irish-related case of relevance is that of Judith Ward, who was convicted in 1974 for delivering the bombs that resulted in twelve deaths on a British Army coach.[27] The conviction was once again undermined by the unreliability of the forensic evidence (Skuse's name appears once more) and of the confessions she made (although this time more because of her mental instability than because of police mistreatment of her). In the background were allegations of non-disclosure by the prosecution of evidence to the defense. Ward's case was referred to the Court of Appeal unilaterally by the Home Office, and she was released in 1992 after the prosecution declined to contest the matter. The Court's judgment was particularly censorious of the nondisclosure of evidence by named forensic scientists and prosecution counsel.

4. Another long-running case was that involving the murder of Carl Bridgewater, a newspaper delivery boy who was killed when he interrupted a burglary at Yew Tree Farm, near Stourbridge. Michael Hickey, Vincent Hickey, James Robinson, and Patrick Molloy were imprisoned in 1979.[28]

The convictions rested largely on the confessions of Molloy, who died in prison in 1981. Molloy, who was denied access to a solicitor, later retracted his confession and claimed he had been tricked by police, who showed him a confession by Vincent Hickey, and his refutation was given credence by later electrostatic tests on the police papers, which revealed the imprint of a fake confession. The case was referred back to the Court of Appeal in 1996 (an appeal had been refused in 1989 following a referral back in 1987). The men were released in 1997.[29]

5. The *Tottenham 3* (Winston Silcott, Engin Raghip, and Mark Braithwaite) were convicted of the murder of Police Constable Blakelock during the Broadwater Farm riot in 1985.[30] On a referral back to the Court of Appeal in 1991,[31] it was shown that notes of the interview were altered by the police in the case of Silcott, that Raghip's confession was unreliable because of his mental state, and that Braithwaite had been unfairly denied a lawyer.

6. Stefan Kiszko was released after an even longer period of imprisonment, thirteen years after his original appeal.[32] His conviction for murder was accepted in 1992 as unsustainable in light of the medical evidence that he was unable to produce the sperm found on the murdered girl. The processing of this evidence by the prosecution counsel also gave rise to concern.

7. As a correction to any impression that miscarriages are a phenomenon in the English legal system confined to previous decades, the final illustration concerns the recent Sudden Infant Death Syndrome (SIDS, or "cot death") cases of Sally Clark and Angela Cannings. The Court of Appeal was faced with evidence that expert medical testimony was far more problematic than previously acknowledged. In the *Clark* case,[33] the precipitating cause of the overturning of the conviction was non-disclosure of expert evidence, although the statistical analysis of the prosecution's chief expert pediatrician, Professor Sir Roy Meadow, was equally called into question. In *Cannings*,[34] the criticism went further, to the value of the scientific bases for the evidence of Professor Sir Roy Meadow. The trials concerned whether the cause of death was Sudden Infant Death Syndrome (SIDS), which, although medically and legally recognized, is not yet fully understood. The prosecution asserted that there had to be some criminal action on the part of the mother, likely to be smothering, in the light of the fact that babies in the same family died in similar equivocal circumstances when in her sole charge. This multiple occurrence was the core of the Meadow thesis—that one sudden infant death is a tragedy, two is suspicious, and three is murder, until proved otherwise—a thesis questioned by other experts in the case. Sally

Clark was released in January 2004, after serving three years of a life sentence for the murder of her two baby sons. Angela Cannings was released in December 2004, having served twenty months of a life sentence for the murder of her two babies. Prompted by the decision in *Cannings*, the Attorney General announced in January 2004 a review of 258 convictions relating to homicide or infanticide of a baby under two years old by a parent within the previous ten years. The Criminal Cases Review Commission (described later in this chapter) identified twenty-eight cases worthy of referral, and, in January 2005, the case of Donna Anthony, who has served eight years of a life sentence for the murder of her two babies, was referred to the Court of Appeal. In a parallel review in civil cases, ordered by the Children's Minister, 5,175 cases were reviewed that had been through the family courts, involving 9,195 children. Of these, 385 cases hinged on expert evidence, but dispute among experts was detected in only forty-seven cases. So far there is only one case in which the local authority changed its care plan as a result of the *Cannings* judgment, although thirty-eight remain subject to change. In a second stage of the review, the authorities have been asked to review about 30,000 care orders already in place. Furthermore, the Minister asked Sir Liam Donaldson, the chief medical officer, to investigate more generally the availability and quality of expert witnesses in the family courts.

Despite the more recent focus on cases involving mothers, and the potential for miscarriages of justice to be occurring unnoticed in the Family Courts, for the time being, it remains the case that the largest catalog of contemporary miscarriages has concerned Irish "terrorist" cases. To these can be added the emergent cases arising from the "war on terror" currently waged both internationally and domestically, which has already given rise to a serious catalog of alleged abuses.[35] Among the reasons behind this tendency to lapse from acceptable standards are, first, that terrorist action creates, and is designed to create, extraordinary tension, fear, and panic. Second, official reaction to terrorism often involves a conscious departure from the normal due process ideology of the criminal justice system and a tendency toward the holding of grand "state trials." Hence, Lord Denning's comment in response to the *Guildford 4* case was that even if the wrong people were convicted, "the whole community would be satisfied."[36] Nevertheless, a great number of miscarriages do not relate to terrorism, with this catalog of cases, in a sense, even more significant since they have occurred in more commonplace circumstances and under "normal" policing regimes. That miscarriages can occur without the pressures induced by terrorism can be illustrated by the SIDS cases. In addition, there is predicted a deluge of "children's home" appeals (where defendants have been convicted on historical abuse allegations made by past residents of children's homes across England and Wales)[37] resulting from the formation in August 2003 of the Historic Abuse Appeals Panel (HAAP) and false abuse allegations more generally in both the civil and criminal courts. More generally, the vastly increased availability of, and reliance on, forensic materials has created dangers of unquestioning and undue trust in this type of evidence.[38]

Typology of Cases

Miscarriages result from a multiplicity of causes, and individual prisoners have often been subjected to more than one form of abuse of authority. However, it is possible from this limited survey to form a picture of the recurrent forms of miscarriage in practice.[39]

1. The most obvious danger is the falsification of evidence. For example, it has been recognized for some time that informers who are co-accused may well have self-serving reasons for exaggerating the role of the defendant. The police are also in a powerful position to manipulate evidence, for example by "verballing" the accused, inventing damning statements or passages within them. The *Birmingham 6* and *Tottenham 3* cases all involve such behavior that is no more excusable because, sometimes, it is said to have been committed in a "noble cause."[40]

2. Both the police and lay witnesses may prove to be unreliable when attempting to identify an offender, especially if the sighting was momentary and in a situation of stress.[41]

3. The evidential value of expert testimony has also been overestimated in a number of instances only for it later to emerge that the tests being used were inherently unreliable, that the scientists conducting them were inefficient, or both. The *Maguire 7*, *Birmingham 6*, *Ward*, *Kiszko*, and "cot death" cases all fit into this category.

4. The next common factor concerns unreliable confessions as a result of police pressure, physiological or mental instability, or a combination of all of these. Examples include the *Guildford 4*, *Birmingham 6*, *Ward*, *Cardiff 3*, and *Tottenham 3* cases.

5. A further issue may be the non-disclosure of relevant evidence by the police or prosecution to the defense. The investigation of a case is by and large reliant on the police; they speak to all possible witnesses and arrange for forensic testing. The defense have neither the financial resources to undertake such

work nor the opportunities in terms of access. Yet several cases—*Guildford 4*, *Maguire 7*, and *Ward*—demonstrate that the police, forensic scientists, and prosecution cannot be relied on fairly to pass on evidence that might be helpful to the accused, despite there being no other agency that might uncover it in the interests of justice.

6. The conduct of the trial may produce miscarriages. For example, judges are sometimes prone to favor the prosecution evidence rather than acting as impartial umpires, as is alleged in connection with the *Birmingham 6* case. A failure to appreciate the defense's submissions either in law or fact can result in unfairness in their rulings or directions to the jury, as in the *Maguire 7* case. Equally, defense lawyers are not always beyond reproach and may not be as competent or assertive as they should be.

7. The next problem concerns the presentation of defendants in a prejudicial manner. An insidious way of achieving this effect is the pejorative labeling of them as "terrorists" or "bad mothers." Similarly, the obvious and heavy-handed security arrangements accompanying trips to court and the defendant's quarantined appearance in the dock inevitably convey an impression of guilt and menace. Prejudice can also arise through media commentaries.

8. There are the problems associated with appeals and the procedures thereafter. Common difficulties include the lack of access to lawyers and limited legal aid funding, so there has to be reliance on extralegal campaigns that may or may not be taken up by the media dependent on factors that have little to do with the strength of the case. The Court of Appeal has made the task even more difficult because of its interpretations of the grounds for appeal.

The Mechanisms to Redress Residual Error

The prime mechanism for consideration of official policies on the redress of residual error has been the Royal Commission on Criminal Justice (the "Runciman Commission"), which reported in 1993.[42] In keeping with many other facets of British public life, Royal Commissions tend to be exercises in bureaucracy and pragmatism rather than philosophy and principle. Accordingly, the Runciman Commission expended little effort on conceptualizing miscarriages of justice. Without much further ado, it simply emphasized the need for "the effectiveness of the criminal justice system in England and Wales in securing the conviction of those guilty of criminal offences and the acquittal of those who are innocent," as well as "the efficient use of resources." The approach of the Commissioners was criticized sharply, as it allowed for lobbying by official interest groups on grounds unrelated to any analysis of past cases and also for greater political freedom for the government of the day to interpret, meld, and select from the reform agenda.

Prior to the Runciman Report, for an appellant who maintained that he or she had been wrongfully convicted but whose appeal under section 1 of the Criminal Appeals Act 1968 had been unsuccessful, the only option available was to lodge a petition with the Home Office under section 17 of the Criminal Appeals Act 1968. The fitful scrutiny by the Home Secretary's back-room staff and the politically charged reluctance to refer cases back to the Court of Appeal contributed to an inadequate review system. A proposal for an independent tribunal eventually came into official favor and the Runciman Report acceded to these pressures, recommending a replacement for the reviews and referrals through the Home Office.[43] The idea was implemented after April 1, 1997 in the shape of the Criminal Cases Review Commission (CCRC)[44] by Part II of the Criminal Appeal Act 1995.[45]

The role of the CCRC with respect to alleged wrongful convictions is in many ways similar to that previously performed by the Home Office. It has no power to determine the outcome of cases for itself but, if certain criteria are established, can refer a case back to the Court of Appeal. However, there are some critical differences between the old and new procedures.

1. *Preparation of the application.* The establishment of the CCRC was designed in part to remove some initial practical obstacles from the petitioner. Although in the vast majority of cases an applicant will still have to bring his or her case to the attention of the CCRC, much has been done to make the application process user-friendly. The CCRC encourages the use of legal advice but will consider applications not supported by legal advice.

2. *Resources.* In addition to the fourteen Commission members, the CCRC employs dozens of case workers. Its initial annual budget of about £7.5 million represented a substantial increase in resources compared to C3. Whether these enhanced resources are adequate can only be determined by experience, and in practice, the CCRC has faced financial and staffing crises that required the budget to be increased from around £3 million to 4 million (i.e., doubled). However, this increase proved shortlived, with substantial budget cuts of 17 percent announced in 2004.[46]

3. *Consideration of the application.* The reluctance of C3 at the Home Office to refer cases because of "political embarrassment" could only be overcome by a body truly independent of the executive. The constitutional independence of the Commission is provided for in section 8(2), whereby it "shall not

be regarded as the servant or agent of the Crown or as enjoying any status, immunity or privilege of the Crown." The Home Secretary is not involved with the selection procedure, does not decide the ways in which the Commission should do its work, and, most crucially of all, is not involved in its decision-making role.[47] At least one-third of the Commission's membership must be legally qualified, and under section 8(6) at least two-thirds "shall be persons who appear to the Prime Minister to have knowledge or experience of any aspect of the criminal justice system." However, there are criticisms that the current Commission membership derives too heavily from prosecution interests and that it also largely reflects the white, male, middle-class background that is so often a feature of judicial institutions in the United Kingdom.

As well as Commissioners, much of the sifting work is undertaken by case workers. A preliminary assessment of all applications is made to establish eligibility on the grounds that appeal rights have been exhausted and that there are grounds on which an appeal would be likely to succeed if the grounds for application were true (if not, the case goes forward as a "short form of review"). If successful, the case then undergoes a more intensive, Stage 2 review, when a case review manager and a commissioner are assigned to work on the case. A case worker peruses the documentation, makes inquiries, and, in consultation with the assigned commissioner, takes a preliminary view on referral. If the case worker is not satisfied that there is a real possibility that the conviction would be reversed were the case referred back, the applicant is sent a "short form" of reasons and is given twenty-eight days to make a response. Rejections are finally made by a single commissioner, in consultation with the case review manager. If, on the other hand, the case review manager and commissioner believe that there may be a possibility of reversal, the case is presented to a quorum of three commissioners who make the final decision as to whether to refer. Following a referral to the Court of Appeal, the CCRC's involvement ceases.

4. *Reinvestigations.* Most applicants will be faced with the problem of trying to persuade the Commission to use its resources in carrying out further investigations. As the quality of reinvestigations under the old reference procedure was heavily criticized, it is vital to the success of the Commission that it is seen to have thorough and, as far as is possible, transparent investigative processes. But the government stood fast against giving the Commission an ability to investigate cases with its own staff:[48]

> The Government has no intention of funding a team in the Commission whose job would be to operate as a mini police force, duplicating work which could, and should, be done by the police. . . .

We envisage its doing investigative work from time to time but, generally the right people to investigate will be the police. . . .

Consequently, there is no CCRC in-house investigative staff. Instead, investigations are mainly carried out by the police under the supervision of the Commission. Under section 19 of the 1995 Act the Commission can require the appointment of an investigating officer to carry out inquiries, and can insist that the investigating officer be from a different police force than the one that carried out the original investigation. The Commission can also direct that a particular person shall not be appointed or, should they be dissatisfied with his or her performance, they can require under section 20 that the officer be removed. As Malet suggests, "In short, the 1995 Act takes a trusting attitude to the police,"[49] and this relationship represents a major concern for the future effectiveness of the CCRC.

5. *Disclosure of evidence.* The Commission has a wide power to obtain documents from public bodies under section 17 of the 1995 Act "where it is reasonable to do so." This, however, means that the Commission rely on noncoerced cooperation in obtaining information from private bodies. As regards disclosure of information to the applicant, in *R v. Secretary of State for the Home Department, ex parte Hickey (no. 2),*[50] Simon Brown LJ ensured through his judgment that when the Home Secretary was minded to reject an applicant's petition on the basis of evidence gathered in any further inquiries, the applicant should be given an opportunity to make representations on such material before a final decision is made. There is no general duty under the 1995 Act to disclose all the information gathered during any reinvestigation, the Government preferring to rely on the flexible standard of fairness in *ex parte Hickey.*

6. *Referral to the Court of Appeal.* To refer a case to the Court of Appeal, the CCRC under section 13(1), must "consider that there is a real possibility that the conviction . . . would not be upheld were a reference to be made." This "real possibility" can be realized through, "an argument, or evidence, not raised in the proceedings." There is no longer a need to provide "new evidence" as interpreted by the Home Office. Yet, the Act left much to be determined through the interpretations of the CCRC and also the receptivity of the Court of Appeal, which have to be second-guessed by the CCRC. More radical solutions would have been to give the Commission the power to determine applications or at least to make recommendations to the Court of Appeal either to acquit or to order a retrial, placing the onus on the judges to find reasons to disagree. However, these ideas could be seen as interfering too much with judicial independence and the finality of verdicts.

In terms of design, the CCRC is an important and innovative reform that does recognize the possibility of residual error and places state facilities on call for their correction. However, there are increasing criticisms leveled at the performance of the CCRC, including their decision-making processes, their resources, and ultimately their remit.

Performance of the CCRC

The CCRC has been widely accepted, in theory and in practice, to be a great improvement on its predecessors, the C3 Department of the Home Office[51] and the equivalent unit in the Northern Ireland Office.[52] Not only is it an independent body, separate from both the executive and the judiciary, but it has enhanced resources, staffing, and even, arguably, expertise. Most important, its receptive approach and attitude are in complete contrast to the reluctance, endemic in the governmental departments, to reinvestigate cases with thoroughness.

The CCRC began work on April 1, 1997 with 279 cases transferred to it from the Home Office and twelve from the Northern Ireland Office. Through December 2004, the Commission had received 7,346 applications, of which 6,606 have been completed (including those that were not eligible for review). Of these applications, 264 referrals have been made to the Court of Appeal, of which 209 have been heard, resulting in 144 quashed convictions or sentence variations. There is now a growing backlog in the Court of Appeal, but the rate of referral compares very favorably to the rate under the Home Secretary

The CCRC has powers under section 19 to appoint an outside Investigating Officer. By the end of March 2004, an Investigating Officer (invariably from the police) had been appointed in just thirty-four cases. The limited use of section 19 reflects the possibility that more limited fact-finding can arise from the commissioning by the case worker (under section 21) of specific independent reports, such as by engineers, forensic scientists, and psychiatrists. In addition, the Commission itself has adopted the practice of carrying out for itself as much fieldwork as is practicable (including interviews with witnesses, lawyers, and the applicant). However, it is a disappointing replication of Home Office practices that police officers have invariably been employed as investigators. It seems that the financial consideration that the police provide their services for free (to the CCRC) will prove weighty both in the short and long term.

The backlog of cases before the CCRC continues to cause anxiety. Even before the CCRC started work in 1997, concern was voiced that it would be swamped with applications. These fears soon materialized. By the end of

December 2004, a total of 740 applications awaited completion, with 414 actively being worked on. A report by the Home Affairs Select Committee in 2004 expressed concern that of the cases processed by the CCRC through December 31, 2003, only 4 percent had been referred to an appropriate appeal court, with around half that number resulting in an overturned conviction.[53] The Home Affairs Select Committee continue to suggest that the CCRC is too dependent on the Court of Appeal in determining the outcome of its reviews and in decisions to refer or reject cases,[54] a position recently reiterated by a CCRC member.[55]

Unease thus persists that the backlog is still too large, itself creating injustice as well as damaging confidence and demoralizing staff. There is also the danger that some of these dissatisfied customers might begin legal action against the CCRC for the injustice of delay. Assuming its own complaints mechanism is exhausted without satisfactory redress, the possibilities include judicial review[56] and an action based on the Human Rights Act 1998. Of perhaps even greater concern is the several years that an investigation can take before a decision is taken on referral. In the case of Donna Anthony, the CCRC has been heavily criticized for taking more than five months to refer the case even after the Attorney General himself expressed concerns directly to the CCRC over the case.[57] In addition, many failed applicants are now voicing their dissatisfaction with the paucity of reasons given for the Commission's refusal to refer their case.

A significant barrier to CCRC referrals also relates to their inherent cautionary approach and their internal decision-making protocols. It takes just a single commissioner to refuse referral, but it requires three to refer, making decisions about whether to refer cases weighted in favor of nonreferral.[58] The cautionary approach of the CCRC to referring cases was extended when a commissioner recently outlined the structural consequences of their referral system.[59] In practice, case review managers, who have the main responsibility for investigating cases, have internalized the "one CM to refuse, three CM's to refer" system to the extent that they have transformed the working practice of the "real possibility test" into "a real possibility of a real possibility test" when deciding whether or not to recommend a referral: the case review manager deciding whether there is a "real possibility" that three commissioners will refer before making his or her own recommendation.

The CCRC then is currently charged with reassessing its approach to referrals; increasing its productivity; increasing, or at least protecting its resources; or some combination of the foregoing. The Select Committee has previously argued that the CCRC could take a changed approach to its investigation of cases in that it could "prune the amount of detailed work done" with no loss of effectiveness, describing its investigative processes as "highly technical and formulaic."[60] This feature, it is contended, has contributed greatly to the large backlog of cases that has now built up. It could be contended that in looking for a "real possibility" that a conviction would be reversed by the Court of Appeal, the CCRC should not be second-guessing the Court of Appeal and only referring those cases that are sure to be overturned; the high success rate in the Court of Appeal combined with the low number of cases referred is indicative of this tendency. However, there are problems with a more cursory review. The risks arise that less obvious grounds for referral will be overlooked so that cases are not referred or referred on weaker grounds than necessary, with no certainty that the necessary investigative work will be undertaken in time by defense lawyers, prosecutors, or appellate judges.[61] If at this early stage in the life of the CCRC the quality of preliminary investigation is reduced, honed down to a mechanical filtration and rejection process with eligibility thresholds being effectively increased, the CCRC will quickly become as discredited as the previous system. In the view of the CCRC itself, it might "perpetuate the very miscarriages of justice that the Commission was set up to review."[62] There is also the danger of incurring the wrath of the Court of Appeal if a sizable proportion of referrals fails.

As regards improvements to the CCRC's working practices suggested by a report of the Home Affairs Select Committee in 1999,[63] the following are the more substantial or more controversial changes that have been advocated. First, the Select Committee have suggested that the CCRC should publicize the availability of legal advice so that a greater proportion of the applications received meet the eligibility criteria.[64] In this way, private lawyers could act as gatekeepers for the CCRC, saving the time of the case review manager, who would otherwise have to check for eligibility (around 25 percent of applications are ineligible, mainly because of the failure to exhaust appeals). To a certain extent, this goal has been pursued through the production of the CCRC's video, "Open to Question," which may have contributed in the increase from 10 percent to 30 percent in applications prepared with legal assistance from 1997 to the end of March 2000. The utilization of private lawyers is not, of course, an overall financial saving to the public if their work is paid for from the Legal Services Commission, but there may savings in regard to the cost of unjust imprisonment.

The Select Committee has also considered various permutations in priorities. In this regard, the CCRC has given little prominence to summary cases (they amount to 7 percent of the workload) but instead has adopted a system of priority that largely favors in date order of receipt those in custody. It also gives priority to cases falling under the short form of review procedure; in other words, weaker cases are accelerated, which must improve the statistical returns but hardly makes much sense in terms of justice. Another aspect of resource allocation has been the priority for those cases transferred from the Home Office and Northern Ireland Office in 1997. Yet one wonders whether so much effort should be expended on old cases that involve files of gargantuan proportions but no live defendants and arguably no live issues for the contemporary criminal justice process. The very first case to be considered was that of Mahmood Mattan, who was hanged in 1952,[65] and huge resources have been expended on cases such as that of Derek Bentley (who was hanged in 1952)[66] and James Hanratty (hanged in 1962).[67]

Another area (not considered by the Select Committee) where savings could be made concerns the establishment on April 1, 1999 of a separate Scottish CCRC. It is arguable that valuable resources and time are being dissipated through the process of institutional establishment and subsequent maintenance, whereas a unified United Kingdom Commission could have operated earlier and more efficiently and effectively through the dissemination of practices and experiences. Although Scotland has a distinct criminal process and does require distinct expertise, its differences should not be reflected in expensive offices and equipment or the reinvention of working systems, especially as its miscarriages of justice relate mainly to the same causes. So, the separation is explained by the pandering to historical symbolism rather than a determination to combat miscarriages of justice.

The principal tone of the Select Committee Report was one of bureaucratic efficiency in which standards could be cut. The appropriate response should have been in terms of a lobby for more resources or the reconsideration of priorities within existing resources. It is heartening that these have indeed been the responses of the CCRC, which agrees with the Select Committee's combination approach, but focusing on productivity and resources. Conversely, it rightly cautions against a more superficial approach to the examination of applications.[68] One important task that the CCRC is still unable to attend to, however, is the analysis of the thousands of cases it has dealt with and the referrals made so far, to discern patterns and to give advice to criminal justice stakeholders. In this way, the CCRC could act as a form of criminal justice inspectorate. One example it has given is the repetition of applications where there is little corroborative evidence in sex-related convictions.[69] Yet, in the latest Select Committee investigations,[70] it was confirmed again that the priority of the CCRC is to clear the backlog and speed up delays, so that analysis of prior cases is not being given a high precedence in the near future.[71]

Performance of the Court of Appeal

Crucial to the success of the scheme must be the receptivity to referrals and a willingness to look again on the part of the Court of Appeal. As already mentioned, the first case to be considered was that of *Mattan*.[72] It is an encouraging sign that Lord Justice Rose expressly recognized that "the Criminal Cases Review Commission is a necessary and welcome body, without whose work the injustice in this case might never have been identified." Similarly, in *R v. Criminal Cases Review Commission, ex parte Pearson*,[73] Lord Bingham asserted that, "It is essential to the health and proper functioning of a modern democracy that the citizen accused of crime should be fairly tried and adequately protected against the risk and consequences of wrongful conviction."

Of the cases to have reached judgment to date, the case of Derek Bentley (who was hanged in 1952),[74] decided in July 1998, was perhaps the most remarkable, not only because of its history but also because it gave rise to the alarming implication that older convictions can become vulnerable simply by the application of current standards of due process. The Court of Appeal relied essentially on the unfair conduct of the trial and directions to the jury by Lord Chief Justice Goddard, an issue that had been raised without success in the appeal immediately following conviction in 1952. This prospect has become less likely since the decision in *Gerald* in November 1998.[75] Lord Justice Rose expressed mild annoyance that the referral (concerning a conviction for grievous bodily harm in 1987) had been made at all: "[w]e venture to express a measure of surprise that, in this case, in which, as will emerge, there is no new evidence and the points which form the substance of the appeal were never canvassed in evidence or argument at trial, the Commission has thought it appropriate to [refer]." A corresponding approach has been established in regard to sentencing referrals in the case of *R v. Graham*.[76] The (Auld) Review of the Criminal Courts in England and Wales called for statutory clarification,[77] but the Court of Appeal itself has provided elucidation in *Hanratty*.[78] Next, as well as puzzling over what tests to apply, the Court of Appeal has expressed objection to the utility of the referral of historic cases. In the unsuccessful appeal in *Hanratty*, Lord Woolf stated:[79]

> We do not consider it would be right to attempt to judge the Commission with the benefit of hindsight in relation to this case. We do however emphasise that there have to be exceptional circumstances to justify incurring the expenditure of resources on this scale, including those of this court, on a case of this age.

In the case of Ruth Ellis,[80] the Court commented that even if the resources of the CCRC were not troubled by the exercise, those of the Court itself certainly were:

We have to question whether this exercise of considering an appeal so long after the event when Mrs Ellis herself had consciously and deliberately chosen not to appeal at the time is a sensible use of the limited resources of the Court of Appeal. On any view, Mrs Ellis had committed a serious criminal offence. . . . The Court of Appeal's workload is an ever-increasing one and recent legislation will add substantially to that load. Parliament may wish to consider whether going back many years into history to re-examine a case of this kind is a use that ought to be made of the limited resources that are available. The exercise of the CCRC's discretion in deciding whether to refer cases is one that is a frequent source of challenge by way of Judicial Review and it may be that an express power to consider factors of this kind would enable the CCRC to take into account more readily the public interest in making its decision.

Interestingly, following this statement, the CCRC refused to refer the notorious case of Timothy Evans, who had been hanged for the murder of his wife and daughter in 1950.[81] His downstairs neighbor was John Reginald Christie, who was the central prosecution witness at the trial of Timothy Evans. Christie turned out to be a serial killer who later confessed to killing Mr. Evans's wife, Beryl. The bodies of six women Christie also murdered were later found at 10 Rillington Place. In *Westlake v. Criminal Cases Review Commission*,[82] the Divisional Court accepted the fact that Evans had been granted a full pardon in 1966 as a valid reason for not taking the case any further since the integrity of the public justice system did not need any further restoration. More generally, and in response, the CCRC has argued that public interest is already considered, with the fact that the subject is deceased being a relevant factor.[83]

Despite the spats over historic cases, the courts have generally shown respect for the CCRC by not unduly interfering in its decision making. This could be done through the mechanism of judicial review,[84] but few cases have resulted in decisions being overturned.[85] The sole adverse decision was *Farnell*,[86] where the CCRC was seen to second-guess under section 13 the views of the Court of Appeal rather than a hypothetical jury. In addition, the process of judicial review is itself not subject to appeal from the High Court, which may cause too much expense and delay for the CCRC.[87]

However, this generally positive picture must be balanced with some difficulties. One problem concerns the meaning of the statutory test for referral. As stated, the 1995 Act provides that there must be a "real possibility" that the original conviction, finding, or sentence[88] would not be upheld as "safe" were the conviction to be referred back to the Court of Appeal. In the case of a conviction, the "real possibility" must be as a result of an argument or evidence not raised in the original proceedings, or of "exceptional circumstances" such as wholly inadequate defense representation. Although "real possibility" itself is not defined in the Act, the leading case on the interpretation of section 13 has been *R v. Criminal Cases Review Commission, ex parte Pearson*,[89] in which it was held that the meaning of "real possibility" "plainly denotes a contingency which in the Commission's judgment is more than an outside chance or a bare possibility but which may be less than a probability or likelihood or a racing certainty." Those standards were applied both to the admission of fresh evidence (where relevant) and also to the assessment of the evidence by the Court of Appeal. The "assessment" for these purposes means ultimately whether there would be impact on a jury and not what the appeal judges themselves would conclude concerning the strength of the case. Whether this formula provides a sufficiently clear signal of society's determination to avoid miscarriages remains to be seen. It still leaves a lot of discretion: some defendants might be lucky to be heard by receptive judges, others might not. One instance of the receptive kind was the long-running saga of *R v. Mills (no.2), R v. Poole (no. 2)*.[90] The defendants' case had initially been rejected by the CCRC, as confirmed by Lord Woolf in the Divisional Court on judicial review.[91] But Lord Woolf expressed the view that "the Court of Appeal could now have a doubt about the safety of the convictions." The result was a referral by the CCRC and a subsequent quashing of the conviction even in the absence of new evidence or new arguments. Lord Justice Auld further refined further the tests to be satisfied by the appellant. In his view, section 13 requires that the CCRC establish either a new argument or new evidence or exceptional circumstances before making a referral.[92] As to the receptivity of the Court of Appeal, the proper exercise of the Court's discretion under section 14(5) involving departure from its previous reasoning should equally be confined to exceptional circumstances.[93] It follows that this restraint of exceptionality does not govern the consideration of grounds rejected by the Commission.[94]

One issue on which the Court of Appeal is clearly irritated, although not so much with the CCRC, concerns section 14(5) of the Criminal Appeal Act 1995, by which "Where a reference under any of sections 9 to 12 is treated as an appeal against any conviction, verdict, finding or sentence, the appeal may be on any ground relating to the conviction, verdict, finding or sentence (whether or not the ground is related to any reason given by the Commission for making the reference)." The effect is to allow an appellant to be able to incorporate any conceivable argument, including any arguments previously rejected by the Court of Appeal.[95] Lord Justice Kay in *R v. Bamber*[96] called this situation "a serious deficiency in the statutory framework," and it was suggested in *R v. Day*[97] that the Court of Appeal's exceptional permission should be required for any ground of appeal other than those referred by the CCRC. This restraint has now been codified by the Criminal Justice Act 2003, section 315, which amends section 14 of the Criminal Appeal Act 1995 by which the appeal may not be on any ground that is not related to any reason given by the CCRC for making the reference, though, at the same time, the Court of Appeal may give leave for an appeal on a ground extraneous to the CCRC referral. The effect is to put an extra onus on the CCRC to investigate cases both quickly and exhaustively, neither of which has been easy to achieve in practice.[98]

Finally, as mentioned, there is a growing backlog in the Court of Appeal. Whereas resources have been poured into the CCRC, the same has not been true of the Court, which "has barely been keeping up with the cases that the Commission refers to it."[99] The additional prosecutorial rights of appeal introduced (primarily of judge-directed acquittals) are also going to put a great deal of extra pressure on an already stressed Court of Appeal, with those making contingency plans conceding that further delays in hearing normal appeals may be inevitable.

Conclusions

The CCRC is undoubtedly an improvement on previous mechanisms for remedying residual error, and has on the whole been well received, as shown by the submissions to the House of Commons' Home Affairs Select Committee's survey of "The Work of the Criminal Cases Review Commission."[100] The Select Committee considered that it had made a "good start."[101] However, a chorus of criticism is growing, with continued dissatisfaction with delays (not likely to be assisted by budget cuts), and a perceived low referral rate. Rejected applicants have also complained that reasons for nonreferral are often cursory, while many researchers are frustrated by the lack of analysis and "value-added" work that the CCRC is so well placed to carry out, or at least facilitate.

In addition, there is an emergent agenda concerning the state of the compensation of the wrongfully imprisoned and abused.[102] Financial compensation can be awarded either under section 133 of the Criminal Justice Act 1988 or on an *ex gratia* basis. By section 133(1), "when a person has been convicted of a criminal offence and when subsequently his conviction has been reversed or he has been pardoned on the ground that a new or newly discovered fact shows beyond reasonable doubt that there has been a miscarriage of justice, the Secretary of State shall pay compensation for the miscarriage of justice to the person who has suffered punishment as a result of such conviction or, if he is dead, to his personal representatives, unless the non-disclosure of the unknown fact was wholly or partly attributable to the person convicted."[103] *Ex gratia* payments are offered "in recognition of the hardship caused by a wrongful conviction or charge and notwithstanding that the circumstances may give no grounds for a claim for civil damages."[104]

Both have been narrowly construed. Section 133 has been said to require that the claimant is not just innocent but is "clearly innocent,"[105] while the *ex gratia* system in practice requires proof of "a period in custody following a wrongful conviction or charge, where . . . it has resulted from serious default on the part of a member of a police force or of some other public authority." There was widespread condemnation of the recent decision not to compensate Angela Cannings after her four-year ordeal at the hands of the justice system, with the reasoning offered (that it was an independent expert's evidence that resulted in her wrongful conviction and she did not fit into any of the discretionary categories for awarding compensation) roundly rejected by commentators.[106] In addition, recent rulings that those previously in receipt of compensation must have deducted from their award the cost of bed and board for the duration of their imprisonment (money that they supposedly "saved" by being incarcerated) have led to considerable legal wrangling.[107] Yet while those serving long sentences in prison are required to undergo "reacclimatization" courses, to assist with reintegration into society, the wrongly convicted are simply freed with no assistance at all. Those released by the Court of Appeal commonly then suffer a great deal of further trauma by their sudden release and lack of support.[108] Yet wider meanings of reparation— rehabilitation, restoration of dignity, and reassurance of nonrepetition—are not presently considered the responsibility of the government.

Further, the Prison Service is under pressure from the numbers of prisoners who are maintaining their innocence, and thereby not "progressing" through their sentence to release. The "parole deal," whereby prisoners admit their guilt and exhibit remorse for offenses they may maintain they did not commit to receive benefits and be eligible for parole, is now creating an impossible situation for the Prison Service and Parole Board with numbers of prisoners refusing to undergo "offender behavior programs" to address their offending, thereby disqualifying themselves from release.[109] Classic examples of the consequences of the parole deal in action are Stephen Downing, who served twenty-seven years after being labelled IDOM (in denial of murder) when ordinarily he would have been released after twelve years,[110] and Robert Brown, who served twenty-five years for a murder, refusing to leave prison until he had his conviction overturned.[111]

Criminal justice systems should be judged, inter alia, on the number of injustices produced by them in the first place, and, second, on their willingness to recognize and correct those mistakes. The British system could improve on both counts. The institution of the CCRC is much to its credit, but the failure to resource it generously or to reform the Court of Appeal may yet undermine its future.

Notes

1. Blackstone, *Commentaries on the Law of England* (1765–1769), Vol. IV, 27.

2. See R. Pattenden, *English Criminal Appeals 1844–1994* (Oxford, UK: Clarendon Press, 1996).

3. See M. Naughton and C. McCartney, "The Innocence Network UK" *Legal Ethics* 7 (2005): 150.

4. Home Office Statistical Bulletin, *Crime in England and Wales 2003–04* (London: HMSO, 2005).

5. Where the perpetrator is identified although not necessarily charged.

6. Crown Prosecution Service, Annual Report 2003–04 (2003–04 HC 710) Annex A.

7. Sections 34–39. See C. Walker and K. Starmer (Eds.), *Miscarriages of Justice* (London: Blackstone Press, 1999), chap. 5.

8. Home Office. *Justice for All* (London: HMSO, Cmnd 5563, 2002), 13.

9. I. Dennis, "Rethinking Double Jeopardy: Justice and Finality in the Criminal Process," *Criminal Law Review* (2000): 933.

10. N. Jorg, S. Field, and C. Brants, "Are Inquisitorial and Adversarial Systems Converging?" in *Criminal Justice in Europe: A Comparative Study,* ed. P. Fennell, C. Harding, N. Jorg, and B. Swart (Oxford, UK: Clarendon Press, 1995), 48.

11. *The Daily Telegraph,* October 7, 1993. See M. McConville and L. Bridges, eds., *Criminal Justice in Crisis* (Aldershot, UK: Edward Elgar, 1994); T. Newburn, *Crime and Criminal Justice Policy* (London: Longmans, 1995), 178.

12. Crown Prosecution Service, Annual Report 2003–04 (2003–04 HC 710), 9.

13. See M. Naughton, "Redefining Miscarriages of Justice," *British Journal of Criminology* (2004, Advance Access): 1. See further M. Naughton, "Reorientating Miscarriages of Justice," in *Beyond Criminology: Taking Harm Seriously,* ed. P. Hillyard, C. Pantazis, D. Gordon, and S. Tombs (London: Pluto Press, 2004).

14. See further S. Greer, "Miscarriages of Justice Reconsidered," *Modern Law Review* 57 (1994): 58.

15. H. L. Packer, *The Limits of the Criminal Sanction* (Stanford, CA: Stanford University Press, 1969), 153.

16. R. Dworkin, *A Matter of Principle* (Oxford, UK: Clarendon Press, 1986), 72.

17. See *Osman v. UK.,* Appl. no. 23452/94, Reports 1998-VIII. Compare *Keenan v. UK,* Appl. No.27229/95, Reports 2001-III.

18. See Police Complaints Authority, Report on the investigation of a complaint against the Metropolitan Police Service by Mr N and Mrs D Lawrence (London: HMSO, Cm. 3822, 1997); Macpherson Report, The Stephen Lawrence Inquiry (London: HMSO, Cm. 4262, 1999).

19. A. McColgan, "Common Law and the Relevance of Sexual History Evidence," *Oxford Journal of Legal Studies* 16 (1996): 275. A response by way of video links and limits on the forms of cross-examination was enacted by the Youth Justice and Criminal Evidence Act 1999, Pt.II.

20. A. L.-T. Choo, *Abuse of Process and Judicial Stays of Criminal Proceedings* (Oxford, UK: Clarendon Press, 1993), 10.

21. For full details and analysis of these and other important cases, see C. Walker and K. Starmer, eds., *Miscarriages of Justice* (London: Blackstone Press, 1999), chap. 2; F. Belloni and J. Hodgson, *Criminal Injustice* (London: Macmillan, 2000); R. Nobles and D. Schiff, *Understanding Miscarriages of Justice* (Oxford, UK: Oxford University Press, 2000); S. Field and P. A. Thomas, eds., Justice and Efficiency, *Journal of Law & Society* 21(1994), special issue.

22. See *R. v. Hill and others* (1975); *The Times,* October 23, 1977. *The Times,* February 28, 1989; *The Times,* October 20, 1989. See P. Hill and R. Burnett, *Stolen Years* (London: Doubleday, 1990); G. Conlon, *Proved Innocent* (London: Hamish Hamilton, 1990); R. Bennett, *Double Jeopardy* (London: Penguin, 1993); Sir John May, *Report of the Inquiry into the Circumstances Surrounding the Convictions Arising out of the Bomb Attacks in Guildford and Woolwich in 1974, Interim Report* (1989–90 H.C. 556), *Second Report* (1992–93 H.C. 296), *Final Report* (1993–94 H.C. 449). Three police officers were acquitted of conspiracy to pervert the course of justice: *R. v. Bow St. Stip. Mag. ex p. D.P.P.* (1992, D.C.); *R. v. Attwell, Donaldson and Style* (1993); *The Times,* May 20, 1993.

23. *R v. Maguire* (1976); *The Times,* March 5, 1976; *The Times,* June 28, 1977; [1992] 2 All E.R. 433. See A. Maguire, *Miscarriage of Justice: An Irish Family's Story of Wrongful Conviction as IRA Terrorists* (Colorado: Roberts Rinehart, 1994).

24. *The Times,* June, 28, 1992; [1992] 2 All E.R. 433. The defendants had all by then served their sentences, but one, Guiseppe Conlon (father of Gerard) had died in prison in 1980. Four police officers were unsuccessfully prosecuted for malpractices: *R v. Bow St. Stip. Mag. ex p. D.P.P.* (1992, D.C.).

25. 1989–90 H.C. 556; 1992–93 H.C. 296. This argument was expressly rejected by the Court of Appeal: *loc. cit.* at p. 444, which judgment the *Second Report* in turn criticizes: *loc. cit.* paras. 1.6–8, 3.16.

26. *R. v. Hill and others* (1975); *The Times,* August 16, 1975; *The Times,* March 31, 1976; *McIlkenny and others v. Chief Constable, West Midlands* [1980] 2 All E.R. 227; *Hunter and others v. Chief Constable, West Midlands* [1981] 3 W.L.R. 906; *R. v. Callaghan and others* [1988] 1 W.L.R. 1; *The Times,* January 29, 1988; *The Times,* March 22, 1988; *R v. Callaghan and others* (1988) 88 Cr. App. R. 40; *The Times,* April 1, 1991; *R. v. McIlkenny and others* [1992] 2 All E.R. 417. Commentaries include B. Gibson, *The Birmingham Bombs* (Chichester, UK: Rose, 1976); C. Mullin, *Error of Judgment,* 3d ed. (Dublin: Poolbeg, 1990); Sir L. Blom-Cooper, *The Birmingham Six and Other Cases* (London: Duckworth, 1997). The prosecutions of three of the detectives involved in the case was abandoned: *R. v. Read, Morris and Woodwiss* (1993); *The Times,* October 8, 1993; J. Rozenberg, *The Search for Justice* (London: Hodder & Stoughton, 1994),314.

27. *R. v. Ward* (1974); *The Times,* November 5, 1974; *The Times,* May 12, 1992; 96 Cr. App. R. 1 (1992); J. Ward, *Ambushed* (London: Vermilion, 1993); J. Rozenberg, "Miscarriages of Justice," in *Criminal Justice under Stress,* ed. E. Stockdale and S. Casale (London: Blackstone Press, 1992), 107.

28. See P. Foot, *Murder at the Farm* (London: Penguin, 1988); J. Morrell, *The Wrong Men* (Birmingham, UK: Bridgewater Four Support Group, 1993).

29. *The Times,* February 21, 1997; *The Times,* February 22, 1997; *The Times,* July 31, 1997; B. Hilliard, "Trial and Error," *Police Review* 105 (1997): 16.

30. See Lord Gifford, *The Broadwater Farm Inquiry* (London: Karian Press, 1986); Cruise O'Brien, "Legal Buffers Needed When Ethnic Groups Collide" *The Times,* July

27, 1991; D. Rose, *A Climate of Fear* (London: Bloomsbury Press, 1992); J. Rozenberg, "Miscarriages of Justice," in *Criminal Justice under Stress*, ed. E. Stockdale and S. Casale (London: Blackstone Press, 1992), 108.

31. *The Times*, December 9, 1991.

32. See 68 Cr App R 62 (1979); *The Times*, February 18, 1992; *The Times*, February 19, 1992; J. Rose, *Innocents* (London: Fourth Estate, 1997).

33. [2003] EWCA Crim 1020. See C. Montgomery, "Forensic Science in the Trial of Sally Clark," *Medicine, Science and Law* (2004): 185.

34. [2004] EWCA Crim. 1. See T. Ward, "Experts, Juries and Witchhunts" *Journal of Law & Society* (2004): 369; C. Walker and C. McCartney, "Case Commentary," *Criminal Law Review* (2005): 126.

35. For alleged abuses at Abu Ghraib, see (Taguba) Report on the Treatment of Abu Ghraib prisoners in Iraq: Article 15–6 investigation of the 800th Military Police Brigade (Washington, DC: Department of Defense, 2004); (Schlesinger) Independent Panel to review Department of Defense detention operations, Final Report (Washington, DC: Department of Defense, 2004); (Fay) Investigation of intelligence activities at Abu Ghraib (Washington, DC: Department of Defense, 2004). For alleged abuses at Guantanamo, see Center for Constitutional Rights, Composite Statement (New York, 2004). A review by Brigadier General John Forlow of treatment of Gunatanamo detainees is now pending further to reports released by the ACLU in December 2004.

36. *The Times*, August 17, 1990.

37. See, for example, *Attorney General's Reference (Nos. 37, 38, 44, 54, 51, 53, 35, 40, 43, 45, 41and 42 of 2003)* [2003] EWCA Crim 2973; *Attorney General's Reference (No.53 of 2004)* [2004] EWCA Crim 1831.

38. See C. McCartney, "Forensic DNA Sampling and the England and Wales National DNA Database: A Sceptical Approach," *Critical Criminology* 12 (2004): 157. Forensic evidence may, of course, be the cause both of a wrongful conviction and its annulment: See *R. v. Jenkins (Sion David Charles)* [2004] EWCA Crim 2047.

39. The Criminal Cases Review Commission, *Third Annual Report 1999–00* (Birmingham, UK: 2000), 9, relates the following causes in the eighty cases referred to the Court of Appeal to date: police or prosecution failings = 27; scientific evidence = 26; nondisclosure = 23; new evidence = 23; defective summing up = 11; defective legal arguments = 10; false confessions = 6; defense lawyer failings = 6.

40. See HM Inspectorate of Constabulary, Police Integrity (London: HMSO, 1999), para. 4.13.

41. See Report of the Departmental Committee on evidence of identification in criminal cases (the "Devlin Report") (1975–76 H.C. 338); *R. v. Turnbull* (1977) Q.B. 224.

42. *Runciman Report* (London: HMSO, Cm. 2263, 1993), chap. 1, paras. 5, 16. Previous high-profile miscarriages of justice had likewise led to significant reforms. Thus, the *Confait Affair* of the late 1970s precipitated the (Phillips) Royal Commission on Criminal Procedure in 1981 (London: HMSO, Cmnd. 8091), which brought about positive reform of the criminal process of England and Wales, especially in the shape of the Police and Criminal Evidence Act 1984.

43. *Runciman Report*, chap. 11. This was considered further in Home Office, *Criminal Appeals and the Establishment of a Criminal Cases Review Authority* (London: Home Office, 1994); Lord Chancellor's Department, Home Office and Law Officer's Department, *The Royal Commission on Criminal Justice: Final Government Response* (London: Home Office, 1996).

44. See http://www.ccrc.gov.uk/.

45. See J. C. Smith, "Appeals Against Conviction," *Criminal Law Review* (1995): 920.

46. The Criminal Cases Review Commission, *Seventh Annual Report 2003–04* (2003–04 HC 9), revealed that the number of cases under review had risen to 418 from 362.

47. Compare the partial reform in Canada: K. Scullion, "Wrongful Convictions and the Criminal Conviction Review Process Pursuant to Section 696.1 of the Criminal Code of Canada," *Canadian Journal of Criminology and Criminal Justice* 46 (2004): 189.

48. House of Commons Debates, vol. 263, cols. 1371–72, July 17, 1995.

49. D. Malet, "The New Regime for the Correction of Miscarriages of Justice," *Justice of the Peace* 159 (1995): 716, 735, at 736.

50. [1995] 1All ER 490.

51. See Home Office, *Criminal Appeals and the Establishment of a Criminal Cases Review Authority: A Discussion Paper* (London: Home Office, 1994).

52. See Northern Ireland Office, *Criminal Appeals and Arrangements for Dealing with Alleged Miscarriages of Justice in Northern Ireland* (Belfast, 1994).

53. See Home Affairs Select Committee, *The Work of the Criminal Cases Review Commission* (2003–04 HC 289-i), Question 34.

54. For example, Home Affairs Select Committee, *The Work of the Criminal Cases Review Commission* (2003–04 HC 289-i), Questions 5 and 8.

55. John Weedon, Commissioner, personal statement at All Party Group on Abuse Investigations Conference, House of Commons, Westminster, London, December 4, 2004.

56. For a successful application, see *R. v. CCRC, ex p. Cleeland*, March 31, 2000, DC (but the appeal failed: *R. v. Cleeland* [2002] EWCA Crim. 293).

57. See *The Times*, February 3, 2003.

58. Criminal Cases Review Commission, *Seventh Annual Report 2003–04* (2003–04 HC 9),32.

59. Laurie Elks, speaking in a personal capacity to the Miscarriage of Justice Stream at the Annual Socio-Legal Studies Association Conference, University of Glasgow, April 2004.

60. Select Committee, *Report,* paras. 26, 44.

61. The Court of Appeal can now direct the CCRC to carry out investigations but, as of March 31, 2004, just eleven matters had been referred under the Criminal Appeal Act 1995 sections 5, 15. A direction may be made on application for leave to appeal as well as on appeal against conviction: Criminal Justice Act 2003, sections 313, 314.

62. *Fourth Annual Report 2000–01* (2001), 26.

63. Home Affairs Committee, *The Work of the Criminal Cases Review Commission* (1998–99 HC 106) and Government Reply (1998–99 HC 569).

64. Ibid., para. 47.

65. *The Times,* March 5, 1998. Other "historic" cases include George Kelly, who was hanged for murder in 1950 ([2003] EWCA Crim. 2957).

66. *The Times,* July 31, 1998. See D. Yallop, *To Encourage the Others* (London: W. H. Allen, 1972); I. Bentley, *Let Him Have Justice* (London: Sidgwick & Jackson, 1995). The Home Secretary's initial failure to consider all relevant forms of pardon was quashed on review: *R. v. Secretary of State for the Home Department ex p. Bentley* [1993] 4 All E.R. 442. Compare the Scottish position in *Boncza-Tomaszewski v. HM Advocate* (2000 SCCR 657).

67. [2002] EWCA Crim. 1141. See L. Blom Cooper, *The A6 Murder* (London: Penguin, 1963); E. F. L. Russell, *Deadman's Hill* (London: Secker & Warburg, 1965); P. Foot, *Who*

Killed Hanratty? (London: Cape, 1971); *Report of Mr. C. Hawser Q.C.* (London: Cmnd. 5021, 1975); B. Woffinden, *Hanratty: The Final Verdict* (London: Macmillan, 1997).

68. *Second Annual Report* 1998–99 (Birmingham, UK, 1999), 7.

69. *Fifth Annual Report 2001–02* (2002), 25.

70. Home Affairs Select Committee, *The Work of the Criminal Cases Review Commission* (2003–04 HC 289-i).

71. See Criminal Cases Review Commission, *Seventh Annual Report 2003–04* (2003–04 HC 9), 30.

72. *R. v. Mattan; The Times,* March 5, 1998.

73. [2000] 1 Cr App R 141.

74. *The Times,* July 31, 1998. Compare the Scottish position in *Boncza-Tomaszewski v. HM Advocate* (2000 SCCR 657).

75. [1999] Crim.L.R. 315.

76. LEXIS February 23, 1999 (CA).

77. (Auld) Review of the Criminal Courts in England and Wales (London: 2001), para. 12.106.

78. [2002] EWCA Crim. 1141 at para. 98.

79. [2002] EWCA Crim. 1141 at para. 214.

80. [2003] EWCA Crim. 3556 at para. 90. It was notable that the appeal was on the basis that the murder conviction should have been reduced to manslaughter rather than that the conviction should be quashed altogether. See further G. Ellis, *A Murder of Passion* (London: Blake, 2003).

81. See *Report of an Inquiry by Scott Henderson* (London: Cmd. 8896 and 8946, 1953); R. T. Paget and S. Silverman, *Hanged and Innocent?* (London: Gollancz, 1953); M. Eddowes, *The Man on Your Conscience* (London: Cassell, 1955); J. Grigg and I. Gilmour, *The Case of Timothy Evans* (London: Spectator, 1956); F. J. Tennyson, *The Trials of Timothy John Evans and John Reginald Christie* (London: Hodge, 1957); L. Hale, *Hanged in Error* (London: Penguin, 1961); L. Kennedy, *Ten Rillington Place* (London: Gollancz, 1961); *Report of an Inquiry by Mr. Justice Brabin* (London: Cmnd. 3101, 1966); J. Eddowes, *The Two Killers of Rillington Place* (London: Little, Brown, 1994).

82. [2004] EWHC 2779 (Admin).

83. The Criminal Cases Review Commission, *Seventh Annual Report 2003–04* (2003–04 HC 9), 17.

84. Another possibility is reapplication, and this route is growing with seventy-nine in 2002–03: *Sixth Annual Report 2002–03* (Birmingham, UK, 2003), 25.

85. Out of fifty-nine applications, just ten have been given leave to proceed. Ibid.

86. *R. (Farnell) v. Criminal Cases Review Commission* [2003] EWHC (Admin.) 835.

87. *R. (Saxon) v. Criminal Cases Review Commission* [2001] EWHC (Civ.) 1384.

88. An additional problem was encountered by Iain Hay Gordon in 1998 (see *Criminal Cases Review Commission's Reference under s 14(3) of the Criminal Appeal Act 1995* [1998] NI 275). A "guilty but insane" verdict under the Trial of Lunatics Act 1883 did not amount to a conviction, finding, or sentence for the purposes of section 10 of the 1995 Act until amended by the Criminal Cases Review (Insanity) Act 1999.

89. [2000] 1 Cr App R 141 at 149 per Lord Bingham. See also *R. (Hunt) v. Criminal Cases Review Commission* [2001] 2 Cr App R 76.

90. [2003] EWCA Crim. 1753.

91. *R. (Mills) v. Criminal Cases Review Commission* [2001] EWHC (Admin.) 858, para. 114.

92. Ibid., para. 56.

93. Ibid. See also *R. v. Ian Thomas* [2002] EWCA Crim. 941; *R. v. Wallace Duncan Smith* [2002] EWCA Crim. 941.

94. Ibid., para. 60. See also *R. v. Garner* [2002] EWCA 1166.

95. The same position has been taken in Scotland: SCCCR, *Fourth Annual Report 2002–03* (Glasgow, 2003), 24; *Campbell, Steele, and Gray v. HMA* (2004 SCCR 220).

96. [2002] EWCA (Crim.) 2912.

97. [2003] EWCA (Crim.) 1060. See also *R. v. Howell* [2003] EWCA Crim. 01 at para. 11: "where such an ancillary ground is, as here, unrelated to the basis for the Commission's reference and has already been dismissed by this court upon an earlier application for leave to appeal, it is very unlikely to receive other than short shrift at the later appeal consequent on the Commission's reference." However, the Court passed no comment in *R. v. Mills (no. 2), R. v. Poole (no. 2)* [2003] EWCA Crim. 1753.

98. See G. Langdon-Down, "Favourable Reviews," *Law Society's Gazette* 101 (2004): 18.

99. (Auld) Review of the Criminal Courts in England and Wales (2001), para. 12.105. Indeed, since the Auld Report the delay has increased, with the average delay between CCRC referral and appeal now standing at twelve months.

100. Select Committee, *Report*, para. 18.

101. Ibid., para. 19.

102. See C. Walker and K. Starmer, eds., *Miscarriages of Justice* (London: Blackstone Press, 1999), chap. 12.

103. This provision is based in the United Nations International Covenant on Civil and Political Rights (1966), art.14(6): "When a person has by a final decision been convicted of a criminal offence and when subsequently his conviction has been reversed or he has been pardoned on the ground that a new or newly discovered fact shows conclusively that there has been a miscarriage of justice, the person who has suffered punishment as a result of such conviction shall be compensated according to law, unless it is proved that the non-disclosure of the unknown fact in time is wholly or partly attributable to him."

104. *The Independent Assessor v. O'Brien, Hickey, and Hickey* [2004] EWCA Civ. 1035.

105. *R. (Mullen) v. Secretary State for the Home Department* [2004] UKHL 18.

106. See *The Times,* January 12, 2005.

107. *The Independent Assessor v. O'Brien, Hickey and Hickey* [2004] EWCA Civ. 1035.

108. See A. Grounds, "Psychological Consequences of Wrongful Conviction and Imprisonment," *Canadian Journal of Criminology and Criminal Justice* 46 (2004), 165.

109. M. Naughton, "Why the Failure of the Prison Service and the Parole Board to Acknowledge Wrongful Imprisonment Is Untenable," *Howard Journal* 44 (2005): 1.

110. See *R. v. Downing* (Stephen Leslie) [2002] EWCA Crim. 263.

111. See *R. v. Brown (Robert)* [2002] EWCA Crim. 2804; N. Hopkins, "Man Wrongly Convicted of Murder Freed after 25 Years," *The Guardian*, November 14, 2002.

11

A COMPARATIVE ANALYSIS OF PROSECUTION IN GERMANY AND THE UNITED KINGDOM

Searching for Truth or Getting a Conviction?

∼

ISABEL KESSLER

The German criminal justice system is based on the inquisitorial tradition of all continental or civil law systems, contrary to the procedure in Anglo-Saxon common-law countries characterized by adversarial principles. The function of the prosecution, its influence on investigations, and its role in pretrial and trial proceedings differ substantially between the two systems. These differences, with regard to the implied risks of miscarriages of justice, are outlined in this chapter. I first outline the German system, followed by a section on the English prosecution service as it developed after recent changes. In the final section, I assess how the two systems favor and check the risks of wrongful convictions.

Germany

Overview of the German Prosecution and Criminal Justice System

The position and structure of the German prosecution service is defined in a law on the organization of the criminal justice system, called Court Constitutional Law (GVG), and further specified in the Code of Criminal Procedure (Strafprozessordnung; hereafter CCP).[1] The duties of the prosecutor as a special magistrate, being in charge of criminal investigations, were adopted under Prussian Justice Ministers von Savigny and Uhlen in 1856.

As custodian of the law, he[2] should have the responsibility not only to bring charges to court, but, during prior operations by the police, to investigate in favor of as well as against the defendant. This idea was expressed in General Prosecutor Isenbiel's statement, made in 1910, that "the prosecution service is the most objective authority in the world." Being a government's branch, it is vested with considerable autonomy from the Ministry, but organized separately and independently from the courts with a hierarchical structure.[3] Throughout Germany as a whole, there are about 5,150 prosecutors[4] who handle about 6.5 million crimes[5] per year.[6] In practice, each prosecution service consists of several officials who act as deputy prosecutors of the first officer (the higher prosecutor). In most cases, prosecutors act independently, but the head of service can require reports and give instructions as to how a particular case should be dealt with to standardize internal policies.[7] These powers of the head of service can be problematic, particularly since, in Germany, the prosecution service has a "monopoly" on bringing charges. To balance these powers, German prosecutors are legally obliged to charge a defendant for the offense he or she actually committed whenever the evidence seems, at first sight, sufficient to obtain a conviction (the so-called legality maxim).[8] In practice, offenses "of every kind" are first dealt with by police officers, although formally under the authority of the public prosecution service. Prosecutors and police officers are expected to lead the investigations as objectively as possible. By law, the public prosecution service is considered to be part of the government, but in practice it is also part of the judicial system. In the following sections, the role of the public prosecutor, particularly with respect to the search for "truth" and "justice," is discussed and critically evaluated.

The Investigation Process

The prosecution controls—as the head of pretrial proceedings—the investigations by the police who need to ask for a special warrant whenever coercive measures (see Table 11.1) are to be taken against a suspect. Whenever serious infringements of civil rights are at risk, prosecutors need a judge's approval.[9] The first interview of the suspect is usually conducted by the police. However, a magistrate's decision is necessary for an arrest warrant. The suspect has to be informed about the offense he is being charged with, of his right to remain silent, and of his right to ask for defense counsel. Statements obtained in violation of these principles cannot be used in court.

When the question of pretrial custody arises, the prosecution decides, after reading the police reports, whether or not the decision should be submitted to an examining magistrate. A custody order requires strong evidence that the offender has committed the offense under investigation, that he might otherwise fail to appear at later court hearings, or that he might destroy evidence or commit new serious offenses. Beyond these specific requirements, pretrial detention must be in line with the constitutional principle of proportionality. In assessing proportionality, the prosecutor considers the likelihood that the defendant will, in case of a verdict, receive an immediate custodial sentence. Before any decision, the judge will interview the defendant on the offense with which he is charged. As long as the defendant remains in pretrial detention, the prosecution has to check for the continuing presence of the reasons for custody. If, at a later stage of the investigation, the conditions for pretrial detention are not met, the prosecutor has to file a petition for the defendant to be released. In this case, the examining magistrate has no power to keep the defendant in pretrial detention even if he does not feel the reasons have not disappeared.

Once the police investigation is concluded, the prosecutor will check whether the investigation can be closed. Often important means of proof, such as hearing witnesses, have not been fully assessed yet. In such cases, the prosecutor, or on his behalf the police, initiate further examination measures. Frequently the prosecutor hears witnesses and, in some cases, the defendant and experts.[10] Moreover, the prosecutor will arrange, before preparing the

TABLE 11.1.   COERCIVE MEASURES, POWERS TO ISSUE
WARRANTS, AND PRECONDITIONS

Coercive Measures	Powers to Issue Warrants	Preconditions
Blood test, etc., § 81a CCP	Examining judge (in urgent cases: prosecution service and the police)	Initial suspicion
Use of forensic science evidence, § 81b CCP	Police, prosecution, or examining judge	Initial suspicion
Confiscation, § 94 CCP	Examining judge, prosecution service, and police in urgent cases	Initial suspicion
Wiretapping, § 100a CCP	Examining judge, prosecution in urgent cases	Qualified initial suspicion (based on facts, restricted offenses)
Searches, § 102 CCP	Examining judge, prosecution service, and police with danger in delay	Initial suspicion
Use of undercover detectives, § 110a CCP	Police with approval of prosecution service and judge	Initial suspicion (restricted offenses)
Pretrial custody §§ 112 CCP	Examining judge	Compelling suspicion of offense based on facts
Preliminary arrest, § 127 CCP	Police or prosecution service	Compelling suspicion of offense
Determining identity, § 163b 1 CCP	Police or prosecution service	Initial suspicion
Lengthy observation, § 163 CCP	Examining judge, if observation is longer than one month, otherwise prosecution service, police in urgent cases	Initial suspicion

indictment, for eventual forensic science (of fingerprints, DNA testing, etc.) and other expert reports (e.g., on the mental condition of the defendant). These reports will be available to the court and the defendant. The code of criminal procedure[11] and a few other laws[12] allow the dismissal of a case. This so-called opportunity principle, or expediency maxim, is an exception to the prevailing legality principle. Prosecutors have the option to drop a case during or at the end of the preliminary investigation. Beyond the opportunity or expediency principle, the prosecutor can also dismiss proceedings because there is insufficient evidence. However, based on the opportunity principle, prosecutors often drop cases, although the evidence might call for a conviction, if the defendant agrees, in return, to meet certain conditions.[13] In this case, the defendant will not have a criminal record, but the case will remain recorded in the files of the prosecution service. Dismissal of a case is possible whenever the defendant's guilt is considered minor, or if the court can see no need for a penalty. Examples are charges of possession of less than ten grams of marijuana as a first-time offender, or first-time or juvenile offenders with low criminal intent and damage, such as shoplifting. Other circumstances are situations where the offense (e.g., shoplifting) is not considered serious in comparison to another offense (e.g., robbery) of which the defendant is likely to be found guilty, or because of peculiarities in the offense, offenders, or victims. The opportunity or expediency principle allows the public prosecution to concentrate on cases of higher priority. In general, the relevant facts are investigated only summarily if the case is likely to be dismissed. Under the German system, the police are not authorized to drop cases. They must refer to the prosecution service, which alone has authority to drop a case.[14]

In about 15 percent of all cases handled by the prosecution service, an indictment is filed before the competent court. An indictment needs to specify clearly the facts with which the defendant is being charged, as well as their legal qualification and the evidence. About an equal proportion of cases ends with a so-called penal order,[15] a conviction by the prosecutor that needs to be approved by the competent court. This simplified procedure is a kind of German version of plea bargaining, since it needs, implicitly, the defendant's approval, and the defendant always has the right to insist on a trial in court. Unlike in the United States, plea bargaining is available, however, only if the sentence does not exceed a suspended custodial sentence of one year (or a fine); that is, for less serious offenses. In line with his impartial role, a German prosecutor may become criminally liable for a felony (§ 339 of the penal code)[16] whenever he files charges although the facts clearly point to the innocence of the defendant[17] or if, in cases where diversion is not a reasonable option, he fails to charge a defendant who is obviously guilty, or to do whatever may be necessary to obtain a conviction given the merits of the case.

The Trial Stage

During the trial, the prosecutor who intervenes during hearings is not necessarily the same person who conducted the pretrial investigation and prepared the indictment. In this case, this "outside" prosecutor not only is less familiar with the details of the case than the judge and the defense counsel, but he may, eventually, also be less motivated to intervene actively during proceedings. In practice, he will contact the colleague who prepared the case before entering an agreement ending the proceedings. Such procedural agreements take on more and more significance, especially in larger and complicated proceedings. It frequently happens that, some time ahead of the hearing, the defense counsel, the prosecutor, or the judge meet to discuss, informally, what sentence might be expected "in case of a confession." The court is primarily interested in an agreement rather than the prosecution. Any such settlement requires a guilty plea by the defendant. If an agreement is reached, the fact that time and costs involved in a trial are being saved is expressly taken into account as a rationale for mitigating the sentence.

According to the guidelines adopted by the Federal Supreme Court,[18] such an agreement is possible only if the following conditions are met: (1) The arrangement must take place among all parties, although preliminary informal talks are not ruled out. If negotiations lead to an agreement, the result is formally introduced into the trial. (2) The terms of the settlement must be ratified in the trial minutes. (3) The court must check the confession to ascertain whether it is credible; hearing of evidence may still be necessary in some cases. (4) The court is not supposed to impose any sentence before the hearing; however, the court may accept an upper limit to any custodial sentence. This limit will be binding, except if unexpected facts are disclosed during the trial. Formally, guilty pleas and waivers of appeal[19] are not permitted; similarly, the legal qualification of the criminal offense is not negotiable.[20]

In sum, these negotiations are similar to plea bargaining under the U.S. system, although prosecutors and judges have far less discretion as to how to settle a case. In practice, such settlements are used only in complicated cases that otherwise might require excessive resources. Critics observe, however, that there might be a risk of "tactical guilty pleas," and that the principle of public hearings as well as the oral character[21] of trial hearings might be undermined.

The criminal procedure in Germany does not rely on parties. The prosecutor on the one hand and the defendant on the other may not offer facts and evidence to the court as parties. To search for the truth, the court is entitled and has a duty to do whatever can reasonably be expected to clarify any aspect of a case, without being bound by petitions from the prosecution, the victim, or the defense.[22] Thus, judges inquire themselves (instruction principle) and proceed on an inquisitorial basis. As a result, they not only lead the trial, but are the "masters of the main proceedings."[23] The prosecution and defense have no control over what evidence is to be heard, and they cannot make facts uncontested by mutual agreement (or silence).[24] A kind of "formal" truth is unknown in criminal procedure. Whenever concrete suspicions point to the presence of circumstances that are of significance for the assessment of the offense, the court must investigate the issue, even without motions to take evidence. In the search for truth, the court is bound to certain rules,[25] but it freely assesses the result of the hearing of evidence.[26] In any case the judge's appraisal of the truth needs to remain in line with established facts and must not be arbitrary, particularly for questions of guilt and punishment where the principle *in dubio pro reo*[27] requires a high degree of certainty. Yet, wide latitude remains. In appeal proceedings, a violation of the rules of evidence[28] is promising only if evidence can be presented that demonstrates, without a new trial, that the facts, as assessed by the lower court, are not in line with evidence and facts presented during trial.[29] Thus, an appeal is unlikely to be successful if it is based on the mere assertion that a witness has made statements, out of court, that are not in line with what he had told the court. Additionally, at proceedings in the regional courts of first or second instance, not even a summary report of the witness and expert statements is presented, with rather rare and narrow exceptions.[30] These rules can jeopardize the finding of truth and narrow the control of decisions through appeal proceedings.

According to the rule *Nemo tenetur se ipsum accusare*, the person accused may not be compelled to take part actively in proving his own guilt. This principle is secured by the defendant's right to remain silent, of which he must be informed before any examination.[31] Essentially, no disadvantageous conclusions can be drawn from silence. On the part of the court and the prosecution, it is occasionally assumed that only guilty defendants and those skilled in court practice make use of their right to remain silent. Therefore, the defendant's silence is (unjustly) understood as a kind of "declaration of war," which at least can have a negative influence on the climate during the trial. The accused is not obliged to remove the reasons for suspicion or to offer evidence for his innocence.[32] The right to remain silent implies that the defendant does not face disadvantage from his silence.[33] Under no circumstances may the fact be taken into account that he did not speak during police examination, only before the judge.[34] If the defendant is silent only before the judge, the examining officer may be used as a witness from hearsay.[35]

The "prosecutor's finest hour" is the pleading. In this speech, all means of proof listed in the trial (and only these) are to be assessed, the watertight factual content shown, and the relevant legal provisions explained, particularly why the facts, as assessed, meet the legal criteria. The pleading closes with a recommendation of a particular sentence and eventual further legal consequences. The rhetorical skills of a prosecutor may have an impact, especially on the assessment of the criminal events by lay judges who, in the magistrates' courts of first instance and in the small criminal courts of the regional District Courts (acting as an appeals court),[36] can outvote the professional judge with respect to the verdict and the sentence. Usually the prosecutor, representing the state authority, is listened to more than the defender, who pleads last and who is often considered "too subjective" by lay judges. Prosecutors should not abuse the impression they usually make on lay judges, but use it in the sense of promoting material justice. If, during the trial, it turns out that the defendant's guilt cannot be proven beyond reasonable doubt, the prosecutor, after exhausting all means of proof, has to honor this outcome in his pleading and, for legal or factual reasons, apply for acquittal, even if this may be difficult to explain to his superior. At this stage, a prosecutor must keep in mind that the result of an oral and public trial does not always match the result of the pretrial investigation,[37] let alone that further evidence presented by the defense may have changed the outcome. Hence, an unexpected outcome is not seen, by a representative of the "World's most objective authority," as a defeat, but as a sign of the fairness of the criminal justice system.[38]

Appeal and Other Postconviction Duties of the Prosecutor

If the court, against the personal conviction of the prosecutor, has reached a verdict of acquittal, the prosecutor is obliged to file an appeal in favor of the defendant.[39] In practice, this is too rarely the case. An appeal in favor of the defendant can be filed by the prosecution without or even against the defendant's will, but only if the verdict has practical negative implications for him. In making his decision, the responsible officer within the prosecution service is in principle bound by guidelines issued for the exercise of discretion.[40] According to these rules, an appeal should only be filed if the defendant has been disadvantaged by a violation of rules of fair trial, by an obvious error of the court, or if the sentence appears too severe taking into account all relevant circumstances. Important public interests and concerns of people involved in the proceedings must be taken into account. Once a verdict becomes final, the prosecutor in charge of the case passes the proceedings to the correctional service. At this stage, he has to decide what to do with any exhibits and other pieces of evidence, such as fingerprints and human cells.[41] Physical evidence of this kind should, contrary to former practice, be retained in the interest of finding the truth, particularly with respect to a later reopening of proceedings.[42] The reopening, although an infringement of the principle that final decisions should no longer be contestable, offers a last resort in cases where final decisions are based on an erroneous factual basis. Petitions for reopening have no chance if they are aimed at correcting errors in the interpretation of criminal law, or at re-evaluating evidence presented during trial. The defense, and also the prosecutor, may apply for reopening of a case in favor of the convicted defendant.[43] There is considerable reluctance toward this "extraordinary" appeal procedure, as it undermines the noble principle of the rule of law, particularly in the eyes of the judiciary. On the other hand, it is not out of line with the role of the prosecutor as the "world's most objective authority." A study conducted during the 1960s[44] identified, over a period of some thirty years, some 1,600 reopened cases.[45]

Nevertheless, the search for material truth is, theoretically at least, best secured by the inquisitorial principle as it operates in Germany. Risk factors leading, eventually, to miscarriages of justice may include the reluctance of courts to hear expert witnesses on the reliability of confessions and eyewitnesses, the widespread use of procedural agreements between the prosecution and the defense counsel, and, perhaps most of all, the broad discretion of judges in assessing evidence[46] that, under certain circumstances, may be hard to verify. The purpose of finding the truth in appeal proceedings is not served by the fact that the course of the trial (either the first or the second instance) before the district court is not tape-recorded.[47] The fact that an appeal can only be based on the minutes of the trial considerably limits its chances of success. Furthermore, enormous local differences with respect to charging and sentencing continue to exist throughout Germany. Some standardization should be achieved through national guidelines.[48]

England and Wales

Every time you stand up in court as a Crown Prosecutor, you'll have to ensure that the case you're prosecuting will stand up too.[49]

The Position and the Role of the Crown Prosecution Service

The Crown Prosecution Service (CPS) is the government department responsible for prosecuting defendants in England and Wales.[50] Created by the Prosecution of Offences Act 1985 and operating since 1986,[51] it is a single independent and nationwide authority that works closely with the police.[52] Up to this point, local police forces had been solely responsible for deciding whether to prosecute particular cases.[53] Hence, prosecutions were either brought by police officers or by hired lawyers acting on behalf of the police.

The principal reasons for establishing the CPS were to encourage greater consistency in prosecution and to provide for independent review of police cases before they reach the trial stage.[54] Its lawyers, although being civil servants, were expected to be independent of government control, although little was put in place to guarantee this.[55] Although formally independent of the police, the CPS has to rely entirely on information provided by the police in making the decision whether to prosecute or not. Unlike its German counterpart, the CPS has no power to institute proceedings, or to direct the police to carry out further investigations.

The Royal Commission on Criminal Justice in 1993 commented that the CPS was hastily conceived and inadequately resourced. Another source of friction with the police, as well as causing frustration for the victims and the court, was the way the CPS could drop cases. These criticisms eventually led to the 1998 Glidewell Report,[56] which recommended its reorganization into forty-two areas largely coinciding with the police operation districts.[57] Each area has a Chief Crown Prosecutor (CCP) managing a team of lawyers and case workers. The CPS is subject to supervision by a central inspectorate, which has employed new practices, applying business-like principles. The Director of Public Prosecutions (DPP) heads the CPS[58] and reports to the Attorney General, who holds parliamentary responsibility for the Service.[59]

As the principal prosecuting authority, the CPS is giving advice to the police any time they seek it. However, and unlike the system in Germany, the CPS has no direct control over the police and their investigations. It reviews cases submitted by the police, prepares cases for court, and presents them there, based on the Code for Crown Prosecutors,[60] which demands cases to be prosecuted firmly, fairly, and effectively wherever the evidence offers a realistic prospect of conviction and if it is in the public interest to do so. Unlike in Germany, however, other authorities also have the power to prosecute,[61] which implies that prosecution may be guided by interests other than those of formal justice as well. Nevertheless, 75 percent of magistrates' court prosecutions and 95 percent of those in the Crown Court are brought by the CPS. In magistrates' courts, a Crown Prosecutor or even a solicitor or barrister[62] from a private law firm may be charged by the CPS to act on its behalf in particular cases.[63] In the Crown Court, cases are presented by barristers instructed by the CPS, or, in cases involving guilty pleas, by higher court advocates (CPS or private practice solicitors). By March 2003, the CPS employed 7,046 people, including 2,267 lawyers and 4,711 case workers and administrators dealing with (in 2002–2003) 1.44 million cases sent by the police, leading to 1.08 million prosecutions in the magistrates' courts and 80,000 in the Crown Court.[64]

According to the government-initiated Glidewell Report, the CPS was considered too centralized and overly bureaucratic. O'Reilly and Stevens[65] claim that by comparison with defense lawyers, prosecution lawyers often appear inadequately prepared in court because of lack of time or opportunity to get familiar with cases.[66] There was also a need to clarify the aims of the CPS and its proper relationships with other agencies of the criminal justice system. The Auld Report,[67] based on a major review of the criminal courts in England and Wales, suggested changes in the procedures for preparation for trial, including a shift in the respective roles of the police and the prosecuting authorities so that in the majority of cases, the CPS and not the police would decide whether to charge and what with. It also recommended that the CPS should have more responsibility for discharging the prosecution's duties of disclosure. Therefore, the Criminal Justice Act (CJA) 2003[68] provides for much greater involvement of the CPS in determining whether proceedings should be instituted and, if so, on which charge. Important previous police roles have thus been taken over by the CPS. For instance, the CJA 2003 provides mechanisms for custody officers to seek advice from the CPS on the correct charge to be made.[69]

The Investigation Process

In the English adversarial or accusatorial system, it is the role of the police and the prosecution on one hand, and of the defense on the other hand, to present opposing accounts of the suspect's blameworthiness. It is left to the jury or the magistrates to pick the winning version. In this system, the police play the central role in the construction of the prosecution's campaign to persuade the fact finders. Their role is not an impartial one, and it is only recently that the police became obliged to inform the defense of any evidence favorable to the defense. Accordingly, the police's view is influenced by traditional values and reflects the prosecutorial role.[70]

As soon as the police challenge any individual they regard as a suspect, an adversarial relationship is formed. On arrest, the suspect is taken to a police station and detained. Here, due process protection including the right of access to lawyers and others should apply, since civil liberties are further eroded by means of interrogation, search of the suspect's home, fingerprinting, DNA testing, and so on. As these actions are only dependent on police discretion, in many cases, their ECHR[71] compatibility is questionable. The police investigation process has been the source of many discussions and legal changes.[72] For example, the practice of "stop and search" on the streets was not legally legitimized before the Police and Criminal Evidence Act (PACE) in 1984, which provided the first nationwide stop-and-search powers that were extended by further acts. Now, it is held that the police must have "reasonable suspicion" founded on an objective basis to exercise, at least as a general rule, arrest and stop-and-search powers.[73] These increased formal powers have led to increased use of this crude instrument of crime control,[74] often based on broad, intangible suspicions.[75] Stop-and-search, as well as an arrest, can be made without juridical warrant and are allowed in most "normal crimes"[76] and the police periodically are given greater powers for more offenses.[77] Furthermore, the Criminal Justice Act 2003 allows in section 4 for police officers, as an alternative to taking detained persons to a police station to arrest them, to bail them to attend a police station at a later date. Failure to answer such police bail may lead to arrest without a warrant.

The CJA 2003 further includes an extension of power to fingerprint and to take nonintimate samples from detained suspects without consent.[78] This can be seen either as a violation of civil rights or as part and parcel of the unprecedented advances in relation to the detection and investigation of crime using new technologies.[79] Even before the new Act, getting objective evidence like DNA was fairly easy and possible without further legal barriers. Unlike in Germany, coercive measures are not dependent on any previous decision by a prosecutor or a judge. Rather, police can make a unilateral decision whether to take samples or not. Recently, DNA samples have been routinely collected from the scenes of both serious and high-volume crimes along with subject samples from individual suspects.[80] A police officer is entitled to question any person from whom he or she thinks useful information can be obtained. This person's declaration that he or she is unwilling to reply does not alter this entitlement. Therefore, police officers are able to carry on with questioning and persuade suspects to change their minds, which results in heavy psychological pressure.[81] The obvious dangers implied in these methods have been exacerbated through the Criminal Justice and Public Order Act 1994 (CJPOA), which provided that the court can draw an adverse inference from a defendant's earlier silence whenever he or she invokes a fact that he or she could have been reasonably expected to mention when questioned by the police. In addition, courts can draw adverse inferences from failures to answer questions in court. Hence, it is most surprising that, despite Article 6 § 2 ECHR,[82] the European Court of Human Rights has ruled these provisions to be in line with the Convention.[83]

Half of all suspects interrogated either confess or make incriminating statements to the police.[84] However, coercion may occur in both formal and informal interrogations. During formal interrogations, a police officer who insists on questioning a suspect despite his or her former refusal may cause psychological strain, whereas informal interrogations are a dubious means of securing confessions outside formal and tape-recorded[85] interrogations and occur mostly on the way to the police station.[86] Formally, the provisions in sections 58 to 60 of PACE 1984 guarantee free legal advice to all suspects who request it, the suspect having a right to be informed of this by the custody officer. In reality, only 40 percent of suspects use this service, at least partly due to missing information.[87] The higher the level of police pressure, the greater the risk of false confessions,[88] because suspects believe, or are influenced to believe, that the benefits of confessing outweigh the costs.[89] This potential cradle of miscarriages of justice is aggravated by the lack of sufficient safeguards.[90] PACE section 76(2) does include a shift in the burden of proof, as it is now the duty of the prosecution to prove that a confession has not been obtained as a consequence of anything said or done that might invalidate it. In several high-profile cases, the Appeal Court was obliged to overturn convictions that rested on confessions that turned out to be false. Between 1989 and 2002, the convictions of twenty-three high-profile murder cases were quashed.[91] According to Gudjonsson,[92] 61 percent of those defendants can be categorized as psychologically vulnerable,[93] but the rest were due to police misbehavior or malpractice. In the case of the Guilford 4 and Birmingham 6, it was discovered, during the reinvestigation, that the police had fabricated evidence concerning some of the defendants' interview records. All of the Guilford 4[94] made written confessions, which they later alleged having accepted under coercion by the police. Paul Hill, one of the Guilford 4, says that he was threatened by a Surrey police officer who pointed an unloaded gun through the hatch in his cell door.[95] The Birmingham 6[96] also alleged that they were physically threatened and assaulted during their custodial interrogation. In the case of Wayne Darvell,[97] whose confession to the police concerning his and his brother's implication in murder, a reinvestigation revealed that his original police interview records had been rewritten in a way that altered their content; in particular, leading questions had been changed to make them appear nonleading.[98] In the Bridgewater case, the police faked a confession from a co-accused and lied about it to extract a written confession statement from another suspect, which resulted in the conviction of four men for the murder of thirteen-year-old newspaper delivery boy Carl Bridgewater.[99] In this context, it should be emphasized that every year, around two million people are arrested by the police.[100] Around half of all suspects admit to offenses afterward. Securing a confession is still regarded as the most important aim of interviewing suspects by the police. Prior to the change in the rules concerning the right of silence, about 10 percent of suspects refused to answer any questions by the police, compared to 6 percent after the revision.[101] This development obviously favors false confessions. On arrest, all suspects should be brought directly to the police station where a custody police officer decides whether or not the suspect should be detained. Not surprisingly, detention is rarely refused.

The CJA 2003[102] provides a new thirty-six-hour detention without charge for all arrestable offenses[103] on condition that an officer of the rank of a superintendent or above must have reasonable grounds for believing that the detention of that person without charge is necessary to secure or preserve evidence relating to an offence for which he or she is under arrest, or to obtain such evidence by questioning him or her. For those suspected of terrorism, detention of up to fourteen days is now legal.[104] Schedule 2 of the CJA 2003 amends PACE and provides that, where a custody officer is deciding whether or not there is enough evidence to charge a suspect in police detention, he must have regard to guidance issued by the Director of Public Prosecutions (DPP), concerning whether the suspect should be released without charge but on bail, released without bail and charged with an offense, and so on. When, under the DPP's guidance, a case is referred to the CPS to determine whether proceedings should be instituted, the defendant must be released on police bail with or without conditions. The guidance is aimed at ensuring that all major decisions, particularly those concerning sensitive cases, are referred to the DPP. (See Table 11.2.)

Cases must be sent to the DPP as soon as possible so that a decision can be made as to what action, if any, is to be taken against the offender. The options open to the DPP when a case is referred are: (1) insufficient evidence to charge (a notice is given to the suspect); (2) sufficient evidence to charge, but a decision is made not to charge (public interest grounds, notice is given to the suspect); (3) sufficient evidence to charge, but caution is appropriate (police *must* caution, they cannot decide not to caution); and (4) charge with offense, either by virtue of provisions under section 29 of the CJA 2003 or by police on answering police bail.

TABLE 11.2. OPTIONS AVAILABLE TO A CUSTODY OFFICER (DPP MAY ISSUE GUIDANCE)

Charge with Offense	Release without Charge and without Bail	Release without Charge but on Bail	Release without Charge and on Bail for the Purpose of Enabling the DPP to Make a Decision under Section 37 B
The police still retain the right to charge a suspect with any appropriate offense. Upon charge, a decision is made either to bail the suspect to court or to keep him in custody and produce him before the next available court.	This ends the investigation, although the suspect may be rearrested if new evidence becomes available.	This is to allow for the release of the suspect on bail while the police undertake further enquiries.	This option is broader than the present "advice file" procedure and is assigned to ensure that the charge (if there is to be one) is correct. Also, conditional bail can be imposed.

The police custody officers will need to have regard to the guidance issued by the DPP when making a decision.[105] In practice, this will be inseparable from questions of when the police must refer a case to the CPS. It is expected that the police will be able to bring charges only in minor cases,[106] as well as in cases where there is an unequivocal acceptance of guilt from the outset, and will probably be disposed of by a magistrates' court. Furthermore, the police will have to charge where envisaged that the defendant would be released on bail while waiting for the CPS's decision. Hence, where a detention seems to be realistic,[107] the police will charge as part of the process through which the defendant is brought before court to seek a remand in custody. Theoretically, the new section 37B of PACE provides the CPS with the power to determine whether the suspect should be charged, and if so, with what offense. The CPS will have to conclude that the evidence is sufficient, or decide that the suspect will be offered a (conditional) caution. Therefore, conflicts may arise regarding the exact role of the police and CPS, with possible negative effects on the actual proceedings.

Before and since the CJA 2003, the relationship between the CPS and the police has been difficult. Both Glidewell and RCCJ[108] have noted the existence of serious tensions, rivalry, and a certain "blame-culture."[109] According to the CPS, their advice was sought in only 5 percent of all cases between 1993 and 1995.[110] The CPS even reported that it was not uncommon for their requests to be ignored or refused.[111] A 1996 pilot scheme that guaranteed the availability of Crown Prosecutors in some selected police stations to provide early face-to-face advice to officers did not encourage police officers to seek consultation.[112] Although the CPS now has to decide whether to proceed with a case, it still cannot demand further investigation or direct police operational procedures.

The Pretrial Stage

Whenever the police charge a suspect, the case file is, according to the CJA 2003, handed over to the CPS. The Crown Prosecutor will then review the evidence and witness statements collected by the police, decide whether the case should go to court, and if so, what the precise charge should be. The CPS can, as already mentioned, only proceed if the available evidence offers a realistic prospect of conviction, and if the prosecution is in the public interest. While the latter corresponds largely to the German opportunity principle, the first requirement has a much higher standard than the pre-CPS test used by the police: Is there a prima facie case?[113] This includes an assessment of how witnesses will come across, and how a jury or magistrate might react. However, there exists evidence that prosecutors do not always adhere to these rules and continue cases that should have been discontinued.[114] Up to now, weak cases have rarely been dropped, and if so, only on the initiative of the police or after several court appearances.[115] The reasons for this were the furtherance of police working rules, the chance of a freak conviction, and the reliance on guilty pleas.[116] Where police working rules pointed to prosecution, the CPS was reluctant to stop the case,[117] a problem unknown in Germany, where the police have no power to charge, caution, or dismiss a case. But the changes established by the CJA 2003 provide at least a theoretical improvement, even though the CPS is still in a structurally weak position, given that the police shaped the case and collected all the evidence.[118]

Contrary to the German system, the CPS does not have the possibility to take over investigations, hear suspects, or expert witnesses, even if a case depends entirely on a key witness's credibility. Hence, the CPS reviews the quality of police cases that are shaped to be prosecutable. The facts are to serve as a support and are, therefore, selected in a way so that weaknesses only appear at trial. Thus, prosecutors often have no chance to know what gaps exist in the information they receive. This situation is exacerbated in cases where the Crown Prosecutor has to rely on very selective police summaries.[119] Hence, on the one hand, the CPS seems to be strongly influenced by police working rules, counting on guilty pleas, and the chance of unexpected "freak" convictions. On the other hand, bureaucratic and economic reasons[120] may prevent an effective prosecution in accordance with the two requirements foreseen in the CCP.[121]

The risk of miscarriages of justice is exacerbated by the tendency of prosecutors to maximize the number of prosecutions in the hope that defendants will plead guilty. Typically enough, the success of the CPS is measured by the number of convictions, which is generally regarded as too low.[122] The lack of objectivity of the CPS in weak cases presents a great risk of miscarriages of justice, particularly in view of unsupervised police investigations and interrogations. This is a general weakness of the adversarial system. The CPS is expected to assist the police in achieving a maximum conviction rate, as opposed to the "neutral" search for truth by German prosecutors. Although the role of the CPS as a police prosecution agency may be inherent in an adversarial system, the costs for a suspect who cannot rely on the CPS for the protection of his or her rights are obviously high.

Another critical point with regard to avoiding miscarriages of justice involves disclosure rules. Such rules must exist and be fully adhered to to provide equality between prosecution and defense in their access to evidence. In the past, the prosecution was blamed for suppressing evidence favorable to the defense, as for example in the cases of the Guilford 4 and Birmingham 6, where such misbehavior went on even at the appeal hearings.[123] Additionally, the reinvestigation in the case of Wayne Darvell[124] cast doubt on the non-disclosure of a blood-stained palm print at the crime scene that belonged to neither of the Darvell brothers. The Criminal Procedure and Investigations Act 1996 (CPIA) created a statutory scheme for disclosure of evidence in criminal proceedings.[125] The prosecution was required to disclose to the defense any material it had knowledge of, which, in the prosecutor's opinion, might undermine the prosecution's case.[126] Part 5 of the CJA 2003 amended the CPIA concerning defense case statements and disclosure by the prosecution to the defense of "unused material," whereas Section 33 of the CJA 2003 amended the defense disclosure requirements, obliging the defendant to provide a more detailed defense statement than under the former law. On the other hand, the prosecutor will have to review prosecution material on receipt of the defense statement and make disclosures as appropriate under a continuing duty. Nevertheless, it is dubious whether a full disclosure by the prosecution, which is indispensable as many miscarriages of justice arise from partial disclosure, is now guaranteed. Greater duties of disclosure for both the defense and the prosecution have been established, but those duties are more onerous for the defense. This inequality may lead to ineffective investigation of the issues on behalf of the defense.

The Trial Stage

Virtually all criminal cases start at the magistrates' courts, with the less serious offenses being settled at that level, and up to 95 percent of all cases proceed under the control of magistrates.[127] More serious offenses are passed on to the Crown Court, to be dealt with by a judge and a jury.[128] As mentioned, the CPS can, before the start of the trial or committal, discontinue proceedings whenever a conviction seems unlikely given the available evidence, or if prosecution is not in the public interest. Alternatively, the CPS can bring different or additional charges whenever it considers that the evidence supports this. Unlike under the German system, there is no bar on any additional charges or facts not mentioned in the indictment. Obviously, weak cases should be discontinued as soon as possible. A study found, however, that the prosecution case was weak in about a fifth of Crown Court contested cases, of which over 80 percent ended in an acquittal (Zender & Henderson, 1993). Moxon and Crisp (1994) detected that only 12 percent of cases were discontinued on or before the first hearing. Prior to the establishment of the CPS in 1985, judge-ordered and judge-directed acquittals accounted for up to 48 percent of all acquittals, but increased to 58 percent in 1990 and stood at 54 percent in 2000,[129] while judge-ordered acquittals have risen from 26 percent to 38 percent of all nonjury acquittals.

This high dismissal rate is said to be due to the weakness of CPS-initiated cases, which may be linked with its ongoing dependency on the police. However, the weakness of some cases cannot be detected as the CPS has no possibility to hear witnesses or to initiate further investigations. Besides, the CPS cannot formally discontinue a case once it has been committed for trial, where a witness may prove to be unreliable, but must ask the judge to order an acquittal. Nevertheless, 80 percent of nonjury acquittals were foreseeable due to weaknesses that were mostly known to the CPS before trial and were often recorded in the file itself. Despite clear indications suggesting discontinuance, prosecutors often failed to do so because either they tended to endorse the initial police view, eventually came under some pressure from the police, or because they hoped to obtain a guilty plea—a hope that often becomes a sad reality (McConville, Hodgson, Bridges, & Pavlovic, 1994; McConville, Sanders, & Leng, 1991).

Criminal offenses fall into three categories: triable only on indictment,[130] triable either way,[131] and summary offenses.[132] On summary trial, the court reads the charge to the defendant and asks whether he or she pleads guilty or not guilty. If a defense lawyer is present, he or she will give the court the defendant's explanation of the offense and any other matters in the defendant's favor. This might include information about an early guilty plea. More than 80 percent of defendants convicted by the magistrate's court plead guilty.[133] In this case, the court will usually hear an outline of the case from the prosecution and then proceed, without any further evidence or interrogation, to the sentencing stage. However, where the defendant pleads guilty and then says something that indicates a defense to the charge or says, for example, that the plea is entered "to get the case over with," the guilty plea must be rejected theoretically.[134] Just over 4 percent of all proceedings are dealt with by the Crown Court. Roughly three defendants in five plead guilty.[135] As at the magistrates' court, in these cases the judge immediately imposes the sentence, and no jury is involved.

In the context of trial proceedings, the problem of plea bargaining arises. Some call this phenomenon the most virulent virus ever to have invaded the criminal justice system,[136] as it seems impossible to solve the inherent conflict of efficiency and fairness. Further, the principle that hearings should be oral and the rights to a fair and public trial are endangered if arrangements are made behind closed doors in negotiations among prosecution, defense, and judge to manage the rising caseload they are facing. Research has revealed that 40 percent of defendants plead guilty under pressure from their defense barrister, even without a specific offer being made to them. [137] Only 29 percent admitted that they were guilty as pleaded, with no deal or pressure having occurred. Hence, plea bargaining is widespread, but few defendants seem to enter truly voluntary guilty pleas. Instead, many defendants seem to admit that, even in the absence of a formal agreement, a guilty plea would be honored under the form of a reduced sentence. The most dangerous consequences of plea bargaining are related to the risks for the truly innocent. The plea-bargaining process hardly distinguishes between those likely to get convicted or those likely to be acquitted. Thus, there is no guarantee that plea bargaining operates only among the guilty and does not threaten the innocent.[138] Even prosecutors themselves regarded one in seven cases handled by plea bargaining as difficult to get a conviction.[139] This obvious risk of miscarriages of justice is exacerbated by the lack of appropriate defense work and the guilty plea orientation of many criminal lawyers.[140] There is evidence[141] suggesting that serious errors by defense lawyers contribute significantly to wrongful convictions that are rarely overturned on appeal. In 1,300 cases of alleged miscarriages of justice,[142] complaints regarding inadequate counsel work arose in 47 percent.[143] Yet, despite repeated condemnations by the Court of Appeal,[144] the attraction of plea bargaining persists.

The trial stage itself is the pivotal point of the process as the facts are established and the law is applied. During this process, the prosecution must do nothing to suggest back-door, secret communication to improperly influence the court.[145] It is for the prosecution and the defense to lead their own witnesses, to test the credibility of the opposition by cross-examination, and to argue their own interpretation of the evidence and the law. As such, the adversarial process is a competition between two opposing parties.[146]

The critical issues are related to evidence. The CJA 2003 made fundamental changes to the admissibility of evidence relating to character evidence and hearsay. The far-reaching section 103 provides for the admissibility of previous convictions[147] either in support of propensity to commit similar offenses or to detect untruthfulness.[148] During the hearings, judges are more than reluctant to exclude evidence.[149] This powerful weapon, able to ruin the case of the prosecution, is rarely applied as most judges are said to be unwilling to see incriminating material excluded.[150] Central due-process rules are the presumption of innocence and the right of silence,[151] but, as already mentioned, defendants who do not take the stand or, after having done so, refuse to answer any question without good cause, are liable to have such adverse inferences as appear proper drawn from their silence. The suspect's silence may be held against him or her, without the suspect's properly understanding the implications of his or her decision whether or not to answer the police's questions. The failure to cooperate may be used against the suspect in the same way as positive evidence, lessening the burden of proof resting on the prosecution, which has to prove each fact "beyond a reasonable doubt."

Considering the string of quashed convictions and miscarriages of justice over the past twenty-five years, the former operation of proceedings certainly was more than questionable,[152] although the responsibility for this lies not just with the trial courts. Many of these cases are associated with police malpractice, such as coercive or oppressive interviews, failure to caution the detainee or to provide him or her with a solicitor on request, alteration of interview records, suppression of exculpatory evidence, perjury, or other factors.[153] Hence, the jury in the infamous miscarriage of justice case of the Birmingham 6 was faced with confessions backed up by alleged forensic evidence relating to the handling of explosives. Others are said to be due to the failures of the Home Office, which, in its former role of predecessor of the CCRC, ignored compelling subsequent evidence. This is highlighted by the case of Stefan Kizsko, where later analysis of the DNA showed that he was innocent.[154] Some blame the Court of Appeal's reluctance to recognize when a conviction is "unsafe and unsatisfactory." Often defendants are convicted despite insubstantial evidence. For example, Winston Silcott, in the Broadwater Farm trial,[155] was not connected to the killing by any forensic evidence, nor any of the thousands of photos and videos at the scene, nor any eyewitness account, but was convicted on the strength of an unsigned statement saying "you can't pin this on me, no-one will talk."[156] The elevated risk of miscarriages of justice may also be blamed on the prosecution, which cannot supervise the police, but should be self-conscious enough to detect independently legal and factual weaknesses, which should be taken into consideration when deciding whether there is a realistic chance of conviction. However, as long as the courts admit improperly obtained evidence, it is unlikely that the CPS will discontinue a weak case, which may well result in a conviction.

The Criminal Appeal System

Appeals in general made a relatively late appearance on the English legal scene,[157] but are now provided by law.[158] Appeals following a magistrate's decision are more common than those against a Crown Court verdict, a difference that reflects a deep trust in jury decisions. Furthermore, Appeal judges have been criticized for being excessively reluctant to overturn jury decisions, and for being unwilling to criticize colleagues in the legal profession for providing poor defense work. The types of errors a criminal trial may give rise to are classified as errors of law, errors of fact, or an irregularity in the trial process causing the loss of a chance of acquittal.[159] Appeals are usually heard by two judges. A further appeal to the Divisional Court to the House of Lords, the country's highest court, is possible. However, appeals following a trial on indictment in the Crown Court are very restricted. The defendant is allowed to appeal a conviction or sentence to the Court of Appeal, where the case is heard by three judges.[160] According to the law,[161] an appeal is open against convictions; whenever the judges think that it is unsafe, it must be quashed, otherwise the appeal must be dismissed. The Court itself confirms the quashing of convictions for cases provoking a "lurking doubt."[162] Whenever a conviction cannot stand, the court is directed to order a retrial, a *venire de novo,* or to substitute an alternative offense for a conviction. Often, the possibility to make no order is chosen. Any further appeal by either party is submitted to the House of Lords. If an appeal is directed not against the verdict, but against the sentence, the case is heard by two judges, mostly without representation of the prosecution. In case of a successful appeal, the Court may impose a different sentence, provided the new one is not more severe than the previous one. The prosecution had no right to appeal a verdict, sentence, or both before 1972. Part 9 of the CJA 2003 expands the prosecution's right to appeal to the Court of Appeal in several respects, to balance the defendant's existing right of appeal against conviction and sentence.

To summarize, there are procedures by which a defendant can try to undo a miscarriage of justice, but many limitations still exist, such as the time limit for appealing[163] or—in general—the adversarial nature of the trial. The latter allows both prosecution and defense to select the facts they will present before the magistrates' or Crown Court, so that Appeal Courts, which are not in search of the objective truth, but must rely on the most convincing presentation, are very reluctant to offer a chance for a retrial, especially after a jury decision. Hence, most of those convicted have to wait to see whether new evidence will turn up (which happens, if at all, mostly after the appeal deadline), or rely on the Criminal Cases Review Commission (CCRC), whose existence slightly mitigates the impenetrable and often insufficient appeal system.[164] It has the power to investigate possible miscarriages of justice and refer appropriate cases to the Court of Appeal, on grounds of conviction, sentence, or both.[165] The CCRC reviews convictions of the magistrates' and the Crown Court to identify whether the conviction may have been unsafe, while reviews of sentences seek to identify whether a point of law was not raised in the court proceedings, or if new information is now available that has a bearing on the sentence. When deciding that a case merits intensive review, it has the power neither to overturn a conviction nor to alter a sentence, nor the resources to conduct its own investigations. However, the police and CPS staff have a public duty to assist the CCRC in carrying out its statutory role. In particular, the CPS must preserve or disclose any material held by the CPS in full and without delay.

The Inquisitorial Versus the Adversarial System: A Critical Evaluation

The risk of wrongful convictions, a well-discussed issue in the United Kingdom, seems higher under the English and Welsh adversarial system than under the German inquisitorial approach.

However, some of the weaknesses in England's and Wales' criminal justice and, especially, prosecution system have been removed, at least theoretically, by the CJA 2003 that strengthens the position of the CPS, particularly with regard to the former unchecked and unbalanced police charging powers. Yet, these reforms may still not go far enough. It should be the duty of the prosecution to make charges in any case, and to decide whether and how pretrial procedures are to be discontinued, to guarantee the independence of investigation and prosecution as well as equality before the law. The police should have no power to charge, dismiss, or even say there is no case, but, as in Germany, each file, even where no criminal act can be proven, should be transmitted to the CPS, which should preside over the final decision.

With regard to the police, the CPS's self-confidence and self-consciousness should be increased. Therefore, the investigation should be controlled by the CPS and for the sake of civil rights, a professional judge. The CPS should be allowed to meet key witnesses before trial or even conduct interrogations, as in Germany. Hence, a more realistic assessment can be made of the further conviction, based on firsthand knowledge. Up to the present, despite the CJA 2003, the CPS is overly dependent on the police as it cannot initiate prosecutions, and has no power to require further, specific investigations like its German counterpart. Consequently, many weak cases proceed to the Courts where plea bargaining is widespread, even among those who are innocent.[166] Although in England and Wales the operational dependency of the CPS and the reluctance of the police to seek advice may have been reduced under the CJA 2003, a new legal culture with mutual consultation still has to grow. Here, Germany, where prosecutors and police officers treat each other as colleagues, may serve as a model.[167] Critical inspection of the police work by the CPS, with the ability of the latter to influence the former, are vital to guarantee defendants the right to fair (pre)trials. To encourage Crown Prosecutors to scrutinize cases more carefully, their work should be measured, as in Germany, by the general workload and not by the number of convictions. Only "waterproof" cases should reach the trial stage. The hope of a guilty plea should not influence the decisions made. At the very least, a system of informal reproofs for not properly assessing the sufficiency of evidence against the accused should be exercised. Furthermore, all CPS lawyers should work exclusively for the Prosecution Service.

On the other hand, the German criminal justice system, where miscarriages of justice or wrongful convictions are not an issue of public debate, could learn from the self-criticism of the English system that, on several occasions, has initiated independent research allowing it to identify shortcomings and to bring about appropriate reforms, such as the CJA 2003. Moreover, the impact of psychological research and expert testimony on law and procedure, police practice, and legal judgments is, following the lessons given by the mass of quashed convictions since the late 1980s, unparalleled to that anywhere in the world.[168] Germany is far from this development. However, it is time for every judicial system to review its procedures and practices, learn from new scientific developments such as those in the area of forensic psychology, and have the courage and willingness to implement the necessary changes. Here, Britain should serve as an example.[169] Another institution worth imitating is the CCRC. Nevertheless, many elements that are typical of the English and Welsh adversarial systems remain potential cradles for miscarriages of justice, particularly in times where priority is shifting away from due process to an overriding concern with the efficient use of resources, and from protection of the defendant to the benefit of "the system."

The Royal Commission's Review on Criminal Justice in 1993, following the overturning of a number of high-profile convictions, disappointed the expectations of system critics once attention shifted from the conviction of innocent people to the avoidance of letting a guilty party be acquitted. Interest in comparative research, and particularly inquisitorial systems, was limited at best. Instead, police powers were increased,[170] and, as in the CJA 2003, the efficiency of crime control, risk management, and system surveillance became priorities. Hence, the suspect is put under even greater pressure to confess, a trend that is particularly threatening given judges' reluctance to exclude evidence. Pretrial resolutions of issues are emphasized and oral tests of evidence have decreased. The restraints on the admissibility of evidence were already reduced in 1994 by the abolition of the mandatory corroboration warning and the curtailment of the right of silence. Police malpractice in fabricating false confessions endangers not only vulnerable suspects, such as juveniles, persons with learning disabilities, and the mentally ill,[171] but also a large number of persons suffering from different types of psychological disorders.[172] Unreliable confessions in general may be caused in various ways, but especially under police pressure. This is particularly dangerous where the position of the prosecution is too weak to control police malpractice appropriately.

Additionally, the disclosure rule may hinder appropriate defense work.[173] The CJA 2003 may further aggravate the situation. In comparison with the inquisitorial system, the main problem is that the defendant has to rely completely on his or her often inadequate defense lawyer, given that the prosecution does not investigate on the defendant's behalf, and that defense lawyers may fail their clients. Finally, appeals are rarely successful. The right of appeal is unduly limited and safeguards for wrongful convictions are missing. The CJA 2003 did not remove the inadequacies of the appeal system.[174] The German inquisitorial system offers more balanced safeguards against wrongful convictions, among which is the strong, nonpartisan status of the public prosecutors who control police investigations. In addition, a wider, supervised pretrial investigation exists, next to greater powers of judges who can extend investigations and thus guarantee inclusion of a wider range of evidence. The prosecution and the defense have less power to determine the case, as the presiding judge leads the questioning of the defendant and witnesses, a system that makes cross-examination widely redundant. Furthermore, the rules of appeal are clear and include, according to the guardian function of the prosecution, the right, and even the duty, of the prosecutor to appeal in favor of the defendant.

To summarize, neither the adversarial nor the inquisitorial systems are perfect, but each system includes many elements borrowed from the other. Hence, the solution may be a hybrid form of both, with regard to providing the fairest possible trial based on checks and balances. A system's performance should not be measured by the number of yearly convictions, but by the number of miscarriages of justice. The risk of such miscarriages seems high in England and Wales, due to the typical weaknesses of the adversarial system. Nevertheless, thanks to critical evaluation and research, the public awareness of the risks of miscarriages of justice is high in England and Wales, whereas the German system seems to trust excessively in its own integrity.

Notes

1. Both laws date back to the years after the foundation of the German Empire. They became effective on October 1, 1879.

2. Or "she"; in the following, without implying gender discrimination, the male form is used.

3. Horizontally: general prosecution service–provincial prosecution services; vertical: the minister of justice–general prosecutor–leading senior public prosecutor–senior public prosecutor–junior prosecutor (in charge of pretrial investigations).

4. 33% female; Frommel (2004).

5. Police Criminal Statistics (2003; http://www.bundeskriminalamt.de/pks/pks2003/index2.html).

6. In each court, there should be a public prosecutor according to § 141 GVG.

7. Meyer-Goßner, 2003, prenote § 141 GVG.

8. See § 170 section 1 CCP; Roxin 1997.

9. The examining judge may become active in investigative proceedings only if the prosecution applies for this.

10. A witness has a duty to appear before the prosecutor (but not the police) and to make a statement, except in a few situations specified by law (close relationship with the defendant, possible involvement in the offense, etc.).

11. Sections 153–154e.

12. Such as the Juvenile Court Act (§ 45 and following) and the Narcotic Drug Act (§ 31a).

13. Once the indictment has been filed, the court is allowed to make such a dismissal, but only with approval of the public prosecutor (Volk, 2002).

14. However, the police may abandon investigations started on their own initiative (after collecting all relevant evidence) if the prosecution is likely to drop the case.

15. Data on the frequency of indictments and penal orders can be found in the European Sourcebook of Crime and Criminal Justice Statistics, 2nd edition, The Hague: WODC 2003, 93–95.

16. The minimum sentence for this offense is one year in custody; the maximum is five years.

17. Cases against former German Democratic Republic judges and prosecutors who prosecuted or convicted political opponents are dealt with under this law.

18. BGHSt 43, 195.

19. BGH NJW 1998, 86; NJW 2000, 536. The Federal Supreme Court (NJW 2000, 526) considers waivers of appeal as void if accepted by the defense in exchange for a particular sentence.

20. Within certain limits, criminal charges may be reduced, however (§ 154 CCP).

21. These principles are expressed in §§ 169–175 and 257 and 261 of the CCP.

22. See §§ 155.2 and 206 of the CCP.

23. Unlike in the civil process, where the negotiation maxim prevails, the court decides independently what issues are to be debated at trial and what evidence is to be heard. Therefore, a confession by the defendant does not bind the court.

24. Although § 239 of the CCP provides for the possibility of cross-examination, the practical importance is minimal under the investigation principle.

25. For example, § 244 CCP.

26. Section 261 CCP.

27. This *in dubio pro reo* principle is the European version of the Anglo-Saxon "beyond reasonable doubt." It is based on Article 6 of the European Convention of Human Rights (ECHR).

28. Section 261 CCP.

29. This is the substance of rulings by the Federal Supreme Court (in NStZ-RR 98, 17 BGH MDR 1991, 704).

30. Sections 273.2 and 273.3 CCP. These restrictions do not apply to magistrate's courts.

31. Section 136.1 CCP. Concerning the trial, § 243.4 CCP.

32. By making statements, the defendant can, under certain conditions, become a means of proof (that will be assessed independently by the court), particularly in the case of a confession or with respect to statements against codefendants (Federal Supreme Court 32 140, 145).

33. No verdict can be based solely on the fact that the defendant remained silent, nor on his mimicry and gestures during the hearing (Federal Supreme Court 1993, 458; Federal Constitutional Court 1995, 505; Kuhne & Esser, 2002).

34. Federal Supreme Court 1994, 413. The same applies to late offers of exonerating evidence, such as evidence presented only after the position of the court has become recognizable. The defender's statement is a means of proof only if explicitly confirmed by the defendant (Federal Supreme Court 39, 305; Dahs, 1999).

35. Federal Supreme Court in NJW 1966, 1514.

36. Composed of one professional judge and two lay judges.

37. In law, a suspicion of an offense, according to § 170.1 and 203 CCP, is "reasonable" and calls for filing a charge whenever the probability of a conviction exceeds 50 percent.

38. Whenever the person found not guilty (or wrongly convicted) has either been detained or has suffered from other material damage during the pretrial investigation, he is entitled to compensation according to the criminal compensation law. The duty to pay criminal law damages operates, at least psychologically, as a deterrent to filing unreasonable charges.

39. Section 296.2 CCP.

40. Guidelines for imprisonment and fine proceedings give instructions for standard cases (No 147 II 1 RIStBV).

41. Section 81a.3 CCP. Forensic expert reports remain part of the files.

42. Sections 359 and following of the CCP.

43. Sections 365 and 296.2 CCP. Chapter 8 of this volume (on Switzerland) offers empirical illustrations of the fact that, under a continental system, petitions to reopen a case are often filed by prosecutors.

44. Peters (1970, 1972, 1974).

45. Prominent examples of successful reopened proceedings are the cases Rohrbach, Brühen, Hetze Lettenbauer, and Weimar-Boettcher. The latter was convicted of murdering her five- and seven-year old daughters in 1988. In the reopening in 1997, she was acquitted as it could not be proven beyond reasonable doubt that she—and not her ex-husband and father of the children (who could not be convicted of the crimes, either)—killed her children. The court was not convinced according to a standard of "subjective personal certainty." This case was highly discussed. The acquitted defendant did not get any compensation for custody, because she had, to protect herself, at least tried to conceal relevant facts (for example, she had known that the children were dead as she reported their disappearance to the police).

46. Based on § 261 CCP.

47. Sections 273–274 CCP.

48. For example, trafficking of five kilos of marijuana by a first-time offender may result in a suspended (i.e., noncustodial) sentence in Nordrhine-Westfalia, whereas in the neighboring state of Rhineland-Pfalz, the sentence may be, under identical circumstances, an immediate custodial term of up to four years.

49. Job description at the official home page of the CPS, 2004 (http://www.cps.gov.uk/vacancies/index.html).

50. Scotland and Northern Ireland have their independent law and jurisdiction with their own Prosecution Services.

51. Unlike Germany, England and Wales has no written penal code or definitive statement of the principles of criminal justice.

52. The CPS started operating only in 1986, nearly a century later than the German one.

53. Hence, the police have a long history of serving as both investigators and prosecutors, which still influences their opinion regarding both activities as one step (Belloni & Hodgson, 2000, 104ff).

54. The sole responsibility of the police for the decision to prosecute was inconsistent with their duty to investigate, as the necessary objectivity to sort out weak cases was missing (Belloni & Hodgson, 2000, 110).

55. Davies, Croall, and Tyrer (2005, 180ff).

56. Review of the Crown Prosecution Service (Glidewell Report), Cm 3960 (1998).

57. Counting the metropolitan and city police areas as one.

58. Which incorporates the former Department of the DPP and Police Prosecuting Solicitor's Departments.

59. With headquarters based in London, York, and Birmingham, the CPS operates under a structure of forty-two geographical areas, each one headed by a CCP who is responsible for prosecutions within the area. Although CCPs are directly accountable for their areas, most of the responsibilities for the efficient and effective administration fall to the area business managers.

60. This code is a set of guidelines on factors to be taken into account in deciding whether to prosecute.

61. The other main organizations allowed to prosecute are Customs and Excise, the TV Licensing Records Office, the Inland Revenue, the Serious Fraud Office, the Department of Trade and Industry, the Driver and Vehicle Licensing Authority (DVLA), the Department of Social Services, the Health and Safety Executive, the Local Authorities, the National Society for the Prevention of Cruelty to Children, and the Royal Society for the Prevention of Cruelty to Animals.

62. There are two kinds of lawyers in England and Wales, barristers and solicitors. The latter advise clients on a number of different issues and prepare cases before they go to court. They may also represent clients in court. Barristers spend a large proportion of their time representing clients in the higher courts. Recent changes have led to solicitors having wider rights of audience in these higher courts.

63. A publicly debated criticism of the CPS has been the staff shortages from which it suffers as a result of low pay and poor image. These shortages are compensated for by using external lawyers as a partial solution, but with high costs in the short term and a failure to develop a coherent organization due to the use of temporary staff. In Germany a prosecutor, as a civil servant, earns the same amount as a judge; many defense lawyers are attracted by a prosecutor's position given its life-term civil servant status.

64. Davies et al. (2005).

65. O'Reilly and Stevens (2002).

66. Crown prosecutors are said to be generally overworked and consequently, some of those who join the service do so merely to get experience and then change to highly paid law firms, where they do defense work. Furthermore, some of the case workers preparing the files are presumed to lack the ability to speak English competently, and are not trained in law (Doherty, 2004).

67. http://www.criminal-courts-review.org.uk/

68. The Criminal Justice Act was introduced into the House of Commons on November 21, 2002 as part of the Government's aim to "ensure that criminal trials are run more effectively and to reduce the scope for abuse of the system" as well as providing a sentencing framework that is supposed to be "clearer and more flexible than the current

one." Home Office 2003. See http://www.hmso.gov.uk/acts/acts2003/20030044.htm or www.cja2003.com.

69. The CJA 2003 is the seventh piece of criminal justice legislation in six years. The Act came partly into force from November 2003 until February 2004. The remaining parts will come into force on dates to be determined by the Home Secretary. Much of the Act is uncontroversial and it deals with practical changes to crime control (see Home Office, 2003b, http://www.homeoffice.gov.uk/justice/sentencing/criminaljusticeact2003/#crimact). However, changes regarding double jeopardy, bad character, and jury trial have all been (unsuccessfully) opposed, especially with regard to due process rights such as the right to a fair trial and the presumption of innocence under the ECHR (Kelly, in Keogh 2004, 8ff).

70. Stephenson (1992, 114ff).

71. European Convention of Human Rights, which became law in 1998 by the Human Rights Act.

72. Williamson (2004, 40ff).

73. Some other important stop-and-search powers do not require reasonable suspicion, such as the power to stop and search for weapons created under section 60 of the Criminal Justice and Public Order Act 1994 (Sanders & Young, 2000, chap. 2).

74. Sanders and Young (2002, 1041ff).

75. Still, ethnic minorities are involved disproportionately, according to police data (Hillyard & Gordon, 1999; McPherson 1999; Miller, Bland, & Quinton, 2000).

76. These include theft, burglary, serious assault, sexual offenses, drug goofiness, public order offenses, and so on.

77. Section 16 (2) of PACE 1984 allows a warrant to stop and search to persons accompanying any constable who is executing it. The CJA 2003 gives accompanying persons the same powers as the constable with respect to the execution of the warrant and the seizure of anything to which the warrant relates. This involvement of nonpolice staff in the search process may violate Article 8 of the ECHR.

78. The reasoning expressed by the government is that this will potentially allow for more crimes to be resolved at an earlier stage, with corresponding savings in police time and cost.

79. Fingerprints can now be taken electronically and the police can confirm within minutes the identity of a suspect if his or her fingerprints are already recorded in the National Fingerprint Database. Similarly, a DNA profile can be screened, through the National DNA Database, (NDNAD) within a very short time.

80. Samples from crime scenes and subject samples are either directly compared or entered into the NDNAD.

81. Hillyard (1993); Choong (1997); Memon, Vrij, and Bull (2002).

82. Which embraces the right to remain silent and not to contribute to incriminate himself or herself.

83. Sanders and Young (2000, 251–268).

84. Bucke, Street, and Brown (2000). According to my experience, this proportion is similar in Germany.

85. Interviews are usually audiotaped, although this is only legally required if the offense in question is indictable or triable either way. Some terrorist and Official Secrets Act offenses are exempt from tape recording. The custody officer may authorize a nonrecorded interview if the necessary equipment or facilities are not available.

86. In January 2002, the Court of Appeal quashed the 1974 murder conviction of Stephen Downing. The police's failure to caution Downing and to provide him with a

solicitor during several hours of interrogation was crucial in overturning his conviction (Hale, 2002).

87. Sanders and Young (2000).

88. See Memon et al. (2002). Suspects may confess knowing that their confession is untrue, as compliance refers to a behavioral change for an instrumental purpose. People also confess to escape the stressful police interview. Paddy Armstrong, one of the Guilford 4, in one of the most famous cases of wrongful conviction in the United Kingdom, has claimed that he confessed for this reason.

89. According to Gudjonsson (1992, 2003), there are four distinct categories of false confessions: (1) People may make confessions entirely voluntarily as a result of a morbid desire for publicity or notoriety, or to relieve feelings of guilt about a real or imagined previous transgression, or because they cannot distinguish between reality and fantasy. (2) A suspect may confess out of a desire to protect someone else from interrogation and prosecution. (3) People may see a prospect of immediate advantage from confessing (e.g., an end to questioning or release from the police station), even though the long-term consequences are far worse (those are the coerced-compliant confessions). (4) People may be persuaded temporarily by the interrogators that they really have done the act in question (the resulting confessions are termed coerced-internalized confessions).

90. It depends on the discretion of the judges to exclude such "evidence." Corroboration evidence is not mandatory (Sprack, 2002, 278ff).

91. Gudjonsson (2002, 335). Five of those cases (Guilford 4, Birmingham 6, Judith Ward, Alfred Allen, and Patrick Kane) were terrorist as well as murder cases; Allen's (one of the UDR Four (Paisley, 1992) and Kane's ("IRA Funeral Murder"; Gudjonsson, 1999) are from Northern Ireland. The others involved terrorist acts in England attributed to the Irish Republican Army (IRA).

92. Gudjonsson et al. (1993; 1999, 334; 2004).

93. This includes a considerable variance, such as borderline intelligence, combined with high suggestibility, memory distrust, psychogenic amnesia, and personality disorder (Gudjonsson et al., 1999).

94. On October 5, 1974, members of the IRA planted bombs in two public houses in Guilford, Surrey. Four people (P. Hill, P. Armstrong, G. Colon, and C. Richardson) were subsequently convicted for the offenses.

95. BBC News, June 6, 2000, 11:03 GMT 12:03 UK.

96. On November 21, 1974, two public houses in Birmingham were bombed by the IRA. Twenty-one people were killed, and six Irishmen were convicted of the bombings.

97. On June 19, 1986, Swansea's Crown Court convicted the brothers Wayne and Paul Darvell of murdering a thirty-year-old woman, who worked as a manageress of a sex shop, relying on Wayne's confession.

98. Gudjonsson (2002, 337).

99. The confession of Patrick Molloy made on December 10, 1978 led to his and three other men's implication in robbery and murder. Molloy died in prison. The convictions of the four men were quashed in 1997 (Gudjonsson, 2003).

100. Sanders and Young (2002).

101. Brown (1997, 114).

102. Section 7 of the Acts amends section 42 (81) (b) of PACE came into force on January 20, 2004.

103. Any offense for which the sentence is fixed by law or for which a sentence of imprisonment of five years or more may be imposed, or any additionally listed offense in Schedule 1 A to PACE 1984.

104. Section 6 of the CJA 2003 even establishes that the reviews of detention can be conducted by telephone.

105. Although there are no coercive measurements foreseen if the guidance is not followed.

106. The exclusive responsibility of the police to decide whether to prosecute was inconsistent with their duty to investigate, as the necessary objectivity to sort out weak cases was missing.

107. Which is up to the police to judge, so that also in major cases, a power-potential remains.

108. Royal Commission of Criminal Justice (1993).

109. Belloni and Hodgson (2000, 111).

110. Belloni and Hodgson (2000, 108).

111. RCCJ (1993, 74), a fact that can be linked with the historical development of the prosecution.

112. Baldwin and Hunt (1998) found that prosecutors—like the police—were operating on intuition and hunches rather than giving a clear legal statement on the case. Besides, those schemes support only those police officers who in fact recognize a legal problem.

113. Rose (1996).

114. Sanders and Young (2002, 1052ff).

115. Doherty (2004).

116. Sanders, Creaton, Bird, and Weber (1997) and McConville, Sanders, and Leng (1991).

117. Gelsthorpe and Giller (1990).

118. This will not change with the CJA 2003.

119. See Baldwin and Bedward (1991), Duff (1997, for Scotland), and Gelsthorpe and Giller (1990).

120. Rose (1996, 135ff), assumes that pre-eminent public interest would be not justice, but cost.

121. The CPS has been so far less a decision maker than a restricted decision reverser. It has been not only passive in relation to weak cases, but even more in relation to cautionable cases. According to McConville et al. (1991), no cases were dropped because of cautionability alone, despite many similar cases that would have been cautioned by the police. Here, too, the CPS seems to adapt to or at least accept police working rules.

122. Belloni and Hodgson (2000, 111).

123. This means that such misbehavior continued after the establishment of the CPS (Gudjonsson, 2002, 337).

124. See note 89 and Gudjonsson (2002, 234).

125. Gibson and Watkins (2004, 41ff).

126. The defense was also given the right to apply for a court order requiring the disclosure of prosecution evidence if there is reasonable cause to believe that undisclosed prosecution material might aid the defendant.

127. In 1998, 1,951,900 defendants were prosecuted in magistrates' courts (including the youth court): 510,500 for indictable offenses (including triable either way), 591,800 for

summary nonmotoring offenses, and 849,600 for summary motoring offenses (Doherty, 2004, 175ff).

128. The involvement of the CPS in Crown Court cases is still restricted as they mostly instruct independent barristers, although recent efforts have aimed for greater participation of the CPS's own lawyers.

129. Belloni and Hodgson (2000, 109) and Baldwin (1997).

130. Those most serious breaches of the criminal law include murder, rape, and robbery and must be tried at the Crown Court. Currently, in the case of indictable-only offenses, magistrates must consider whether there is a case to answer. If the magistrates decide that there is, the case will be committed to the Crown Court. Part 7, section 43f of the CJA 2003 provides for trial on indictment without a jury in two instances. The prosecution may apply for trial without jury in relation to certain fraud trials or those where a danger of jury tampering exists.

131. Triable either way offenses may be tried either at the Crown Court or at a magistrates' court and include criminal damage where the value is £5,000 or greater, theft, burglary, and drink driving. Magistrates have to decide whether to handle the case themselves or commit the case for trial at the Crown Court. In 1998, 28 percent of committals to the Crown Court for trial for triable either way offenses were a result of defendant election (Doherty, 2004, 169ff).

132. Summary offenses are triable only by a magistrates' court. This group is dominated by motor vehicle offenses, for some of which fixed penalties can be issued, but it also includes offenses such as common assault and criminal damage up to £5,000.

133. Belloni and Hodgson (2000, 108ff) and Doherty (2004, 173).

134. McConville (2002, 360ff).

135. Doherty (2004, 173).

136. McConville (2002, 376ff).

137. Baldwin and McConville (1981).

138. McConville (2001, 371).

139. McConville (2001, 369ff).

140. McConville et al. (1994).

141. Submitted by JUSTICE (1993).

142. Which JUSTICE (1993) researched over three years (January 1990–December 1992).

143. These complaints included short, last-minute encounters with defendants and pressure to plead guilty. Twenty-eight percent were dissatisfied with case preparation by their solicitors.

144. Grive (1977) 66 Cr. App.R. 167; Atkinson (1978) 2 All ER 46; McConville (2001, 361); Patterson (2002).

145. CPS (2004; see http://www.cps.gov.uk/legal/section15/chapter_j.html#_Toc44 662308).

146. The judge does not have an investigative role. Indeed, he or she should know nothing about the case at the start of the trial (while his or her inquisitorial counterpart has the duty to know the whole file) so that he or she can act as the umpire, spelling out what evidence is inadmissible, ruling as to the interpretation of the law to be applied and to explain the issues involved to the jury, who must then decide on the facts.

147. Since December 2004, judges are expected to reveal to the juries if a defendant has prior convictions for the same offense with which he or she is charged. For child sex offenders the new measures are more wide-ranging (Batty, 2004). In Germany, the juries

and the public have always had the right to hear all previous convictions if not deleted in the public records according to the legal regulations.

148. In either case, this would negate common-law rules in relation to the admissibility of bad character evidence. Thus, hearsay evidence is now admissible where there is a sound, statutory reason why the person who originally made a statement cannot be present in court or the court otherwise considers that to admit the hearsay would be appropriate in the interest of justice. This underlines the practical focus of the CJA, which implies the concrete danger of undermining the rights of the accused.

149. Which is mandatory if a confession is found to be unreliable or obtained by oppression (76 PACE) and discretionary if according to the court, the inclusion of the evidence would adversely affect the fair trial.

150. Belloni and Hodgson (2000, 83).

151. As there is no written code of procedure yet in England and Wales, a new Committee was charged, during the summer of 2004, to establish such rules for all criminal courts in England and Wales, including the Court of Appeal. Since fairly recently, the application of the ECHR, which contains many of the inquisitorial procedure rules, is guaranteed in the domestic courts due to the Human Rights Act 1998.

152. An overview can be found in Williamson (2004, 45) and MOJUK (2004; see http://www.mojuk.org.uk/).

153. Williamson (2004, 42ff); Gudjonsson (2002, 336; 2003).

154. Convicted of the (sexual) murder of eleven-year-old Lesley Molseed in 1976, Stefan Kiszko spent sixteen years in prison until he was released in 1992. He died of a heart attack the following year (age forty-four); his mother, who had waged a long campaign to prove her son's innocence, died six months later. Stefan Kiszko suffered from XYY syndrome, a condition in which the human male has an extra Y chromosome. Such males are normal except for—sometimes slight—growth abnormalities and minor behavioral disorders. One of Stefan Kiszko's "behavioral abnormalities" was jotting down the registration numbers of a car if he had been annoyed by the driver. This led, in part, to his wrongful conviction: He had at some point prior to the murder unwittingly jotted down the number of a car seen near the scene of the crime. It was argued that only someone at the scene could have known the registration number of this car. As part of his condition Stefan Kiszko would have been physically incapable of the sex crime of which he was convicted, something that was never disclosed to his defense (Rose, Panter, & Wilkinson, 1998).

155. In 1987, Winston Silcott, Mark Braithwaite, and Engin Raghip were convicted of murdering Police Officer Keith Blakelock on the 1985 riot-torn Broadwater Farm estate in Tottenham, North London, but all three were cleared in 1991 when their convictions were quashed by the Court of Appeal. Forensic tests suggested evidence against Silcott may have been fabricated by police officers. Former Detective Chief Superintendent Graham Melvin and ex-Detective Inspector Maxwell Dingle were cleared at the Old Bailey in 1994 of fabricating evidence. Winston Silcott is serving a life sentence arising from a separate matter—a crime he maintains was committed in self-defense—for which he has already served his "tariff." He has not been granted parole. Winston Silcott received £17,000 in compensation after his conviction was quashed in 1991. In October 1999 he was awarded £50,000 compensation for malicious prosecution by the Metropolitan police in the Blakelock case (Dodd, 1999).

156. Rose (2004).

157. It was not until 1907 that there was anything resembling a proper system of appeal following trial in the Crown Court (White, 2002, 14).

158. Such as the Magistrates' Court Act 1980, The Criminal Appeal Act 1968, the Administration of Justice Act 1970, and the Supreme Court Act 1980.

159. There are many possibilities such as a biased judge or a jury who used a ouija board during an overnight adjournment of the trial to contact the deceased (*R. v. Young* [1995] QB 324).

160. The appeal takes the form of a rehearing although the court tends to act more like a court of review.

161. Section 2(1) of the Court of Appeal Act 1968.

162. *R. v. Cooper* (1968) 53 Cr. App. R 82, 86.

163. Usually twenty-eight days from the date of the decision of the trial court.

164. Which was established by Part II of the Criminal Appeal Act 1995, following the RCCJ's recommendations. On the CCRC, see also Chapter 10 of this volume on England and Wales and, on a similar review system, Chapter 7 on Canada.

165. It has similar powers to investigate and make references to the Crown Court in summary cases and it may also be asked to investigate issues by the Court of Appeal in an appeal.

166. Referring to this, both systems suffer from inherent weaknesses in the non-strictly codified rulings of plea bargaining, which pose a great risk of convictions of innocent people, although in Germany, at least the trial stage must be entered and the judge should not rely on the confession, but to seek corroborative evidence.

167. Furthermore, regular meetings and workshops are held to create a forum for criticism and communication.

168. Gudjonsson (2002, 332).

169. This conclusion may be true for other continental countries as well. See the chapters on France (Chapter 12), the Netherlands (Chapter 9), and Switzerland (Chapter 8) in this volume.

170. The CJPOA 1994, for example, classified saliva as nonintimate so that it might be taken by force.

171. Hodgson (1997).

172. Gudjonsson, Clare, and Rutter (1994) and Gudjonsson, Rutter, and Clare (1995).

173. The prosecution is still overly dependent on police accounts due to the absence of any external supervision.

174. Belloni and Hodgson (2000, 193) refer to the case of the Birmingham 6, which was treated unsympathetically by a judiciary declining police's wrongdoing and becoming more intense in the assumption of the guilt of the convicted.ˈ

References

Baldwin, J. (1997). Understanding judge ordered and directed acquittals in the Crown Court. *Criminal Law Review, 12,* 536–555.

Baldwin, J., & Bedward, J. (1991). Summarising tape recordings of police interviewing. *Criminal Law Review, 6 ,* 671–679.

Baldwin, J., & Hunt, A. (1998). Prosecutors advising in police stations. *Criminal Law Review, 13,*521–536.

Baldwin, J., & McConville, M. (1981). *Confessions in Crown Court trials* (Research Study No. 5, Royal Commission on Criminal Procedure). London: HMSO.

Batty, D. (2004, November 24). Juries to hear of previous convictions. *The Guardian.* Retrieved January 1, 2005, from http://society.guardian.co.uk/crimeandpunishment/story/0,,1335775,00.html

Belloni, F., & Hodgson, J. (2000). *Criminal injustice: An evaluation of the criminal justice process in Britain*. Chippenham, UK: Palgrave.

Brown, D. (1997). *PACE: Ten years on: A review of the research* (Home Office Research Study No. 155). London: Home Office.

Bucke, T., Street, R., & Brown, D. (2000). *The right of silence: The impact of the CJPO 1994* (Home Office Research Study No. 1999). London: HMSO.

Choong, S. (1997). *Review of delay in the criminal justice system*. London: Lord Chancellor's Department.

Dahs, H. (1999). *Handbuch des Strafverteidigers* [Manual of the criminal defense lawyer] (6th ed.). Köln, Germany: Dr. Otto Schmidt-Verlag.

Davies, M., Croall, H., & Tyrer, J. (2005). *Criminal justice: An introduction to the criminal justice system in England and Wales* (3rd ed.). Harlowe, UK: Pearson Longman.

Dodd, V. (1999, November 16). Cleared Silcott gets 50,000 pounds. *The Guardian*.

Doherty, M. (2004). *Criminal justice and penology* (2nd ed.). London: Old Bailey Press.

Duff, P. (1997). Diversion from prosecution into psychiatric care. *British Journal of Criminology, 37*, 15–34.

Frommel, N. (2004). Frauen [Women]. In R. Northoff (Ed.), *Handbuch der Kriminalprävention* [Manual of criminal prevention], p. 124. Baden Baden, Germany: Nomos.

Gelsthorpe, L., & Giller, H. (1990). More justice for juveniles: Does more mean better? *Criminal Law Review, 5*, 153–164.

Gibson, G., & Watkins, M. (2004). *Criminal Justice Act 2003: A guide to the new procedures and sentencing*. Chippenham, UK: Waterside Press.

Gudjonsson, G. H. (1992). *The psychology of interrogations, confessions and testimony*. Chichester, UK: Wiley.

Gudjonsson, G. H. (2002). Unreliable confessions and miscarriages of justice in Britain. *International Journal of Police Science and Management, 4*, 332–343.

Gudjonsson, G. H. (2003). *The psychology of interrogations and confessions: A handbook*. Chichester, UK: Wiley.

Gudjonsson, G. H., Clare, I., & Rutter, S. (1994). Psychological characteristics of suspects interviewed at police stations, a factor-analytic study. *Journal of Forensic Psychiatry, 5*, 517–525.

Gudjonsson, G. H., Clare, I., Rutter, S. & Pearse, J. (1993). *Persons at risk during interviews in police custody: The identification of vulnerabilities* (The Royal Commission on Criminal Justice Research Study No. 12). London: HMSO.

Gudjonsson, G. H., Rutter, S. C., & Clare, I. C. H. (1995). The relationship between suggestibility and anxiety among suspects detained at police stations. *Psychological Medicine, 25*, 875–878.

Gudjonsson, G. H., Sigurdsson, J. F., Bragason, O. O., Einarsson, E., & Valdimarsdottir, E. B. (2004). Confessions and denials and the relationship with personality. *Legal and Criminological Psychology, 9*(1), 121–133.

Hale, D. (2002). *Town without pity: The fight to clear Stephen Downing of the Bakewell murder*. London: Century.

Hillyard, P. (1993). *Suspect sommunity*. London: Pluto.

Hillyard, P., & Gordon, D. (1999). Arresting statistics: The drift to informal justice in England and Wales. *Journal of Law and Society, 26*, 502–522.

Hodgson, J. (1997, August 29). Justice undermined. *Criminal Justice Matters (CJM)*, pp. 4–6.

Home Office (2003). Criminal Justice Act 2003, London: HMSO. Retrieved February 1, 2005 from http://www.homeoffice.gov.uk/justice/sentencing/criminaljusticeact 2003/#crimact

JUSTICE. (1993). *Negotiated justice: A closer look at the implications of plea bargains.* London: Author.

Keogh, A. (2004). *Criminal Justice Act 2003: A guide to the new law.* London: The Law Society.

Kühne, H. H., & Esser, R. (2002). Die Rechtsprechung des Europäischen Gerichtshofes für Menschenrechte [Jurisprudence of the European Court for Human Rights]. *Strafverteidiger, 8,* 383–392.

Macpherson, Sir W. (1999). *The Stephen Lawrence inquiry* (Cm 4262-I). London: Stationary Office.

McConville, M. (2002). Plea bargaining. In M. McConville & G. Wilson (Eds.), *The handbook of the criminal justice process* (pp. 353–376). Oxford, UK: Oxford University Press.

McConville, M., Hodgson, J., Bridges, L., & Pavlovic, A. (1994). *Standing accused: The organisation and practices of criminal defence lawyers in Britain.* Oxford, UK: Clarendon.

McConville, M., Sanders, A., & Leng, R. (1991). *The case for the prosecution.* London: Routledge.

Memon, A., Vrij, A., & Bull, E. (2002). *Psychology and law: Truthfulness, accuracy and credibility.* Chichester, UK: Wiley.

Meyer- Goßner, L. (2003). *Strafprozessordnung* [Criminal procedure code] (46th ed.). Munich, Germany: Beck.

Miller, J., Bland, N., & Quinton, P. (2000). *The impact of stops and searches on crime and the community* (Police Research Series Paper 127). London: Home Office.

MOJUK (2004). Miscarriages of justice UK. Retrieved March 1, 2005, from http://www.mojuk.org.uk

Moxon, P., & Crisp, D. (1994). *Case screening by the Crown Prosecution Service: How and why cases are terminated.* London: HMSO.

O'Reilly, J., & Stevens, J. (2002, March 10). Bandit country UK: Why criminals win. *Sunday Times.*

Paisley, I. J. R. (1992). *Reasonable doubt: The case for the UDR Four.* Dublin: The Mercier Press.

Patterson, S. (2002). Criminal appeals: The purpose of criminal appeals. In M. McConville & G. Wilson (Eds.), *The handbook of the criminal justice process* (pp. 487–504). Oxford, UK: Oxford University Press.

Peters, K. (1970–1974). *Fehlerquellen im Strafprozess: Eine Untersuchung der Wiederaufnahmeverfahren in der Bundesrepublik Deutschland* [Sources of errors in criminal proceedings: A study of cases of successful petitions of revision in the Federal Republic of Germany] (3 vols.). Karlsruhe, Germany: C. F. Müller.

Rose, D. (1996). *In the name of the law.* London: Vintage.

Rose, D. (2004, January 18). The Observer special reports: "They created Winston Silcott, the beast of Broadwater Farm. And they won't let this creation lie down and die." *The Observer.* Retrieved XXDATE, from http://observer.guardian.co.uk/race/story/0,11255,1125536,00.html#top

Rose, J., Panter, S., & Wilkinson, T. (1998). *Innocents: How justice failed Stefan Kiszko and Lesley Molseed.* London: Fourth Estate.

Roxin, C. (1997). Zur Rechtstellung der Staatsanwaltschaft Damals und Heute [The legal status of the prosecution service then and today]. *Deutsche Richterzeitung,* 109–121.

Royal Commission on Criminal Justice. (1993). *Report,* Cm 2263. London: HMSO.

Sanders, A., Creaton, J., Bird, S., & Weber, L. (1997). *Victims with learning disabilities: Negotiating the criminal justice system.* Oxford, UK: Centre for Criminological Research.

Sanders, A., & Young, R. (2000). *Criminal justice* (2nd ed.). London: Butterworth.

Sanders, A., & Young, R. (2002). From suspect to trial. In M. Maguire R. Morgan, & R. Reiner (Eds.), *The Oxford handbook of criminology* (3rd ed., pp. 1034–1075, Oxford: Oxford University Press.

Solbach, G., & Klein, H. (1998). *Anklageschrift, Einstellungsverfügung, Dezernat und Plädoyer* [Charging, cautioning, leading the department and pleading] (11th ed.). Düsseldorf, Germany: Lange Verlag.

Sprack, J. (2002). *Emmins on: Criminal procedure* (9th ed.). Oxford, UK: Oxford University Press.

Stephenson, G. M. (1992). *Criminal justice.* Oxford, UK: Blackwell.

Volk, K. (2002). *Strafprozessrecht* [The law of criminal procedure] (3rd ed.). Munich, Germany: Beck.

White, C. A. (2002). The structure and organisation of criminal justice in England and Wales: An overview. In M. McConville & G. Wilson (Eds.), *The handbook of the criminal justice process* (pp. 5–10). Oxford, UK: Oxford University Press.

Williamson, T. (2004). USA and UK responses to miscarriages of justice. In J. Adler (Ed.), *Forensic psychology,* pp. 39–57. Cullompton, UK: Willian Publishing.

Zender, M., & Henderson, P. (1993). *Crown Court study: Great Britain* (Royal Commission on Criminal Justice). London: HMSO.

12

WRONGFUL CONVICTIONS IN FRANCE

The Limits of "Pourvoi en Révision"

~

NATHALIE DONGOIS

T he French judiciary system, following the continental tradition, provides many detailed rules. Unlike the American system, continental procedural laws insist on the binding character of final decisions. To achieve this, continental systems protect final decisions, by a multitude of formal rules, from being challenged. Such a formalistic framework not only protects final decisions but contributes to the legitimacy of the whole criminal justice system. If so few petitions of revision succeed in France, the reason may be that these rules are so strict that it becomes virtually impossible to obtain a new trial.

The French judiciary system has two degrees of jurisdiction (trial and appellate jurisdiction), and, on top of these two, the appeal to the Supreme Court (*Cour de cassation*). Appeal allows a review of the case in all aspects, including facts; that is, the substance of the case. On cassation, judges only check whether formal rules have been violated.[1] Despite the guarantees given by such a system, judges can always err by acquitting a guilty person or convicting an innocent person. However, only the latter qualifies as judicial error and may therefore justify a petition of revision.[2] The French judiciary system is not concerned with the acquittal of guilty persons; only the fact that an innocent person is convicted for a crime that he or she did not commit is perceived as an error against which there must be a remedy at law. Thus, the revision aims at errors of fact[3] in the case of final decisions. Verdicts become "final" once the time limit for an appeal has expired, or if all remedies normally available have been exhausted.

The *pourvoi en révision* (petition to obtain a new trial after a final verdict) is considered necessary since it would be inappropriate to let judicial errors stand. It nevertheless challenges the validity of final decisions. For this reason, to preserve the credibility of the judiciary system, there have to be limits to the possibilities to file a pourvoi en révision. One first limit consists of not qualifying as judicial errors the acquittal of guilty persons, based on the argument that they benefit from the error. In doing so, the very definition of judicial error becomes limitative per se, the pourvoi en révision being only available against errors that lead to a prejudice for the concerned person. This judiciary concept can best be illustrated by the famous proverb "Better one hundred guilty in liberty than one innocent convicted." Since the "Seznec" law of 1989,[4] 2,080 demands have been filed with the *Commission de révision*, a special body of senior judges in charge of examining new evidence. Of those, 1,987 have been decided, and only fifty-four transferred to the Commission de révision. Of those fifty-four demands, the *Cour de révision*, which reviews cases where new evidence may call for a new trial, has rejected nine, and thirty-two have led to a repeal of the verdict. Since the establishment of the pourvoi en révision, only six of the reviewed trials have led to an acquittal.[5] This illustrates the extreme "filtering" function of the rules governing the petition on revision.

As every wrongful conviction directly conflicts with the human dignity of the person concerned, it is important that procedural requirements do not interfere with finding the truth. In today's reality, however, the formal prerequisites for as well as the procedure of the petition both severely limit the further reopening of "closed" cases. The analysis of judicial errors by means of the pourvoi en révision illustrates how difficult it is to find the equilibrium between, on one hand, the human desire for justice, and, on the other hand, the national investment in preserving the validity of final decisions. In addition, in this chapter I give a review of the formal conditions, the procedure, and the effects of the pourvoi en révision through infamous examples of wrongful convictions.

The Conditions of Applicability
of the Pourvoi en Révision

The pourvoi en révision (Articles 622 ff. of the Code of Criminal Procedure, hereafter referred to as CPP) is available against final decisions in criminal cases if the defendant has been found guilty of a felony (*délit*) or a crime. Minor offenses (so-called *contraventions*) are excluded except when they are connected with a crime or a felony.[6] Further limiting conditions are enumerated in the CPP.

Decisions Against Which the Pourvoi en Révision Is Available

A decision is "final" (i.e., *res iudicata*) if it is "irrevocable" and "not subject to opposition."[7] Consequently, no verdict of a trial court can be challenged through a pourvoi en révision, as long as it is not "irrevocable"; that is, as long as neither an appeal nor a *pourvoi en cassation* (appeal to the Supreme Court) have been filed. Moreover, any verdict against an absent individual found guilty of a crime[8] cannot lead to a pourvoi en révision (provided that the absence can be excused), but must be challenged first by asking for a new trial. In such cases, a new trial is routinely granted because the accused has the right to defend himself or herself and because the possibility to challenge a verdict has its grounds in the principle of *procédure contradictoire* (contradictory procedure). Further, as long as a decision is subject to any form of appeal, the pourvoi en révision is unavailable. However, it may nonetheless be open if, at the trial court level, criminal prosecution has been stopped by an amnesty, but the appeal as to the civil action (for damages) is still pending.[9] Furthermore, the pourvoi en révision is available only if there is no other legal remedy to correct the error, such as rectification of the police record[10] and the like.

The Law of June 15, 2000[11] created another legal remedy, apart from the pourvoi en révision: the *réexamen d'une disposition pénale* (reexamination of a criminal disposition; Article 626–1 ff. CPP) subsequent to a decision of the European Court of Human Rights, if the Court finds that French courts have violated the European Convention on Human Rights.[12] In the case of Omar Raddad,[13] once the petition had been rejected, Maître Vergès, counsel for Raddad, decided to bring his client's case before the European Court of Human Rights, hoping that the new legal remedy created by the Law of June 15, 2000 would permit repeal of the guilty verdict.[14] The case is still pending in the European Court.

The pourvoi en révision is available only against a verdict relating to a felony (délit) or a crime. A request in a misdemeanor case does not fall into the scope of the Article 622 CPP:[15] The underlying policy is that a misdemeanor (contravention), as such, is not serious enough to justify a révision procedure, except in cases where the misdemeanor (contravention) at issue is indivisibly intertwined with crimes or even felonies that, taken for themselves, would be subject to the révision.[16] In the case of an acquittal, the révision is available only if the court ordered the defendant to pay civil damages.[17]

Preconditions for a Révision

The pourvoi en révision is limited to the following preconditions, as specified in Article 622 CPP: (1) if, after a conviction for homicide, there is sufficient evidence suggesting that the alleged victim is still alive; (2) if, after a verdict for a felony (délit) or a crime, a third party, in a separate proceeding, has been convicted based on the same facts, and that, since the two verdicts cannot be reconciled, the resulting contradiction proves the innocence of one or the other convicted party;[18] (3) if one of the witnesses heard is subsequently charged and found guilty of perjury against the accused, the witness convicted for perjury cannot be heard in a retrial of the case;[19] however, the revision will not be available if the trial for perjury leads to discharge of the witness;[20] and (4) if, after the verdict, new facts or an element unknown at the time of the trial are found, and if it is likely that the new evidence will raise doubt about the guilt of the convicted defendant.[21] Until 1989 (i.e., before the "Seznec" law), the Minister of Justice had the competence to decide about the advisability of a petition for révision. On June 12, 1989, a law (created at the initiative of Robert Badinter) required that petitions be examined by a commission of five judges of the Cour de Cassation,[22] and, more important, that the révision be available when "the facts, by their nature, are capable to raise a doubt on the guilt," and not only when they prove the innocence of the convicted person.

Consequently, there are two requirements for a pourvoi en révision. On the one hand, new facts have to be invoked; the elements known at the time of the verdict cannot justify a révision by themselves. On the other hand, since 1989, there have to be one or several facts capable of raising doubt about the guilt of the convicted person. The step made from the establishment of innocence to the raising of doubt about guilt lowered the threshold of the second requirement. More precisely, any new document coming to the attention of the judge after the verdict that contains an element that could have left a decisive impression on the judge's mind has to be considered capable of establishing the innocence of the convicted person.[23] In the light of that definition, a new interpretation of a question of law does not constitute a new fact capable of establishing the innocence of the convicted person, as several decisions have ruled.[24] Conversely, a new fact (i.e., an element yet unknown to the judge but capable of establishing the innocence of the convicted person) was held to exist in the case of a person convicted for insubordination who, in reality, had lost his French citizenship[25] and in the case of a soldier convicted for desertion during wartime, who, in reality, was a prisoner of war, a circumstance unknown to the judges at the time of the trial.[26] The révision was also granted to admit a new fact where, after a verdict, it was discovered that the convicted person was mentally incapacitated at the time of the crime[27] and in a case where the convicted, at the time of the crime, had been hospitalized far from the scene of crime and an unidentified third party had assumed his identity.[28]

This said, and at a first look, the legal principle seems well established: Any demand invoking new facts that do not have sufficient probative value to convince the Cour de Cassation of the innocence of the convicted person[29] has to be refused. However, there is a downside to this principle: It leaves the judge with a considerable margin of interpretation regarding the probative value of the new fact invoked. This margin of discretion also plays an important role when it comes to deciding whether a new fact is capable of raising doubt as to whether a convicted defendant is guilty. The fact that the doubt as to the guilt of a person is mainly based on the subjective appreciation of a judge may be subject to criticism.

Assessment of New Facts by the Judge

There are, of course, cases where the answer is logical—for example, when a judge has to decide whether the death of the convicted person only a few hours after the commission of the crime of which he or she has been found guilty is sufficient to raise a doubt as to his or her guilt. In such a case, the death following the commission of the crime, by itself, does not permit one to objectively establish innocence. However, there are cases where the rejection of a petition for révision is based on the subjective appreciation of the situation. For example, a new (and especially a late) declaration of a party in a civil trial will almost never have sufficient probative value to convince the Cour de Cassation that it establishes sufficient doubt as to the guilt of the convicted person.[30] The trial court necessarily takes into consideration the credibility of the accusation of the victim. Therefore, no new trial will be granted as long as the verdict remains substantially unchallenged. In other words, the judges base their refusal of the petition for révision on what—subjectively—appears plausible to them.

In the case of Omar Raddad,[31] the commission in charge of filtering the demands decided on June 25, 2001 to have the case heard by the Cour de Révision. It decided that the presence of "a DNA different from the one of Omar Raddad" on the scene of the crime constituted a new fact. That element, although not sufficient to prove the innocence of the convicted person, indicated the presence of a third party at the scene of crime, which, as such, was sufficient to raise doubt as to the guilt of Omar Raddad. However, other arguments made by Maître Vergès were rejected, such as the fact that the son of the victim was believed to have a bad relationship with his mother. The commission rejected this argument because the only relevant testimony was contradicted by the totality of other testimonies, which made the commission conclude that the credibility of the declarations made during the first trial was not sufficiently challenged by this new element.

Such appreciation of the credibility of a witness also played a role in the matter of Dils.[32] In fact, the presence of the serial killer Francis Heaulme at the scene of the crime created the likelihood that Heaulme was involved in the commission of the child murder for which Patrick Dils had been convicted. Doubt about the guilt of Patrick Dils was raised when the serial killer Heaulme was questioned in 1994. During that interview, Heaulme admitted having been present at the time of the crime, and having had an argument with the two child victims.[33] Even though there was still doubt as to the direct responsibility of Francis Heaulme for these homicides, his simple presence was established against any doubt. The credibility of Heaulme's statement, together with the verification of his presence at the scene of crime, raised sufficient doubt, and the Cour de Cassation ruled that Dils be granted a new trial.

The discovery of a new fact is the most often used grounds for a petition of revision, the three other possibilities set forth in Article 622 CPP being too specific and thus too restrictive. Consequently, one can say that the scope of that fourth possibility—the existence of a new fact being capable of raising a doubt as to the guilt of the convicted person—is a definitive advantage for these who were wrongfully convicted. However, formal requirements often are such that the new provision falls short of its effectiveness, as the filtering system of the pourvoi en révision tends to make it difficult to obtain a new trial. Once again, the equilibrium between, on the one hand, the validity of final verdicts (i.e., the preservation of the social order) and, on the other hand, the commitment to repair—as far as possible—every wrongful conviction (i.e., the official recognition of truth) is difficult to maintain.

The Procedure of the Pourvoi en Révision

Article 623 CPP reinforces the filtering function of the Commission de Révision: The commission can decide on its own to have the Cour de Révision hear a certain "demand which seems admissible" pursuant to the terms of the article. The wide range of discretion of the commission, therefore, constitutes the first obstacle in the way of a petition's chances of success. Even thereafter, the opening of a revision proceeding still requires that the Cour de Révision come to the same conclusion as the commission regarding the admissibility of the demand. Finally, the fact that only a limited circle of persons may demand révision limits procedural relevance even further.

Persons Qualified to File a Petition of Revision

The Seznec case illustrates the latter limitation. Guillaume Seznec was found guilty of a murder he had always denied, and he was sentenced in 1924 to compulsory labor for life. Even though he had been found guilty of the murder of his friend and *Conseiller général* Pierre Quémeneur, numerous inconsistencies in the investigation led several persons to claim judicial errors.[34] However, his attempts to rehabilitate his grandfather, Denis Seznec, grandson of Guillaume, hit a substantial obstacle: He was not allowed to file a demand for révision. In fact, pursuant to Article 623 CPP, the revision may only be demanded by the Minister of Justice, by the convicted person (or, in the case of incapacity, by his legal representative), and, after the death or formally declared disappearance of the convicted person, by his spouse, children, parents, heirs, or any person who had been expressly mandated to do so, but not by the grandson as such.[35] In the matter of Seznec, the Minister of Justice, Madame Marylise Lebranchu, formally filed a demand for revision on March 30, 2001, and asked for a retrial, arguing that a new element (i.e., the testimony of Colette Noll[36]) raised doubt about the guilt of Guillaume Seznec. On April 11, 2005, the Commission de révision referred the case to the Cour de révision.

Without its specific political background, the matter of Seznec would undoubtedly have been forgotten a long time ago. The reason for renewed interest was that Guerdi, a key figure in this case, was thought to have been connected with Inspector Bonny from the Gestapo during 1944. This constituted a new fact, reason enough to raise a doubt about Seznec's conviction. Nonetheless, one cannot conclude that this will necessarily lead to the rehabilitation of Guillaume Seznec. For this to be the case, the Cour de Révision must subsequently come to the same conclusion.

The Filtering of the Demands

A second procedural obstacle consists of the filtering of the demands by the Commission de Révision. In practice, this commission of five judges of the Cour de Cassation is in charge of transferring the cases that seem admissible to the Chambre Criminelle that functions as the revision court. Article 623 CPP states that the commission may undertake, directly or indirectly, any useful investigations, hearings, confrontations, and verifications, and hear the pleadings of the demanding party, as well as the Ministère Public. The motivated decision of the commission is final and binding, not subject to any legal remedy. The case of Rida Daalouche[37] illustrates the importance of these investigations, confrontations, or verifications, and, even more important, the public interest in permitting not only the prosecution to bring new elements to the knowledge of the judiciary, but also the defense, if such elements are proven. In fact, Daalouche was acquitted after his family, during the supplementary investigation ordered by the commission de révision, produced a check-in ticket, two medical certificates, and a check-out ticket from the Edouard-Toulouse Hospital in Marseille. This element proved that Daalouche had not been capable of committing a crime at a football stadium at the same time. Faced with this new element, the Commission de Révision transferred the case to the Cour de Révision and ordered that the execution of the sentence be suspended pursuant to Article 624 CPP. This possibility is also open to the Cour de Révision. If the commission orders a suspension, it can only be done on the basis of a sufficient probability that the Cour de Révision will finally admit the petition of revision.[38] Even if this criterion (the sufficient probability of admission of the demand) is very vague, it underlines the decisive role of the Cour de Révision. In fact, the ruling of the Commission de Révision undoubtedly constitutes a significant obstacle insofar as the commission has full discretion to decide whether or not a demand fulfills the legal requirements of the revision, and to reject the demand if the answer is negative. However, if a petition seems admissible to the Commission, it has to be transferred to the Cour de Révision, which is the final instance to judge whether there is doubt from a legal point of view.[39] The supremacy of that court is also illustrated by its authority to order a supplementary investigation if it considers the case insufficiently clear.[40] Ultimately, the court hears, examines, and decides the case. No appeal is permitted of its decision (Art. 625 CPP). The Cour de Révision rejects a demand if it is not sufficiently well founded. If the court concludes to the contrary, it revokes the sentence and considers whether it is possible to grant a new trial. The Cour de Révision examines not only questions of law, but all issues related to facts brought up by the parties. If a new trial seems possible, the former verdict is canceled. In this case, the Cour de Révision has the power to find the convicted person innocent or guilty again, or to confirm the previous verdict. However, the new decision may in no event be more severe than the original verdict. If it is impossible to grant a new trial (i.e., according to Article 625 CPP, in the case of amnesty, death, dementia, or absence of one or more of the convicted persons), the Cour de Révision repeals verdicts that seem unjustified.[41] This is what happens when the innocence of the convicted person is recognized, even if, by his own erroneous declarations, he shares some responsibility in his wrongful conviction.[42]

The Effects of the Pourvoi en Révision

In Principle

If the former verdict is overturned, either by the Cour de Révision or by the court that had been in charge of a new trial, any criminal record (at all levels, from the police to courts) is deleted. Any fine that the convicted person may have paid will be paid back and all legal acts that he or she performed on his or her own, as well as the donations he or she could have made or received while legally incapacitated, will be validated. Any civil damages and interests, to the extent that they were based exclusively on the criminal responsibility of the convicted person, will be revoked retroactively. However, such retroactive effects may not lead to any prejudice for third parties, insofar as any legal act made by the custodian for and on behalf of the convicted person will remain valid.[43]

Compensation in Cases of Wrongful Conviction

Finally, the judicial error that led to the wrongful conviction entitles the victim of any such error, as well as any third party who suffered a prejudice because of it, to damages. Nonetheless, there are exceptions, as it would be unfair if the victim of a wrongful conviction, or the third party who subsequently suffered harm, contributed to the nondisclosure of the truth or, more specifically, to the court's lack of knowledge of the new element that constituted grounds for the revision (Article 626, CPP).

Repair is of a moral nature and consists in a demand that the decision of revision be proclaimed and published in the local newspapers as well as the official journal, at the expense of the state. The goal is to rehabilitate the wrongfully convicted. However, repair is also monetary; that is, the state has to pay damages to the wrongfully convicted person for the material as well as the moral harm. Damages are decided by the commission, or, at the request of the interested party, by the court of the new trial. In any case, damages are at the expense of the state, which may in turn sue the third party or parties whose fault caused the wrongful conviction (e.g., the civil party or parties, the whistleblower, or the witness who had committed perjury). The repair of judicial errors is necessary and symbolizes that justice is being done, even if, ultimately, it does not always appear justified, because liberty has no price. Nevertheless, the issue of quantifying the indemnity leads to problems, given the considerable amounts at stake. Such indemnities are justified in two ways: On the one hand, the years lost while in prison are difficult to value in monetary terms, and on the other hand, the importance of the allotted amounts underlines the exceptional character of the recognition of wrongful convictions and corroborates the principle of the validity of final rulings.

The quashing of the conviction of Patrick Dils led to damages of one million Euros. The French criminal justice system, in a certain way, had to "buy back" the fifteen years he spent in prison. One year's time due to this judicial error, therefore, cost the French government 66,666.66 Euros. This could well be interpreted by taxpayers as a new form of injustice to them. Such concerns, although more prosaic than the ideal of justice, may explain the reluctance of the judiciary and governmental bodies to grant revisions easily, especially in cases of alleged wrongful convictions involving deceased victims.

The Importance of Appeals and the Pourvoi en Révision

The scope of the pourvoi en révision is limited by the fact that it is an exception to the *res iudicata* principle provided in the French Civil Code (article 1351). It means that decisions become final or *res iudicata* once they are no longer open to appeal. Thus, the practical role of the petition of revision and the *res iudicata* principle can only be assessed in the light of the functioning of the appeal procedure. A statistical overview of the outcomes of all procedures before the thirty-three French Courts of Appeal in 1998[44] shows that, of 418,045 verdicts, appeals were filed in only 6.2 percent of the cases. Many of these appeals were, as in many other European countries, directed against the sentence and not the verdict as such. In 89.6 percent of all cases, the lower court's verdict was confirmed. Only 6 percent of verdicts were overturned by the Court of Appeals. The proportion of acquittals overturned on appeal by the prosecution was nearly the same. Approximately the same proportions hold true for appeals after verdicts by juries. There is some variation across jurisdictions, but the overall picture is rather even across space and stable over time.

Conclusion

In sum, and compared to other countries,[45] the proportion of decisions overturned through appeals is rather modest in France. Given the extremely narrow scope of the pourvoi en revision as outlined here, the conclusion seems warranted that many judicial errors go undetected or, at least, uncorrected, under the French system—at least if one does not wish to believe that the quality of lower courts' rulings is far superior in France than elsewhere on the continent. Of course, the impact of wrongful convictions depends also on the type of sentences that apply. From this point of view, prior to 1981 the death penalty, as an irreversible sanction, gave special importance to the issue of wrongful conviction. Gilles Perrault, author of *The Red Pull-Over*,[46] a book about the death sentence of Christian Ranucci,[47] said, "The honor of justice consists of admitting that it may fail." The execution of an innocent person as a result of a wrongful conviction must multiply moral concerns as long as the death penalty is maintained. Therefore, it is most fortunate that the death penalty was abolished in France in 1981, the last nation in Western Europe to do so.

Notes

1. All these appeals have to be exhausted if a defendant wants to file a petition of revision (*pourvoi en révision*).

2. Thus, the French procedure retains the ban on double jeopardy, whereas others European countries admit revision not only in favor of the defendant, but also in favor of the accusation.

3. The revision is different from the appeal to the Supreme Court, which aims at errors of law.

4. L. no. 89–431, June 23, 1989.

5. The six trials reviewed are:

1. Patrick Dils was sentenced in 1999 to life imprisonment for the homicide of two children. A pourvoi en révision was opened then he was rejudged and finally acquitted on April 25, 2005.

2. Rida Daalouche, a Tunisian, had been convicted in 1991 for murder. He was rejudged and acquitted in 1999, after being imprisoned for more than five years.

3. Guy Meauvillain was sentenced to eighteen years of imprisonment for the homicide of an old woman and was rejudged and acquitted in 1985.

4. In 1973, Roland Agret was sentenced to fifteen years of imprisonment for the homicide of a mechanic. After a hunger strike, his trial was reviewed and he was acquitted in 1985.

5. Jean-Marie Deveaux was sentenced to twenty years of imprisonment in 1963 for the homicide of his employers' daughter. In a new trial, he was acquitted in 1969.

6. Jean Dehays, accused of the homicide of a farmer, was sentenced to twenty years of compulsory labor in 1949. He was rejudged and acquitted in 1955.

6. Crim., November 5, 1987: Bull. Crim., no. 392.

7. Crim. April 8, 1967: Gaz. Pal. 1967. 2 .40.

8. This precision is justified since the opposition to a *jugement par défaut* is possible in *matières correctionnelles* as well as *matières de police* (in a *matière criminelle*, the opposition is unavailable; the *purge par contumace* is foreseen and responds to different principles), whereas the pourvoi en révision only aims at final judgments regarding felonies (délits) and crimes.

9. Crim. November 17, 1997: Bull. Crim. no. 387.

10. Crim. July 21, 1966: Bull. crim. no. 209.

11. L. no. 2000.516, June 15, 2000.

12. In that case, the demand comes to the attention of a commission of seven judges of the *Cour de Cassation,* which may remand the case either to a jurisdiction of the same level as the one having first decided the case, or to the *Cour de Cassation.*

13. In 1994, Omar Raddad was sentenced to eighteen years of imprisonment for the murder of his superior, Ghislaine Marchal, a rich widow of sixty-five years. Writing made of blood, *Omar m'a tuer* (i.e., Omar killed me), which was discovered next to the body of the victim, had put the police on the track of Raddad. In 1998, Raddad was released due to a presidential pardon granted by Jacques Chirac. In 1999, Raddad filed a petition for revision. It was finally rejected by the Cour de révision and Raddad will not benefit from a new trial.

14. It has to be noted that the pardon is an individual measure that is in the exclusive competence of the President of the French Republic. However, contrary to the amnesty, the pardon does not erase the verdict. In consequence, because the decision was final, Maître Vergès had the intention to bring three arguments before the European Court of Human Rights: first the fact that this court requires that the "avocat general" communicate the reasons for his or her pleadings to the parties; second, the fact that the director of the investigation had published a book with the title *Omar m'a tuer,* in which he presented his synthesis report much like a list of charges; and third, Maître Vergès asked the court to hear the declarations of a witness to a judge in Grasse (southern France) as to a possible involvement of the sect "Ordre du temple solaire" in that murder.

15. Crim., May 5, 1994: Bull. crim. no. 172.

16. Crim., November 5, 1987: Bull. crim. no. 392.

17. Crim., April 27, 1989: Bull. crim. no. 172.

18. Crim., March 5, 1931: Bull. crim. no. 65; Crim., April 28, 1975: Bull. crim. no. 112; Crim., November 5, 1987: Bull. crim. no. 392; Crim., February 8, 1989: Bull. crim. no. 62.

19. Crim., May 16, 1952: Bull. crim. no. 127; Crim., November 13, 1968: Bull. crim. no. 296; Crim., April 27, 1989: Bull. Crim. no. 172.

20. Crim., January 26, 1994: Bull. crim. no. 37.

21. The *Code d'instruction criminelle* of 1808 included only three restricted grounds for a revision: It was only in the matter of Dreyfus that the insufficiency of these three grounds was proclaimed. A law of June 8, 1895 created a fourth ground for a revision, of which the law of June 23, 1989 (L. no. 89–431) extended the scope.

22. The collegiality can limit the risk of wrongful convictions as, contrary to a single person who can be motivated by interests other than equitable ones, five persons cannot err simultaneously.

23. Ch. Réun., June 3, 1899: DP 1900. 1. 180, rapp. Ballot-Beaupré.

24. Crim., August 5, 1915: DP 1916. 1. 123; Crim., June 4, 1970: Bull. crim. no. 186; Crim., April 28, 1997: Bull. crim. no. 150.

25. Crim., June 26, 1991: Bull. crim. no. 283.

26. Crim., November 25, 1991: Bull. crim. no. 434.

27. Crim., May 3, 1994: Bull. crim. no. 163; Crim., May 27, 1997: Bull. crim. no. 205.

28. Crim., June 28, 1994: Bull. crim. no. 258.

29. Crim., October 21, 1976: Bull. crim. no. 297; Crim., January 13, 1981: Bull. crim. no. 21.

30. Crim., January 26, 2000: Bull. crim. no. 47.

31. For a brief summary of the facts see note 13.

32. In 1989, Patrick Dils was sentenced to imprisonment for life for the murder of two children in Montgny-lès-Metz in 1986. An adolescent at that time, Dils had admitted the two murders but revoked his admission a few days later. After fifteen years of imprisonment, a revision procedure was opened and it ended with his release on April 25, 2002.

33. A new fact exists, for example, if it appears that a person other than the convicted was present at the scene of the crime at the relevant time, and that this person, having altered his testimony as to his whereabouts on that day, had already been convicted for two murders that were similar to the one for which the convicted person was accused. Crim., April 3, 2001: Bull. crim. no. 92; D. 2001. 2227, note Defferrard.

34. It has to be noted that the media coverage of this affair even led to a new law, the law of June 23, 1989, which had the purpose of rehabilitating Guillaume Seznec, since

the révision became possible at the discovery of a new fact that, by its nature, is merely capable of raising doubt, although not necessarily establishing the innocence of the convicted person.

35. Comm. révis., March 24, 1994, Bull: no. 115.

36. The existence of that woman had been known, but she had always refused to testify. Consequently, her testimony was a new fact capable of raising doubt about the guilt of the convicted insofar as it rendered incontestable the existence of Gherdi, a collaborator with whom Pierre Quémeneur had had a meeting in Paris to handle the cars by which they organized the traffic.

37. In November 1991, Rida Daalouche was sentenced to fourteen years of imprisonment for murder after the body of a dealer had been discovered in May 1991 at the finals of the European football champions' cup. The revision procedure was opened in 1997, and Daalouche was acquitted in 1999, after Daalouche's family produced evidence that Rida, at the time of the crime, had been hospitalized.

38. Crim., May 11, 1976: Bull. crim. no. 152.

39. Comm. révis., June 25, 2001: Bull. crim. no. 157.

40. Crim., February 26, 1997: Bull. crim. no. 80.

41. Gaston Dominici, sentenced to the death penalty in 1954 for the murder of three English campers in Lurs, was pardoned in 1960. He died in 1965. When Mme. Lebranchu, Minister of Justice, used her powers to reexamine the Seznec case, Dominici's family wanted the Commission des revisions to accept a new reexamination of their case. A similar issue was raised by the family of Christian Ranucci, sentenced to the death penalty and beheaded in 1976 for the murder of a young girl, Maria-Dolorès Rambla. However, Christian's mother, still alive, saw a new chance in the reexamination of the Seznec case due to the Minister of Justice's action. She asked, for the fourth time, for the revision of her son's case, at the end of 2004.

42. Crim., December 2, 1937, DH 1939, Somm. 20.

43. In the same way, a divorce for fault decided against the convicted person—insofar as the infliction of a painful punishment is considered a fault that can justify a divorce—may not be deleted retroactively. The repeal of the divorce would not only harm the ex-spouse of the convicted person, but probably also the new spouse of both former partners, as well as their offspring.

44. All figures used here are from Noémie Goyet, *L'erreur judiciaire dans la justice pénale française*. MA dissertation, Ecole des sciences criminelles, University of Lausanne (2005). Her data derive from several statistical materials published on the Web site of the Cour de cassation, unpublished materials collected by her, and some materials published in C. Rizk and J. Torterat (2003), *L'appel en matière correctionnelle: Analyse par juridiction*, Paris: Ministère de la Justice (Direction de l'Administration générale et de l'Equipement, Sous Direction de la Statistique, des Etudes et de la Documentation).

45. See the percentages given in the chapters on Germany (Chapter 11) and Switzerland (Chapter 8) in this volume.

46. G. Perrault,"L'honneur de la justice est d'admettre qu'elle peut se tromper," *l'Humanité,* February 3, 2001.

47. Soon after Ranucci's execution (the last one in France; see note 39), doubts about his guilt were expressed. So far, no decision on the petition of revision has been reached.

13

THE SANCTITY OF CRIMINAL LAW

*Thoughts and Reflections on Wrongful
Conviction in Israel*

~

ARYE RATTNER

Does It Really Happen?

D uring the 1980s and the early 1990s the conscience of many of
us, in several countries including the United States, Canada, the
United Kingdom, Israel, and many others, was shaken by a number
of instances that cast doubt on a cherished belief: that innocent people are
seldom, if ever, convicted, and they are certainly not executed. Almost as if
orchestrated in the way they came to public attention, completely unrelated
cases of miscarriages of justice, not in which the guilty were freed but in which
the totally innocent were severely punished, became front-page news and the
subject of frequent discussion in the media. Thus, it is not a coincidence that a
great deal of attention has been devoted since then to the subject of wrongful
conviction from a rather more academic and scientific point of view.

Until the 1980s those who wrote on the subject, or who gave it serious
thought, relied on newspaper accounts that surface, not infrequently but in
numbers sufficiently small to make one believe that the prisons are over-
whelmingly filled with the guilty; yet not so infrequently that the problem
can be disregarded as a tragedy so ominous as to touch the nerve centers and
the basic tenets of a criminal justice system. These newspaper accounts were
collected by several authors (Borchard, 1932; Frank & Frank, 1957; Gardner,
1952; Radin, 1964), who usually added other cases gleaned from such sources
as interviews with attorneys, court records, interviews with victims of false
convictions, interviews with victims of crime, and firsthand knowledge. Their

works almost always consisted of a series of anecdotes, with each case a small horror story in itself; yet they provided no data that might give an estimate of the magnitude of the occurrence, or legal analysis as to how it happened. It was only later, during the 1990s, that a series of books and articles provided a more analytic framework for understanding the problem of wrongful conviction (Huff, Rattner, & Sagarin, 1996; Radelet, Bedau, & Putnam, 1992; Scheck, Neufeld, & Dwyer, 2000).

Resulting from the series of comprehensive studies conducted on wrongful conviction, a body of knowledge has been advanced, attempting to understand what goes wrong in our criminal justice systems that each year produce what may be a substantial number of false positives, even though it has so many apparent safeguards against wrongful conviction, and can boast of more elaborate mechanisms to protect defendants than any other system in the world. These studies have yielded a body of knowledge pointing at some key elements that have been detected as leading causes of wrongful conviction, among them eyewitness identification; perjury by witnesses as well as perjury by criminal justice officials; negligence by justice officials; false and coerced confessions; forensic errors; the use of jailhouse "snitches"; and several other factors that have led innocent people to be wrongfully convicted. Hence, while most of the attention has been indeed directed to the question, "How could this have happened?" much less attention has been devoted to related issues dealing with the legal procedures leading toward the exoneration of those who have been wrongfully convicted.

Criminal procedures do have, though, built-in formal legal mechanisms that allow the review of a case. The trial process represents a forum in which official abuses of power often occur; therefore, appellate review represents both a safeguard for the individual accused and an opportunity to elaborate on the rights of the individual, or the possibility that an error has occurred somewhere along the process. Hence the rigidity of the system in determining what constitutes a reversible error, as well as the limit on the number of appeals, creates in many instances a barrier, especially where reasonable concern about errors exists, and all postconviction avenues have been exhausted. Under such circumstances where the review of allegations of miscarriage of justice is sought, either by the defendant himself or herself or any other party, application procedures for a new trial (or retrial) have been set up. Most of the critiques that have been raised pointed out that review bodies should be independent and transparent and ready to consider any error as reversible. In this chapter, I attempt to show how, despite the existence of a review mechanism in the Israeli criminal justice system, a general attitude exists that judicial errors and mistakes rarely happen, thus defending what one may call the "sanctity of the criminal law."

Exonerating Innocents in Israel

Until October 1995 the main avenue for holding a retrial in the Israeli judicial system was an application that had to be submitted to the State Attorney General, who had to review and determine whether the following accumulated requirements were fulfilled as stated in Sec. 31 of the Court Law:

- The existence of a piece of evidence that was presented in the case and believed to be false or forged and there is reason to assume that without this evidence, the outcome of the trial would change in favor of the accused.
- New facts or new evidence were discovered that, alone or together with the material that was brought before the first court, would be likely to change the outcome of the trial in favor of the accused, and at the time of the first trial, such evidence was not available or was unknown to him or her.
- Another person has in the meantime been convicted of committing the same criminal act, and revealed at the trial that the person who was convicted first for the offense did not commit it.

Not only did the accumulation of these requirements create in many instances a judicial barrier, but adding to it was the general attitude of the court expressed in what can be termed as the "rule of finality." The rule of finality assumes that the final decision of the court, authorized to deal with a given case, represents the truth. Although the legal system does not presume or claim that a final and decisive verdict does, indeed, reflect the real truth, the finality of its decision creates the image of truth or, at least, a proxy of a truth that cannot be disputed. The rationale underlying this rule originates in the wish of all of us, laymen and lawyers alike, to believe that the legal system has succeeded in extracting a truth that is acceptable to all parties involved, even if they do not agree with it. Thus the rule of finality can be regarded as a type of legal fiction, one that receives its support through the voice of the court in some cases. In the case of Amos Baranes (Retrial 6731/96 *Amos Baranes v. the State of Israel*) the court made it clear the "he who had his day in court, and has been judged, should see this as the end of the road. Trials should not be reopened after they have been finished. The verdict has to be stable and able to serve the matters of other accused persons waiting for legal clarification." In his analysis, Feller (1968) indicates that the principle of finality does not draw its strength only from the needs of the judicial system or the criminal enforcement system: "Its strength lies also in the educational and deterrent needs that stand at the basis of a verdict." On a different occasion, Feller (1960) makes it clear that "the final judgment is vital—this is the judgment and no aspiration for retrial should be allowed. Apart from this, the final verdict has to be characterized by almost absolute stability; otherwise, the efficiency of its educational and deterrent effect is likely to be comprised." Indeed the rigidity of Section 31 of the Court Law, with the requirement for accumulated conditions, including the need for completely new evidence, combined with the recognition of the principle of finality, has led to a situation wherein judicial errors have hardly been recognized by the judicial system in Israel, where only three retrials of convicted persons have taken place during the entire history of the judicial system over fifty-two years! Even in these three cases, not one of the defendants was exonerated on retrial, despite grave doubts as to guilt within the legal community. Nevertheless, in two of the cases the persons who were convicted were granted amnesty by the president of the state of Israel, who stands outside of the court system, and were released from prison as a result of the doubts about their guilt.

Thus, a growing pressure exists to see the trial process as a forum in which official abuses of power often occur, and that any suspicion of miscarriage of justice should be sufficient grounds for a retrial. This has led to the amendment of the Court Law. In October 1995, the Israeli Parliament adopted an amendment to Section 31 of the Court Law. According to the amendment, a retrial could be ordered by the Supreme Court when real suspicion exists that the accused has suffered a miscarriage of justice. The amendment indicates that every piece of evidence, new or old, can be used as the subject of the application for a retrial as long as it has its own potential to exonerate, thus justifying such an application. In addition, this section indicates now, after the amendment, that every time there is doubt and concern that a miscarriage of justice may have occurred, that doubt can be a sufficient and justified cause for a retrial.

It would appear that the addition of subsection 4 to section 31 was intended to represent a real revolution in the matter of retrial. It was no longer necessary to prove accumulated conditions of one kind or another, or to attempt to prove something from nothing because the new evidence can lead to the acquittal of the accused, and the very "wide basket" rule provides a remedy for all those who have been wrongly convicted. Further examination of subsection 4 reveals that the legislature chose two vague terms: "real suspicion" and "miscarriage of justice." These two terms, which have to do mainly with subjective determination of the court, could potentially pave the way for many more convicted persons to enjoy the right to an additional opportunity to prove their innocence.

The amendment of section 31 of the Court Law has been adopted, but its effect on the attempts to exonerate people who claim innocence have not been evaluated. Toward that end, we retrieved all legal cases, since the amendment of the law, that involved decisions of the Supreme Court regarding retrials. The search revealed eighty-five requests for retrial that were submitted to the Supreme Court after the amendment to section 31 of the Court Law; of these, retrials were ordered in seven cases. Three of these were widely publicized cases[1] in which the crimes that were committed had a devastating impact throughout the country at the time they were committed and they resurfaced each time requests to hold a retrial were turned down by the Supreme Court. In two of these cases the people who were convicted were fully exonerated; in the third, the conviction was not overturned.

Examination of the records showed that only in four additional cases did the Supreme Court agree to order a retrial. In the case of Mr. Tamir Flink (Retrial 8777/99—*Tamir Flink v. the State of Israel*) the Traffic Court found that the applicant was responsible for a fatal road accident in which three people died and six others were injured. The Supreme Court, not without reservations, determined that

"In the end, the complainant was injured in the traffic accident. He lost his memory. He was convicted at the time (without even remembering the details of the accident) on the basis of an expert opinion determining that he was the driver of the vehicle responsible for the accident." Nevertheless Mr. Flink claimed that his memory returned and that it was another person who drove the car. His claim was supported by at least one expert opinion, and even the Attorney General did not dispute its veracity. Indeed, the Supreme Court in this case stated that the return of his memory and the testimony of an expert make it clear that on the face of it:

> Facts or evidence, that are likely, either alone or together with the material brought to the first court, to change the outcome of the trial in favor of the accused are sufficient in the spirit of section 31(a)(2) of the Court Law to order a retrial. There is also a real suspicion that the applicant suffered a miscarriage of justice (in the spirit of section 31 (a) (2)of the Court Law. The Attorney General might be justified in arguing that whether the applicant drove the car himself or another person without a license drove it, without a doubt, the guilt still falls upon him (legally and morally). However, it seems that in the eyes of an external observer (not to mention the applicant himself) there is a clear distinction between the two situations. Under these circumstances, the applicant is entitled to a retrial—on the basis of his restored memory and on the basis of the expert opinion in his possession. Under these circumstances, I find it appropriate (as already mentioned, not without reservations) to order a retrial.

In a different case (Retrial 1114/00, *Dina Bar-Yosef v. the State of Israel*) the applicant was charged in the Magistrates Court in Tel Aviv with the theft of 450 shekels from her employers' home (the complainants) while working there as domestic help. She was charged after a private investigator, acting at the request of the complainants, discovered monetary notes in her possession that had been marked by florescent paint. Paint marks were also found on the hands of the applicant. The applicant was convicted of the offense according to section 384 of the Penal Code (1977) and she confessed to the charges against her in the framework of a plea bargain. The complainants submitted a request to the Israeli Police for the applicant's conviction to be cancelled after discovering that money continued to be stolen from their house even after she stopped working for them. The Supreme Court determined that:

> . . . Indeed, as noted by the Attorney General, the grounds enumerated in section 31 (a) of the Court Law did not exist. However at the same time, taking in consideration the fact that the complainants and the applicant claim that the applicant is innocent, and in consideration of the circumstance of the request before me, as well as the position of the Attorney General, I found it appropriate to order a retrial as requested.

In yet another case (Retrial 7324/96—*Muhmad Adel Hayat v. the State of Israel* (3)97, 281) the applicant was convicted, on the basis of confession, of membership in the Islamic Jihad Organization, conspiracy to murder the guard stationed at the building of the traffic department of the Jerusalem Municipality, and attempted murder of the guard after supplying to two other persons the knife used to perform the attack. He was also convicted, on the basis of confession, of setting fire, together with another person, to a commercial vehicle belonging to a Jew. The applicant received a twelve-year sentence for the first set of charges (excluding the membership in the Islamic Jihad Organization) and a three-year prison sentence (two of them combined) on the arson charge. The applicant did not appeal the verdict of the District Court. The Supreme Court decided that:

> In the matter before us, we were presented with facts or evidence likely to change the outcome of the trial in favor of the applicant. These facts or evidence, as well as the confession of the applicant to arson, are false and it is proper to overturn the conviction for this charge. This new situation is likely to have a direct effect on the conviction of the applicant for the attempted murder. This conviction, too, is based on the confession of the applicant. The new situation according

to his confession on the matter of the arson is false—the State agrees with this determination. All these matters were not brought before the District Court before and thus it is proper to allow the court to reexamine them. It seems to me that the proper way is a retrial. The applicant is entitled to have his conviction cancelled and have his case discussed in a retrial.

Despite the change of the "judicial mood" expressed in these cases, out of eighty-five requests, the Supreme Court ordered retrials in only seven cases, three of which, as mentioned, were exceptional high-profile cases. Indeed, although the decisions of the Supreme Court, after amendment of section 31 of the Court Law, are assumed to be more reasoned, in actual fact, most of them follow exactly the same pattern as that which characterized the decisions of the Supreme Court before the amendment.

What Can Be Done?

The examination of the situation before and after the amendment of section 31 of the Court Law gave rise to a number of poignant questions regarding the mechanism of correcting judicial errors leading to the conviction of innocent people. The major question is whether any change has been achieved through the amendment of the Court Law. At least from a quantitative point of view, one may doubt that seven cases in which a retrial has been ordered indeed reflect the entire body of cases in which miscarriage of justice is suspected. If the answer is positive, then one may wonder if the Israeli legal system is almost free of mistakes. The answer has been given already in our earlier study (Huff et al., 1996), wherein we reported that even the most conservative estimated error rate of 0.5 percent of all felony convictions in a given year would yield thousands of erroneous convictions in any large Western society. Thus the number of cases that are being referred to retrial indicate that the existing situation is far from satisfactory and, therefore, there is room to consider a number of additional changes to give those who have been wrongly convicted a chance to prove their innocence.

Similar problems have been identified in other legal systems, leading to some considerations of the review process. Such was the situation in the United Kingdom. The old British system was similar to the current Canadian process where applications were made to the Home Secretary under a provision of their criminal code.[2] In March 1997 the Criminal Cases Review Commission in England was set up as a publicly funded, independent body for investigating suspected miscarriages of justice. It has twelve commissioners who come from various backgrounds including law, law enforcement, academia, the business world, and social service agencies. In the first two years of its operation, 2,416 applications were made and 793 were completed. The commission referred forty-four cases to the court of appeal, of which thirteen had been heard, resulting in ten convictions or sentences being quashed and three upheld. By the end of June 1999, 2,065 applications had been made; 961 had been completed and fifty-three cases had been referred. Thus the major change that was introduced there was the adoption of an inquisitorial approach by an independent body.

Examination of the process in Israel, even after the amendment of the Court Law, reveals that the Supreme Court places considerable importance on the attitude and the recommendation of the Attorney General regarding requests for retrial. As noted, according to Court Law (judgment orders in retrials), in his response to the retrial request, the Attorney General attaches his reasoned opinion regarding the existence of one of the grounds for retrial. The assumption is that the opinion of the Attorney General and his representatives, as officers of the court, is based on serious, impartial examination of the case, and that their position also represents the interests of the applicant. In light of the problems surrounding retrial already enumerated, and based on the examination of more than 200 cases (Huff et al., 1996) we suggest that every review procedure by officials from inside the system has significant implications for the production of false convictions. We call this phenomenon the "ratification of error." That is, the criminal justice system, starting with police investigation of an alleged crime and culminating in the appellate courts, tends to ratify errors made at lower levels in the system. The further the case progresses in the system, the less chance there is that an error will be discovered and corrected. Thus an internal procedure might be another step in error ratification.

The fact that both the Attorney General of Israel and the Supreme Court are part of the review procedures puts them under the same umbrella. Hence, by leaving the review process in the hands of the system, any change, such as the one that has been introduced by the Israeli Legislature, will not increase the chances of an error being detected and thus an innocent person being exonerated. Those who are familiar with Israeli criminal law are under the impression that amending several sections in it is almost impossible, even when there is a public outcry, and even when public inquiry committees recommend doing so. Not only that, but when certain amendments are being adopted in the right direction, one would still confront a wall of resistance (mainly from the side courts and prosecutorial authorities) when trying to give them practical meaning. Criminal law in Israel is in many ways an exception; it suffers from many deficiencies and from a great deal of unwillingness to admit its own errors to an extent that makes some wonder about the sanctity of the criminal law. According to the Jewish tradition, even God can be mistaken, but according to the Israeli judicial tradition, the Israeli courts do not err.

Notes

1. Amos Baranes (Retrial 3032/99), Ahmed Kozli and others—the murderers of the child, Danny Katz (Retrial 7929/96), and Gideon Harari and others—the Ma-atz affair (Retrial 966/98).

2. The situation in Canada allows appeal courts to review cases when there has been an error of law in the lower court. section 690 of the Criminal Code allows the justice minister to order a new trial after a review of an application from a convicted person has been completed.

References

Borchard, E. M. (1932). *Convicting the innocent: Sixty-five actual errors of criminal justice.* Garden City, NY: Doubleday.

Feller, S. Z. (1960). *Basics of criminal law,* vol. 1. Institute of Legislative Research, Jerusalem:Hebrew University.

Feller, S. Z. (1968). *Basics of criminal law,* vol. 2. Institute of Legislative Research, Jerusalem: Hebrew University.

Frank, J., & Frank, B. (1957). *Not guilty.* Garden City, NY: Doubleday.

Gardner, E. S. (1952). *The court of last resort.* New York: William Sloane.

Huff, C. R., Rattner, A., & Sagarin, E. (1996). *Convicted but innocent: Wrongful conviction and public policy.* Thousand Oaks, CA: Sage.

Radelet, M. L., Bedau, H. G., & Putnam, C. E. (1992). *In spite of innocence: Erroneous convictions in capital cases.* Boston: Northeastern University Press.

Radin E. (1964). *The innocents.* New York: William Morrow.

Scheck, B., Neufeld, P. J., & Dwyer, J. (2000). *Actual innocence: When justice goes wrong and how to make it right.* New York: Doubleday.

Cases Cited

Dina Bar-Yosef v. the State of Israel, retrial 1114 (2000).

Muhmad Adel Hayat v. the State of Israel, (3)97, 281, retrial 7324 (1996).

Tamir Flink v. the State of Israel, retrial 8777 (1999).

14

WRONGFUL CONVICTIONS IN POLAND

From the Communist Era to the Rechtstaat Experience

~

EMIL W. PLYWACZEWSKI, ADAM GÓRSKI,
AND ANDRZEJ SAKOWICZ

Before assessing research on wrongful convictions in modern Poland, some general background information on the country and its criminal justice system may be helpful. Poland is one of the larger countries in central Europe, sharing borders with Germany, the Czech Republic, Slovakia, Ukraine, Belarus, Lithuania, and the Kaliningrad region of the Russian Federation. With a surface area of 312,683 square kilometers (120,725 square miles) stretching some 650 kilometers (405 miles) from north to south and 690 kilometers (430 miles) from east to west, Poland ranks seventh in size among countries in Europe. The population of Poland is 38.659 million, placing Poland eighth among European countries and thirty-eighth in the world.

In Poland, there were 7,304 lawyers as of 2001; of these, 5,300 were practicing. Law is also practiced by legal advisers, who primarily provide legal services to the poor. There are about 15,000 legal advisers in Poland, who can represent clients in court in certain fields, including criminal trials. Only about 7,000 legal advisers may work with individual clients (persons); the rest work in the business sector and in public administration.

Poland has a typical continental criminal justice system. The judiciary consists of a Supreme Court, common courts, administrative courts, and military courts.

The Supreme Court is the cassation court, located in Warsaw. The court handles cassation, which is a legal redress directed against sentences or decisions of courts of appeals. Petitions of cassation are limited to technical legal issues, alleged violations of procedural rules that might have had an impact on the verdict, or violations of substantive criminal law, but it never reviews facts or sentences. Petitions of cassation are not open in all cases; they must be filed by a lawyer admitted at the bar.

In addition to criminal procedures, the courts of appeals and regional and district courts handle cases of civil, commercial, and family law, as well as cases related to minors, labor relations, social security, bankruptcy, and corrections. Common courts consist of two instances:

1. Courts of first instance
   - District court (including municipal court)
   - Regional court
2. Courts of second instance
   - Regional court
   - Court of appeals

In Poland, there are forty-three regional courts located in all major cities. Regional courts hear appeals of district court decisions; thus, they function as courts of second instance. They also handle certain serious cases (e.g., serious crimes) as courts of first instance. Poland has ten courts of second instance (courts of appeals) that review decisions by lower courts in legal as well as factual respects. They can confirm, change, or cancel rulings by lower courts. As of July 2004, Poland had 310 district courts, which are the judicial units closest to citizens. These courts handle all cases, except cases reserved for the regional court. In most district courts there are municipal divisions (also known as municipal courts). There are 369 municipal divisions countrywide (as of July 2004) that handle minor civil and criminal cases, including misconduct.

The Revision of Final Verdicts in the Polish Code of Criminal Procedure

Final decisions cannot generally be challenged again once all legal redresses have been unsuccessfully used. The exception is the so-called extraordinary revision that allows a case to be reopened and a verdict to be reviewed. In the context presented here, the most important reason to obtain a new trial is the existence of new evidence, the so-called revision *de novis* (or *propter nova*). This can occur whenever new evidence that had not been available at the time of the verdict tends to show, at least hypothetically, one or both of the following:

1. The defendant had not committed the crime he or she had been found guilty of.
2. The sentence was increased because the court wrongly excluded factual circumstances that would have called for a less severe sanction or because it wrongly admitted facts calling for a more severe penalty.

Beyond these two circumstances, extraordinary revision is also possible in cases where the defendant had not been convicted, but where, assuming his or her guilt, the case had been dismissed under certain conditions with which he or she had to comply.[1] Moreover, revision is possible if the verdict was based on a legal provision that a constitutional court or an international body (e.g., the European Court of Human Rights) has declared invalid.

Before December 30, 1995, only the Ministry of Justice (the General Prosecutor) or the Ombudsman (the Commissioner for Citizens' Rights Protection) had the right to file a petition of extraordinary revision.[2] The Ombudsman supervises all sectors of public services including courts and corrections. One of the important duties of the Ombudsman, in this context, is to file petitions of extraordinary revision whenever he or she is convinced that a verdict does not withstand scrutiny in the light of new evidence. Generally, citizens and foreigners may approach the Ombudsman in cases involving violations of constitutional rights and liberties. A motion to the Ombudsman is free of charge and does not demand any special form. The only necessary contents are full name and address of the applicant. The Ombudsman may inform the applicant of his or her rights. If the Ombudsman finds a violation of constitutional rights and liberties, he or she may take the case himself or herself or pass it on to relevant departments. If, after examining the case, the Ombudsman finds no violations, he or she informs the applicant of the findings. If the Ombudsman recognizes a need for action, he or she may undertake legal action on behalf of the individual or group of persons. The Ombudsman may demand the filing of a civil claim and take part in it, in which case the Code of Civil Procedure regulations on the participation of a public prosecutor are applicable. The Ombudsman may also demand other proceedings, whether administrative, criminal, or disciplinary. If an offense is found, the Ombudsman may submit a motion for punishment. He or she is also entitled to file cassations, extraordinary appeals from judgments of the Chief Administrative Court, and complaints to the Constitutional Tribunal in individual cases.

In 2003, the staff of the Ombudsman's Office saw a total of 3,504 clients and conducted 16,244 telephone conversations giving explanations and advice.[3] In that year, 33,016 new individual cases were examined. Proceedings were completed in 22,678 of the cases taken up by the Ombudsman. A satisfactory solution was obtained in 21 percent of those completed cases, meaning that an individual problem was solved in accordance with the applicant's expectations.

Wrongful Convictions and Dealing with the Past

Dealing with wrongful convictions in Poland is, as in the Czech Republic, in Slovakia, or in Russia, far more complicated than in a country with no need to "deal with the past" through legal instruments. Poland has utilized two approaches to revise wrongful convictions: extraordinary revision (as described earlier) and the Rehabilitation Act, a special law dealing with wrongful political convictions that declares some categories of former verdicts invalid. Both approaches require a closer look, based on currently available research.[4]

Poland (as well as other Eastern European countries) experienced what is often called "a lawful revolution."[5] However, nullifying all verdicts of the past, even those most cruel and unjust, was never envisaged after the change of the political system. Instead, Poland sought to develop proper legal principles that would deal with the problem as decently as possible. Obviously, new laws never really allow justice for the past. In this chapter we try to point out the most insoluble difficulties Poland faced, namely how to optimize the law that would declare certain verdicts invalid, and, at the same time, how to offer adequate compensation to the victims of wrongful convictions.

The idea of nullifying and compensating for wrongful convictions emerged right after the change of the Polish political system in 1989. However, legal remedies at hand did not suffice to deal with the problem. Poland, therefore, needed to pass a new law choosing between two approaches, namely reopening verdicts reached under the communist regime *ad meritum* (i.e., by examining each case again in the light of the available evidence, hardly possible now), or declaring void a class of verdicts, provided certain conditions are met. Some scholars pointed out that reexamining each case would raise the question of which law to apply: the communist (or even Stalinist) one, or current laws that would then be applied retroactively. Finally, the idea prevailed to declare criminal verdicts of the Stalinist period as generally null and void, provided certain conditions were met. Czarnota and Hofmański observed that, at first glance, it seemed impossible that all those verdicts were outrages against the law. At that time, a very useful legal concept was developed, namely the material element of the crime, or more strictly, the lack thereof.[6] In the Rehabilitation Act of 1991, any sentences meted out against people in connection with their activities in favor of the independence of Poland were declared void. Declaring a verdict invalid automatically implies declaring the defendant not guilty. This approach solves the formal as well as the moral side of the problem. The Rehabilitation Act declares void any rulings by courts made between January 1, 1944 and the end of the year 1956 (when the first political change occurred in Poland). The law was not limited to court judgments only. It also included the decisions of "special commissions" that, despite their role in political procedures, cannot be regarded as courts.

In objective terms, the law states that the incriminated conduct was an activity in favor of Poland's independence. At first glance that criterion is not sufficiently clear and is thus subject to numerous court interpretations,[7] which are discussed later. In a verdict dated November 20, 1991,[8] the Supreme Court stated that only the analysis of the intention of the convicted person (i.e., the defendant's will) can demonstrate whether conduct falls within the scope of conducts as foreseen by the Rehabilitation Act. If so, how should the case of someone who has already passed away be decided?

Whereas some cases raise no doubt under the Rehabilitation Act, such as a plot against the Communist regime, many cases discussed by Czarnota and Hofmański are much less straightforward. Illegal weapon possession, for example, although it might have to do with fighting for independence, may not necessarily be driven by such motives, particularly in the aftermath of World War II when almost everyone had access to weapons. Convictions for telling political jokes offer further examples: The Supreme Court held that "not every one claiming freedom of expression can be considered fighting for Poland's independence."[9]

A vivid and transparent example of breaking the basic rules of criminal law is offered by the so-called Special Commission aimed at combating economic damages against the socialist state. Without going further into the full scope of the Commission, it dealt with crimes such as "speculation," social and economical sabotage, "hooliganism," and "work repugnance." Countless of its "verdicts"[10] flouted both material and procedural law. Hardly any features of this state organ, although it played the role of a court, show similarities to courts, given the absence of all major safeguards of a fair trial, its very inquisitorial structure, often abusive pretrial detention, and, as often stressed, the presumption of guilt rather than innocence[11] in its verdicts.

The Commission functioned between 1945 and 1954 and imposed severe punishments and other penal measures, raising serious doubts about the safeguards of the accused, but also about the very legitimacy of its existence;[12] often "measures" were imposed for conduct that did not fulfill the standards of the *nullum crimen sine lege* principle. Often the Commission violated rules of criminal procedure, such as the ban on *reformatio in peius*.[13]

After that period, further violations of basic criminal law principles, including the nonretroactivity principle, took place. As to the latter principle, it is only necessary to mention the discussion of the criminal law implications of the decree of December 14, 1981, imposing martial law in Poland. On that occasion, the Supreme Court of Poland held that one should be aware of the criminality of conduct not from the time of publishing of the decree, but from the time the public media is informed about it. The later verdict, being a visible overinterpretation of the basic rules of criminal jurisprudence, was very harshly criticized.[14] Despite the criticism, this interpretation of (non)retroactivity was widely followed by the courts.

A related problem is finding a way to offer decent compensation. As a consequence of proclaiming certain verdicts invalid, Section 8 of the Rehabilitation Act makes it possible to offer both material and moral compensation for the damage caused by a wrongful verdict. The problem is—and to a certain extent this is inevitable—that a considerable amount of damage caused by repression has nothing to do with any legal procedure; it is a crime with no "legal excuse."

Compensation for Wrongful Convictions

The problem of adequate compensation for wrongful convictions in Poland, as in any country, has always existed, both before and after the collapse of communism. However, it fully emerged after the change of the political regime. The problem itself is rooted both in civil and criminal law and, therefore, is complex. Poland confronts a legal situation in which a strictly civil-law problem has been handed over to criminal courts, and where rules of compensation for wrongful convictions have developed gradually. Up to the nineteenth century, as far as Poland is concerned, no responsibility of the state for wrongful conviction existed. The first Polish Act of Criminal Procedure (dated 1928) provided for compensation only in cases of a wrongful verdict (remaining silent about other cases of wrongful convictions). The *largo sensu* compensation for wrongful convictions was introduced by a law enacted in 1956, followed by a code of criminal procedure dated 1969. As far as compensation was concerned, the law of 1969 envisaged it for cases of wrongful verdicts as well as clearly wrongful detention.

Under the People's Republic of Poland, as Poland was called, compensation for wrongful convictions played a marginal role at best, mainly because the requirements were far too narrowly defined. The newly enacted Code of Criminal Procedure of 1997 was a broad response to the democratization of the political and legal system, including criminal justice. By and large, it broadened the scope of compensation for wrongful convictions, for example, by no longer requiring that any party claiming compensation would, to qualify, have to prove a state official's fault.

In addition, Poland is a party to the European Convention of Human Rights, with its Article 5(5) providing that "anyone who suffered from detention or conviction contrary to the wording of that article has the right to compensation." Polish legislation is now, as far as wrongful convictions are concerned, in compliance with the European Convention.

Wrongful Convictions Identified by the Ombudsman: A Review of Exemplary Cases

To illustrate the considerable importance of exonerations and compensation in Poland in recent years, a few qualitative and quantitative indications are helpful. Some cases are summarized here, based on work by Bulenda.[15] It should be stressed that wrongful convictions that had to do with the Communist system were paid special attention by the Polish Ombudsman right after the political change in 1989.[16] It can also be seen by the Ombudsman's activity concerning petitions based on the Rehabilitation Act of 1991. Bulenda gives examples of compensation for wrongful convictions as well as less frequently for a prolonged rehabilitation procedure.[17] In the case of this so-called professional cassation (i.e., filed by the Attorney General and the Ombudsman), the thirty-day deadline is irrelevant, contrary to ordinary cassation.[18] Therefore it was possible to react to wrongful verdicts with cassation, and that means of revising wrongful verdicts fits within the definition of those verdicts.

In 1985, the Regional Court in Węgrów[19] found Leszek A. guilty of launching a strike, and he was sentenced to six months in prison, suspended for three years. In 1994[20] as a result of extraordinary revision in favor of the convicted, Leszek A. was declared not guilty because, as the court argued, he committed no crime. Leszek A. demanded approximately €20,000 of compensation for material and moral damage, caused by unjustified pretrial detention. As the defense pointed out, a strike was at that time legal, according to the trade union laws, and Leszek's behavior could by no means be regarded as any illegal form of strike because he merely provided information about a strike. Leszek A. was exonerated by the Supreme Court, which did not regard his conduct as a crime. However, the compensation demanded by Leszek A. was said to be highly overestimated, as "the period in which Leszek A. was detained was moderately short." The compensation for moral damage given was approximately €12,000, much less than claimed.

In a case (Walentyna N.) involving cassation applied by the Ombudsman, a claim for moral compensation was forwarded when Walentyna N.'s mother,

Franciszka E., was still alive. In the Ombudsman's opinion, Walentyna N. was entitled to a claim for both the material and moral damage caused as a result of wrongful conviction. The cassation was admitted (V KKN 533/97).

In another cassation applied for by the Ombudsman (RPO/260091/97/II) in favor of Józef J., it was pointed out in cassation, that the court had omitted (in counting the amount of compensation) five years of exile to Siberia. The cassation was admitted with a judgment (II KKN 92/98).

In yet another cassation applied for by the Ombudsman (RPO/269249/98/ II) in favor of Czesław A., it was decided that the court had wrongly judged that the imprisonment that resulted from a wrongful verdict did not involve any measurable material damage, whereas the imprisonment had actually made it impossible for Czesław A. to finish school or get a proper job. The cassation was admitted with a verdict signed III KKN 289/98.

In yet another interesting case, the Supreme Court proclaimed that:

> with regard to the mode of assessing (measuring) compensation as stipulated in art. 487 par. 1 of the code of criminal procedure there is no justification of compensating for unlawful decision concerning the execution of penalty. The wording of art. 497 does not allow (entitle) for the interpretation that compensation should be given to anyone who was unrightly deprived of liberty. If the penalty temporarily suspended was wrongly executed (with court's decision) it is not equal to wrongful conviction.

Another interesting case is that of the Witnesses of Jehova, declared guilty of taking part in an illegal organization whose existence and purpose were

TABLE 14.1.   TOTAL AND SUCCESSFUL PETITIONS OF CASSATION FILED BY THE OMBUDSMAN IN CRIMINAL CASES IN POLAND, 1992–2003

Year	Total Petitions Filed	Successful Petitions
1992	23	11
1993	14	9
1994	11	8
1995	23	17
1996	20	17
1997	48	39
1998	102	46
1999	61	45
2000	—	60
2001	—	38
2002	—	33
2003	—	—

Note: Complete data available only through 1999.

concealed from the authorities. At that time, belonging to any such organization was a crime, according to the so-called little penal code.[21] Witnesses of Jehova convicted under this statute were rehabilitated (declared not guilty) in the year 2000.[22]

For the period between 1992 and 2003, the number of cassations applied by the Ombudsman on the basis of wrongful convictions was quite substantial (see Table 14.1) and the annual compensations paid averaged about €200,000.

Summary and Conclusions

In Poland, exoneration of those wrongfully convicted for political reasons is regulated by the Rehabilitation Act. Many cases have been brought under this law. It should be noted that the Rehabilitation Act was meant to be an extraordinary means of overturning final verdicts in favor of defendants or their descendents. Some observers argue that this law is often invoked by relatives of wrongfully convicted persons with the sole purpose of obtaining compensation. Often they may have no idea of what their relative's damage and suffering had really been.

No complete survey has been undertaken in Poland to investigate the number of wrongful convictions. In particular, little is known about the role of new evidence in reversing wrongful convictions. The most complete source is the Ombudsman's archives (see Table 14.1).

The cases reviewed in this chapter tend to prove that laws dealing with wrongful conviction in Poland are far from being merely laws on the books, despite some difficulties in interpretation faced by the Supreme Court. However, the compensation awarded was usually much lower than what was claimed.[23] Courts may thus underestimate damages and suffering related to wrongful convictions. Hopefully, better knowledge of the number of wrongful convictions and their impact on the lives of those concerned will increase the courts' awareness of this risk of judicial decision making.

Notes

1. For closer commentary see P. Hofmański E. Sadzik, and K. Zgryzek, *A Commentary on the Code of Criminal Procedure* (Warsaw, Poland: C. H. Beck, 1999), 870–873.

2. Changes to the Code of Criminal Procedure of June 29, 1995 (effective January 1, 1996) removed regulations about extraordinary revision and put into effect cassation, in which the Minister of Justice, the General Prosecutor, the Ombudsman, and other parties have the power to file a cassation in favor of the defendant against every legally valid court judgment or decision.

3. See www.brpo.gov.pl.

4. The first author is currently attempting to collect full statistical data on how wrongful convictions have been dealt with over this critical period.

5. See, for example, A. Czarnota and P. Hofmański, "Prawo, Historia i Sprawiedliwość" ["Law, History and Justice"], in *Current Problems of the Penal Law and Criminology*, ed. E. W. Pływaczewski (Białystok, Poland: Temida, 1998), 138.

6. It indicates that conduct is not a crime if it lacks relevant "social jeopardy" (or "damage") to any legally protected legitimate interest).

7. See, for example, P. Mierzejewski, "Orzecznictwo Sadu Najwyższego na tle tzw. Ustawy Rehabilitacyjnej" ["The Jurisdiction of the Highest Court in Relation to the Rehabilitation Act], *Studia Iuridica* 38 (1996): 74.

8. I KZP 25/91, OSP 1992, no. 3–4, poz. 22.

9. Decision of 03.07.1992, II KRN 90/92.

10. Quoted and explained by P. Fiedorczyk, *Komisja Specjalna do Spraw Walki z Nadużyciami i Szkodnictwem Gospodarczym* [*The Special Commission for the Fight with Commertial Abuse and Damage*] (Białystok, Poland:Faculty of Law and Administration at the Warsaw University, 2002). For the structure and competence of the commission, see therein.

11. *Ibid.*, 322.

12. As to the latter, *ibid.*, 47–53.

13. Under continental law, Courts of Appeal are usually not allowed to modify the verdict or the sentence of the lower court in a way that is unfavorable to the defendant, except if the prosecutor has filed an appeal.

14. See especially J. Kochanowski and T. de Virion, "A Gloss Concerning the Verdict of the Highest Court of Poland Dated 1.03.1982," *Państwo i Prawo* 9 (1982), 148–151. The vast report on that subject by J. Kochanowski could only be published officially eight years later.

15. See K. Bulenda, "Odszkodowanie za niesłuszne skazanie (Problematyka społeczno—prawna)" ["Wrongful Convictions: Social and Legal Problematic"] (master's thesis, Institute for Applied Social Sciences, University of Warsaw, 1999).

16. See alsoBulenda, "Odszkodowanie," 86.

17. Numerous such information is provided by the Ombudsman Bulletin (Biul RPO) 1996/29, 155ff; 1998/35, 33; 1999/37, 36; 2000/39, 31–32; 2001/43, 52; Cited after Bulenda, passim.

18. Article 520 says that "Parties shall have the right to bring a cassation appeal." The next Article (521) adds that "The Attorney General and also the Commissioner for Citizens' Rights Protection (the Ombudsman) may bring a cassation appeal from any valid and final judgement concluding the court proceedings." According to Article 524 § 1, "The time-limit for filing cassation by the parties shall be 30 days from the date on which the judgment with reasons was served. The motion requesting the service of the judgment with reasons should be filed with the court which rendered the judgment within the final time-limit of 7 days from the date it is announced. Article 445 § 2 shall be applied accordingly. § 2. The time-limit set forth in § 1 shall not be applied to the cassation brought by the Attorney General and the Commissioner for Citizens' Rights Protection (the Ombudsman). § 3. No cassation to the prejudice of the accused may be accepted after 6 months from the date on which the judgment became valid and final."

19. II K 450/85.

20. II KRN 144/93.

21. See "Mały kodeks karny" (so-called Small Criminal Code), a decree of June 13, 1946 on crimes particularly dangerous in the postwar period.
22. II KKN 376/99.
23. See Bulenda, "Odszkodowanie," 111.

References

Bulenda, K. (1999). *Wrongful convictions: Social and legal problematic.* Masters thesis, Institute for Applied Social Sciences, University of Warsaw, Poland.

Bulsiewicz, A. (1965). Stanowisko Poszkodowanego w Procesie o Odszkodowanie za Niesłuszne Skazanie lub Bezzasadne Tymczasowe Aresztowanie [The legal status in the process of compensation for wrongful verdict or unjustified detention]. *Nowe Prawo, 10,* 21–36.

Bulsiewicz, A. (1968). *Proces o Odszkodowanie za Niesłuszne Skazanie lub Oczywiście Bezzasadny Areszt Tymczasowy* [The process for compensation for wrongful verdict or manifestly unjustified detention]. Toruń.

Bulsiewicz, A., & Hofmański, P. (1981). Materialnoprawne Warunki Odpowiedzialności Skarbu Państwa za Szkodę Spowodowaną Oczywiście Niesłusznym Tymczasowym Aresztowaniem [Conditions for state's responsibility for damage caused by manifestly unjustified detention]. *Palestra, 10–12,* 37–49.

Czarnota, A., & Hofmański, P. (1997). Law, history and justice. In E. W. Pływaczewski (Ed.), *Current problems of the penal law and criminology* (pp. 137–160). Białystok, Poland: Temida.

Daszkiewicz, W. (1990). Problem Rehabilitacji i Odszkodowań za Bezprawne Represje Karne [The problem of the rehabilitation and indemnities for illegal penal repressions]. *Państwo i Prawo, 3–18.*

Hofmański, P., Sadzik, E., & Zgryzek, K. (2004). *A commentary on the code of criminal procedure.* Warsaw, Poland: C. H. Beck.

Małecki, J. (1989). Niektóre Cywilnoprawne Aspekty Odpowiedzialności Skarbu Państwa z art. 487 k.p.k.—Wybrane Problemy [Chosen issues of state's compensation for wrongful convictions upon art. 487 of the (previous) code of criminal procedure]. *Palestra, 8–10,* 84–134.

Mierzejewski, P. (1996). The jurisdiction of the highest court against a background of the so-called Rehabilitation Act. *Studia Iuridica, 31,* 117–146.

Paprzycki, L. K. (1987). Przesłanki Zasądzenia Odszkodowania za Oczywiście Niesłuszne Tymczasowe Aresztowanie w Doktrynie i Orzecznictwie Sadu Najwyższego [Grounds for compensating for manifestly wrongful detention in legal doctrine and jurisprudence]. *Nowe Prawo, 2,* 44–51.

Stanowska, M. (1993). The jurisdiction of the highest court in the rehabilitation cases in 1988–1981. *Archiwum Kryminologii, 19,* 133–165.

IV

CONCLUSIONS

15

Wrongful Conviction

Conclusions from an International Overview

~

C. RONALD HUFF AND MARTIN KILLIAS

The risk of wrongfully convicting the innocent is not merely a matter of an innocent defendant being confronted with evil, incompetent, or lazy decision makers who place their own interest above the interest of avoiding miscarriages of justice. If eliminating unqualified people from key positions within the criminal justice system remains a permanent and uncontested goal, the fact is that procedural structures can far more easily and permanently be amended than can the morality of individuals. For this reason, this project has been undertaken with the purpose of discovering factors related to procedures and practices in all sectors of criminal justice that might, with some regularity, contribute to wrongful convictions. In the foreground of our project is the risk of convicting innocent people for offenses they did not commit. Obviously, there are many more forms of miscarriages of justice, such as violations of procedural rules, errors in the interpretation of relevant laws, excessive or otherwise inappropriate sentences, or even the failure to convict a guilty person (certainly a miscarriage of justice from the perspective of the victim). Although these issues are far from irrelevant, addressing the problem of wrongful convictions of innocent people deserves first priority, particularly in an international perspective, because such errors may be less idiosyncratically related to specific characteristics of national laws, and because it is, in any respect, the most serious type of miscarriage of justice.

As the chapters included in this volume have shown, the risk of convicting innocent people is probably not equally distributed across nations, nor is it necessarily the same at all levels of national systems. In this concluding chapter, we look more closely at the lessons that can be learned from the preceding chapters.

Focus on Finding the "Truth," or on Obtaining Convictions?

A first and important aspect is, of course, the extent to which the criminal justice system is devoted to finding the truth. Of course, almost everywhere prosecutors and police officers are obliged to search for the "truth," or to "get" the guilty and to save the innocent. However, as long as such declarations of intent are not embedded in a setting of institutional safeguards shaping the legal culture, they will probably be no more efficient than codes of ethics of bar associations that state that all lawyers admitted to the bar should contribute to finding the truth, and should never "lie" in court.

Whenever American lawyers speak about the continental system, they are usually well aware of its inquisitorial traditions. However, they may be far less aware that the continental procedure in *civil* lawsuits shares many features of the American criminal justice model. One could say that the specifically inquisitorial tradition of the continental system is limited to the field of criminal law. Here, indeed, it has always been the understanding that establishing truth is the court's business, and that parties and their lawyers are expected to assist the court in this task. One consequence of this *officiality maxim* (*Offizialmaxime*)[1] is that the court never may rely on what the parties present, but has to verify the facts by its own means. This system of "balanced" fact-finding efforts on the side of the judiciary is entrenched in the continental inquisitorial tradition. It first appears, expressively, in the code adopted by the German *Reichstag* in 1532 under Emperor Charles V. In section 47 of this *Constitutio Criminalis Carolina* (CCC; Kohler & Scheel, 1900/1968), judges are warned to consider all relevant facts, including those favorable to the defendant, never to rely only on what the parties declare, and to be critical about confessions. This rule still applies in countries maintaining a continental system, and may be the most fundamental difference from American criminal procedure. The latter is focused much more on the respect for formal rules than on outcomes.[2] Obviously, postmedieval continental legislators (as the legal advisers of Charles V) were concerned about the risks of wrongful convictions. The bad reputation of the inquisitorial system is certainly due to the abuses in connection with witchcraft trials, where the guarantees of the CCC (against torture[3]) did not apply due to the "enormous seriousness of the offence" (Schmidt, 1965, 209–211)—a justification not unfamiliar in modern times where due process guarantees are often set aside in "very serious" (e.g., terrorist) cases, or whenever moral panics tend to remove formal guarantees of due process, as described in Chapter 2 by Grometstein. In such cases, "coordinated" testimony by several victim-witnesses can also lead to devastating consequences (Crombach, 1999).

The *officiality maxim* has far-reaching consequences. It means that police officers and prosecutors who fail to collect or disclose evidence that might be favorable to the defendant are subject to criminal prosecution. Although such cases are rare, the mere existence of such rules may work as an efficient deterrent for individuals concerned about their careers and any scandal of this sort. Chapter 11 on German prosecutors and Chapter 8 on Switzerland both provide illustrations about the potential of such rules, including in discovering wrongful convictions and following exonerations that sometimes are initiated by prosecutors or police officers. In the debate on the role of forensic scientists (see Chapter 3 of this volume), the question of whether they should be independent of the police cannot be adequately debated without reference to the role of the police in general and the officiality maxim. If the police must also search for evidence that may turn out to be favorable to the defendant, any police officer and any specialist employed in the forensic science unit of the police is per se entitled to come forward with whatever evidence he or she finds. The answer may obviously be different if police laboratories are embedded in a "partisan" police organizational culture where the hierarchy has the power to suppress undesirable findings, or if they are organized as private companies concerned with their clients' interests. Therefore, one may question whether private laboratories will really be the answer if they end up "selling" whatever evidence they understand will best serve the cause of those who are going to pay them. In sum, a rule of impartial, disinterested search for the truth may—if it is endorsed by ethical guidelines on police, prosecutorial, and experts' conduct and backed by appropriate sanctions—be a promising way of dealing with some sources of errors.

The Role of Plea Bargaining

Plea bargaining, or "justice without trial" (Newman, 1966), has always been found to be a major source of wrongful convictions. Several chapters in this book offer new and compelling illustrations. When the defendant risks being punished more severely by the court if he or she does not accept an offer by the prosecutor, the probability is that innocent people will be "lured" into entering an "Alford"[4] guilty plea simply to avoid an even worse outcome at trial. Several conclusions can be drawn from some of the preceding chapters concerning how to reduce the risk of such outcomes. As noted by Huff, Rattner, and Sagarin (1996), the threat of a death sentence may be a powerful incentive for a defendant to enter a guilty plea to avoid the worst of all possible outcomes. In addition, verdicts leading to capital sentences are not always beyond doubt, as the many exonerations of death row inmates in American prisons have illustrated (see Chapter 6 of this volume and Huff, 2002). Even in Europe, the last defendant (Ranucci) beheaded in France—the last country on the "old" continent to abolish the death penalty (in 1981)—may have been innocent, as noted by Dongois (Chapter 12).

Plea bargaining should be restricted to minor offenses (traffic violations, minor thefts, possession of drugs, etc.) where the sentence at stake does not exceed a few months or one year at most; where the facts are obvious; and where the legal qualification does not raise any difficulty. Under such circumstances, it certainly is legitimate to divert the system's scarce resources to more important cases. This form of "justice without trial" (including "convictions by the prosecutor" or "penal orders") exists under many different names[5] in virtually all countries. The Netherlands has an equivalent system of "transactions with the prosecutor," implying that a certain amount is being paid to the treasury or any other agreed-on body; other countries (e.g., France, Belgium, Germany, and Italy) combine the two systems.

The experience with wrongful convictions suggests, however, that there should be a number of additional procedural safeguards. First, there should be a rule that the sentence the defendant receives if he or she insists on a court hearing does not exceed the one the prosecutor had offered (thus, *reformatio in peius* should be ruled out). Second, since many defendants accept a penal order (or a transaction) merely because this procedure is not public and, therefore, does not attract public attention, the rule should be that the court hearing is not public whenever the defendant requires his or her case to be heard behind closed doors. Further, a penal order (or transaction) should never be issued as an option to downgrade serious crimes. Finally, such a decision should never be possible without a hearing of the defendant by the prosecutor.[6] Indeed, the evidence (see Chapter 8 on Switzerland) suggests that exonerations are not infrequent if prosecutors have not heard defendants before issuing a penal order, in most cases because the relevant facts (including the suspect's identity) have not been sufficiently verified. Even if such errors concern mostly minor offenses and often trivial sanctions, their combined effect on the legitimacy of the criminal justice system should not be underestimated, since they concern many more people than the few exonerations in murder or other serious cases.

The Role of Confessions

False confessions have, since the time of the *Constitutio criminalis carolina* of 1532, been recognized as an important source of wrongful convictions.

Several chapters in this book offer convincing illustrations that this problem has not been solved in modern times. The most important lesson to be learned from this experience is that confessions should not have the same far-reaching consequences in criminal procedures as they do in civil cases (e.g., those involving damages) or under American law. If a defendant admits (in a police interrogation) having committed an offense, the police should try to obtain from him or her as many details as possible to search for evidence corroborating that the crime happened in exactly the way the defendant described. In no way should any confession "close" a case (as, for example, in a damage suit). In particular, a confession should never make a court hearing unnecessary except in minor cases (as already described). If facts are uncontested, the focus may turn, of course, to legal issues or the sentence in countries where the court decides the verdict and the sentence during the same hearing. The confession itself should, at best, be a mitigating circumstance of limited impact on the sentence.

The devastating role of false confessions can also take unexpected forms that might become of even greater interest in the context of the "war on terrorism." As Marcelo Fernando Aebi (2003) described in a presentation during a workshop that we held in Switzerland, terrorist defendants with ETA connections in Spain, when facing a life sentence due to other uncontested or presumably well-established offenses, tend to admit a number of other terrorist attacks actually committed by other (unknown to the police) members of their organization, to make prosecutors and the police believe that they have solved more attacks than they actually did. In such cases, false confessions (and what Aebi calls a sort of "voluntary wrongful conviction") will protect other terrorists, and may make the police drop investigations that are necessary to prevent further terrorist actions. This is not unlike the practice of "taking the rap" for someone higher in an organized crime network.

Rules on Disclosure and the Right to Be Heard

Zalman (Chapter 5) and others point to the critical role of "disclosure" of evidence before trial. Under the Anglo-Saxon system, such disclosure is the exception, although the number and scope of such rules have increased over recent decades. Under the continental system, full disclosure of the entire file of the prosecution is the rule, and is based on the constitutional principle of any citizen's "right to be heard" before any decision is made about his or her case. As a result, the defendant (and his or her lawyer) has the right to comment on all relevant aspects of the file.

To reduce the risk of wrongful convictions, the full file of the police or the prosecutor should be made available to the defense before the case goes to trial. Having an opportunity to see whatever charges are in the file allows one to come forward with contrary evidence before the trial begins. In continental countries where these rules are routinely applied, defense counsel is discouraged from abusing their privileged information because they are expected to announce, before trial, all exonerating evidence they can reasonably provide. Although the defense is not bound by the right to be heard (that applies only to the government and, thus, the prosecutor and the police), defense lawyers typically come forward with potentially exonerating—even speculative—hypotheses during the police investigation. In case they do so only at trial, the court will likely interrupt the hearing and order a complementary investigation. Such rules may quite efficiently assist courts in avoiding the conviction of innocent people, but also in avoiding the acquittal of guilty defendants. Both Type I and Type II errors are, as Forst (2004) has noted, "errors of justice" that compromise public safety.

Limiting the Role of the Defense

Wherever the full disclosure of the prosecution's file is the rule, the role of the defense is more limited in the establishment of the relevant facts. In continental law countries, defense lawyers typically do not conduct their own investigation. Whenever they believe that the police have neglected evidence that might be favorable to the defendant, they will ask for an extension of the police investigation, usually when the case is being heard at a pretrial hearing by the examining magistrate or the prosecutor (*Staatsanwalt, procureur*). In practice, police investigations often involve long and energy-consuming searches for evidence for or against alternative (including speculative) hypotheses advanced by the defendant or his or her counsel.[7] For example, police and prosecutors always have to envisage the possibility that a crime has been committed by a third party. This rule applies even if the defense does not establish any evidence in this respect, and the police often invest considerable resources to rule out the existence of any third party. In sum, such rules help reduce the risks of convicting innocent defendants resulting from incompetent or inadequately equipped counsel (Schmid, 1993; Trechsel and Killias, 2004).

Given the risks involved in poorly resourced or incompetent counsel, judicial errors may, ironically, more easily be reduced by limiting the role of the defense. If the defense does not need to do much more than to raise—even speculative—alternative explanations, and if the prosecutor and the police share the burden of investigating and ruling out any such possibilities raised by the defendant, it may be more difficult to convict an innocent person than if the prosecutor wins his or her case whenever the defense fails in its efforts to come forward with a successful alternative investigation. In terms of error management, it may indeed be preferable not to rely excessively on the "rights" and, in the result, the ability of the defense. Zalman (Chapter 5) offers convincing evidence in this regard.

The Role and the Hearing of Witnesses

Under the Anglo-Saxon system all witnesses, including experts (e.g., physicians, coroners, forensic scientists) are cross-examined by both parties, whereas under the continental system, it is the presiding judge's duty to do this. Under any system, unpleasant comments concerning witnesses, particularly the victim, should, whenever unwarranted, be labeled as attorney misbehavior and discouraged by appropriate sanctions. Such rules may, in turn, make current rules barring certain questions (e.g., those concerning the victim's former sexual conduct; see Ries, 1984) far less necessary. They may also increase witness and victim satisfaction, particularly if these individuals find an opportunity to present their story without being permanently interrupted by attorneys (Pizzi, 1999). Attorneys should also be discouraged from meeting potential witnesses before trial, not to mention "rehearsals." Finally, the role of defendants and codefendants as witnesses should be seriously restricted. Many instances illustrate the risks of convictions based on the testimony of witnessing codefendants.

The System of Appeals

According to our definition of *wrongful convictions* adopted throughout this book, a judicial decision is wrongful only if an innocent person has been convicted and if this error has not been corrected through appeals. Therefore, the frequency with which innocent people are convicted may depend also on the checks that exist in the system and the possibilities of getting such a decision overturned through appeals and other legal remedies. The scope and frequency of appeals seem to vary greatly among countries. However, the frequency of appeals may also depend on whether or not they may be brought against the sentence imposed. In European countries, most appeals are focused on or even limited to the sentence, an understandable situation since European judges have very wide discretion at that stage, and because most defendants do not contest the facts, but rather hope for a relatively lenient sentence. Another variable is whether or not appeals are available to the prosecution and not only to the defense. To the extent that prosecutors are also entitled to file an appeal, their success rate seems to be not much different (or even higher) than those of defense counsel, at least in France, Germany (Jehle,

2003), and Switzerland.[8] Overall, it appears that roughly one in three decisions brought before a higher court is amended, although appeals are rarely successful on issues related to fact finding by the lower court.[9] Of course, one must bear in mind the number of lower court decisions that are routinely appealed; again, the variety among Western countries is almost unlimited, ranging from far less than 10 percent to fully one-third. From these figures (and keeping in mind the English and the Israeli experiences, as described in earlier chapters of this volume), it would seem that higher courts in France, Germany, and Switzerland review decisions brought before them rather critically. Obviously, risks of wrongful convictions can be reduced if many errors are discovered and, eventually, corrected through appeals to higher courts. A high risk of having a decision overturned by a higher court may also be a strong incentive for lower courts to avoid errors of all kinds.

A low rate of decisions that are overturned by courts of appeal can be interpreted in several ways. It could mean that lower court rulings are relatively uncontested, or hard to contest because they obviously fit the facts rather well. It could, however, also reflect what Huff et al. (1996) called "the ratification of error" and what Brants (in Chapter 9 on The Netherlands) describes as "tunnel bias," a tendency among all decision makers to routinely confirm whatever has been decided at the preceding step—obviously the easiest way to manage a high caseload with limited resources.

It may not be easy to overcome such confirmation bias. However, a few other conclusions seem quite straightforward. First, every verdict should be subject to appeal. If fact finding by lower courts cannot be contested before a higher court, judges and juries may be far less concerned about careful fact finding. Appeals on facts are also necessary to correct the effects of any "surprise tactics" by both parties, witnesses, or experts. If statements can be contested (and have, eventually, to be repeated in a higher court), bluff and surprise will be far less promising as a strategy at trial. Barring the prosecution from filing an appeal seems less warranted if any wrongful decisions—including acquittals of guilty defendants—are to be prevented. Indeed, acquittal of guilty defendants may often do great injustice to victims, as Forst (2004) rightly points out. If we share his view that errors are unavoidable to some—at best, minimal—extent, error management becomes the central issue. In this sense, appeals may be considered a built-in system of error control and elimination.

Rules on Exoneration and New Trials

National systems vary greatly in the extent to which "final" judicial decisions ever become really incontestable and, thus, executable. According to a fundamental principle in continental law, any ruling in any legal field, once all appeals are exhausted, is called *res iudicata*, meaning that it cannot be challenged again, except under a few exceptional circumstances. In other words, habeas corpus or other remedies are not available once the verdict and the sentence have become final. Therefore, a "final" ruling is more final in Europe than in the United States,[10] a difference that explains why scientific (technical) evidence is far less often preserved over extended periods of time in Europe than in America.[11]

One of the exceptional circumstances that allows, under continental law, the appeal of a verdict after it has become legally effective is when evidence presented at trial turns out to be untrue, or when any relevant new evidence can be found that was not available at trial. For example, a witness may have lied, or an expert may have drawn wrong or excessive conclusions from the material he or she had at hand, or a DNA test conclusively proves that the defendant cannot be guilty. In all these situations, all European countries allow for a procedure by which the defendant can file a "petition of revision" (usually to a higher court) by which he or she can ask for a new trial. The terminology varies greatly,[12] but the basic conditions are fairly similar across Europe. Further, *double jeopardy* is possible in most continental countries (except in France) if, on the prosecution's petition of revision, the court cancels a former (final) decision by which the defendant was found not guilty.

To prevent wrongful decisions from remaining uncontested, every civilized country should allow for such a procedure and should not, as for example in France, make the process excessively difficult. If we accept that some innocent people are being convicted every year, the rate of successful petitions of revision should not, as in the French case, be depressed by a multitude of formalistic obstacles. The merits of the case and the facts should guide the outcome of such procedures, rather than concerns for the "majesty of the law" or the "prestige" of the criminal justice system. Exonerations are, along the lines of Brian Forst's (2004) approach, something like the last safety valve once all other built-in mechanisms of error control and management have failed.

Some countries have developed extremely detailed rules as to how wrongful convictions can be corrected, and how the damage suffered by the defendant has to be compensated. Given the extremely low frequency of exonerations in France, Canada, and Israel (to name just a few countries), the multitude and the high complexity of rules as to the kind, mechanisms, and extent of damage compensation appears to be highly disproportionate given their almost complete irrelevance, statistically at least, in practice. Perhaps such prolific rules serve an ideological purpose, in the sense that they may make people believe that the criminal justice system cares considerably about correcting errors, although the opposite may be true. Some countries, however, face the problem of thousands of applicants for compensation, particularly after the collapse of dictatorships, as in Poland after 1989. As described by Plywaczewski, Górski, and Sakowicz, in Chapter 14, hundreds of rulings became invalidated because the laws under which the applicants had been convicted were declared contrary to fundamental principles of human rights. If a country follows this line, the issue of how far back and how extensively compensation should be paid—in terms of time, degrees of proximity of the applicant to the victim of a wrongful conviction, and so on—becomes dramatic. Similarly, many defendants may have been wrongfully convicted under dictatorships for ordinary crimes, but based on political reasons and doubtful or manipulated evidence. Other countries that made the transition from dictatorships to democratic societies, such as Germany, Greece, Turkey, Spain, Portugal, and many others, have not known comparable challenges, probably because the idea of compensation was far less popular at the time of their transition to democracy.

The Role of Forensic Science and Expertise

In connection with this project, we have confronted the issue of wrongful convictions in many common-law and continental law countries. Despite the fact that wrongful convictions are a commonly debated subject in all countries, the impression we got is that exonerations—particularly those based on DNA evidence not available at the time of the trial—may be far more common in the United States than in Europe. According to recent U.S. accounts, a total of 328 exonerations were found over a recent fifteen-year period, mostly of people sentenced either to death or to very long prison terms (Gross, Jacoby, Matheson, Montgomery, and Patil, 2005). This represents about twenty exonerations per year. Controlling for population differences, these figures would, in Europe, equal about seven exonerations each year for people serving life sentences in Germany,[13] and perhaps five in France, whereas the actual numbers, as described in the chapters by Kessler (Chapter 11) and Dongois (Chapter 12), fall far short of such proportions.[14]

An easy conclusion would be that wrongful convictions are less frequent under the continental system, because several mechanisms described in this and the preceding chapters may more efficiently protect against such errors, including less reliance on the competence of defense counsel, more unbiased police and pretrial investigations, a strong focus on technical-scientific evidence, a limited role of eyewitness and other personal testimony including confessions, a more active role of neutral judges during trial, the wider availability of appeals on issues of facts, and so on. Although we do not rule out the possibility that these characteristics of the continental procedural system may indeed limit the risk of wrongful convictions, one should not ignore a number of fundamental differences in the way forensic evidence is stored after the trial. Indeed, critical items of physical evidence are often destroyed in Europe once a case has become *res iudicata* (i.e., it has been definitively decided by the courts[15]). If critical items are no longer available, no DNA analysis or any other recent technology will ever allow the discovery of errors. It is indeed surprising that no exonerations of convicted defendants are reported in the "continental" chapters of our book,[16] although this technology is widely used in Europe as well. Thus, it is equally possible that no physical evidence is available in Europe to retest the items presented during the first trial. Given the thousands of annual convictions for serious offenses throughout Europe, it is simply impossible to believe that no innocent people are among those convicted. Thus, forensic science units and coroners should be required to preserve physical evidence over extended periods, long beyond when the case becomes *res iudicata* and at least as long as the convicted person remains in prison or until a test can be completed.

U.S. observers usually call for independent forensic science experts. There are obviously many advantages in institutionalized independence of laboratories and institutes, although private firms may not necessarily guarantee high quality. Intentional deception and manipulation occur but appear to be the exception,[17] whereas classical (and often trivial) errors are far more common, as Schiffer and Champod show in Chapter 3. Against this type of errors, institutionalized independence is of little help, however. To overcome risks of that kind, it may be more important that the defendant has access to a second opinion. In contested cases, and even if no substantiated suspicion may challenge the first expert's conclusion, second opinions should, therefore, become part of a standard procedure of quality control. Beyond high standards of fairness, medical and forensic examiners should develop a culture of *quality control*. This implies that second opinions should no longer be regarded as a form of distrust, but as part of routine and good practice. Recent developments in the medical field concerning error management and appropriate ways of dealing with cases of malpractice may offer useful models to adopt in forensic science. So far, not much has been done in this respect.

With all these problems with forensic evidence and its role in criminal procedures in mind, one should not forget that identification through forensic evidence is far less vulnerable to risks of errors than is eyewitness testimony. Whenever witnesses are mistaken, it is rarely because they lie or misrepresent facts, but mostly because they misidentify people. Since misidentification of persons is, according to U.S. as well as European research (Huff, 2002; Huff et al., 1996; Peters 1970–1974), the most prominent single factor in wrongful convictions, forensic evidence should be preferred over personal testimony as far as possible. Moving away from heavy reliance on eyewitness accounts and increasing the accuracy and use of forensic evidence should make an important contribution to avoiding wrongful convictions.

Conclusions

The chapters of this book and the cases presented all illustrate the role of procedural systems and their characteristics. The conclusions we have presented in this final chapter go far beyond the simplistic alternative of favoring either an adversarial or an inquisitorial system. Zalman's (Chapter 5) warnings are illustrative in this context, as are Brants's (Chapter 9) cautions and Italy's experience in shifting to an "accusatorial" procedural system, which has not eliminated judicial errors (Gualco, 2003).

Beyond forensic experts, coroners, and police officers, prosecutors should develop and stick to ethical guidelines, violations of which should become an offense. Criminal justice officials of all fields and levels who, knowingly, fail to collect or disclose evidence that might be favorable to the defendant, or who fail to initiate procedures to exonerate a person whom they discover has been wrongfully convicted, should be liable to criminal prosecution, or at least some serious sanctions (Huff, 2002). In this connection, "winning" his or her case should not be the prosecutor's top priority; doing everything possible to ensure fair and just verdicts should be that priority instead. Perhaps Europe's less politically ambitious prosecutors may be better "losers" than their American colleagues who, often, aim to initiate a political career after a few years in office. This final warning should remind us that rules, laws, and jurisprudence are all part of a judicial culture that often differs—and sometimes also matters.

Notes

1. The opposite in continental law would be the parties' maxim (*Maxime des débats, Parteimaxime*) that largely prevails in civil (except family) law cases. It may help Europeans to know that American criminal procedures operate by and large like continental proceedings in civil (contract) law cases.

2. For a discussion and comparisons with Norway and the Netherlands, see Pizzi (1999).

3. It should be kept in mind that torture was allowed only when "strong evidence" was available—comparable to the standards of proof required for a conviction today. Since courts could not convict without a confession, however, torture was "unavoidable" before about 1750, when that requirement was removed and courts were allowed to convict even without admission of guilt (Langbein, 1977).

4. 400 U.S. 25 (1970).

5. In Italy, it is called *patteggiamento* (transaction); *ordonnance pénale* in France, *Strafbefehl* in Germany, and so on.

6. In several European countries (Germany, parts of Switzerland) this practice is widely used despite its apparent contradiction with the constitutional right of "being heard," but generally not seen as unconstitutional as long as the defendant remains entitled to ask for a full-fledged (court) hearing.

7. As a rule, the burden of proof lies with the prosecution in showing that "alternative" explanations, or potentially exonerating circumstances (for example, any alibi), cannot be true.

8. A higher success rate of appeals by prosecutors may not necessarily mean that courts are more sympathetic to prosecutors' views, but may reflect the fact that prosecutors may file an appeal less often.

9. It should be kept in mind that in some jurisdictions, in Europe as well as in the United States, appeals are not available on issues of fact, but only on legal or procedural issues.

10. See Gerberding (2005, 142–158).

11. This may, in part, explain why cases of exoneration are less common in Europe than in the United States, as shown later in this chapter.

12. In Germany, the petition for a new trial is called *Wiederaufnahme-Gesuch*. In France the term used is *pourvoi en révision*.

13. There are some 100 life sentences in Germany per year (*European Sourcebook* 2003, 158–159).

14. A similar survey undertaken in Germany during the 1960s (Peters 1970–1974) reached similar conclusions.

15. In France, evidence used by forensic medical experts is routinely destroyed one year after delivery of the expert's opinion (Professor Malicier, University of Lyon, personal communication). In other European countries, rules seem to be less standardized, but evidence is usually destroyed once a case has reached the stage of *res iudicata*.

16. A high-profile exoneration, described by Brants in Chapter 9 on The Netherlands, occurred there in 2004 and did indeed involve DNA, but in the opposite sense. In that case, a man convicted of rape and murder (serving a sentence of eighteen years) was exonerated after another man confessed to the offense. Ironically, the error would not have happened if the mismatch of DNA traces collected on the bodies of the victims and the suspect's DNA profile had received more attention. The exoneration, as such, was unrelated to DNA.

17. The American experience may differ in this respect; see Gross et al. (2004).

References

Aebi, M. F. (2003, August). *Thinking about wrongful convictions in Spain*. Paper presented at the International Workshop on Wrongful Convictions, Breil/Brigels, Switzerland.

Crombach, H. (1999). Collaborative story-telling: A hypothesis in need of experimental testing. *Psychology, Crime and Law, 5*, 279–289.

European Sourcebook of Crime and Criminal Justice Statistics (2nd ed.). (2003). The Hague, Netherlands: WODC.

Forst, B. (2004). *Errors of justice: Nature, sources and remedies*. New York: Cambridge University Press.

Gerberding, P. (2005). *Das Rechtsmittelsystem im US-amerikanischen Strafverfahren* [The system of appeals in American criminal procedure]. Frankfurt, Germany: Peter Lang.

Gross, S. R., Jacoby, K., Matheson, D. J., Montgomery, N., & Patil, S. (2004). Exonerations in the United States 1989 through 2003. *The Journal of Criminal Law and Criminology, 95*(2), 523–560.

Gualco, B. (2003, August). *An example of a wrongful conviction in Italy.* Paper presented at the International Workshop on Wrongful Convictions, Breil/Brigels, Switzerland.

Huff, C. R. (2002). Wrongful conviction and public policy: The American Society of Criminology 2001 presidential address. *Criminology, 40*(1), 1–18.

Huff, C. R., Rattner, A., & Sagarin, E. (1996). *Convicted but innocent: Wrongful conviction and public policy.* Thousand Oaks, CA: Sage.

Jehle, J.-M. (2003, August). *An overview of the German appeal system.* Paper presented at the International Workshop on Wrongful Convictions, Breil/Brigels, Switzerland.

Kohler, J., & Scheel, W. (1968). *Constitutio Criminalis Carolina* (reprint of text edition). Aalen: Scientia. (Original work published 1900)

Langbein, J. H. (1977). *Torture and the law of proof: Europe and England in the ancient regime.* Chicago: The University of Chicago Press.

Newman, D. J. (1966). *Conviction: The determination of guilt or innocence without trial.* Boston: Little, Brown.

Peters, K. (1970–1974). *Fehlerquellen im Strafprozess. Eine Untersuchung der Wiederaufnahmeverfahren in der Bundesrepublik Deutschland* [Sources of errors in criminal proceedings: A study of cases of successful petitions of revision in the Federal Republic of Germany] (3 vols.). Karlsruhe, Germany: C. F. Müller.

Pizzi, W. T. (1999). *Trials without truth.* New York: New York University Press.

Ries, P. (1984). *Die Rechtsstellung des Verletzten im Strafverfahren* [The victim's position in criminal procedure]. Munich, Germany: Beck.

Schmid, N. (1993). *Strafverfahren und Strafrecht in den Vereinigten Staaten: Eine Einführung* [Criminal procedure and criminal law in the United States] (2nd ed.). Heidelberg, Germany: Müller.

Schmidt, E. (1965). *Geschichte der Deutschen Strafrechtspflege* [History of German criminal procedure]. Göttingen, Germany: Vandenhoeck & Ruprecht.

Trechsel, S., & Killias, M. (2004). Criminal law/criminal procedure. In F. Dessemontet & F. Ansay (Eds.), *Introduction to Swiss law* (3rd ed., pp. 245–286). The Hague, Netherlands: Kluwer Law International.

CONTRIBUTORS

About the Editors

C. Ronald Huff is Professor of Criminology, Law and Society and Sociology and Dean of the School of Social Ecology at the University of California, Irvine. He previously taught at Ohio State University (1979–1999), where he directed both the John Glenn School of Public Affairs and the Criminal Justice Research Center and was a Fellow in the Center for Socio-Legal Studies (Ohio State and Oxford University). He also taught at Purdue University and served as a visiting professor at the University of Hawaii. His previous twelve books include *Convicted but Innocent: Wrongful Conviction and Public Policy* (with Arye Rattner and Edward Sagarin), which received an Academic Book of the Year award, and three editions of *Gangs in America*. He is a Fellow and Past President (2001) of the American Society of Criminology. His other honors include the Donald Cressey Award from the National Council on Crime and Delinquency, the Paul Tappan Award from the Western Society of Criminology, and the Herbert Bloch Award from the American Society of Criminology. He is a member of the advisory boards of the National Youth Gang Center (Tallahassee, Florida) and the Center for Juvenile Law and Policy (Loyola Law School, Los Angeles); a former member of the California Attorney General's research and policy advisory board; and has served as an expert witness in numerous cases as well as a consultant to the attorneys general of Ohio and Hawaii, the U.S. Senate Judiciary Committee, the FBI National Academy at Quantico, and the U.S. Department of Justice.

Martin Killias obtained MA degrees in law and in sociology as well as his PhD in the sociology of law from the University of Zurich. After three semesters spent at the University at Albany (New York) School of Criminal Justice, he directed the Institute of Criminology and Criminal Law at the University of Lausanne (Switzerland) for twenty-five years. During those years, he held visiting positions in Canada, the United States, the Netherlands, England, and Italy. In 2006, he became Professor of Criminal Law and

Criminology at the University of Zurich. His research has focused on international and comparative empirical studies, as well as on experimental evaluations in the area of corrections and treatment. He received the prestigious Sellin-Glueck Award from the American Society of Criminology in 2001. He was the first President of the European Society of Criminology, co-founder of the International Crime Victim Surveys, and Chair of the European Sourcebook of Crime and Criminal Justice Statistics. Since 1984, he has also served as a part-time judge in the Federal Supreme Court of Switzerland.

About the Contributors

Chrisje Brants is Professor of Criminal Law and Criminal Procedure at Utrecht University in The Netherlands. She started her career as a journalist and, being British by birth and bilingual, later also became an interpreter and translator (Dutch–English) accredited to the courts in Amsterdam. As a professor of criminal law, she teaches a variety of subjects. Her main research interests are comparative work with an emphasis on crime and the media, as well as criminal policy and human rights. She is the author of a number of books and many articles on these subjects. She has also lectured widely in different countries, including the United Kingdom, the United States, Russia, and China, and she has represented Amnesty International and the Council of Europe at conferences and training sessions in the Netherlands and at the EU-China Human Rights Dialogue in Beijing.

Kathryn M. Campbell is Associate Professor in the Department of Criminology at the University of Ottawa, Ontario, Canada. Professor Campbell's research focus has been mainly on issues of social justice, including explorations of miscarriages of justice, youth justice, and Aboriginal conceptions of justice. She has written extensively on the Canadian experience of wrongful convictions and has published several articles and book chapters on this topic.

Christophe Champod received his MSc and PhD (summa cum laude), both in Forensic Science, from the University of Lausanne. From 1999 to 2003, he led the Interpretation Research Group of the Forensic Science Service (UK), before taking a professorship position at the School of Criminal Sciences, Institute of Forensic Science, at the University of Lausanne in Switzerland. He is deputy director of the School and is in charge of education and research on identification methods (detection and identification). He is a member of the International Association for Identification and in 2004 he was elected as a member of the FBI-sponsored SWGFAST. His research is devoted to fingerprint detection techniques and the statistical evaluation of forensic identification techniques.

Nathalie Dongois holds a Doctor of Law degree and is currently Replacement Professor at the University of Lausanne in Switzerland, where she teaches courses on criminal law and wrongful conviction. She also teaches an introduction to French law, which allows her to do some comparative surveys. Her primary interests lie in criminal law and criminal procedure, as well as identifying the sources of wrongful convictions and comparing different criminal justice systems.

Adam Górski is Adjunct Professor and Chair of Criminal Procedure at Jagiellonian University in Poland, where he is also an Alexander von Humboldt and Max Planck Fellow.

He specializes in criminal law, criminal procedure, and medical law. He is the author of some fifty publications on the Europeanization of criminal law and medical law.

Randall Grometstein is Assistant Professor of Criminal Justice at Fitchburg State College in Massachusetts. She is interested in social construction and moral panic theory, ethics, biosocial perspectives, and corrections. She is the author of "Prosecutorial Misconduct and Noble Cause Corruption" (*Criminal Law Bulletin*), and is a co-author of *Managing Relationships with Industry: A Physician's Compliance Manual*, forthcoming in 2008 from Elsevier.

Talia R. Harmon obtained her PhD degree from the School of Criminal Justice at the State University of New York at Albany. She is currently Associate Professor in the Department of Criminal Justice at Niagara University. She has published work on death qualification, wrongful convictions in capital cases, wrongful executions, racial discrimination, and innocence. Her work on wrongful capital convictions has appeared in *Justice Quarterly*, *Crime and Delinquency*, *Criminal Justice Policy Review*, and *Criminal Justice Review*.

Isabel Kessler studied law and criminology from 1993 to 1998 in Cologne, Germany, and in Lausanne, Switzerland. She completed her PhD degree in law and criminology at the University of Cologne. From 2002 to 2004, she was an assistant district attorney at the district court of Koblenz, Germany, before becoming a lecturer at the University of Middlesex in Great Britain, where she earned a Master of Science in Criminology and Forensic Psychology in 2005. She then worked as a research assistant in criminology at the European Institute of Social Science at the University of Kent. In 2006, she became a judge in the district court of Hamburg and then, in April 2007, she returned to work as an assistant district attorney in the field of juvenile delinquency.

William S. Lofquist is Professor and Chair of Sociology at the State University of New York at Geneseo. His current research focuses on the relationship between historical practices of race-based social control and contemporary patterns of punishment. One line of this research is examining the history of the death penalty in the Bahamas, a former British slave colony that retains the death penalty. An article addressing this issue is forthcoming in the *Caribbean Journal of Criminology and Social Psychology*. A second line of this research focuses on the regional and racial patterning of death penalty use in the United States. Publications presenting this research have appeared in the *Iowa Law Review* (2002) and the *Journal of Ethnicity in Criminal Justice* (2006, with Margaret Vandiver and David Giacopassi). He has also published a range of works examining the production of wrongful convictions in capital cases.

Carole McCartney is a lecturer in criminal law and criminal justice at the University of Leeds. She previously studied and taught at Bond University, Queensland, Australia. She has written on Australian justice, innocence projects, and DNA and criminal justice, including *Forensic Identification and Criminal Justice: Forensic Science, Justice and Risk*. She established and directs an Innocence Project at the University of Leeds. She was project manager for the Nuffield Council on Bioethics report *The Forensic Uses of Bio-Information: Ethical Issues*. She is currently working on a project to teach forensic practice to law students and is researching the regulation of forensic science in the United Kingdom.

Emil W. Plywaczewski is Professor of Criminal Law and Criminology on the Faculty of Law at the University of Bialystok, Poland, where he also serves as Director of the Chair in Criminal Law, Head of the Department of Substantive Penal Law and Criminology, and Vice-Dean of the Faculty of Law. His research has produced 280 publications in Poland and other nations, including a number of monographs. He has served as a visiting professor or guest lecturer at thirty-nine universities in Australia, Austria, Germany, Lithuania, Greece, India, Italy, Japan, China, the Netherlands, New Zealand, South Korea, the United States, and Switzerland. He was the recipient of the Distinguished International Scholar Award, presented by the International Division of the American Society of Criminology in 1997. Since 2001 he has been serving as a United Nations consultant for the implementation of its project, "Assessment of Organized Crime in Central Asia." He also serves as Chief Coordinator of the Polish Platform for Homeland Security.

Arye Rattner is Professor of Sociology and Criminology at the University of Haifa, Israel, and Director of the Center for the Study of Crime, Law, and Society. He also served until recently as Dean of the Faculty of Social Sciences. He has held visiting positions at Carleton University in Ottawa and York University in Toronto. He has published numerous articles on wrongful conviction and is co-author (with C. Ronald Huff and Edward Sagarin) of *Convicted but Innocent: Wrongful Conviction and Public Policy*. He has also published numerous articles and a book, *Legal Decision Making among Jews and Arabs in the Israeli Court System*, as well a series of articles on legal culture in Israel.

Andrzej Sakowicz is an Adjunct Professor in the Department of Criminal Law at the University of Białystok, Poland. His research interests lie primarily in criminal justice cooperation in the European Union, criminal law and criminal procedure, and human rights (especially the right to privacy). He is the author of some sixty publications, a member of the Foundation for Polish Science, and a Max Planck Fellow.

Beatrice Schiffer is a PhD candidate in the School of Criminal Sciences at the University of Lausanne in Switzerland, where she also works as a research and teaching assistant. Her research concerns how forensic sciences can lead to, prevent, or help discover miscarriages of justice. Part of her research has been financed by the Swiss National Science Foundation, as part of a larger project entitled "Wrongful Convictions in Switzerland in Comparative Perspective." She also served as a forensic assistant for the United Nations International Independent Investigation Commission in Beyrouth, Lebanon, which was mandated to investigate the assassination of former Prime Minister Rafic Hariri.

Clive Walker is Professor of Criminal Justice Studies and former Dean of the School of Law at the University of Leeds. He has written extensively on criminal justice issues, with many published papers in the United Kingdom and several other countries. He has served as a visiting professor at George Washington University, the University of Connecticut, Stanford University, and Melbourne University. His books have focused on miscarriages of justice, and he is the author of *Justice in Error* (Blackstone Press, London, 1993) and *Miscarriages of Justice* (Blackstone Press, London, 1999) as well as many academic papers on the subject. He has also published on terrorism and emergencies, with recent books including *The Anti-Terrorism Legislation* (Oxford University Press, 2002) and *The Civil Contingencies Act 2004: Risk, Resilience and the Law in the United Kingdom* (Oxford University Press, 2006). He has frequently been called on to provide advice to

UK Parliamentary committees on terrorism and to the UK government's independent adviser on terrorism and, in 2003, he was a special adviser to the UK Parliamentary Select Committee.

Marvin Zalman is Professor and Interim Chair in the Department of Criminal Justice at Wayne State University. He authored a text on constitutional criminal procedure (Prentice-Hall) and has conducted research on topics in criminal law, criminal procedure, and criminal justice policy, including physician-assisted suicide, drug asset forfeiture, domestic violence, jail crowding lawsuits, civil liberties, and judicial sentencing. He recently published (with Brad Smith) a study on the attitudes of police executives toward *Miranda* and interrogation policies (*Journal of Criminal Law and Criminology*). His recent research includes articles on wrongful conviction research and policy and a forthcoming work on the incidence of wrongful conviction.

INDEX